PISTOL & REVOLVER DIGEST

Second Edition

Edited by
Dean A. Grennell & Jack Lewis

Follett Publishing Company / Chicago
T-1274

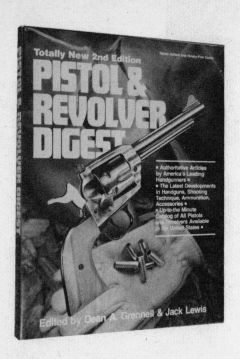

THE COVER: The front cover features the Interarms' Virginian Dragoon, Model 3823, in .357 magnum with six-inch barrel. The back cover guns, from left: Star Model PD, caliber .45 ACP; Star Model BM in 9mmP, chrome-plated with simulated pearl stocks; Star Model BKM, 9mmP, with anodized aluminum alloy frame. Respective Model Nos.: 3030, 3033 and 3032.

Produced by

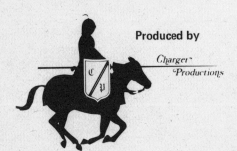

Charger Productions

Editorial Director
JACK LEWIS

Art Director
MALCOLM WILSON

Production Director
BETTY BURRIS

Contributing Artists
SONYA KAISER
JOHN VITALE
JOHN THOMPSON

Associate Publisher
SHELDON L. FACTOR

ISBN 0-695-81274-2   Library of Congress Catalog Card Number: 76-23196

CONTENTS

INTRODUCTION

Those of us engaged in its production have fallen into the habit of referring to Pistol & Revolver Digest by the initials of its title: PARD. Welcome to PARD-II and our sincere thanks to those of the book-buying public who made the first edition a success.

In some ways, 1976 — when the first edition appeared — seems like only yesterday. It was the nation's bicentennial year, heralded with boisterous fanfares. Suddenly, here we are, well launched toward the tricentennial. Time flies on remarkably swift wings!

It's been almost a tricade (if we may coin the word) since the first PARD was tied up and sent off to the printer. Not surprisingly, many things have changed. The field of firearms in general and handguns in particular is noted for its rapid fluxing and shifting. On any number of mournfully remembered occasions, a book such as this has been completed in the most meticulously up-to-date manner imaginable and, during the few weeks before it came off the press, several things were no longer quite as they had been described. It is one of those things that cause authors and publishers to do a great deal of frowning and muttering to themselves.

Perhaps the most impressive — though not encouraging — change in the tricade is the price explosion. A gun we used to value at $75 to $100 now fetches up to $500 and you may have to put your name on a waiting list and be patient. Along the way, ammunition costs have kept pace or forged ahead and the end is not even remotely visible. Only yesterday, a man employed by one of the leading makers of bullets and ammunition remarked that the price of lead was up again, likewise the price of copper. That, in turn, dictated an increase for bullets and loaded ammo. In the tricades to come, we'll have to dole out our shooting expenses with all possible care, meanwhile devoting efforts toward maintaining the right to own and operate firearms in a lawful manner. We hope PARD-II will be helpful to you in that respect.

So thanks again, and Good Shooting, all of you!

Dean A. Grennell   Jack Lewis

Capistrano Beach, California

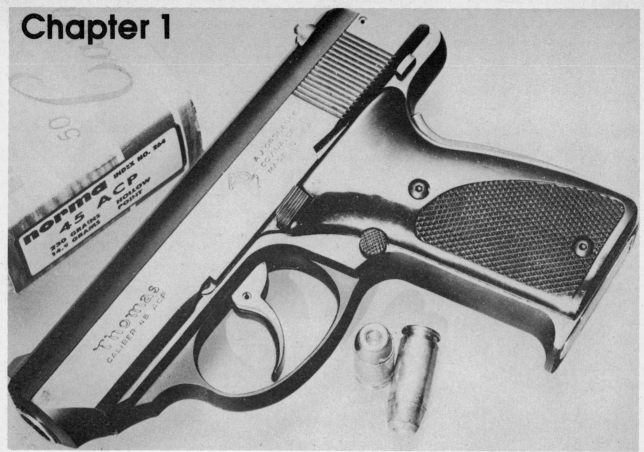

The Thomas .45 appeared since our previous edition and has since been dropped from production. Opposite page shows OMC .380 Back Up; Colt Model 1911A1; Browning BDA; Star PD; Thomas .45; Detonics .45 and S&W Model 59.

NEW HANDGUNS

News And Notes On Progress In The Field Since Our Last Edition

By Dean A. Grennell

THE FIRST EDITION of the work at hand went off to the printer on September 24, 1976, according to my informal record-keeping system on such weighty matters. The two years and a bit intervening have seen the introduction of several new handguns and, in at least one instance, a design that surfaced and sank. That was the Thomas .45, a singular item of ordnance that warrants discussion for the sake of future arms historians and other interested parties.

In terms of a comparable design apt to be familiar to most readers, the Thomas was only slightly larger than the Model PP Walther and bore a moderate resemblance to the little German pocket auto. The Thomas, however, fed upon the .45 Auto Colt Pistol (ACP) cartridge, rather than the daintier fare of the Walther.

Handing the Thomas to a safety-minded handgunner produced instant frustration. The first thing such a person will do is check to make sure the chamber is empty. That involves holding the grip in one hand and dragging the slide back with the other. As it turned out, you couldn't do it with the Thomas.

There was a movable insert at the rear of the grip, pivoted at the bottom, that appeared to be a fairly conventional grip safety. It was not a grip safety. When depressed by grasping the Thomas in normal firing mode, it cammed up two obtuse-angle locking lugs that engaged

Each round fired from the Thomas required a full double-action pull of the trigger, as discussed in text.

Below, because of Thomas locking system, this hold was used in retracting slide. Bottom, the Thomas between a Colt M1911 and a Walther Model PP, to compare sizes.

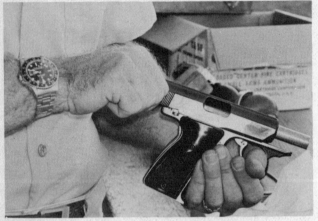

mating notches in the lower edges of the slide to lock the action solidly in a closed position. The Thomas' operating principle was that recoil pressure against the lever at the rear of the grip kept the action locked until the bullet left the barrel, at which time the slide moved rearward to perform the reloading cycle. Although it sounds a bit unlikely, the system worked quite reliably in actual operation.

About the only way to drag back the slide on the Thomas .45 involved hooking a thumb in the front of the trigger guard for support and then dragging the slide back.

The Thomas did not have an exposed hammer, nor did it have a safety in the usual manner of autoloading pistols. It had a slide release catch, a magazine release button and a trigger; that was all.

The magazine held six rounds of .45 ACP, with the option of carrying a seventh round in the chamber. Its barrel measured 3.5 inches and was solidly affixed to the receiver. The suggested retail price, during its all-too-brief career, was $375, with one magazine. The later versions incorporated an adjustable trigger stop that improved its rather dubious trigger-haul by useful increments. Its empty weight was two pounds on the dot and it measured 6½ inches in length and 4½ inches in height.

Every round fired from the Thomas .45 required a full double-action pull of the trigger. That got away from one frequent objection to guns such as the Model 39 or 59 Smith & Wesson, with double-action for the first shot, shifting to the single-action mode for subsequent rounds. On the Thomas, the trigger pull stayed the same, shot after shot. That was the good news. The bad news was that the trigger pull was somewhat pediculous. Pediculous is one of the politer synonyms for lousy.

The Thomas seemed to have been bred for the 230-grain full metal jacket (FMJ) .45 ACP load, performing at its best when thus fed and rarely well with any other load. When fired with care from a steady rest, the Thomas would hold 230-grain FMJ loads within about a three-inch cluster from

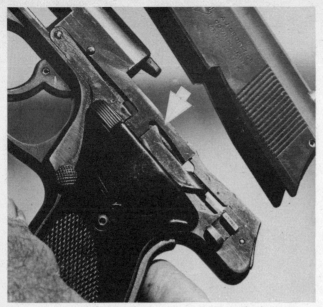
Lever at rear of the Thomas grip is pivoted at the bottom.

When depressed, it cams the locking lug up into slide.

a distance of twenty-five yards; entirely adequate for a gun of its basic design. Considering that it was quite a bit more compact than the hallowed M1911 and capable of holding seven rounds of .45 ACP against the M1911's eight, the Thomas seemed to stack up quite creditably for itself. Nor was its price outrageous in terms of the current economy.

Frankly, I'm at a loss to explain why it didn't survive longer in the marketplace. Perhaps it was not merchandised with the aggressiveness of a starving piranha, as seems to be a requisite these troubled times. At any rate, it was a novel and innovative concept, admirably capable by reasonable standards. It was remarkably well suited as a gun for

The .45 Detonics is a compact .45 auto based upon the familiar M1911 Government Model design.

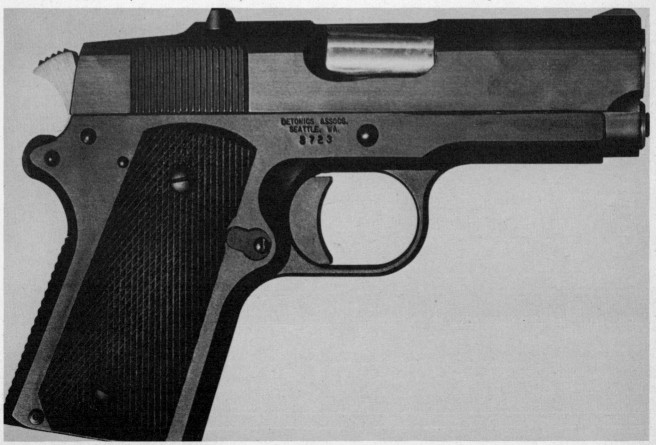

The Model LM-4 Semmerling is a manually actuated repeater, not an autoloader. After each shot, the slide is pushed forward and moved rearward by hand to put a fresh round in the chamber; its trigger is double-action.

off-duty police and non-uniformed law enforcement personnel; a market area to which a great deal of thought and effort has been devoted in recent times.

Two comparable designs have been worked up and marketed in hopes of seining in goodly sales from the same market area: the Detonics .45 and the Semmerling LM-4. Like the ill-fated Thomas, both are chambered for the .45 ACP cartridge and both are quite compact. The Detonics .45 is, basically, a trimmed-down modification of the Model 1911; an autoloader in the conventional sense. The Semmerling is anything but conventional.

The Semmerling could be termed a pump-action repeater, or a manually actuated repeater. Like the Thomas, its every round is set off by a full double-action pull of the trigger. Unlike the Thomas, it does not eject its spent case and rechanber a fresh one. To do so, the operator must move the slide forward and then back to battery before making a fresh DA pull of the trigger. One of the more astounding aspects of the Semmerling LM-4 is its suggested retail price, starting at $645, as of early 1979 and escalating briskly from that point as options are selected. The empty weight of the gun is twenty-six ounces, bringing the net cost to $24.80 per ounce before sales tax.

The traditional single-action revolver design has continued to receive its share of attention from gunmakers, with assorted approaches to one of the basic problems of such mechanisms. I refer to the SA revolver's tendency to set off the round under the hammer if the hammer spur receives a sound thump, even without cocking the hammer and pulling the trigger. At best, this can be a highly disconcerting trait; at worst...

The time-honored approach for circumventing such hazards has been to leave the chamber beneath the hammer empty, thereby making a five-shooter out of the nominal sixgun.

Sturm, Ruger & Company has devoted a lot of their advertising toward informing the public as to the hazards of carrying conventional single-action revolvers with live rounds in all six chambers. Meanwhile, a few years ago, they redesigned their own SA models to incorporate a patented transfer bar to prevent firing when the hammer is forward. Starting about 1977, they included a roll-imprinted notice on the side of the barrel warning the user to become familiar with the instruction manual and offering to send a free copy of same upon request.

That's an endless and perplexing problem for

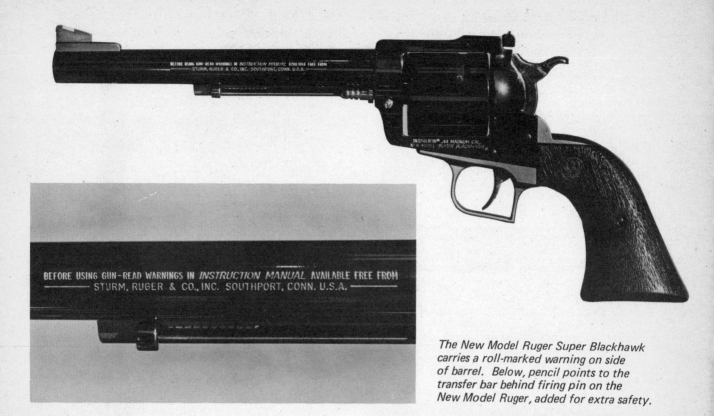

The New Model Ruger Super Blackhawk carries a roll-marked warning on side of barrel. Below, pencil points to the transfer bar behind firing pin on the New Model Ruger, added for extra safety.

manufacturers in the shooting industry, as well as in other areas: All too many purchasers not only neglect to read the instructions, they usually throw them away and proceed to sell the gun, or trade it in, denying subsequent owners the cautionary guidance of the instruction booklet — assuming they'd read it if they had it.

The instruction manual that accompanies the Interarms' Virginian Dragoon SA revolvers, for example, states, "One cylinder chamber has a visible dot on each side so that when it is aligned with the bore a dot appears on each side of the frame. This added safety feature is provided as a guide when loading. *Always leave this chamber empty and under the hammer when carrying the gun loaded.*"

The Virginian Dragoon provides a further arrangement, termed the "Swiss-safe," consisting of a second groove in the base pin — the rod on which the cylinder rotates — so the base pin screw (latch) can be pressed inward and the base pin pushed rearward to engage the latch in the forward or Swiss-safe notch. Doing so leaves the rear tip of the base pin protruding against the lower shank of the hammer to prevent the hammer nose from touching the firing pin.

The Swiss-safe can be engaged as an auxiliary safety measure when the hammer is at half-cock for purposes of loading or removing live rounds from the chambers. The maker does not seem to advocate use of the Swiss-safe as a means for carrying a live round under the hammer because the instructions are quite positive on that score, as quoted.

The Virginian Dragoons are offered in three calibers — .357 magnum, .45 Long Colt and .44 magnum — in barrel lengths ranging from five to 8-3/8 inches, all with adjustable, target-type rear sights. There's also a twelve-inch .44 magnum for handgun metallic silhouette competition.

Since the introduction of handgun metallic silhouette competition, about 1974, interest in this new and highly

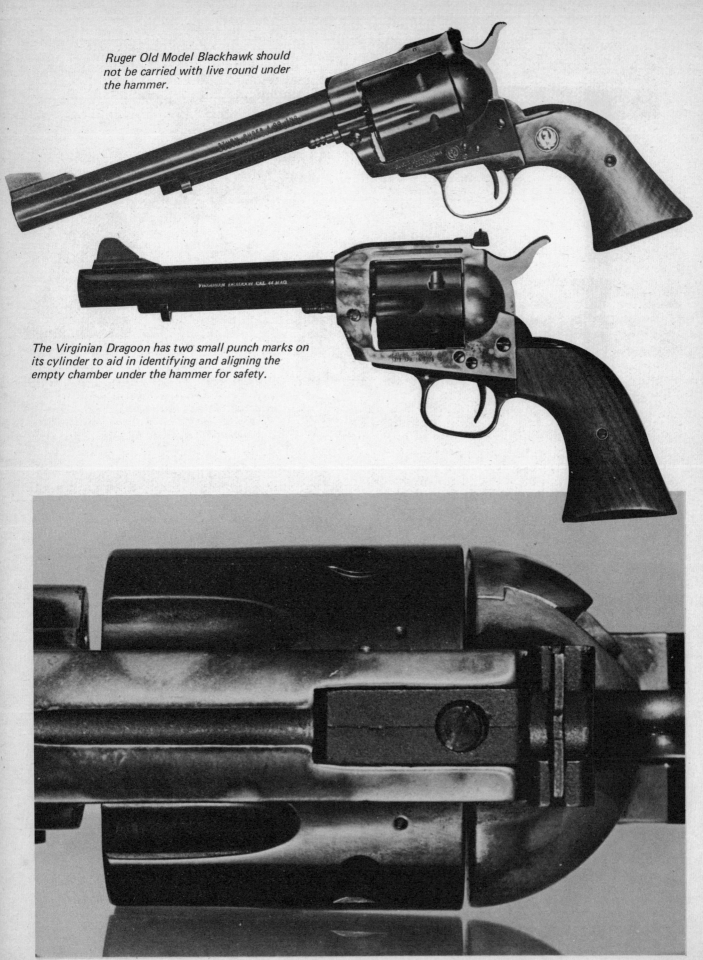

Ruger Old Model Blackhawk should not be carried with live round under the hammer.

The Virginian Dragoon has two small punch marks on its cylinder to aid in identifying and aligning the empty chamber under the hammer for safety.

challenging field has grown by lusty leaps and bounds. As detailed elsewhere in the present volume, many innovations have resulted from the basic need to deliver substantial quantities of foot-pounds to precise points from goodly distances, with a high degree of repeatability. For one of the first times in the long history of handgun competition, it has become important to do more than merely make a hole in a paper target at extended distances.

The metallic silhouette targets are cut from heavy steel plate, and must be physically knocked off their supporting rails in order to score as a hit. The largest of the four targets, the ram, at a full two hundred meters (656.166 feet) from the firing line, is the toughest. Merely creating a hit with an audible clang is not enough. If the massive mark doesn't go over and crash to earth, it counts as a miss.

As a direct result, shooters and arms designers have had to revise their thinking quite drastically. New cartridges — the .45 Winchester magnum, for an outstanding example — have been developed and traditional rifle cartridges, such as the .35 Remington, have been adapted to handgun use. There has been a trend toward longer handgun barrels, for the sake of added velocity and lengthened sight radius. The net result has been a marked improvement of the breed, with vastly increased capability for hunting the larger, more elusive game species as a direct spinoff.

An outstanding example of such competition-accelerated

Swiss-safe feature of Virginian Dragoon (arrow) can be seen, here in extended or safe position, below the firing pin; details are discussed in text. Below, handgun metallic silhouette sport has given great impetus to development of new guns.

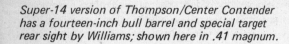

Super-14 version of Thompson/Center Contender has a fourteen-inch bull barrel and special target rear sight by Williams; shown here in .41 magnum.

developments is the Super 14 barrels for the Thompson/Center Contender pistol. Introduced early in 1967 as a single-shot, break-open design with the innovative feature of interchangeable barrels and ability to switch from rimfire to center-fire by means of rotating an insert on the front face of the hammer by a half-turn, the handgun metallic silhouette game was made to order for the Contender, and vice versa. Ample time is allotted so that the single-shot feature poses no handicap and the basic Contender lockup design is such that it can cope with peak pressures typically encountered in the hotter rifle cartridges.

Full exploitation of the potentialities of the Contender concept commenced about 1973 when Steve Herrett and Bob Milek developed the .30 Herrett cartridge. When I visited Herrett in 1970, he was already exploring such possibilities in the form of various wildcat (i.e., nonstandard cartridge designs) configurations based upon the .44 Remington magnum case. He abandoned that approach after deciding the .44 case did not possess the needed strength about the head and rim to withstand the extreme pressures encountered and shifted his attention to the .30-30 WCF (Winchester Center Fire) case, instead.

The .30 Herrett that eventually resulted is made up from .30-30 WCF brass, shortened, blown out and formed with

Steve Herrett's early wildcatting explorations were based on the .44 magnum case, here with .17, .22 and .30 bullets in place. He abandoned the .44 because it did not have as much strength about the head as the .30-30 round used for the .30 and .357 Herrett rounds.

the aid of die sets available from Omark/RCBS. Later, Herrett and Milek went on to create the .357 Herrett, likewise based upon .30-30 brass, but slightly longer and with larger powder capacity.

The rimmed case of the .30-30 offers easy, positive extraction in the Contender design, although the designers are quick to point out that optimum accuracy is obtained solely when care is taken to form the case so that it is supported within the chamber by contact between the case shoulder and the mating surface of the chamber, rather than by the front face of the rim, itself.

In the course of developing the .30 Herrett, Thompson/Center offered bull barrels as an option in place of the lighter, octagonally fluted barrels of the original design and the heavier, round barrels offered a further gain in accuracy, together with reduction of apparent recoil. As it turns out, the Contender bull barrel shows a distinct advantage, even with the cartridges of smaller bullet diameter. The most accurate Contender barrel in the author's possession is a ten-inch bull design in .22 Hornet, capable of holding groups down around one-half-inch at fifty yards.

Except for unlimited events, the rules of handgun metallic silhouette competition specify open iron sights of standard factory offering and that, in turn, has stimulated development of the Foolproof receiver sight for the Contender, as made by Williams Gun Sight Company of Davison, Michigan. The new sight is available in four basic configurations: choice of open notch or aperture peep combined with slotted screw or knurled knob adjustments.

Contender fans are pretty much unanimous in agreement that, if you're denied the use of optical (scope) sights, the Williams Foolproof constitutes one of the most useful gains in Contender performance to the present date. Capable of shrugging off as much recoil stress as the human hand can endure — and then some — the Williams sight offers the ultimate in rock-solid, precision adjustment, all without adding much to the weight and bulk of the gun on which it's mounted.

When not proscribed by competition regulations, the scope sight still represents the ultimate plateau of accuracy potential for the Contender and comparable handguns and it does not seem overly probable that any fresh innovation is going to come along to require modification of such evaluations. One of the few alternatives in the current state of the art is the laser, which projects a tight beam of intense red light. For the present, the laser does not seem to be the elegant, final solution that one might wish. Under bright light conditions, the little red spot is not readily visible at extended distances. In total darkness, it's intensely visible, of course, but the problem is that you can't tell upon what it's shining. Further, the beam-generating mechanism plus the needed power source is rather heavy, bulky and — worst of all — expensive to the tune of several hundred dollars a copy in the present scheme of things. I've worked with some of the current patterns of laser gun sights and can only report that their day of glory has yet to dawn.

One further sighting system shows considerable promise, however, It's typified by the Insta-Sight, marketed by Thompson/Center for their Contender and available, by

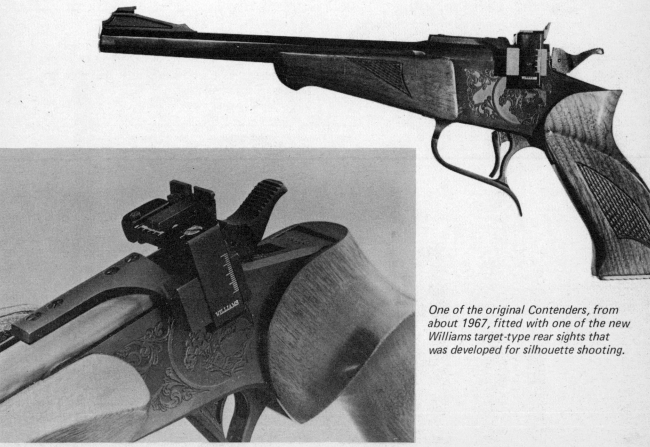

One of the original Contenders, from about 1967, fitted with one of the new Williams target-type rear sights that was developed for silhouette shooting.

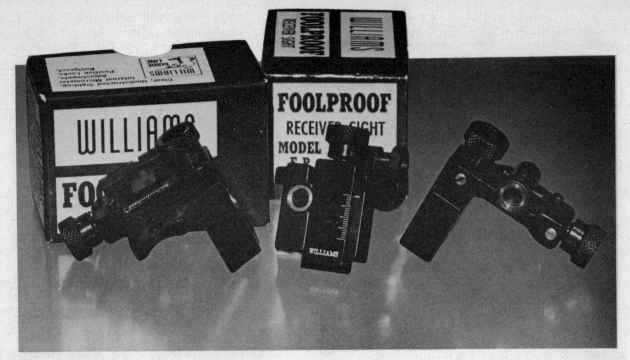

means of suitable mount bases, for use on a number of other popular handguns. The Insta-Sight is compact and light in weight, projecting a white crosshair against a crimson background when the target is viewed through it. Adjustable by means of two turrets, much in the same manner of conventional scopes, in both windage and elevation, the Insta-Sight does not magnify the image. It has the further advantage of being on the same apparent focal plane as the target.

That has long been the great plaguing weakness of conventional iron sights: The human eye is totally incapable of focusing simultaneously upon rear sight, front sight and target. When firing open-sighted handguns, one tries to keep the front sight in focus and align the equally blurry rear sight and target with it.

Conventional telescopic sights offer a useful solution to

Williams Contender sight is offered in four versions: with open notch or peep aperture and with knurled or slot-head adjusting screws, giving the shooter an attractive choice.

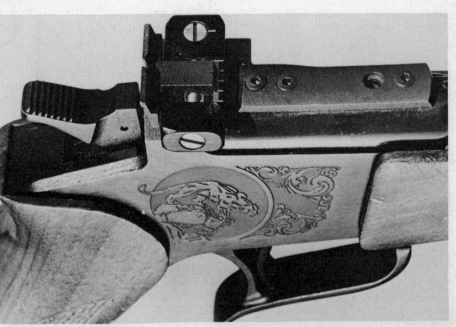

Thompson/Center's Insta-Sight does not magnify the image. Light and compact, it can be adjusted for elevation and windage, provides outstanding accuracy.

the multi-focal problem, of course, though at the cost of increases in bulk and weight of the handgun. If the shooter is willing to put up with these relatively minor handicaps, a scope on a handgun offers the advantage of the most accurate aiming approach currently available.

A scope sight designed primarily for use on rifles is of little or no use on handguns because of the considerable

difference in the length of eye-relief involved. Rifle scopes are designed to position the aiming eye about two inches behind the objective lens or eyepiece, while handguns require an eye-relief on the order of eighteen to twenty-four inches. One of the earliest of the long-relief designs was the Nickel scope, made in Germany and rarely seen in this country. Among the first of the domestically distributed handgun scopes was the Bushnell Phantom, offering a 1.5X magnification and, later, a 3X version. Thompson/Center introduced their Puma and Lobo scopes. Leupold brought out the first of their M8-2X scopes, perhaps the first model based upon the one-inch tube diameter that has come to be accepted as standard for rifle scopes in this country and later added an improved version with an eyepiece that could be adjusted for maximum sharpness, with the M8-4X as their latest offering. More recently, Thompson/Center has marketed a 1.5X and 3X

Here's what the shooter sees through the T/C Insta-Sight. The overall image is rose-tinted with the reticle lines appearing uncolored.

Bushnell Phantom scope on Bushnell mount atop S&W Model 57 proved remarkably accurate, showed no problems from recoil of the .41 magnum round. Load listed develops about 1130 fps.

T/C's Lobo 3X scope, here in two views
on Contender with .22 Hornet bull barrel,
is capable of holding ½″ groups at 50 yards.

Auto Mag in .357 AMP, with M8-2X
Leupold scope on Herringshaw mounts
will group about 1½″ at 50 yards.

handgun scope called the Silhouette, likewise with one-inch
tube diameter for use on conventional scope mounts and
rings. The newest entry in the field is a compact design
from Hutson and, with the growing market potential, it's
probable that other makes and models will make their
appearances.

The growing interest in and acceptance of heavier
handgun calibers accented the problem of coping with
extremes of recoil and various solutions have been offered
to help us live with that. In the early Seventies, Larry Kelly
patented his Mag-na-port concept, which involves using an
EDM (Electrostatic Discharge Machine) to mill small
trapezoidal openings in the barrel near the muzzle. By
diverting jets of high-pressure powder gases at this point,
both recoil and muzzle up-flip are reduced by useful
degrees, without affecting the accuracy or ballistics of the
barrel significantly.

T/C Insta-Sight, showing mount and windage adjustment turret.

Right, High Standard Victor, with Leupold M8-4X scope on discontinued Weaver rings. Below, a novel solution to the problem of machine-resting handguns without need for massive anchoring bench. Movable rest is realigned for each shot, using Weaver scope.

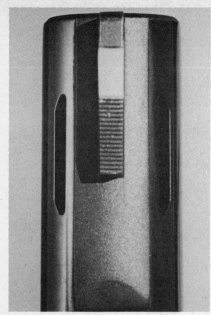

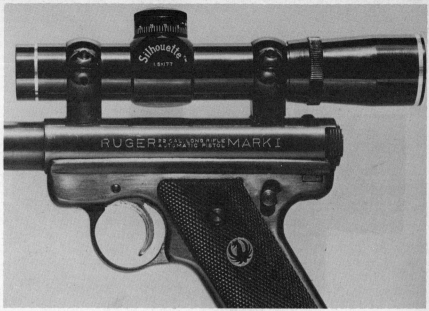

Left, Mag-na-port modification on muzzle of Ruger Super Blackhawk, showing two trapezoidal slots milled by means of electrostatic discharge machine to control recoil and muzzel jump. Right, a T/C Silhouette scope mounted on receiver of Ruger Mark I bull barrel .22 auto, using a pair of the discontinued Weaver steel rings.

This bull-barreled .41 magnum Contender carries a late-model Leupold M8-2X scope on the Herringshaw Maxi-Mount rings.

A further approach has taken the form of modifying handgun stocks to relieve the effect of apparent recoil. Examples include Steve Herrett's Controller stock for the T/C Contender and a comparable design from Schiermeier; both firms based in Twin Falls, Idaho. A minor objection to such stock designs, to the present, is that they are offered in right-hand or left-hand versions but not for comfortable use in either hand. Herrett is reported to be working on an ambidextrous version of his Controller stock, but the final results aren't in, for the present.

The obvious advantage of the ambidextrous stock is that it can be fired by those shooters who favor or are forced to use their left hand, as well as by the northpaw majority. Further, as many have found, hunting situations sometimes arise when there is simply no choice other than making the shot with the weak hand.

It was only natural to devote attention to the possibilities of exploring the limbo between handguns and fully stocked shoulder arms in an effort to obtain the best of both worlds. In an earlier day, there was moderate interest in the use of detachable stocks for handguns, often taking the form of a device that could be used as a holster attached as a stock. Federal regulations, passed about 1934, brought such devices into the "other firearms" category and required the payment of a $200 transfer tax plus considerable red tape when sold.

It is illegal to make a handgun by modification of a conventional rifle or shotgun — or, perhaps more accurately, such modifications must be made under control and approval of the concerned governmental agencies — but the reverse is not necessarily the case. It is permissible to modify a nominal handgun into a rifle or shotgun, provided the rifle barrel is sixteen or more inches in length, the shotgun barrel is eighteen inches or more and the overall length of either is in excess of twenty-six inches. Thus, when Remington introduced their Model XP-100 bolt-action, single-shot pistol in the early Sixties, they were able to go on and modify the basic action to create their Model 600 rifle on it.

Homer Koon, a Dallas-based gun dealer, took a long, thoughtful look at the various restrictions in force and

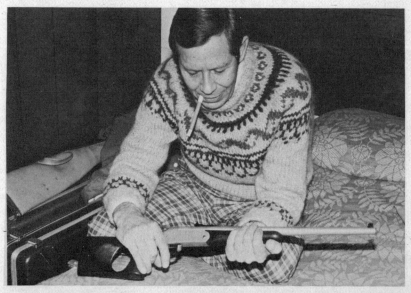

Above, typical 100-yard groups fired with Remington XP-100 pistol, M8-2X Leupold scope on Weaver mounts, laminated thumb hole stock by Fajen. Left and below, Homer Koon with his remarkable .410 Snake Charmer.

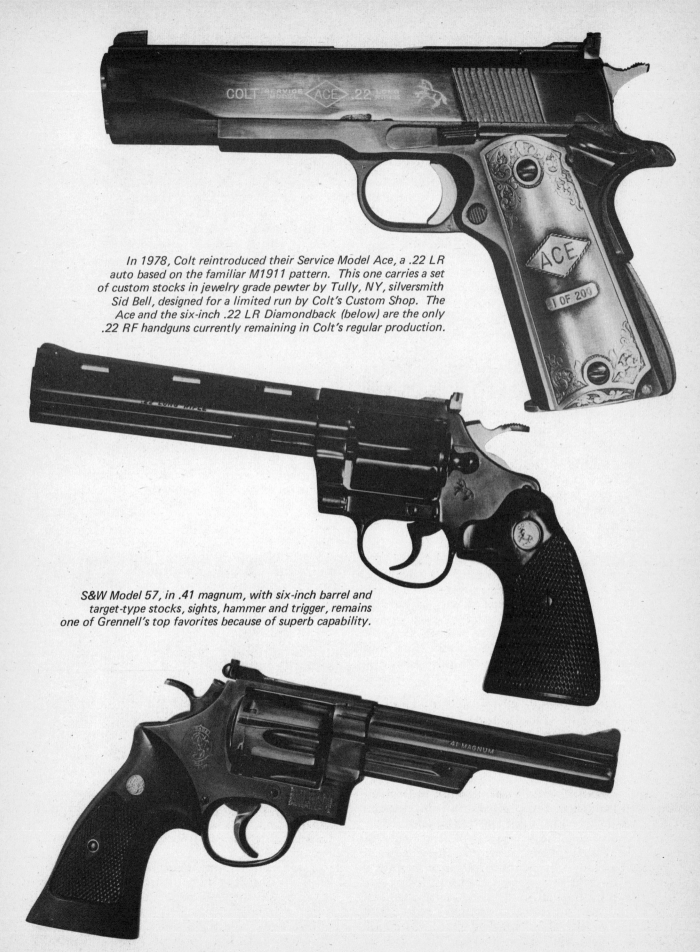

In 1978, Colt reintroduced their Service Model Ace, a .22 LR auto based on the familiar M1911 pattern. This one carries a set of custom stocks in jewelry grade pewter by Tully, NY, silversmith Sid Bell, designed for a limited run by Colt's Custom Shop. The Ace and the six-inch .22 LR Diamondback (below) are the only .22 RF handguns currently remaining in Colt's regular production.

S&W Model 57, in .41 magnum, with six-inch barrel and target-type stocks, sights, hammer and trigger, remains one of Grennell's top favorites because of superb capability.

Sterling Arms' Mark II stainless .380 double-action
auto is compact but capable. Introduced late in 1978,
it is one of several such guns slanted for off-duty police.

came up with a unique gun he calls the Snake Charmer. It's a break-action, single-shot .410 shotgun with a smoothbore barrel 18-1/8 inches long, chambered for the three-inch .410-bore shotshell (with the option of using the standard 2½-inch shell) and it carries an abbreviated thumb hole stock that brings the overall length to twenty-eight inches. The stock and forend are of black Nylon and corrosion-resisting alloys are used for the metal parts. Some of the parts, it should be noted, resist corrosion more successfully than others.

The public acceptance of the Snake Charmer was enthusiastic, to state it mildly. More than 20,000 units were sold in the first year after its introduction. Koon considered the possibility of offering barrels for center-fire cartridges such as the .22 Hornet but, at latest report, has sidetracked that for the present.

Another Texas designer, Frank Kendrick of Houston, organized the firm of Texas Contenders to market barrels of twenty-two-inch length that can be substituted for the usual ten- or fourteen-inch barrels of the T/C Contender. With rifled barrels of length greater than sixteen inches, it requires no further complexity or permit to substitite a conventional shoulder stock for the original handgun grip and Kendrick's firm offers the stocks as an additional option, enabling the Contender owner to convert it into a handy and graceful little single-shot rifle of exceptional accuracy capability. Similar conversion kits for the

Introduced for use in the Wildey auto (opposite page),
the 9mm and .45 Winchester Magnum cartridges are
capable of remarkable performance. Thompson/Center
offers barrels for their Contender in .45 WM, but not 9mm.

Contender are offered by Marsha and Alan Beckstead of Preston, Idaho.

There seems to be no restriction as to maximum barrel length for a handgun and the longer barrels can be used on the Contender with the handgun stock attached, should the owner so desire. The visual effect is a bit arresting, however.

Colt dropped their Woodsman .22 auto pistol from production and, by way of offering replacements,

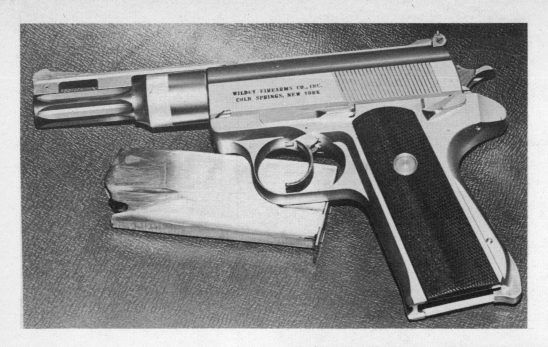

Still not in production at press time, discussed elsewhere in this book, the Wildey may yet reach its full potential.

Lee Jurras, of Hagerman, NM, works up special custom versions of the Contender for the five very robust rounds based on .500 Nitro Express brass.

reinstituted their Service Model .22 Ace and .22 LR version of their Diamondback DA revolver. The Ace resembles the M1911 .45 service pistol, incorporating the floating chamber feature to boost the effective recoil of the smaller cartridge for reliable functioning of the heavy slide. At the same time, it offers reasonably valid practice for shooters of the big service auto at drastically reduced ammunition cost.

The Colt .22 Diamondback closely resembles the Colt .357 Python in general appearance, although built to slightly smaller dimensions. At present, the .22 Diamondback is offered solely in six-inch barrel length. It's built on the same basic frame as the popular Colt Detective Special and stocks are interchangeable between the two.

Terry and Marcy Hudson, at Crown City Arms (Box 1126, Cortland, NY 13045) are marketing a no-frills version of the M1911 pattern of the .45 auto pistol, as well as a variety of parts for such guns so that owners can repair or customize guns currently in their possession.

Mossberg has another .45 auto currently under development, to be termed the Mossberg A.I.G.

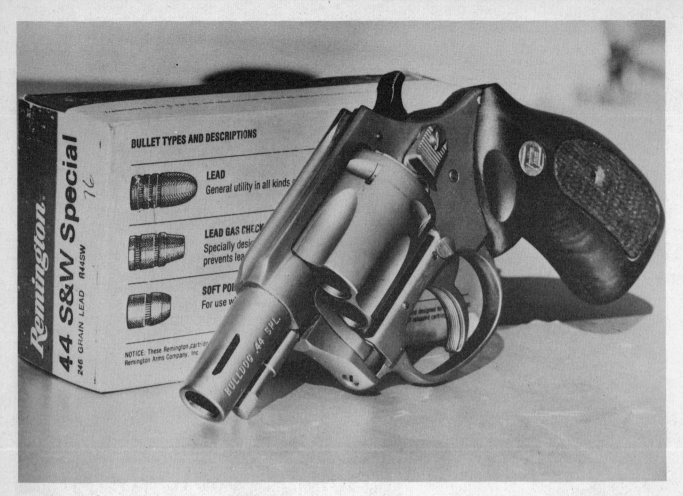

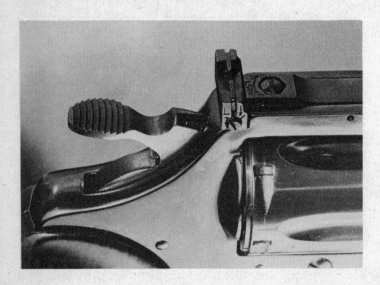

Mag-na-port "Backpacker" is a custom modification of the Charter Arms .44 Bulldog, one of the few guns currently chambered for the .44 Special cartridge. Below, markings on Colt Diamondback rear sight.

The .460 Jurras, left, with a .45-70 cartridge for size comparison. This probably represents the upper limit of practical power for a handgun cartridge and some might be inclined to voice the view that it exceeds it.

26

Browning Model BDA .45, above compared to the 9mm Browning Hi-Power, has an unusual hammer decocking lever, shown at left in operation. Same gun is shown below with its slide locked back. It has no safety in the usual sense, on the same reasoning that omits the safety on typical double-action revolver designs.

Military-Combat Model. Made of stainless steel, it will have a redesigned and relocated safety catch operated by dual levers on each side of the rear of the slide, together with a small spur on the lower front of the trigger guard for convenience of firing from the two-handed hold favored in police silhouette competition.

New auto pistol designs are also under development at Sterling, with DA versions in both .45 and .380 patterns. Again, in line with manifest public preference, the trend is to employ stainless steel for the sake of corrosion resistance.

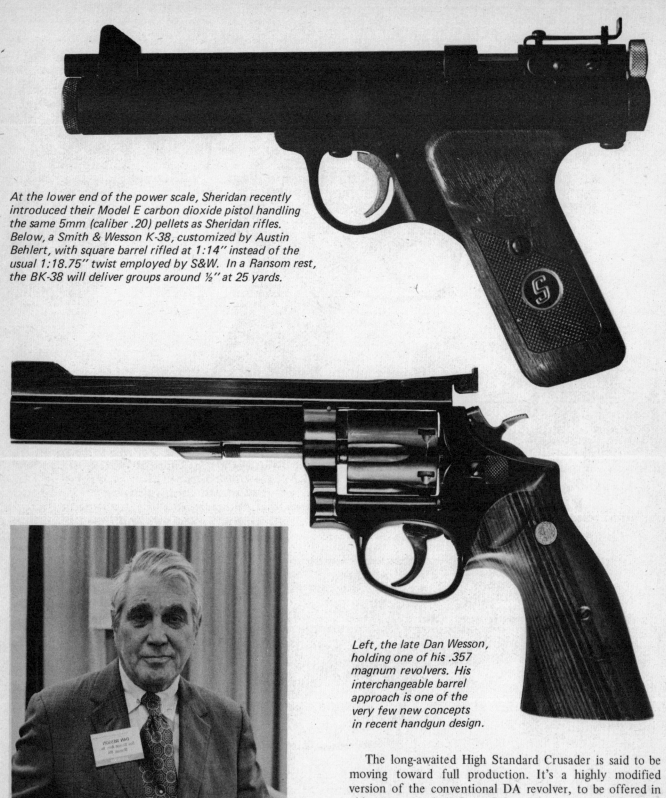

At the lower end of the power scale, Sheridan recently introduced their Model E carbon dioxide pistol handling the same 5mm (caliber .20) pellets as Sheridan rifles. Below, a Smith & Wesson K-38, customized by Austin Behlert, with square barrel rifled at 1:14" instead of the usual 1:18.75" twist employed by S&W. In a Ransom rest, the BK-38 will deliver groups around ½" at 25 yards.

Left, the late Dan Wesson, holding one of his .357 magnum revolvers. His interchangeable barrel approach is one of the very few new concepts in recent handgun design.

The long-awaited High Standard Crusader is said to be moving toward full production. It's a highly modified version of the conventional DA revolver, to be offered in .44 magnum and .45 Long Colt.

Sturm, Ruger & Company has prototypes of a DA revolver on a heavier frame than their Security Six, currently in .44 magnum chambering and possibly to be offered in other suitable calibers such as .45 Long Colt, .45 Auto Rim/ACP and (possibly) .41 magnum.

The Wildey gas-operated auto pistol likewise is in pre-production phases as this book goes to press. A DA design, also in stainless steel, its external appearance resembles what might result if a Model 1911 Colt were

A rather unlikely specimen, highly unusual, at least, is this .45 auto assembled on an aluminum alloy frame from A-R Sales. It incorporates one of the Caraville Double Ace cocking systems, with a Springfield Armory slide that has been custom-fitted with an adjustable rear sight from a Smith & Wesson K-38. The stocks are of ivory-colored epoxy. Hammer is shown in normal carrying mode for the Double Ace. To fire, rear grip lever is squeezed in, bringing hammer to full cock.

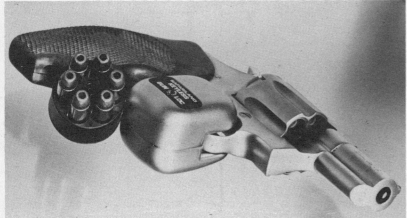

Keyless Gun Loc, by Safariland, can be removed quickly and easily by an adult, but it defies efforts at removal by Bill Grennell, age 12 at time of photo.

crossed with a Walther P'38. It handles two new cartridges, the 9mm and .45 Winchester magnums and features staggered box magazines, interchangeable barrels and a knurled control collar for handling light or heavy loads, with the option of switching to a manually actuated repeater if you don't wish to hunt for spent cases in the tall grass.

Also newly introduced since the previous edition is the Model BDA Browning, designed by S.I.G. and built by Sauer. Originally offered in 9mmP, .38 Colt Super and .45 ACP, only the last caliber remains in current production. Browning continues to make and market their Model 1935 9mmP auto, familiarly known as the Browning Hi-Power.

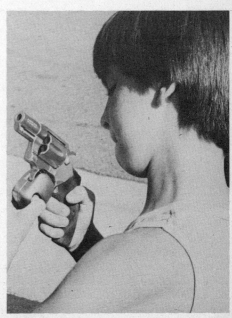

S&W Model 59 is a fat-butt version of their DA Model 39 in 9mmP. Its staggered column magazine has a capacity of fifteen cartridges.

Colt's 3d Model Dragoon is a modern re-creation of a legendary sixgun by its original maker. They picked up the serial numbering where it had left off when the Dragoon was discontinued in the 19th Century.

After having test-fired all three original calibers of the Browning Model BDA, I remain highly impressed by the astonishing reliability of its feeding and functioning. In the course of firing several hundred rounds in the three chamberings, we encountered exactly one round that chambered but did not fire when the trigger was pulled. On examination, it turned out that the reloaded cartridge had its primer seated open-side-out and thus the gun could hardly be blamed for the lone malfunction. No, if you were about to ask, it was not one of my reloads.

At the lower end of the handgun power scale, Sheridan Products was purchased by Benjamin and, not long after, introduced their long-awaited pellet pistol powered by carbon dioxide. It shoots the same 5mm (caliber .20) skirted pellets handled by the line of Sheridan pneumatic and carbon dioxide rifles and the general design of the

Sheridan pistol is highly similar to a carbon dioxide-powered Benjamin pistol made several years ago. Whether or not Sheridan will ever bring out a pneumatic handgun design in 5mm is a moot question for the present.

As we continue to inch through the final quarter of the Twentieth Century, it's a bit disappointing to contemplate the paucity of really notable breakthrough-type innovations appearing in the field of handguns or, for that matter, in firearms as a general class. It has been a long interlude of minor refinements, for the greater part. The caseless cartridge concept has been explored rather perfunctorily and the rocket pistol, a la Buck Rogers, made a brief appearance in the shape of the Gyro-Jet, only to be phased out quickly because of the fire hazard it presented. Another concept, much beloved by science fiction writers — the nonlethal, disabling "stun gun" — has appeared under the

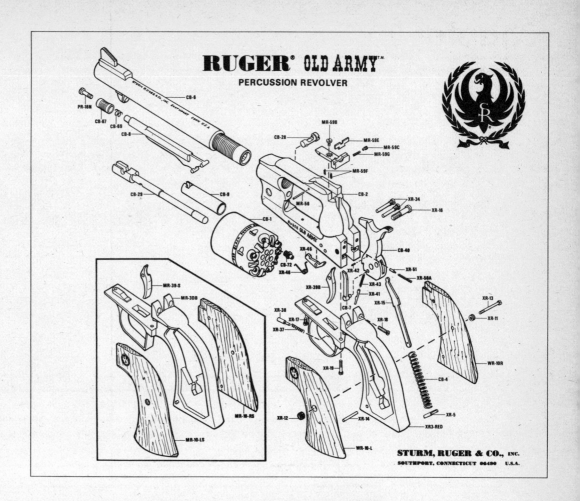

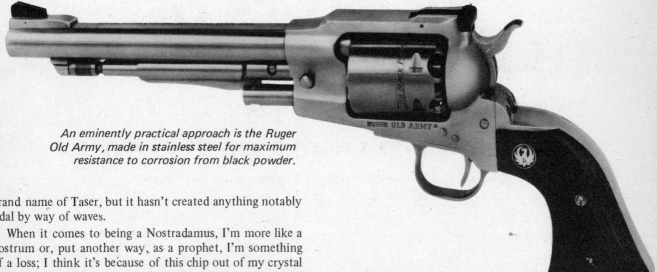

An eminently practical approach is the Ruger Old Army, made in stainless steel for maximum resistance to corrosion from black powder.

brand name of Taser, but it hasn't created anything notably tidal by way of waves.

When it comes to being a Nostradamus, I'm more like a nostrum or, put another way, as a prophet, I'm something of a loss; I think it's because of this chip out of my crystal ball. I recall trying to predict future handgun developments in the previous edition and now, a bit over two years later, the foregoing is about the status of the quo. We can deliver a few more foot-pounds, to increased distances, with a modest gain in overall accuracy. We have a few new bullet designs, a few new cartridges, essentially the same old propellants and a modest sprinkling of gun designs that represent little more than minor refinements of earlier models. As for being on the brink of breathtaking breakthroughs, I'd have to concede that your guess is at least as good as mine.

Enthusiasm or apathy on the part of the buying public is the key catalyst, when all's said and done. It was public acceptance that made the Snake Charmer quite possibly the most noteworthy handgun development (by a slightly stretched definition) since last edition. It was public apathy, among other things, that turned the fairly innovative Thomas .45 auto into a sort of instant collector's item. As someone wryly observed, apathy is one of the worst problems we face today, but who cares?

Chapter 2

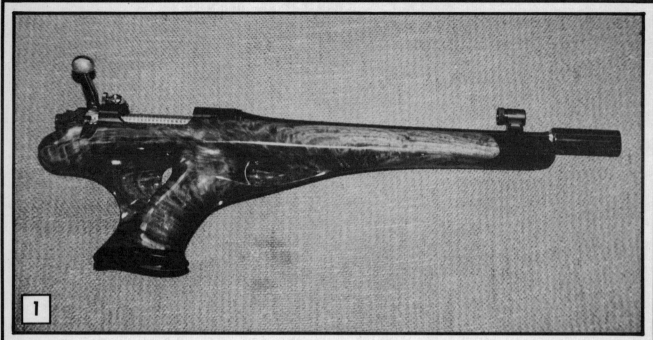

Photo 1: Remington XP-100 customized by Nels Largent of Boise, Idaho. Caliber .30 Remington, full length. Stock is Fajen blank, finished by Largent. Sights: Lyman 57 rear, 17-A Lyman front globe sight. Muzzle brake designed by Largent. Stock is finest grade American claro walnut. Engine-turned bolt. Considerable reduction of recoil from custom muzzle brake.

THE BASICS OF SILHOUETTE HANDGUNNING

This New Sport Is Sweeping The Country's Shooters... So Learn How It's Done!

By Elgin Gates

METALLIC Silhouettes! The most exciting game for handguns that has ever come down the pike!

There are half-inch-thick steel chickens at fifty meters, javelina at one hundred meters, turkeys at 150 meters and rams at two hundred meters; all made of heavy steel, all life-size silhouettes of the real thing.

Try it once and you likely will be hooked for good. Even minor success will bring instant gratification. On the other hand, you may feel a sense of frustration and near impotence. You probably will walk away from the firing line with the sudden realization that your big magnum isn't as potent as you thought. You may feel a bit ineffectual; at least thoughtful and subdued. And you can hardly wait to try it again!

It opens up a whole new world of handgun ballistics that will add new pages to the loading manuals. During the past year, more progress has been made in long-range handgun shooting as regards equipment, loads and techniques than in all the years since the handgun was invented.

As a spectator sport, it has no equal in the shooting world. Punching holes in paper targets at short distances heretofore has been the accepted technique in handgun competition. Silhouette shooting adds a new dimension.

With over five thousand members on the roster of the International Handgun Metallic Silhouette Association (IHMSA), and more flooding in at the rate of over one hundred per week, every manufacturer of handguns and related equipment in the country is giving this new sport a hard, practical look. Already, new products, equipment and

Photo 2: The Wichita Unlimited Silhouette pistol marks the first factory-built unlimited to appear on the market. It is built of the highest grade chrome-moly steel with fluted precision three-lug, recessed bolt, hand-lapped for perfect chamber alignment. Stock is of strongest fiberglass available or custom walnut, with glass-bedded action. Comes with custom Lyman sights, and left or right-hand bolt. Calibers are 7mm IHMSA International, .308x1½, .308 full-length and 7mm PPC. Barrel length and sight radius is fifteen inches, it weighs 4½ pounds and has an adjustable trigger. Firing pin fall is three-sixteenths-inch. Conforms to IHMSA Unlimited rules.

Designed for the serious metallic silhouette shooter who insists upon extreme accuracy and master craftsmanship. In this photo, Gates discusses features of the Wichita with Nolan Jackson, left, and Skip Nelson, center.

Photo 3: Custom XP-100 by Ron Power, one of the top custom masters in the field, whose S&Ws won almost all the championships in 1976 at the Combat Nationals. Unique two-hand stock was co-designed by Power and one of Fajen's shop foremen after Power came up with the original idea. This is a full-house silhouette model chambered for the .357 Auto Mag Pistol (AMP) cartridge and is throated to take the 250-grain rifle bullet. This gun has a Lyman 66 rear sight.

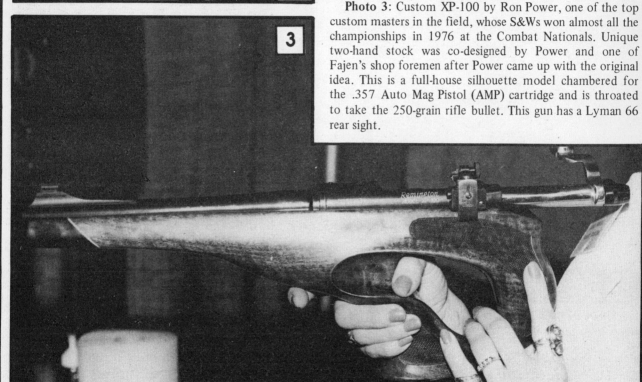

gun designs are in the works to meet the growth and demand of this phenomenal handgun game.

Competition, as established by the IHMSA, founder of the sport, is in two categories: production guns and unlimited guns.

Let's start with production guns. As the name implies, these are models as sold over the counter and may not be altered mechanically in any way. Barrel length is limited to 10¾ inches and weight to four pounds.

Only two changes are allowed: Any catalog grip available to the general public and specifically offered for a certain model may be used. Front and/or rear sights may be painted any color to contrast against the normally black silhouettes. Other than these, no modifications are allowed.

As in all shooting sports, there is a small band of "legal cheats" who perpetually try to bend and beat the spirit of the rules or search for loopholes to get an edge for their own personal advantage.

Officers of IHMSA, in response to the overwhelming demand from the rank and file members, are taking steps to deal with these professional cheats to prevent handgun silhouette from going down that long dreary road of continual modification that leads to super sophisticated and expensive equipment that has plagued and ultimately ruined virtually every shooting sport in existence. First, there is the excitement of bending the rules and getting an edge on the next guy. Soon, it takes $500 to get the edge, then $1000. In the meantime, the great mass of interested shooters have quietly dropped out.

NRA Rifle silhouette is a perfect example. It started as a

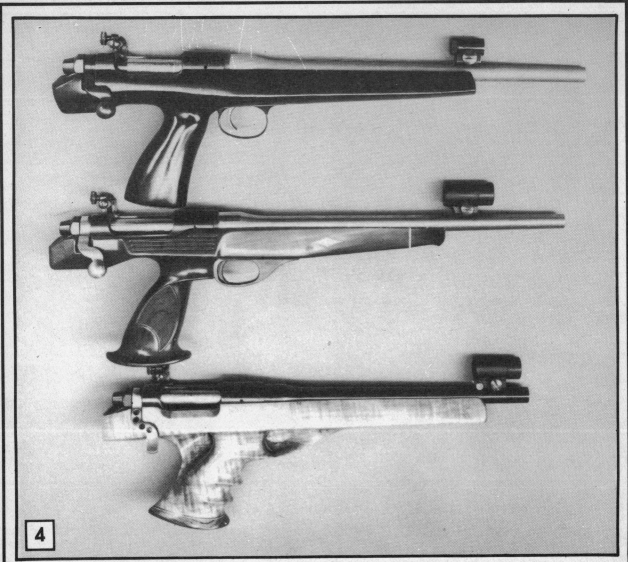

Photo 4: Jack Dever, Oklahoma City, builds custom Unlimited silhouette pistols on XP-100 actions. Top is a 7mmX250, fifteen-inch Shilen stainless barrel, Remington 600 bolt, Lyman 57 rear sight, Merit adjustable disc, Redfield globe front sight. Fiberglass stock designed by Dever and manufactured by Brown Precision. All the extra refinements have been done to the action. Center gun: .223X7mm (7X45) fifteen-inch Shilen octagon bore chrome-moly barrel, Redfield International big bore front sight, Lyman 57 rear sight, Merit adjustable disc. Factory stock cut to fit longer barrel with epoxy reinforcement in areas of front lug and rear stock screw. Bottom gun: .30 Maxi-Mag. (.30/222 mag with forty-degree shoulder and .250-inch long neck) 12¼-inch Douglas chrome-moly 1:12 twist barrel, Lyman 57 rear sight, Merit adjustable disc. Redfield International big bore front, Dever bubble level & crosshair insert added to sight. Action lightened (see bolt handle), Peterson birch stock blank, Devcon bedded stock, almost hollow to make weight.

deer rifle or hunter's sport. The silhouette rifles now used to dominate the game resemble nothing you would take into the woods on a real hunt, and you'd better figure on spending in the neighborhood of a thousand dollars if you want to be in the game.

This is the basic reason IHMSA created the unlimited category: to allow unlimited modification to suit any owner's or shooter's fancy. By the same token, there is solid determination to keep the production class just that — production.

Right now, there are two distinct types of production

guns in competition, revolvers and repeating guns such as the Auto Mags, and several single-shots.

Among revolvers, it is a horse race with no particular make or brand dominating the competition at present.

Freestyle shooters — any position other than standing — prefer the longer barrel models. Thus, Smith & Wesson models 27, 57 and 29, in .357 magnum, .41 magnum and and .44 magnum respectively, with 8-3/8-inch barrels are the most popular of the S&W line. The same model Smiths with six or 6½-inch barrels are preferred by offhand shooters because of better balance — less weight at the

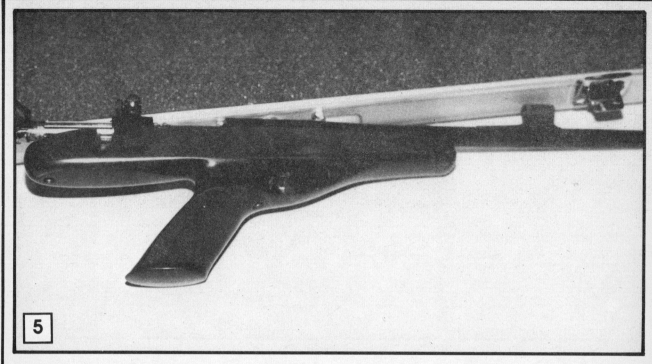

Photo 5: Weatherby Unlimited silhouette pistol, prototype as displayed in the 1978 NRA convention. Built on the Mark-V action with custom stock by Chuck Murray of Weatherby's. Chambered in 7mm or the Weatherby .224 belted magnum case. Tests with this gun, using a 154-grain Hornady, averaged 2650 fps with better than minute of angle accuracy at one hundred yards. Note: Weatherby has just announced their entry into the Unlimited silhouette handgun market, the first major manufacturer to do so, with a custom model, probably in .308 full-length. Full details will be available by writing to Weatherby's. IHMSA, by the way, has the first twenty-five guns on order as one of their Limited Edition series.

muzzle end of the barrel.

Dan Wesson's Pistol Pak with interchangeable barrels from 2½ to eight inches in .357 magnum is a popular combination with the six and eight-inch barrels being switched by many shooters competing in standing and freestyle production gun events. The optional, and also interchangeable, ten-inch barrel is in considerable demand among freestyle silhouette competitors.

Colt's venerable Python in .357 has done well in silhouette competition; a six-inch model holding the standing production record of 27X40 as we go to press. The Mark III Trooper appears on match reports now and then among the trophy winners. As a note of interest, IHMSA now is negotiating for a Limited Edition Special Silhouette model Python with eight-inch barrel as part of the IHMSA Limited Edition series.

With Colt's new look at the handgun market, it is hoped they will come on with heftier models for the .41 and .44 magnum cartridges.

The Ruger Super Blackhawk in .44 magnum with 7½-inch barrel has been one of the most popular revolvers used in metallic silhouette competition. The low price and toughness, combined with dependable performance, is an excellent combination. At this writing, a Ruger holds the revolver production record of 35X40 which has been tied recently by a Model 29 Smith and a Dan Wesson .357.

Some of the early Rugers, now collector items, are doing well in competition including the .256 Hawkeye and the ten-inch .44 flat top.

As a semi-trade-secret, Ruger has in the works — motivated, at least in part, by handgun silhouette — a new stainless double-action, large-frame revolver that could be the first new and revolutionary revolver design offered in the past fifty years.

Some of the other single and double-action revolvers appear in silhouette matches from time to time. Included are the Interarms Dragoon, Navy Arms Frontier, Astra, Charter Arms, and a few others.

United Sporting Arms is building a fifty-unit Special Limited Edition silhouette model of their Eldorado for IHMSA. It will be an all stainless, 10½-inch barrel, single-action piece with the IHMSA logo engraved on the frame with serial numbers 01 to 50. On the back strap will be engraved *1 of 50* on each gun. This is but one of a number of limited silhouette editions being manufactured for IHMSA.

The Auto Mags are still in silhouette competition and doing well in spite of the on and off production runs. At this writing, another run of about five hundred units is in the works.

The first and second scores of 30X40 ever achieved by a production gun were shot by Elgin Gates with a .357 Auto Mag with a ten-inch barrel in June 1977. Gates thus became the first silhouette competitor to achieve the classification of AAA.

Inherently, any single-shot, bolt-action or break-open

Photo 6: Remington XP-100 action re-barreled for the .458 Winchester magnum cut down to 1½ inches. Walnut stock by George Petersen of Western Gunstock. Micro sights on the rear, ramp with hood on the front. Note Mag-na-porting to cut down muzzle jump and recoil.

Photo 7: Mike "Earthquake" McElroy of Catalina Island, owner of the XP-100 .458x1½ magnum, points to huge splash where one of his .458 bullets hit the ram from two hundred meters. This combination puts them down, hard!

gun has an edge over the revolvers. Add to this the ever-increasing sums being spent by a handful of "legal cheats" who are violating the spirit of the production gun rules as originally conceived and intended, and the matter has created great concern among the wheel gunners. So much so, that a referendum vote will be taken by IHMSA to resolve the matter once and for all.

The most popular and successful of the single-shot production guns is the Thompson/Center Contender. So successful in fact that the new Super 14 is doing quite well in unlimited class competition against the most exotic handguns ever devised.

The ten-inch bull barrels in several calibers are quite popular among production-gun silhouette shooters.

As a special note, the steel chickens, pigs and turkeys respond well to average handgun ballistics, starting with the .357 magnum. Bert Stringfellow, IHMSA's Western executive director, achieved AAA classification with a .357 S&W magnum, being the first revolver shooter to do so.

The problem always has been the fifty-two-pound steel rams at two hundred meters. Bullets from any production handgun are rapidly running out of gas at that range.

In the early days of silhouette shooting, because of the difficulty of knocking down rams, it was thought the only way to go was with the .44 mags and the biggest slug you could lob downrange. In simple terms, hit those

fifty-two-pound steel rams with the biggest chunk of lead you could load in the cylinder and hope it did the job if you got a hit. It wasn't long before better scores were being shot with T/Cs chambered for rifle cartridges such as the .30-30, then the .35 Remington, and Steve Herrett's cut-down .30-30 cartridges, the .30 and .357 Herretts. The flatter trajectories, higher velocities and increased striking energy combined to knock down more rams.

This is where part of the controversy came in, the revolver shooters claiming unfair advantage having to shoot against the combination of the single-shot guns *plus* rifle cartridges.

On top of everything else, there was the little band of

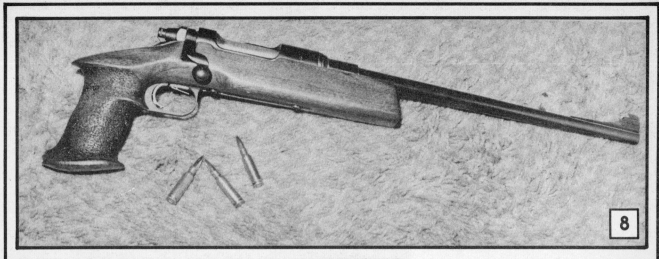

8

9

Photo 8: 7mm International from the collection of Elgin Gates, executive director of IHMSA. This gun epitomizes the ultimate development of the unlimited metallic silhouette pistol. Gun is chambered for the new IHMSA 7mm, with rear grip stock and electronic trigger by Frank Green of Melrose, Colorado.

Photo 9: Lineup of the five IHMSA International calibers on a common case designed by Elgin Gates, the first time several competitive calibers have standardized this way. Left to right, 6.5mm, 7mm, .30, 8mm, .35. Overall length of the case is 1.855-inch; trim length 1.840; head diameter, .474. Shoulder, thirty-eight degrees. Extensive computer analyses indicate an ideal case capacity for silhouette competition.

legal cheats working overtime on expensive modifications to the single-shot guns in violation of the spirit of the rules which has gone a long way toward alienating the honest men with their honest guns.

Thompson/Center has updated their Contender with regular production parts so that accurizing is available to all shooters at modest cost. This is progress in a true sense — improving the breed, if you will, and is welcomed by IHMSA because it is a standard production change on a production gun.

The Remington XP-100, almost phased out a few years back, now has found an application far beyond the wildest dreams of Remington and its designers. The production

version, in .221 Fireball, qualifies for the production category, and makes a good gun for women and juniors because of its light recoil. In the hands of a good shooter, its accuracy is such that scores in the high 30s (out of 40) have been achieved. The big handicap is, of course, the light 50 to 55-grain bullets that often will not knock down the fifty-two-pound rams at two hundred meters, or sometimes the pigs and turkeys, even with perfect hits.

Another break-open gun giving good performance is the Merrill Sportsman with nine-inch barrel, offered in a variety of calibers. A recent production change incorporating Micro sights as the standard and only sight available, should help its performance.

Photo 10: IHMSA headstamp on prototype cases. Flash hole hasn't been drilled on these prototypes. Cases are being manufactured by Federal on contract with Gates.

Photo 11: Two Unlimited Thompson/Center Contenders from the Gates collection. Top gun, with custom forearm and special fifteen-inch heavy barrel, is chambered for one of the early prototype .30 Gates cartridges now designated as .30 IHMSA. This gun was built over a year before T/C introduced their Super 14, and in fact is a forerunner of the Super 14. Lower gun is an experimental Unlimited prototype on a T/C frame chambered for the first 7mm Gates cartridge in 1976, and used to set the Unlimited silhouette record of 34X40 on January 9, 1977. Gates then raised it to 38X 40 on May 14, 1977. This cartridge is now officially the 7mm IHMSA International.

IHMSA is in favor of progress and improvement at the manufacturing level, providing any and all changes are available as standard equipment or accessories at a modest price to all shooters.

The unlimited category has spawned some remarkable handguns, both in appearance and performance. Never before has handgun design and development undergone such a startling transformation in such a short period.

Let me set the scene and tone for a complete update:

At the 1978 NRA convention in Salt Lake, I was in one of the display booths examining a new unlimited pistol. As I turned around, still holding it in my hands, to ask a question, I almost bumped into the classic version of the little old gray-haired lady in tennis shoes. She took one startled look at the exotic pistol and stepped back, wide-eyed.

"Oh, my!" She exclaimed, hand going to her mouth. "That must be one of those laser guns they had in *Star Wars.*"

She wasn't all that far off. Already, the IHMSA metallic silhouette game has developed its own slang and jargon.

Photo 12: Top gun is .308x1½ with a 14-inch barrel on an XP-100 action using the cut-off nylon factory stock and utilizing a tube sight installed by Elgin Gates. Bottom gun is chambered for the full-length .308 Winchester case necked down to 7mm, utilizing a German hammered barrel and Lyman sights.

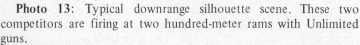

Photo 13: Typical downrange silhouette scene. These two competitors are firing at two hundred-meter rams with Unlimited guns.

Photo 14: Scott Lindley, IHMSA's office manager, foreground, and Frank Hough, of Inkom, Idaho, in shootoff for the Idaho State Unlimited championship after both men fired perfect 40X40 scores in competition. This peculiar "Creedmoor" position is favored by many top rank shooters although due to safety considerations, a vote of the IHMSA technical committee may be taken to rule that no part of the shooter's anatomy may be in front of the muzzle. Lindley won the shootoff by downing eight chickens at two hundred meters to Hough's five. Lindley was using one of the new IHMSA 7mm prototypes.

Photo 15: Unusual Unlimiteds include: (top) Ruger standard .22 grip frame. Barrel extension and rotary bolt head from M-16. Receiver, barrel and barrel nut and bolt carrier are custom by Robert Ballard.

Barrel quick detachable, caliber, .30/223. Single-shot, straight pull rotating bolt lock. (Center) Unlimited revolver, 1917 S&W frame, .45 Long Colt. Twelve-inch barrel patterned after Practical Pistol Course (PPC) barrels and extended to twelve inches. Astra .357 sights. (Bottom) Barrel blank by P.O. Ackley, mounted and machined by Ballard. One-inch diameter heavy barrel, T/C frame with modified sight. Forearm with adjustable forward grip, caliber, .30-30.

Laser, or Star War piece, is slang for a full-house unlimited gun. When you "firewall it" you are max-loading. So, if you hear an expression like this: "Man, he firewalled that laser and daylighted the steel," it translates that he was using maximum loads in one of the new exotic silhouette unlimited pistols and was punching holes in the silhouette targets.

I hasten to add that such loads are not allowed where mild steel targets are being used. IHMSA match directors have the authority to bar such loads that create target damage.

In addition to the guns shown here, mostly by custom gunsmiths, several manufacturers other than Weatherby and Wichita are getting interested. Remington is testing prototypes of its own XP-100 in several of the more desirable high performance unlimited cartridges. In 1979, a new unlimited version may be on the market.

As IHMSA's membership climbs above five thousand, and this wildly exciting sport of handgun metallic silhouette shooting continues to burgeon, there is little doubt that more production and unlimited handguns are in the offing. They will be welcomed by all hands.

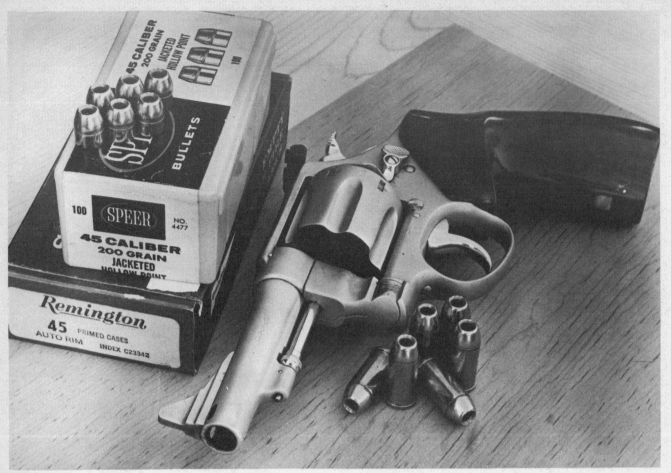

Reloading offers versatility, besides saving money. In .45 Auto Rim, hollow-points can't be bought but can be loaded.

Chapter 3

By Dean A. Grennell

HANDGUN RELOADING

It's Fun; It Saves Money; It Lets You Do A Lot More Shooting — But Observe A Few Sensible Precautions!

FOR ANYONE who fires more than a few rounds of handgun ammunition on rare occasions, reloading has come to be a way of life. The cost of factory ammunition has become substantial. The empty

cases represent a value that's also substantial. Even if you're not into reloading at present, those fired hulls are well worth saving. Someday, you may shift viewpoints on the matter. Meanwhile, you can swap or sell the fired cases to

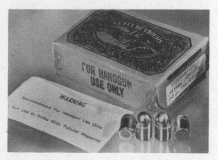

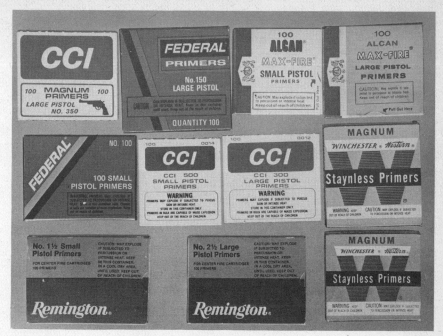

Top, .38 Special, shown with cast bullet before being lubricated, is the most popular round for reloading. Above, jacketed bullets, such as these by Sierra in .4295″ diameter, require no lubrication before loading. Above right, pistol primers come in two diameters; small pistol (.175″) and large pistol (.210″), as needed.

other shooters who reload. If all other considerations make no impression, discarding fired brass constitutes littering, an indefensible act at best.

Anyone who employs the phrase, "cheap and brassy," has not had occasion to purchase brass in recent times. Its cost is impressive and the same goes for tin, so "cheap and tinny" is at least equally dubious. As a rough average figure, one fired brass cartridge is worth at least a dime (in the latter Seventies — someday that will have an archaic ring).

In this country today, according to several firms that make and sell reloading equipment, the .38 Special cartridge is the odds-on leader in terms of die sets sold and, probably, in rounds reloaded. It accounts for sales equaling the next two or three runners-up, combined. So let's discuss reloading the ubiquitous .38 Special cartridge case, with the stipulation that the procedures are fairly well applicable to several other handgun cartridges, as well.

To reload the .38 Special, there are certain basic prerequisites, by way of equipment and components. You will need:

empty cases (.38 Special or whatever)
primers (small pistol size for .38 Special)
powder (nitro type, also called smokeless)
bullets (.357 if jacketed, .358 if lead)
a loading press or loading kit
dies and shell holder for the press
a powder measure and/or powder scale
reloading manuals/handbooks; one, at least
competent instruction
the ability to follow simple directions

In a loaded cartridge, the case neck grips the base of the bullet with a degree of tension. It has to do so, otherwise the bullet would work loose. That's especially true in

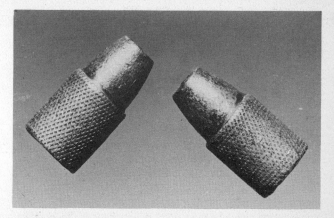

Top, lead semi-wadcutters by Hornady have novel type of knurling on driving band to keep the lube in its place. Above, slip in box warns against use of full metal jacket (FMJ) bullets in guns having tubular magazines, tells why.

ammunition for revolvers. The recoil of each shot slams the gun rearward. In turn, that imparts a lot of momentum to the rim of each remaining, unfired cartridge in the cylinder.

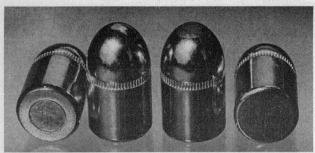

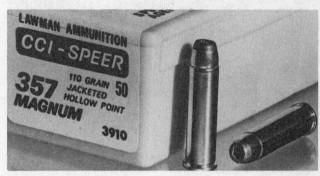

Left, Sierra FMJ and jacketed soft-point (JSP) are similar except for base and tip. Top right, Speer offers their 200-grain jacketed hollow-point (JHP) as component or in the form of ready-to-use factory ammunition. Right, note 5-sided cavity that Speer terms their "Penta-Point."

The natural inertia of the heavy bullet makes it tend to remain motionless while the case moves rearward under recoil stress. Unless the case neck grips it firmly, the bullet can migrate forward to the point where one of the last few rounds will permit the bullet tip to project from the front of the cylinder. That will hang up cylinder rotation and leave the gun temporarily inoperable. To prevent that, we arrange for the case neck to grip the bullet base fairly snugly, as noted.

At the time of previous firing, pressure from the burning powder gases forced the case walls outward until movement was arrested by the walls of the chamber. Brass is not particularly elastic, though it's much more so than lead. Thus, after firing, the case necks will grip a bullet sloppily, if at all.

Since there is a small but significant variation in metal thickness at the case neck — particularly from make to make — and it's important to achieve a precise inside diameter before seating the bullet, the usual procedure involves sizing down the outside diameter to a point a bit too small, then running an expanding plug into the neck to work it back out to the desired inside diameter (ID). Two other necessary steps are performed at the same time: A depriming pin affixed to the end of the expander plug goes down through the flash hole in the case head to push out the spent primer and a tapered area at the top of the plug

produces a slight bell or flare at the case mouth to assure easy seating of the new bullet.

The resizing may be performed down the entire length of the case — or only for a fraction of an inch at the neck — respectively termed full-length and neck resizing. So long as the outside diameter (OD) of the case is small enough to permit easy chambering, either course is acceptable.

Having restored the case to desired dimensions, it remains to seat a fresh primer in the primer pocket, add a suitable amount of the appropriate powder, seat the bullet and turn the flare at the neck back in to restore proper OD at that point. The neck flare may be turned back in as a crimp to further secure the bullet in place, provided the bullet has a corresponding crimping groove at that point.

All of the foregoing operations can be carried out by use

Above, photo taken over 10 years ago shows a typical assortment of powders, most of which were used in reloading handgun ammo. Right, Olin has phased out their 231, replacing it with 230. Such substitutions are not uncommon.

Left, a pair of the old hand-type full-length resizing dies in .44 and .38 Special. They worked after a fashion, but at heavy cost in effort and time consumed. Right, a lubricated cast bullet being seated in case whose neck has been flared.

of a reloading press and matching die sets or by use of one of the inexpensive reloading kits that operate by tapping the cases into and out of the sizing chamber by means of a mallet. Use of a reloading press is the fastest, handiest approach. Use of one of the kits entails the least cash outlay for equipment.

A typical reloading press generates a prodigious amount of leverage and reduces the effort of resizing to comfortable levels. I still have a small full-length resizing die for the .38 Special, made by Lyman, that I bought very early in my reloading career. It was designed to be used without a press. The case — suitably lubricated on the outside — was to be tapped into the die with a mallet, after which the die was reversed and the provided knockout pin was used to drive it back out. The efforts involved were substantial, even for the relatively small .38 Special case. Getting the case head flush with the rear die surface required vast amounts of pressure. I tried using a large bench vise with degrees of success that hardly could be termed indifferent. A friendly filling station proprietor let me use a huge arbor press in his

shop and I've memories of endlessly chinning myself on the end of the six-foot steel lever of the big arbor, all in vain as the small but oversized cases resisted total entry into the die with remarkable stubbornness. Memory of such furious but futile efforts made for extravagant appreciation of my first full-scale reloading press — a C-press by C-H Tool & Die Corporation — when I finally took over its ownership.

Properly cared for, a reloading press stands up to the years remarkably well. Press choice is a matter of individual preference, but selection merits careful consideration. For the past twenty years, I've been using one of the old RCBS Model A-2 jobs and, so far as I've been concerned, I've *had* my loading press, with scant motive to seek further afield. Unfortunately, this paragon of virtues hasn't been made for the past several years. It was superseded by the RCBS design currently termed their Rock Chucker, which I regard as a nice press, but not an A-2.

What's so special about the A-2? Its ram is hollow in the center so that the spent primers drop down out of sight, to be caught neatly in a tin can resting on a shelf below the

Left, Olin 630 and 296 are that maker's current handgun powders, in addition to the 230 on opposite page. Above, if desired, reloading gear can be taken to the range so that various combinations can be made up and tested on the spot.

Left, Grennell's first full-scale loading press was this C-H C-type, capable of resizing .30/06 cases easily when same operation was a strain with a big arbor press. Above, Pacific Durachrome die set, with tungsten carbide sizer.

press. Its frame is an O-type, open at both sides, with plenty of room for putting cases into the shell holder with the left hand and removing them with the right in effortless motion flow. Its design incorporates a novel but efficient compound linkage that multiplies leverage progressively as the handle is operated.

The compound linkage feature remains available today on various top-of-the-line presses such as the RCBS Rock Chucker, the Pacific Multi-Power C, and the C-H CHampion. The CHampion is probably the closest duplicate

of the A-2 still in current production. It retains the hollow ram feature to deposit spent primers neatly into a container positioned beneath it and has ample working room on either side. Its ram is of well hardened steel so that you don't distort the flanges that hold the shell holder, even if employing extreme efforts, as in bullet swaging operations.

The Bonanza Co-Ax press is another of those rare designs that keeps the spent primers under close control. On the Co-Ax, they drop through a slender tube to be caught in a little plastic jar that rides up and down beneath the shell holder. Another admirable feature of the Co-Ax is its universal shell holder that fairly well handles any center-fire cartridge you choose to reload.

Most reloading presses just let the spent primer pop forth to find its own course. Some offer a plastic primer catcher, to be affixed to the press by means of a rubber

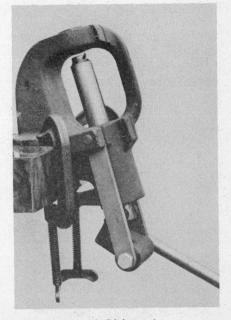

In this sequence of photos, function of the compound leverage system of loading presses can be noted. Right and left photos are of the C-H CHampion, while center press is the Rock Chucker, by Omark/RCBS, shown here with sizing die in place at the top and the case being resized placed in the shell holder on top of ram; both are O-types.

The Bonanza Co-Ax press, shown close-in and mounted on a portable mini-bench which works out extremely well. The Co-Ax catches all of the expelled primers and also features an automatic shell holder accepting all sizes.

band. Such devices often succeed in entrapping a percentage of the spent primers, but others make it over the wall and onto the floor. Policing up scattered primers has never been one of my favorite hobbies. Control of such messy, gritty little artifacts, however, is not the end-all and be-all of press design, surely and I don't wish to seem to over-emphasize it here.

Most handgun cartridges require relatively modest amounts of effort in reloading. The .44 magnum is one of the few exceptions. Massive press leverage is more useful if you get into reloading the larger rifle cartridges, as many may. I apologize to readers in general and press manufacturers in particular for inflicting my personal foibles at this point. My excuse is that, after previous such writeups have been published, readers have written me to point out that I said nothing about what sort of press I preferred, and why. The foregoing discussion is an attempt to rectify such omissions and forestall further critiques on that score.

In point of fact, I know of no really unsatisfactory reloading presses that remain on the market as a new decade dawns over the eastern horizon. There have been some thoroughly dubious designs introduced in the past — one with the unlikely designation of the Eagle Cobra comes to mind as a sterling example — but all such are out of production, to the best of my knowledge. The free enterprise system has a way of dealing rather implacably with such things, in the manner of Mother Nature and survival of the fittest.

The pertinent consideration, I think, is that just about any reloading press is incomparably better than no press at all. Witness the vast improvement in my own facilities when I managed to scrounge up the cost of that C-H press, back in the waning days of the Truman administration. True, it

Here, the big C-H CHampion O-type press has been set up for swaging JHP bullets with C-H No. 101 swage dies.

strewed spent primers about the floor in blithe abandon, but it sure beat trying to get cases back to size on the local garage's arbor press!

Elsewhere in this volume, Skeeter Skelton deals with the Lyman No. 310 tong tool, often termed the "nutcracker." I cut my reloading teeth on one and then went on to buy one of the little Lyman Tru-Line Junior presses because it also used the same thread size of loading dies as the No. 310 (5/8-40, I believe, as opposed to the 7/8-14 employed on most other dies). The Tru-Line had a four-station turret head and I reloaded vast quantities of cartridges with it. The problem lay in the fact that it did not — at that time — have the capability for full-length resizing. Eventually, I accumulated a lot of cases that entered the chamber reluctantly, if at all. That was how I came to try the full-length chamber with the arbor press.

Lyman offers little adapter bushings so the 5/8-40 dies can be used in 7/8-14 presses and some of those early-acquired dies are still very much in business. One in

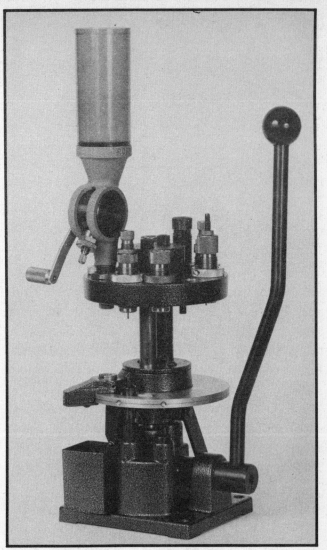

New P-200 Metal-Matic from Ponsness-Warren accepts standard 7/8-14 dies and regular shell holders. Turret can be set up for five dies each in two calibers at once.

Grennell has been using this RCBS A-2 press since 1959, appreciating its hollow ram that drops expelled primers into the bean can shown here. It's also handy for feeding cases in with the left hand and plucking them out with the right. RCBS has replaced the A-2 with the Rock Chucker.

particular is the mouth-expander die for the .45 ACP, with a round-ended punch that does a superb job of preconditioning dinged and battered hulls from the autoloader prior to the pass into the full-length resizing die. I usually keep that one installed on the Hollywood Senior Turret press that I customarily use for the .45 ACP round and find it so handy I wonder why such a die isn't in general use.

Apart from its light weight and compact size, I'm not terribly infatuated with the Lyman nutcracker tool. It soaks up a lot of time and patience for switching those little dies about. In the area of compact and inexpensive reloading systems, I'd prefer the kits offered by Lee Precision or Lee Custom Engineering. They take up little space, cost less and are, I think, simpler and faster in use. They require a small mallet or, in a pinch, you can make do with a stick of wood. Current cost is a touch under fifteen bucks. New kits are sold with thoroughly adequate instructions for their use. If you get such a kit in a horse trade without instructions, by all means, request a fresh set of instructions from the maker (Lee Precision, Highway U, Hartford, Wisconsin 53027 or Lee Custom Engineering, 46

Another example of the familiar C-type press is this one from Hornady-Pacific, here held to bench with C-clamps.

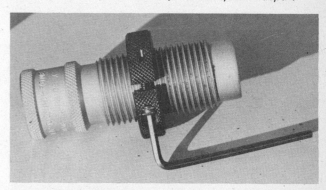

Below, locking ring on Pacific die loosens with hex-wrench. Bottom, Pri-Mike, from Zenith, measures primer depth.

East Jackson Street, Hartford, Wisconsin 53027), specifying the cartridge for which your kit is intended. Either maker, I'm sure, will be glad to supply instructions free on request. By all means, refrain from using such kits until the instructions are at hand. A few overly intrepid souls have come to grief through the use of such kits with the wrong kind of powder.

Both versions of the Lee kits employ small dipper-type measures for dispensing the powder and both offer separate measure kits with the complete line of dippers plus a slide rule table listing the charge weight delivered by each dipper for a large variety of different powders. The Lee Custom Engineering dippers are designated by a number on the handle representing a decimal fraction of one cubic inch. Thus, for example. the No. 039 dipper has a capacity of

0.039-cubic inch (early versions of this particular size were designated as the Special H).

The moulded plastic dippers supplied by Lee Precision in their loading kits and measure kits are designated by their capacity in cubic centimeters (cc). For example, the dipper supplied with the Lee Precision kit for the .38 Special is marked .3cc and dispenses 3.2 grains of Winchester 231 or Hodgdon HP-38 powders to drive bullets of 140 to 150 grains at respective velocities of 850 and 800 feet per second (fps).

How do you get the old primer out? The decapping pin goes through the flash hole as in this cross-section.

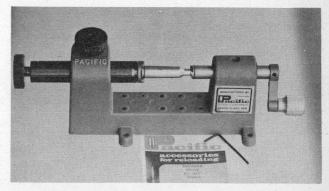

Case trimmer by Pacific accepts standard shell holders, uses pilots of appropriate size in the center of cutter.

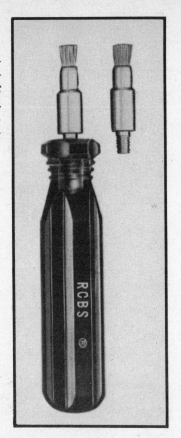

RCBS brush for cleaning primer pockets. RCBS Rock Chucker, with catch tray. RCBS 3-die set.

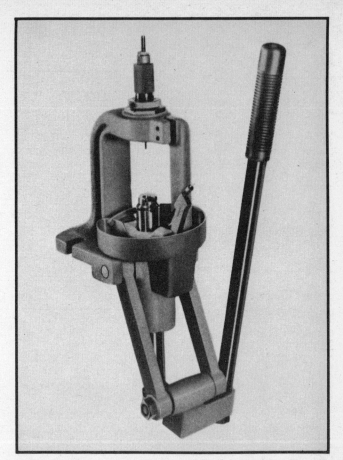

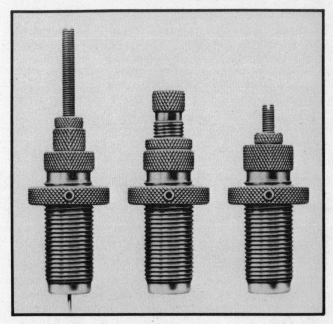

By way of explaining a potentially confusing situation regarding the plurality of Lees in the reloading kit field, Richard J. Lee originally invented and developed the kit concept in this particular format and worked with Lee Custom Engineering for several years before organizing Lee Precision, Incorporated as his own company. Lee Precision remains under Lee's direct supervision to the present but he is not currently connected with Lee Custom Engineering.

I couldn't even begin to estimate how many reloaders have started out with one of the Lee kits, though I'm certain it's an impressively large number. For several years, the kits were priced at $9.95 each and it offered a financially painless entry into the field. The shooter was offered a chance to try out the operation, with the option of going on to more elaborate and expensive equipment if it proved rewarding.

Repeating for emphasis: The kit approach to reloading offers several practical advantages, including modest initial cash outlay but you *must* have the appropriate set of instructions at hand for that particular cartridge before you commence reloading with a kit. Operating without the instructions is a guaranteed downhill shortcut to disaster, never forget it!

The shooter who turns to reloading today may not appreciate the wealth of data and information now available. It was not always so easy or simple to obtain the information needed. About 1948, when I first took an interest in the resurrection of empty brass, we had the late Phil Sharpe's *Complete Guide to Handloading,* a massive and exhaustive work still meriting study, even today, though a lot of the items discussed have been obsolete for decades. Then there were the Lyman/Ideal handbooks. The line of Ideal reloading equipment started out under that

name, apparently close to the turn of the century. My earliest copy of the Ideal Handbook is the No. 24 edition, dating from about 1910. In the foreword, it announces that Ideal had just been taken over by the makers of Marlin rifles. Lyman had started as a maker of gun sights, recently observing their centennial year. Apparently, they acquired the Ideal reloading equipment operation some time after 1910.

A decade or so ago, I visited the old Lyman plant at

Left, RCBS taper crimping die does a good job of conditioning case necks after seating bullet. Below, RCBS case trimmer, showing cutter pilot.

Top, RCBS primer tray. Above, changing shell holder and shell holder in place, ready to accept given case.

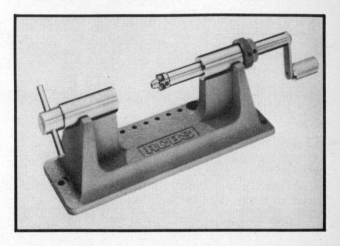

Middlefield, Connecticut; a picturesque holdover from a distant era, it still had a huge water wheel for drawing power from the adjacent river, with a network of jack shafts and pulleys about the ceiling from which belts were used to drive the equipment. It had been converted to electric motors, long before my visit, but the water-powered facilities made an interesting glimpse into Nineteenth Century manufacturing approaches.

The first of the Speer Manuals was copyrighted in 1954. The ninth edition has been used since 1974 and another is due for publication at this writing. Between the eighth and ninth edition, there occurred a marked reduction in several of the listed maximum charges. This caused minor ripples of dismay in reloading circles, but it was for the best. It brought peak pressures within the upper limits set by the Sporting Arms and Ammunition Manufacturers Institute (SAAMI) for the given cartridge.

Every now and again, some reader writes in to request an explanation for the fact that handbooks and manuals on reloading do not agree precisely upon the maximum weight of this or that powder for a particular bullet weight in a given cartridge. The reason is simple enough. The data is generated by people, using test guns. The people vary on an individual basis and, quite definitely, so do the guns.

In developing the data, the lab workers probably started low and worked up by cautious increments until reaching what seemed like a judicious cutoff point. The joker in that particular deck is the fact that even nominally identical guns do not necessarily generate absolutely identical results when identical loads are fired in them. A few years ago, I owned a pair of Smith & Wesson Model K-38 revolvers, both .38 Special (of course), both with six-inch barrels. One of the warmer loads out of the No. 8 Speer Manual worked just fine in one of the K-38s but, if you fired the same load out of the other K-38, it measured substantially lower velocities through the chronograph and, at the same time, the case would stick in the chamber so that it had to be coaxed out with a short length of wooden dowel gently tapped with a mallet.

Fired cases that extract with difficulty from revolver chambers are a positive indication that something is seriously wrong. Either the load in question developed far too high a peak pressure or, alternately, the chamber has been bulged out of shape by a previous firing of an overloaded round. If cartridges loaded to modest pressure levels resist extraction, you need to replace the damaged

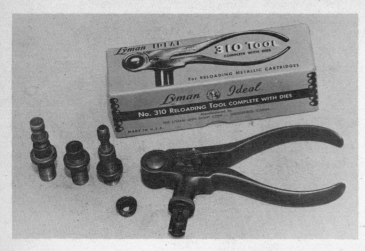

Lyman's No. 310 tong tool, or "nutcracker" used smaller, 5/8-40 thread dies that went into socket on tong arm. Compact and light in weight, it made a good portable reloading facility, although a bit slow in production.

Top right, tong tool set up for seating primers. Lower right, after decapping, a hook grabs rim or extractor groove to pull decapped case back out. Below, as discussed, Grennell has the No. 310 mouth expanding die for .45 ACP installed in an adapter bushing for use in standard presses, finds it handy for ironing out the dented case mouths commonly encountered in cartridges such as .45 ACP.

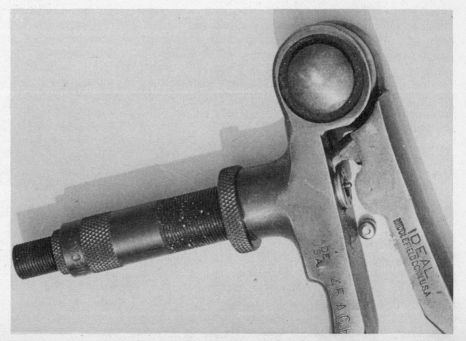

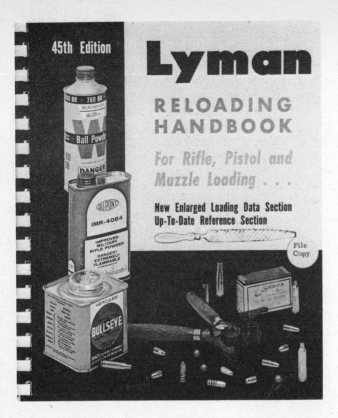

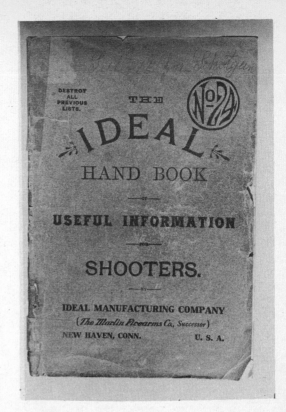

Above, current No. 45 edition of Lyman Reloading Handbook. Above right, cover of the No. 24 Ideal Hand Book, published about 1910, before Lyman bought the Ideal reloading line. Right, sample entry from 1910 Ideal Hand Book, showing a semi-wadcutter design, No. 429336, new to the line at that time, having been made for C.E. Heath. Today, it's customary to refer to SWC bullets as "Keith type," since Elmer Keith did much to popularize the use of them.

Requires No. 3 tool with double adjustable chamber only and separate mould.

Price of Single Mould . . . . Special List, $1.50

429336. For .44 S. & W. SPECIAL and COLT'S NEW SERVICE REVOLVERS. Made for C. E. Heath of the Boston Revolver Club. Cuts a clean hole in the target. When cast one part tin to thirty parts of lead weighs about 255 grains. Powder charge 4 grains' weight Hercules "Bullseye" or 5½ grains' weight DuPont "R. S. Q." Requires No. 3 tool with double adjustable chamber only and separate mould.

Price of Single Mould . . . . Special List, $1.50

429352. SQUARE NOSE BULLET for .44 S. & W. RUSSIAN and .44 S. & W. SPECIAL. Made for M. L. Holman of St. Louis. When cast one part tin to thirty of lead weighs about 245 grains. Powder charge 4 grains' weight of Hercules "Bullseye" or 5½ grains' weight of DuPont "R. S. Q." Requires No. 3 tool with double adjustable chamber only and separate mould.

Price of Single Mould . . . . Special List, $1.50

429348. SQUARE NOSE BULLET for .44 S. & W. RUSSIAN and .44 S. & W. SPECIAL. When cast one part tin to thirty of lead weighs about 176 grains. Powder charge 3 grains' weight of Hercules "Bullseye" or 4 grains' weight of DuPont "R. S. Q." F. Bilderbeck, So. Edmeston, N. Y., says: "It carried perfectly true and accurate up to and including 200 yards. I expected to use the bullet only on the 20 yard range on account of the points to be gained by the large perfect hole it cuts and was exceedingly surprised to find I could spot the shots at 50 yards with as much regularity as I could with the Anderton bullet." Requires No. 3 tool with double adjustable chamber only and separate mould.

Price of Single Mould . . . . Special List, $1.50

cylinder. If the cases stick on a once-only basis, the gun's okay but your charge weights are in drastic need of reduction.

Much has been written and discussed about the possibility of reading pressures by examination of the primer after firing. I'm not inclined to regard that as a reliable approach. I've seen primer cups flattened extravagantly by loads that were within acceptable limits by any other standard and I've seen other primers that still looked quite healthy as I tried to coax the case out of the chamber.

The point to all this rambling is that there is no acceptable substitute for consulting a reliable handbook or manual — synonymous terms implying no distinction — for determination of the proper weight of a given powder for the application at hand. Buy at least one manual (handbook), several, if possible. The load data booklets published by powder suppliers such as Hercules, Winchester-Western, Norma, Du Pont, Hodgdon, et al., often can be obtained at no charge from your local dealer or on request from the supplier so there is no excuse for failing to consult them on dubious grounds of economy.

Close may count in horseshoes, but loading manuals mean exactly what they say. At some point in the mid-Seventies, Winchester-Western discontinued their No. 630P powder and replaced it with a modified version termed No. 630. Data for the two are not interchangeable. If, for example, you try loading .41 magnum ammo with 630 powder, using the charge weights prescribed in the first edition of the Sierra Manual for No. 630P powder, it will cause hazardous pressures, even if you load to less than the maximum listed weights.

Most manuals list a fairly wide variety of powders under each bullet weight for the different cartridges and this raises a question in the beginner's mind: How do you know which powder to use? Assorted considerations apply, including availability of the powder in your locale, economy in terms of cost per load, ease and uniformity of measurement and

Lee Precision powder measure kit includes fifteen dippers and slide card showing drop of each dipper when used with 95 different powders. Two dippers are shown below, center.

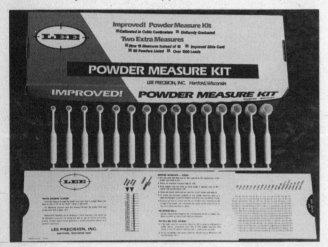

so on. One of the best approaches is to let the individual gun choose the powder it likes best.

The procedure for doing that involves making up a series of test loads, using two or more of the sanctioned powders, in different listed charge weights behind bullets varying as to make, weight and design. Need we repeat that all loads should be within recommended limits as given in the handbook(s)? Label the test loads as you make them up and fire them at targets off a good, steady rest — sandbags, shooting bench or the like — and keep records so you can mark the groups on the target with the pertinent load data.

It's typical to find that any one particular gun will deliver markedly superior accuracy with one or more powders in comparison to its performance with others. There is only one way to find out which powder the gun likes best and that is try as many different loads as possible and practicable in it. True, you have to buy at least one can apiece of all the powders you try, but it's the only reliable way to extract optimum performance.

Loaded ammunition costs money these days, substantial hunks of the handy stuff. The same is true of tailor-made bullets. If you reload your fired brass cases, you recapture most of the considerable cost of producing the case in the first place. If you acquire the ability to produce your own bullets, further worthwhile savings become possible. It's quite impractical to produce your own powder and/or primers, if you were about to ask.

There are two basic techniques for home bullet production: casting and swaging. Casting requires a bullet mould, a supply of suitable lead alloy and facilities for melting and pouring the molten metal into the mould. You'll also need some manner of arrangement for lubricating the finished cast bullet.

Swaging bullets involves squeezing lead into the desired dimensions and shape under a considerable amount of pressure, using especially made bullet swaging dies. Often the operation is performed in a regular reloading press

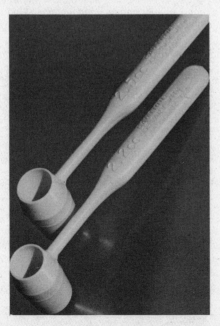

Left, Richard J. Lee, photographed in 1975 with a table covered with his reloading kits. Center, the 2.2cc and 2.5cc powder measuring dippers. Right, current reloading kit for .357 Magnum, from Lee Precision, Inc.

Left, the revised and enlarged second edition of Sierra's Reloading Manual was published in 1978. Above, first edition of Speer Manual made appearance in 1954.

although there are specialized presses available solely for bullet swaging. Besides the dies and press, swaging requires a supply of lead wire for bullet cores, a core cutter for chopping the wire into the desired length/weight, and a supply of copper alloy bullet jackets.

Having long ago acquired fairly comprehensive facilities for casting bullets, my own approach usually involves casting bullets in moulds, using dead-soft lead, of appropriate weight, diameter and shape, then using the lead castings in place of chopped-up segments of lead wire for the cores needed in bullet swaging. In my own estimation,

this method works extremely well, apart from the investment in both casting and swaging equipment.

For swaging bullets to be used in cartridges such as the .38 Special — that is, of .357-inch diameter — my favorite core mould is a four-cavity Lyman in their No. 311316 design. That's a little flat-nosed gas check number nominally intended for reloading the .32-20 Winchester cartridge. When swaged with a jacket of .434 to .500-inch length, it produces finished bullets with a typical weight of about 136 grains. I load such bullets in accordance with data given in the No. 9 Speer Manual for that maker's

First and current editions of Lyman's Cast Bullet Handbook. Hercules Reloaders' Guide covers only their powders.

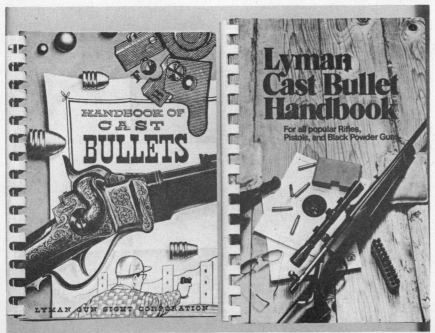

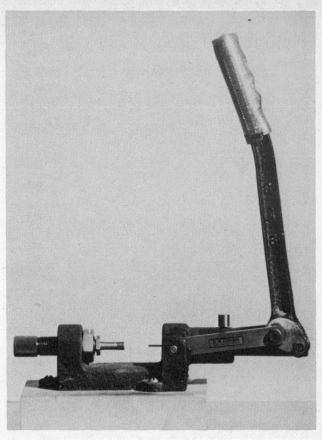

Corbin's Mity-Mite bullet swaging press is designed solely for bullet production and its compound leverage design is capable of generating high working pressures.

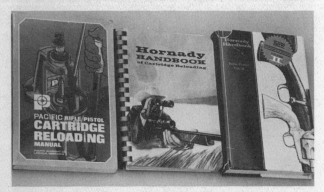

Data books from powder suppliers, such as Hodgdon or Du Pont, concentrate solely on their line. Bottom, Pacific Manual and its successors, the two Hornady Handbooks.

140-grain jacketed hollow point (JHP) design.

The bullet swaging rig I use most frequently these days is a Mity-Mite press from Corbin Manufacturing & Supply, Inc. (Box 758, Phoenix, Oregon 97535). It is designed solely for bullet swaging and performs that operation in a most satisfactory manner.

The complete setup for swaging bullets is not cheap, running well over a C-note for the press and die set. The usual procedure consists of swaging all the cores to uniform size and weight in the core swaging die, with some small amount of excess lead bleeding off through the small holes provided. Replacing the core swaging die with the one for core seating, each core is placed in a jacket and cycled through the press to seat it to a firm fit within the jacket. Then replace the core seating die with the nose forming die and run them all through that operation, after appropriate adjustment.

There is a hasty shortcut approach to which I'm partial when I need a quantity of jacketed bullets and don't mind ending up with round-nosed full metal jacket (FMJ) versions. Starting with a quantity of .500-inch jackets and the cast pure lead No. 311316 bullets for cores, I install and adjust the nose forming die in the Mity-Mite, then feed each core and jacket into the die, with jacket base at the end of the die that forms the nose. After stroking the press handle, the finished bullet emerges ready to load in one pass. I'm

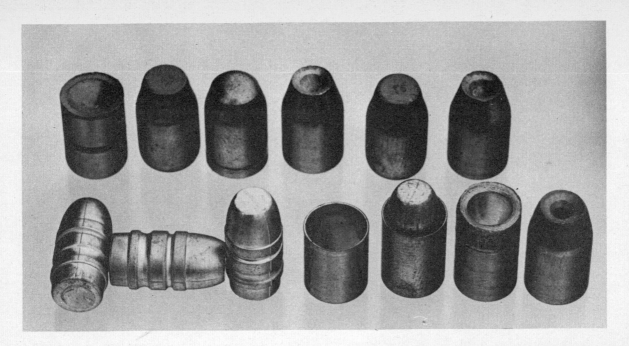

Above, some of the Lyman No. 311316 bullets, cast from soft lead for use as cores in bullet swaging, with some of the variations produced on the Mity-Mite. At right are some bullets made up with the No. 101 C-H swaging dies. At lower right, applying a cannelure with C-H's tool.

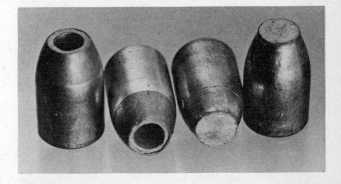

not certain if Dave Corbin sanctions this approach, but I think it works just fine.

Swaging is a highly versatile technique, permitting production of bullets in a bewildering, nearly infinite variety of weights and designs. You can make hollow-points, soft-points, cup-points, full-wadcutters, semi-wadcutters, steel-points (with an air rifle BB imbedded in the nose), disintegrators (using a quantity of fine shot instead of the solid lead core) multi-projectile assemblies or...?? Just about the only limit that governs is your own ingenuity and sound judgment. Swaging bullets can prove so intriguing you hate to spare the time to load them into cases and shoot them.

Casting bullets has many attractive aspects also, not the least of which is the economic factor. The initial equipment costs considerably less than the basic swaging setup and the cost of your raw materials is determined in large degree by your craft and guile at obtaining lead alloys suitable for use. You may be able to obtain automobile wheel weights at costs ranging from free to a dime a pound or so. Wheel weight metal, by itself, is less than pluperfect for casting bullets. By the book, it's supposed to contain a small percentage of antimony plus a trace of tin. I've reason to suspect that the tin gets left out, more often than not. Pure tin is an expensive commodity these days and I'm sure the producers of wheel weights couldn't possibly care less if their output can be transmuted into good bullets.

Bullet moulds from Saeco Reloading usually are furnished in 4-cavity type.

Let's look at the properties of the three metallic elements most commonly used in casting bullets:

Metal	MP	SG	CI/G	CS
Lead	327C/621F	11.37	2873.5	Pb
Antimony	630C/1166F	6.71	1695.4	Sb
Tin	232C/450F	7.29	1842.4	Sn

MP is the melting point, on the Celsius and Fahrenheit scales; SG is the specific gravity, weight compared to an equal volume of water; CI/G is the weight of one cubic inch in grains; and CS is the chemical symbol. It's hardly a moment too soon to note that a grain is a unit of weight. There are 7000 grains in one pound (avoirdupois system)

A Lyman mould, showing aligning pins, scored lines in the block for air venting and the sprue cutter swung to one side.

Formula 99 is a dip-and-dry bullet lubricant from H-R Research, Box 25888, Los Angeles, CA 90025. Photo at right shows half of a single-cavity Lyman bullet mould, with its sprue cutter pivoted partially.

Left, bullet mould from RCBS. Above, stirring beeswax into the molten bullet alloy to flux it and remove impurities.

and 437.5 grains in one ounce. A common paper match weighs roughly one grain, a gummed cigarette paper weighs about one-tenth grain.

An alloy of lead with small amounts of antimony, such as your typical wheel weight, may feel impressively hard when probed with an exploratory thumb nail. The problem arises from the fact that, as the molten metal cools, the antimony crystallizes before the lead. You end up with a bullet composed of tiny antimony crystals surrounded by pure lead. If you fire such bullets, it's likely you'll be plagued by excessive lead fouling in the bore. Adding a small quantity of tin to the mixture keeps the lead alloyed with tin right to the final solidification and relieves the problem most usefully.

I sigh to recall how simple life used to be. Not too many years ago, one could make friendly overtures to affable tradesmen such as plumbers, printers and telephone linemen and barter them out of scrap lead pipe, wiped plumbing joints (a rich source of high-tin alloy), old beer coils (pure tin!), linotype metal (a superb casting material, as received or mixed with wheel weights), cable sheathing and similar good stuff. Every year, such transactions become more difficult to consummate. Most of today's homes have plumbing pipes of polyvinyl chloride (PVC) that doesn't cast into bullets for sour owl sweat and linotypes with their lovely alloy seem to be on their way to join the dodo and the nickel beer with free lunch on the side.

When recycling wheel weights, it's best to melt them all down as an initial step, skimming off the dross and little steel clips from the surface with an old spoon. Then pinch off a fingernail-sized lump of beeswax, drop it onto the skimmed surface and stir it in thoroughly to flux the metal. That assures uniform composition and helps to separate impurities such as road grit and similar unwanted materials.

When working with molten lead, ASSURE ADEQUATE VENTILATION! Always wash your hands thoroughly after working with lead, before eating, smoking or trying to dislodge that pesky raspberry seed from between your back molars. Lead is a poison and even small traces of it are eliminated from the human system slowly, if at all. For the same reason, ventilation is mandatory for indoor target ranges and the like. As lead bullets strike steel backstop baffles, small quantities of lead particles become airborne

Grennell's less-than-immaculate bullet foundry operates with an open door to the left for necessary ventilation. Bausch & Lomb shooting glasses provide eye protection. Sprues are knocked into one shallow cardboard tray and the finished bullets go into the larger tray at left. The stand raises lead pot to handy working height.

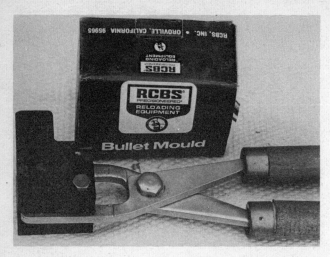

As with several other makes, RCBS moulds are designed to permit mould blocks to be interchanged on the same set of handles. Right, Saeco's excellent lube/sizer, with Grennell's unpatented modification via rubber band.

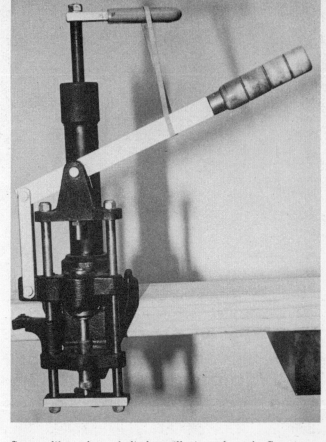

and can be inhaled with highly hazardous effect. Keep this paragraph ever in mind and pass the word to fellow shooters who didn't read the book.

Other metallic elements that pose hazards when melted include zinc, cadmium and arsenic, plus more exotic examples less apt to be encountered as trace impurities in vaguely lead-like alloys.

Once you've produced some cast bullets of lead alloy — without getting laid low from painter's colic, it's hoped! — there remains the process of sizing them and lubricating before they're ready to load. Typical bullet moulds for the .38 Special are dimensioned to produce bullets of about .360-inch diameter, allowing a trifle of excess for the pass through a .358-inch bullet sizing die to arrive at the prescribed diameter. For this operation, I use a Saeco lube/sizer and find it eminently satisfactory. You're welcome to purloin my unpatented modification. I put a rubber band between the operating handle and the grease piston handle to keep the punch from dropping onto my

fingers like a berserk little guillotine; the sole flaw in an otherwise wholly admirable gizmo.

The bullet grease comes in small sticks, hollow or solid, depending on the make of lube/sizer you use. When the hollow stick is placed in the Saeco's reservoir, a spring-loaded piston is brought to bear against the top of the grease and forces the grease through passages in the sizing die to end up in the grooves cast into the sides of the bullet. It's just a matter of giving the piston handle a few turns every dozen or so bullets, to maintain the proper

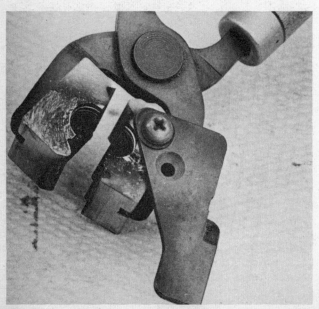

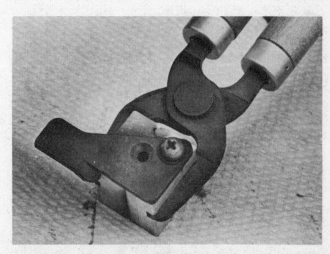

Moulds from Lee Precision have aluminum blocks and usually work better if cavities are lightly smoked.

Left, a 4-cavity Lyman mould, with sprue cutter knocked over and four No. 35887 wadcutters ready to tap free. Below, Lyman No. 410426, as cast, as size/lubed and loaded in .41 Mag case.

compression. Don't forget to replace the rubber band.

Having touched all too briefly on the matters of preparing the fired cases and producing some bullets, there remain the matters of replacing the primer and dispensing the powder charges.

Most reloading presses incorporate a small pivoting primer arm, with provisions for switching priming punches between the two common primer diameters (.175 and .210-inch). Personally, I dislike that approach for seating primers and usually remove the little priming punches, carefully setting them to one side and promptly forgetting where I put them. I prefer to seat the primers as a separate operation and, since its introduction recently, I usually use the Lee Precision Auto-Prime because it's the quickest, handiest approach I've seen to date.

My adjustable powder measure is an old RCBS Uniflow that has seen hard use since about 1959. You can't buy one quite like it anymore, illustrating the futility of writing to ask what I use myself. There are good measures in the lines of nearly all the makers and I'm sure most of them work at least as well as my ancient Uniflow. It's just that it's an old friend and I'm accustomed to it.

My powder scale is an old Lyman/Ohaus, dating to the Eisenhower administration although I've been trying to switch myself over to an RCBS Model 5-0-5 scale of current pattern. Again, there are many makes and models of powder scales on the market, all good to the best of my knowledge. A good powder scale is an absolute must, in my book. It's at least as indispensible as a library of reloading manuals and handbooks.

Given a scale against which to check it, you can make your own little dipper-type powder measures and, properly calibrated and employed, they can give good service until you decide you're ready to afford an adjustable rotary powder measure. A spent .32 ACP case, soldered to a short piece of brass welding rod and perhaps given a handle for convenience, will dip up roughly 3.8 grains of Hercules Green Dot powder. But don't take my word for it: Check it

Three .45 bullets at left are home-moulded production, fourth is a lead factory one from Speer, likewise the maker of the JSP bullet at right; all shoot quite well.

A lead semi-wadcutter (SWC) bullet, as cast, after a dip in Formula 99 lube and as loaded into a .45 Auto Rim.

Lyman No. 35887 wadcutter, cast and size/lubed in the usual manner, then swaged to form cavity in its nose.

out on your own scale. Most manuals that list Green Dot seem to agree that 3.8 grains of Green Dot is a sensible charge for use in the .38 Special behind solid-base wadcutters weighing about 148 grains. The No. 9 Speer Manual cites 3.8 grains of Green Dot as their suggested starting load for 148-grain bevel base wadcutters or 158-grain semi-wadcutters, quoting velocities of 815 and 784 fps, respectively.

An empty .25 auto case usually scoops about 3.3 grains of Hercules Bullseye and I made up many hundreds of .38 Special loads early in my career, using such a dipper. Again, if you want to try it, check it out on your own scale, consult a manual to be sure you're on safe ground and — need I say it? — before commencing to solder, be darned certain your little case doesn't have a live primer in the pocket!

If the discussion seems heavily interlarded with cautionary notes, apologies are offered. I hate to sound negative and I'm not trying to frighten you away from a

really great hobby activity. It's just that prudent handloaders avoid a lot of nasty surprises. If you'll forgive, here are a few more such points to watch.

All gunpowders — nitro, black or Pyrodex are highly flammable substances. If they weren't highly flammable, they'd be useless for the purpose. Do not smoke around open powder or primers. Consider Copenhagen snuff or a cud of Plow Boy, if you really can't get along without tobacco for a bit.

Alcoholic beverages and other less legal euphoriants impair your mental acuity and should be avoided when handloading. It's just too easy to think you're filling the powder measure with Hercules 2400 and not notice that it's really Bullseye. Unlikely? It happened to a friend of mine, once.

Keep all flammable materials, including powder and primers, well removed from bullet casting operations. A random spatter of hot lead can set it off. If it falls through the open mouth of a fifteen-pound drum of powder, you've

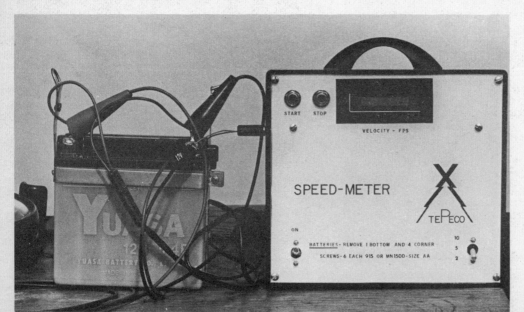

Speed-Meter chronograph for clocking velocities of reloads. MTM makes many types of plastic ammo boxes, as below.

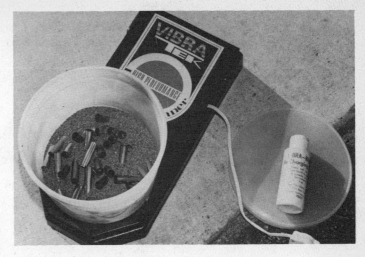

Vibra-Tek case cleaner removes residue and tarnish, restores bright finish; not for use with loaded cartridges. Left, as mentioned, two other books from same publisher provide full details on all aspects of handgun handloading.

got a goshawful problem; so do your neighbors.

If the lead in the pot is quite hot, adding beeswax to flux it can produce a flare-up for a few feet above the alloy surface. Find some other place to store that old pine needle wreath between holiday seasons. Don't hang it on a nail above the melting pot.

Primers merit all the cautious respect you can muster. If set off unenclosed, by heat or percussion, the cup flies one way and the tiny anvil the other, both at velocities hot enough to imbed them in flesh, including in an eye. Handle primers with care and leave them in the compartmented shipping tray until ready to be used. Never dump them in large, loose quantities. They can go off and raise pure hell.

Consider storing your powder supply in a lightweight, moderately sturdy cabinet, with handles on each side, so that it can be evacuated to a place of safety if the building should catch fire. Consider a separate, similar cabinet for your supply of primers. Learn the local regulations for storage of primers and powder and maximum amounts permitted. Obey the law.

Always put unused powder and primers back into their original, labeled container. Never leave unidentified components lying about.

The publishers of the work at hand can supply two other books the size of this one – *Handloading for Handgunners*, by the late Maj. George C. Nonte and *ABC's of Reloading*, by the present writer. Both go into considerably greater detail on the matter than space permits here. The foregoing discussion was intended to acquaint you with a highly rewarding activity and to help you avoid learning about some of the more obvious pitfalls the hard way. Try it, you'll like it!

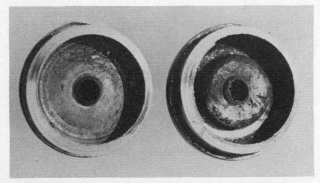

Modern web-head cartridge design at left, with the older balloon head type at right. Cull latter and set them aside.

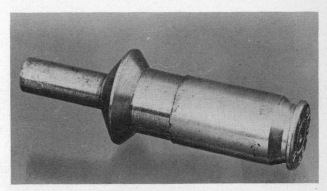

Home made case spinning mandrel can be spun in drill for fast, easy and effective cleaning/polishing of cases.

THE ANTI-HANDGUN GHOSTS ARE REAL

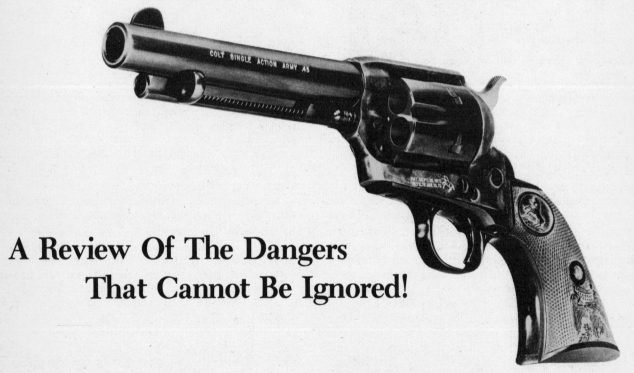

A Review Of The Dangers That Cannot Be Ignored!

Chapter 4

By Neal Knox,
Executive Director NRA Institute For Legislative Action

A CENTURY ago, handguns ranked equally with rifles and shotguns as a chief means of survival. Handguns today mean that and more to many people.

Particularly for women, a handgun is the firearm of choice for self or home defense. For collectors, they are prized and treasured possessions. Law enforcement officers value them as critical peace-keeping devices. Hunters know them as relatively inexpensive and sporting means of taking small and medium-size game. Competitors fire them over a wide number of national and international courses. And, whether they are used or not, shopkeepers see them as one more layer of insurance and security.

Unfortunately, of late, handguns also have found themselves labeled (libeled would be more accurate) as "murder machines" that should be forever banished from social commerce. Handguns have become vilified to the point that they — not their users — are blamed for virtually all types of crime: robbery, rape, even punctuating the final word in alcohol-doused domestic arguments.

The public relations campaign leveled against handguns has had surprising success. Some shooters and some within the industry itself actually feel they must apologize for the existence of handguns and for the actions of a minority of criminal handgun misusers. In essence, they have bought the big lie, they have bought the hard-peddled concept that there is such a thing as a "bad" gun.

What has not been considered is that there are polls, including those not produced by gun organizations, which indicate that up to fifteen percent of the public has used a firearm for defense of life or property. The anti-gun propagandists repeatedly say that a handgun is useless for self-defense, but I don't believe it for a moment — and neither does my wife. Those (usually hidden) poll results show a startling frequency of non-military, non-police gun use for defense — and the defense must have been successful, since those who had used a gun for protection were around to answer the pollsters' questions.

The "bad" gun story is a most effective propaganda gimmick. To the non-gun-owning public and to a large segment of the media, "bad" guns or so-called Saturday Night Specials conjure visions of weasel-eyed thugs lurking, pistol in hand, in an unlit inner-city alley. Those with only rudimentary knowledge of firearms think of a potmetal popgun more likely to disintegrate than to shoot straight.

Both images were played up three years ago by the press and backers of the infamous Saturday Night Special bill — H.R. 11193.

Publicity surrounding H.R. 11193 would have had the public believe it was aimed solely at "bad" guns. Yet when the National Rifle Association pressed the Bureau of Alcohol, Tobacco and Firearms for specifics, BATF admitted that the so-called Saturday Night Special bill would have included more than seventy-five percent of all models of handguns currently in the United States. That list included the Colt Single Action Army, the Buntline Special, and the Hammerli free pistol.

That bit of probing behind the headlines points exactly to the fallacy in the thinking of those who would offer handguns as a Judas goat to be sacrificed at the altar of the federal anti-gun bureaucracy — in hopes of staving off future government strictures on long guns. Such readiness to compromise is a dangerous solution.

To illustrate that point, examine the present anti-handgun strategy. Handgun critics, who would have the public believe that crime statistics would plummet if handguns disappeared, base their case primarily on the fact that a handgun is physically smaller — more concealable — than long guns. Get rid of the little guns and we'll leave your rifles and shotguns alone, they reason. Yet, they well know that the one tool necessary to convert any long gun into an "easily concealable" weapon can be purchased from any hardware store for less than a dollar. That tool? A seventy-five-cent hacksaw blade.

Less than a year after Canada banned handguns, the Montreal Star pictured an M-1 carbine on its front page with the inscription that the gun was "light, easy to handle...and can be cut down to make it easier to conceal." Dubbed a "favorite tool of the underworld," the carbine was described as the next target of that nation's gun-banning politicians.

Some of our gun-owning brethren, wanting to appear "reasonable," say they don't mind a registration law, "because I don't mind if government knows that I have a gun." They feel that those of us who see registration as a prelude to confiscation are being irrational. They are also speaking with a lack of knowledge.

No study, either in the U.S. or any foreign country, has shown registration laws to reduce crime. Instead, the only "advantage" that can be cited is that police know where the firearms are, and who has them — as if that were a worthwhile goal in itself. Actually, any objective study will show that the only guns registered with police are those in the hands of the law-abiding, for not only does a criminal not bother to register his gun — the Supreme Court says that he doesn't have to register it. In *U.S. vs. Haynes,* the court held that fear of self-incrimination was a justifiable defense for a person prohibited from owning a handgun — convicted felon, narcotics addict, etc. — from having to register it.

The immediate result of that decision was the Chicago registration ordinance requiring registration of all firearms *except* by persons who may not legally own them. Yet convicted felons, et al., are those at whom the law was supposedly aimed. The only ones hit are the law abiding — which should make you wonder why it was passed.

Historically, the only effect of firearms registration laws is to allow the confiscation of those registered firearms. That isn't paranoia, that's a fact. It has happened right here in the United States. In Cleveland, a registration law was followed by an attempted ban on so-called Saturday Night Specials, then the city attempted to require those who had registered guns fitting that definition to turn them in. Similarly, in Washington, D.C., a registration law was passed in 1969. In 1975, the city prohibited certain classes of firearms — including defining any firearm capable of more than twelve shots without reloading as a "machine gun." Individuals who had duly registered now-prohibited semi-automatic rifles, including (that I know about) an M-1 carbine registered with a ten-shot magazine, were told by city police to turn them in, or get rid of them.

It should be mentioned that the present Washington, D.C. law — which the National Rifle Association is fighting to repeal — prohibits anyone from possessing a handgun not registered to him in 1975, and re-registered each year since then. In other words, when I moved into the District of

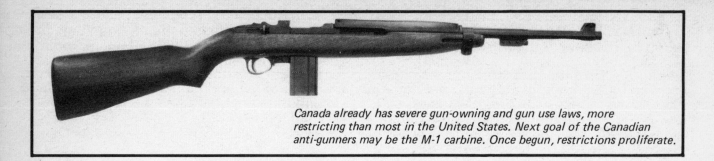

Canada already has severe gun-owning and gun use laws, more restricting than most in the United States. Next goal of the Canadian anti-gunners may be the M-1 carbine. Once begun, restrictions proliferate.

Columbia, I could neither buy a handgun nor bring any of my handguns from Arizona. There is and was no provision for me — or a new Congressman for that matter — to legally have a handgun under any circumstances.

And I've been told by a D.C. police officer, who shall remain nameless, that attempting to register a rifle or shotgun "isn't worth the trouble," which is one good reason why I moved outside of D.C.

But I stopped too soon when I said that no study has shown registration laws to reduce crime. *It is an absolute fact that no type of firearm law has resulted in decreased crime rates.*

In debate after debate, in speech after speech, I have asked: "Where has a gun law reduced crime?" The other side gnashes its collective teeth, and ignores the question.

The basic premise of all gun laws is that they will reduce crime, but they haven't. Therefore, why enact any type of new gun law, when every type of gun law has been tried — and failed to work.

The reason such laws have failed is that they do not address the issue: The issue is not *possession* of guns; the issue is *misuse* of guns. And laws against misuse, such as guaranteed minimum punishment for use of a gun in a crime of violence do work. Such laws do reduce crime.

In many ways, the fault for allowing the anti-handgun campaign to gain so much ground falls squarely on gun owners. Too many of us — hunters, competitors, gunowners in general — have sat back for too long and allowed the anti-handgun rhetoric to take hold by virtue of our remaining silent.

Our collective silence must end. Firearms owners, regardless of their feelings about handguns, must not allow the next guy to fight the fight. Handguns are no different than any other firearm. They just happen to be on the hot seat at this time. Handguns are every bit as useful and honorable as a fine deer rifle or presentation grade skeet gun. It is vital to the preservation of all our gun rights to meet anti-handgun arguments head-on.

For example, critics claim "handguns have but one purpose: to kill people." Nonsense. There are as many legitimate reasons for owning handguns as there are handguns owned by responsible, law-abiding citizens — over fifty million.

The most obvious error in the anti-handgun rhetoric can be shown using their own statistics. Based on their figures of handguns criminally or accidentally misused, only .52 percent of all privately owned handguns bear such a taint. That means a full 99.48 percent of all handguns are not used in crime each year. To put it another way, handguns are more pure than Ivory soap.

Again, if killing people was a handgun's only purpose,

why would so many states be instituting handgun hunting seasons? Why would Mexico's gift to hunters in search of a great way of honing their shooting skills off season — metallic silhouette shooting — be catching on with handgunners? And why would the ranks of the nation's handgun competitors be increasing?

As to a handgun's value as a defense weapon, here again handguns have suffered from the most blatant of anti-handgun lies. Quite beside the point that all law enforcement officers carry handguns for just that reason, the topic of handguns and self or home defense when broached with anti-handgun types runs from the ironic to the ridiculous.

Nelson Shields of Handgun Control, Incorporated (formerly the National Council to Control Handguns), insists that shotguns are the most preferable home defense gun. During one televised debate, I asked Shields if that meant he advocated homeowners killing intruders? I pointed out that a shotgun fired in the home at an intruder was almost guaranteed to kill. I emphasized the fact that the object of self or home defense was not to kill but rather to deter or, and only if necessary, to disable. Shields, I am

There is no such thing as a little restriction or a little confiscation to some legislators. Under one proposed law, guns such as the Hammerli free pistol, Colt Buntline and Single Action Army would be banned.

confident, had not considered the lethality of a shotgun. Nor had he considered that a high-velocity rifle bullet capable of penetrating walls, if fired under similar circumstances, stood a good chance of killing not only the intruder but also an innocent person in the next room or even the next building.

All things considered, a sound argument can and should be made that a properly loaded, short-barrel handgun which could be easily concealed from small children yet readily available and easily handled by responsible adults, regardless of age, sex or strength, may prove just the ticket for home or self defense.

We not only need to refute anti-handgun rhetoric, but we also need to underscore our points with programs of direct action. We need more firearms training and self-defense courses aimed at women, the retired, homeowners and shopkeepers. We need more handgunners ready and willing to share their knowledge and skills with the uninitiated.

It is well documented that increased public involvement with handgun training not only provides a greater sense of inner security, but is a real step toward reducing handgun misuse and crime.

For example, a police-sponsored (and well advertised) self-defense course for women in Orlando, Florida, a few years ago saw that city's rape rate drop by half and also saw dramatic declines in armed robbery and burglary. A similar program for shopkeepers in Detroit saw grocery store robberies drop from eighty-six to ten per month. And, a Highland Park, Michigan, program for merchants saw a four-month period where robberies went from one and a half per day to *none*.

All segments of the shooting community — shotgunners, muzzleloaders, plinkers, collectors, et al. — must stand united against giving the least credence to the "bad" gun syndrome. My own response to those who would even casually entertain the idea that the government should set standards to cull shoddy merchandise from the market is that I have never seen a bad gun, only guns that I would own and guns I would not own.

Rest assured the anti-gun organizations understand perfectly the concept of divide and conquer. They know that if they can gradually erode our resistance through offering "moderate" proposals they will ultimately win the war.

Three years ago Nelson Shields outlined his ultimate plan in three steps: the first, to "slow down the number of handguns being produced and sold in this country," then "to get handguns registered," and finally "to make the possession of all handguns and all handgun ammunition...totally illegal."

Today he claims to have tempered that position. He says he seeks a ban only on "bad" guns, the so-called Saturday Night Special. Divide and conquer.

The situation faced by gunowners today reminds me of a quotation penned by Martin Niemoller reflecting on the rise of the Nazis in his native Germany.

"...They came for the Jews and I didn't speak up because I was not a Jew. Then they came for the trade unionists and I didn't speak up because I was not a trade unionist. Then they came for the Catholics and I was a Protestant, so I didn't speak up. Then they came for me...by that time there was no one to speak up for anyone."

If we are silent today, if we allow handguns to be sacrificed, there is no tomorrow for those of us who would safeguard our right to keep and bear arms.

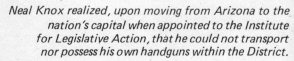

Neal Knox realized, upon moving from Arizona to the nation's capital when appointed to the Institute for Legislative Action, that he could not transport nor possess his own handguns within the District.

CARE & CLEANING OF HANDGUNS

Chapter 5

...Or The Basics
Of Saving Money
And Repairs

By Jack Mitchell

HANDGUNS, LIKE most other products in today's society, continue to increase in price. Although many are purchased for protection, hunting, target shooting, or just plinking, they comprise an excellent investment. Many handguns are worth much more now than the day they originally were purchased. Thus it makes good sense to take proper care of them.

Unfortunately, many gunowners think that slapping a bit of oil on a gun whenever the thought occurs is enough effort to protect it. The rationale here is that, with today's modern technology and space age materials, little or no effort is sufficient.

To clean a gun properly we must accomplish three functions. First, we want to protect it against rust. Second, the working parts of a gun have metal moving against metal so we must reduce drag for a smooth operation. Third, after firing any handgun, powder residue and corrosive particles build up in areas that, unless removed, can cause wear of parts and influence accuracy.

Even with all the different gun designs, sizes, calibers, etc., their basic function is to shoot. The three most important characteristics of any gun are reliability, durability and accuracy. All three can be greatly enhanced by proper cleaning and maintenance.

Let's deal with the problems of rust. Gun metal tends to rust without proper and regular care. One important consideration is how much cleaning and lubricating is necessary in your immediate locale. Hot humid locations such as Florida and Hawaii will rust a gun faster than a dry location such as Arizona, for example. The culprit is moisture combined with oxygen. It is wise to clean handguns regularly and provide a good rust preventive oil on them while in storage.

Merely handling a handgun can cause corrosion. Our fingerprints can leave acids and salts on the metal. The salts, when exposed to moisture, will begin the rusting process immediately. Remember, just moving from an outside location to an inside one can cause moisture to condense on metal surfaces and cause rust. Therefore, it is important

that, after handling handguns, they should by wiped down thoroughly.

I use a G96 Gun Mitt which is like an oversize mitten. It's simple to use, and has rust inhibitors which will protect the gun.

Also, never store your firearms inside a soft case of the leather or vinyl type over any length of time. Moisture gets trapped in the case and only speeds up the corrosion process. I get ill when I hear of folks leaving their firearms in the trunks of their cars over periods of a week or more. If the trunk has a leak in it which traps moisture after rain, it is like storing the gun in a steam closet.

Actually, the ideal place to store guns is in a clean, dry location. One of the best ideas, in addition to a well lubricated gun during storage, is to keep a product called Hydrosorbent in the storage area right next to your guns. It is a packet of silica gel crystals which absorb moisture from the air. This product has been used aboard ship by the Navy for years and is both effective and inexpensive. For more information write to Hydrosorbent, Box 675, Rye, New York 10580. To reactivate the packets, simply heat in an oven to remove the moisture and return them to the storage closet.

The standard blue-steel finish found on the majority of handguns will not prevent rust. Stainless steel handguns such as the Ruger Security-Six or the Smith & Wesson Model 66 will retard rusting much longer than conventionally blued guns but they too require cleaning and maintenance. Although these two particular handguns are less likely to rust than the regular blued types, their accuracy and reliability may be reduced by metal fouling and corrosive particle buildups from firing.

If you have an old favorite handgun that is rusted, but otherwise functional, the Texas Gunshop, 299 Arapaho Central Park, Richardson, Texas 75080, offers a new plating process called Ni-Tex. This is a process of plating that results in a brushed stainless steel look that can be applied over just about any metal surface and is said to be rust resistant. The resulting appearance is impressive and it

An assortment of typical cleaning solvents for firearms includes Hoppe's No. 9, which aids in detecting metal fouling; Casey Gun Scrubber uses high pressure to remove loosened particles.

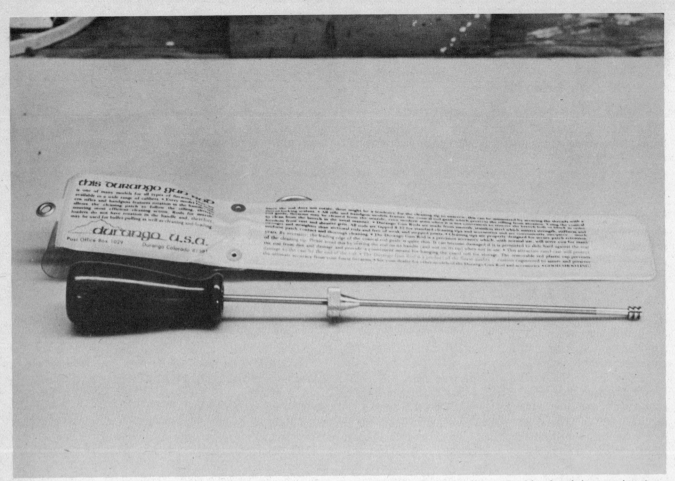

Durango cleaning rod comes in assorted lengths, with replaceable tips for the various calibers. Rod is of stainless steel and swivels freely in the handle. The sliding, tapered brass collar assures accurate centering inside the muzzle during cleaning.

Here are four lubricants that incorporate molybdenum disulfide for reducing drag between moving parts.

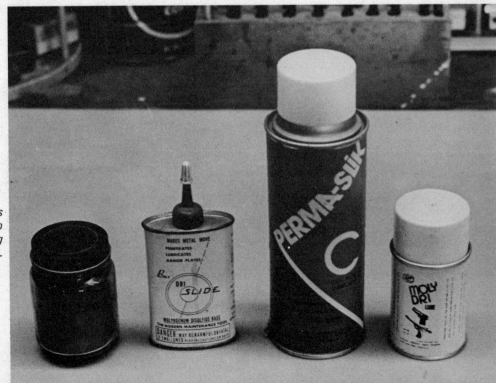

This S&W Model 36 has had its sideplate removed by loosening the screws with a properly fitted screwdriver, followed by tapping the frame around the plate gently and patiently with the butt of a screwdriver until the plate loosens for removal. Never remove the sideplate by direct prying. The internal parts are exposed for cleaning and lubrication; reassemble carefully!

may give new life to guns that have been subjected to all sorts of harsh conditions.

When lubricating handguns to protect them from rust, remember that before they are to be taken to the field they should be cleaned and the protective lubricants may have to be removed. This is especially true in cold temperatures which may cause the lubricant to gum up and create malfunctions. Once back to the house, it is of paramount importance to get that rust-preventive substance back on the piece. It makes good sense to spend the time and effort to keep any handgun in the best condition possible.

The next important consideration is optimum reliability. This means each working part of the gun performs its assigned function to the best of its ability. This is accomplished more efficiently if the gun parts are clean and lubricated to prevent drag. Any time we have metal bearing against metal we need something that will reduce drag and continue to perform without breaking down under adverse conditions. I have found one of the best single lubricants to be molybdenum disulfide. It is excellent for reducing drag, does not break down in hot or cold temperatures and does, to a certain degree, act as a rust preventive.

On the minus side, it is difficult to remove from hands or clothing if used in a powder state and is about as attractive as mud, especially when it oozes out the bottom of the revolver frame around the trigger. It is available commercially from companies such as Dri-Slide, Perma-Slik,

and Engarde. When the molybdenum disulfide is suspended in a liquid it is simple to use and less messy than in powder form.

I recently have begun using a product called Break-Free on the working parts of guns. Although it has a Teflon base rather than the molybdenum disulfide, initial results have been just short of utterly amazing. It is much cleaner to use than the molybdenum-based products and also is an excellent rust preventive. Break-Free is relatively new to the market so for more information write to: San/Bar Corporation, P.O. Box 11787, Santa Ana, California 92711.

I think the least understood, yet the most important part of cleaning and lubricating pistols and revolvers is the proper removal of powder residue and corrosive particles left after firing the guns. This buildup, unless removed, will adversely influence accuracy, impair reliability, and destroy the gun itself. Granted, smokeless powder is much cleaner burning than anything up to its invention but it is not totally foolproof and can cause problems.

Modern non-corrosive primers contain certain elements that can leave a residue causing a degree of harmful rust. Once in a while we come across ammunition with the older, corrosive primers. They contain potassium chlorate which loses oxygen upon ignition, leaving a residue of potassium chloride. The effect is similar to table salt; add a bit of moisture and the rusting process begins.

Lead fouling in pistols and revolvers is detrimental to

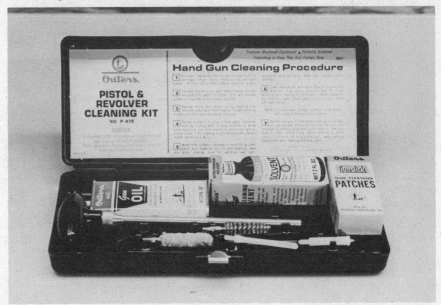

Outers markets this compact but complete gun-cleaning kit that includes swab, brass bristle brush, patches, patch loop and jag with cleaning rod, plus a can of Outers gun oil and a bottle of their bore cleaning solvent, ready for field use.

Amsoil MP metal protector is one of the many compounds offered for lubrication plus rust prevention.

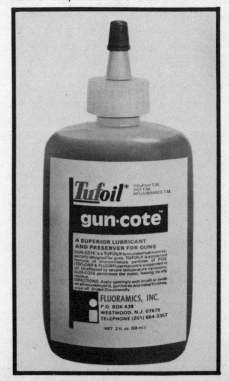

Tufoil Gun-Cote is another compound that lubricates and protects. It is made up with microfine particles of Teflon and Fluon in a permanent state of suspension and it works well.

Five of the multi-purpose compounds described in the text for combination use in cleaning, lubricating and preventing corrosion on steel and other metal parts.

accuracy. Looking down the bore, the fouling can be seen as darker streaks between the lands and grooves. Such fouling usually is quite prevalent near the rear of the barrel. It also builds up in revolver chambers just forward of where the cartridge case mouth ends when the cylinder is loaded. The lead must be removed, as it can actually cause the gun to malfunction. (How to remove this will be explained later in this chapter.)

Cleaning pistols and revolvers is not too difficult in most cases, unless metal fouling is present. Copper-jacketed bullets can cause metal fouling, although not as severe as the lead fouling. In extreme cases of metal fouling, metallic mercury — often called quicksilver — is an effective remedy. However, it is difficult and expensive to obtain. Another method of fouling removal involves an old gunsmith formula that works effectively. The formula includes 112 grains ammonium persulfate; 52 grains ammonium carbonate; 480cc distilled water; 720cc ammonium hydroxide.

To use, place the gun muzzle upward and plug the chamber with a tapered rubber stopper. Pour the solution down the barrel and let sit for about thirty minutes. This system works well, I find.

I do not recommend cleaning handguns using steel wool. When working on revolvers, steel wool and/or bristles from cleaning brushes may get caught between the ejector star and rear of cylinder, which can interfere with the cylinder lockup.

Birchwood-Casey's Gun Scrubber is a handy solvent and cleanser to have around. It is under a great deal of pressure and literally blows dirt and corrosion out of working parts which would otherwise be difficult to reach. It is sort of a combination airgun and cleaner. Hoppes' Cleaner No. 9 has been around longer than most. It contains an ingredient which will stain the cleaning patch a greenish-blue if copper fouling is present in the bore. If there is copper fouling, just let the pieces soak in the Hoppes overnight and the fouling will come out easily the next day. It is an excellent solvent, but does not have any rust preventives in it. Outers' pistol kits and rifle kits contain quality products and everything one needs is right there in one place. The same may be said for other gun cleaning kits such as Marble Arms.

To clean pistols and revolvers correctly, begin with a good solvent. If the gun is badly corroded let it remain in the solvent for twenty-four hours. It will make the job much easier. Clean the barrel using a cleaning rod and a patch soaked with solvent first.

After soaking the barrel, change from a patch to a solvent-soaked bronze or brass wire brush and run it through the barrel several times. Run another solvent-soaked patch through the barrel and finish with dry patches. Examine for metal or lead fouling and repeat the process again, if necessary.

On revolvers, this cleaning step will have to be repeated on the cylinders to clean thoroughly. Since gas escapes between the barrel and cylinder, powder residue and corrosive particles build up between barrel and cylinder. Clean this area carefully or functioning problems may develop. Examine the revolver frame just above the rear of the barrel, the firing pin channel, hammer nose and the hammer groove in the frame. These areas must be cleaned and all traces of buildup removed.

After all metal parts have been cleaned thoroughly, they should be dried with a lint-free cloth. On internal working parts of revolvers or the slide rails of automatics, I apply either a molybdenum disulfide solution or the previously-mentioned Break-Free. If the gun is to be stored, I apply a liberal coating of a good rust preventive such as G96 Gun Treatment. Do not store handguns in holsters, as this speeds up corrosion and may ruin the holster as well.

If you live in a cold climate, wipe off excess oils as they can gum up and cause sluggish operation. When returning the gun to a warm room after zero-type weather outside, moisture will build up on the metal so it must be removed and the gun re-oiled before storage.

In hot, humid climates handguns should be kept well-oiled during storage and wood grips rubbed down with either linseed oil or a commercial product like Stock-Slick. Be careful not to let linseed oil get into the metal working parts, as rust may ultimately result.

In hot, dry climates, dust or sand can get into the working parts. Before taking the gun out to shoot, wipe it down inside and out as oil and sand can cause drag and/or damage during the firing cycle. Wooden stocks will have a tendency to dry out. They should be wiped down regularly with either linseed oil or Stock-Slick.

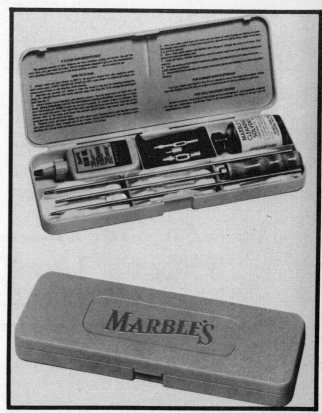

This complete gun-cleaning kit from Marble's contains a multi-jointed rod for cleaning rifles, but similar kits with handgun-length rods are also available from same maker.

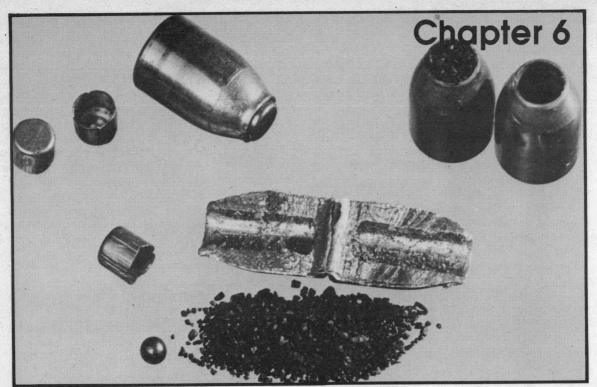

Chapter 6

Above, example of early production, cross-sectioned, with percussion caps and powder. Author warns of extreme danger in attempting to disassemble the bullet or remove it from the loaded round. Opposite page, cross-section of this bullet shows that the drill bit nearly penetrated the base of the gilding metal jacket.

THIS THING CALLED VELET

There Are Pros And Cons On This Exploding Bullet For Law Enforcement Work

By Bob Steindler

THE SEARCH FOR a better performing handgun bullet began with Lee Jurras and his Super Vel ammunition. The light bullet and high-velocity concept made a lot of converts, but it also created the usual nonsensical hue and cry about hollow point or "dum dum" bullets.

The Glaser Safety Slug, a highly effective round that is individually tailored for performance in various length revolver barrels, made believers out of many law enforcement officers, especially when they learned that, unlike any other bullet, the Glaser effort would not ricochet under any circumstances.

Now, borrowing an idea from the old artillery shells and fuses, we have the Velet ammunition. A fuse has been

defined as a device containing an explosive component that is activated by the impact of the projectile on the target. At least, this is one definition and the one concerned with here.

The Velet round, offered in .380 ACP, 9mm Parabellum, .38 Special, .357 magnum and .45 ACP, looks like any other cartridge in many aspects, except that the hollow point in the bullet contains an explosive percussion cap.

The Velet people say that they will sell this ammunition over the counter and I suspect that may offer problems. It's a combat load and should be limited to law enforcement sales.

According to a report in the venerable *Los Angeles Times,* Los Angeles police have been rounding up explosive

ammunition that had been sold to gunowners through local sporting goods stores.

The ammunition, manufactured under the names *Velex* and *Velet* is illegal in California, since it is considered a destructive device.

Admittedly, the store owners did not realize the ammo was illegal, until the police classified it, and other dealers have been warned it is illegal in the state for civilian use. Other states, we understand, have taken similar actions.

In contrast to other hollow-point bullets where the cavity extends only a few millimeters into the lead core, the cavity in the Velet bullet extends all the way down to the base of the jacket. As a matter of fact, in some of the bullets examined, it became apparent that the cavity had been drilled out of the lead core on a lathe, with the bullet being fastened in the headstock chuck. A number of the bullets showed where the drill in the chuck of the tailstock began to bottom out, creating a little protrusion where the tip of the drill bit began to push through the jacket base.

In this cavity is loaded one No. 4 or No. 5 shot pellet, plus a small amount of fine-grained black powder that appears to be FFFFg. When the pellet moves forward from its position at the front of the cavity, it strikes the inside of the percussion cap, which detonates, and thus starts the small powder charge burning. The percussion cap is sealed into the bullet by means of a red lacquer, which is soluble in acetone. Because of the internal construction of the Velet bullet, disassembly of the Velet cartridge must *not* be attempted with the help of an inertia bullet puller.

Disassembly of the Velet rounds calls for extreme care and requires safety precautions not readily available to most shooters. In short: forget it!

The makers of this ammunition have had their problems. We tested the original product, which was marketed under the name, Velex, rather than Velet. Since then, there have been some required design changes. Originally, black powder was used in the explosive charge in the nose of the bullet. As a result of pressure from the Bureau of Alcohol,

The entrance hole in the piece of test plywood, above, is clean. Right, .45 ACP Velet fragments surrounding exit hole in plywood.

Right, Velet would be classed as incendiary ammunition and, as such, its use would be prohibited in areas of high forest fire hazard. Below, current specs on the Velet ammunition.

TRACER AMMUNITION PROHIBITED

UNLAWFUL TO POSSESS OR DISCHARGE ANY TYPE OF TRACER OR INCENDIARY AMMUNITION

CFR TITLE 36, SEC. 261.2 (0)

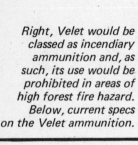

Caliber	Bullet Weight (gr)	MV (fps)	ME (ft/lbs)
.380 ACP	87	1092	230
9mm Para.	92	1373	385
.38 Spl. (4")	101	1144	294
.357 mag (4")	101	1439	465
.45 ACP	200	972	420

Tobacco and Firearms, the makers have incorporated Pyrodex as the bursting charge.

Moreover, to reduce impact sensitivity, the percussion cap in the bullet nose has been replaced with either a rifle or a pistol primer, depending upon the caliber of the bullet. The percussion cap is seated 0.017-inch below the rim of the bullet jacket, and is 0.157-inch high with the diameter of 0.180 to 0.189-inch (all caps removed from live rounds were somewhat deformed, hence the variation in diameter) According to the Velet brochure, the cap is a

In all calibers tested, bullets shed jackets 95% of the time.

SAN ANTONIO POLICE LABORATORY

"discriminating impact fuse," but during tests, it was not possible to discern just what the fuse or cap is supposed to discriminate between or against.

The propellant charge in the cartridge case consists of a gray flake powder, and most of the charges were of the compressed type. The bullet in the .38 Special round weighs 102.8 grains on the average, and is pushed along by 7.4 grains of the above-mentioned powder. We ran only limited velocity tests since we did not have enough ammo for testing, disassembly and chronographing. The velocities recorded for the .357 magnum and the 9mm Parabellum rounds were fairly close to those listed by Velet, as indicated in the accompanying chart.

Velet, Incorporated, headquartered in Spokane, Washington, is working currently on the development of loads for the .44 magnum, the .44 Special and the .38 Super, with special emphasis being placed on deep penetration for hunting loads in .357 magnum and .44 magnum.

According to Velet, the explosive charge delivers the available bullet energy violently within the intended target and Velet bullets are said to fragment better than any other type of bullet. In view of these claims, we conducted a number of bullet expansion and penetration tests. All test firing was done at five feet under controlled temperature and humidity conditions on an indoor range. Two rounds of each caliber were fired into separate test blocks or units.

Velet bullets do not completely penetrate a five-pound block of Duxseal or a block of modeling clay. One round from a .380 did punch through two, two-inch thick, soaking-wet telephone books and no large parts of the bullet were recovered. In the Duxseal and clay blocks, bullets fragmented completely, but penetration was only three inches at the deepest point.

A Velet bullet from a 9mm Browning Hi-Power fired at ten feet into a one-gallon plastic jug filled with water exploded the container dramatically. Only two lead core fragments were recovered from inside the bottle, which

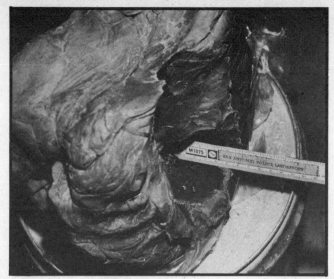

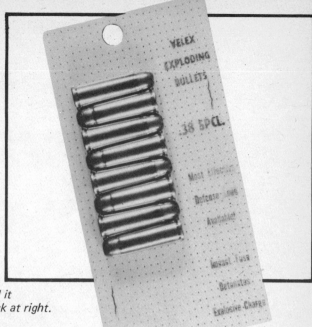

Above, impact cavity in Duxseal for the 9mmP Velet load showed it to possess almost as much power as the .357 magnum. Bubble pack at right.

showed no indication that the bullet or any fragments of it exited from the bottle. All five calibers were tested, one shot each, in the standard pine baffle penetration box. All shots penetrated through the fourth three-quarter-inch pine baffle, with the burning of the bullet charge appearing regularly on that fourth board. The wood blackened but did not burn, and no bullet or core fragments were recovered.

One of the best media for testing bullet expansion is a mixture of grease, resembling cup grease in consistency, and molten paraffin wax, cast into two-foot square blocks that are 1½ inches thick. The Velet rounds penetrated to the third block and started a small fire there, melting parts of the third block.

The Velet ammo for semiautomatic pistols ran smoothly

through a variety of guns, as did the six-gun ammo. Ammunition for self-loaders comes packaged ten rounds per plastic bubble pack, while the revolver ammo comes in eight-round packages. The packaging is simple, effective and fairly easy to handle, although why such odd number of cartridges are sold per pack escapes me. The .38 Special ammo costs about $7 for eight rounds, the two smaller pistol rounds sell for $8 per ten-pack, while the .357 magnum and the .45 ACP retail for $9.50 per eight and ten rounds, respectively.

Going back to our shooting notes when we did some rather extensive and elaborate testing with Super Vel ammo and the Glaser Safety Slug, and then comparing test results from the Velet ammo with those data, it would appear that the Velet ammo is as effective as the Super Vel load

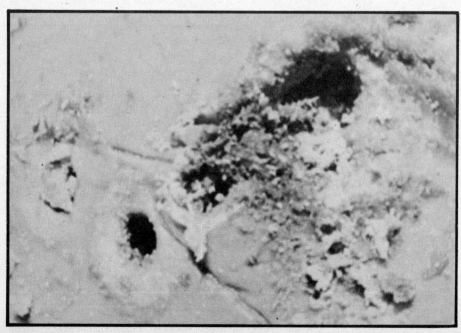

This hole, almost one inch in diameter, is from .380 Velet, fired into mixture of grease and paraffin.

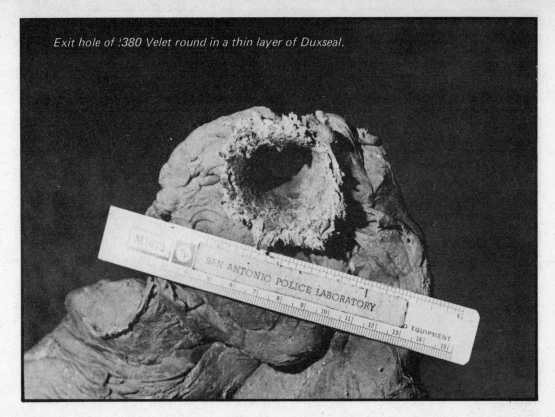

Exit hole of .380 Velet round in a thin layer of Duxseal.

perfected by Lee Jurras. Some preliminary tests of the currently manufactured Super Vel ammo from the H&H Cartridge Corporation appear to indicate that the new Super Vel ammo not only packs a bit more punch, but that bullet expansion seems to be somewhat better or at least more consistent. The Glaser Safety Slug fails to exit from such test targets as plastic bottles and, of course, it does not ricochet — a great advantage for any type of ammunition, especially combat ammo.

Ideally, any two brands of combat ammo should be tested and compared under identical conditions in living tissue. Unfortunately, we have not had the chance to hunt with either the Glaser Safety Slug or the Velet ammo, therefore cannot report success or failure. As mentioned, we cannot find that the impact "fuse" is really a fuse or that it is discriminating, but the explosive effect is certainly dramatic and does help in fragmenting the bullet.

We did dissect a 9mm Luger and a .45 ACP round and found that only the .38 Special and the .357 magnum round contain the shot pellet. The rest of the rounds depended solely on the impacting of the fuse or percussion cap to get things going.

Nylon and other synthetic fibers have the disconcerting habit of melting if you drop live coals from a cigarette, cigar or pipe on your shirt or slacks. Having a shirt wrecked that way, and needing an excuse to get rid of it, we shot the last of the Velet ammo into and through it. No fire or melting was noted either with the naked eye or under the microscope, and the piece of material was mounted first on a yielding surface, then on a piece of pine board from the baffle box.

Velet assigns high relative stopping power (RSP) values to its ammunition, calculating the RSP from measurements of bullet fragmentation deceleration. Neglected or discounted in the RSP calculations is the hydrostatic effect

or shock that is highly tissue destructive. It would not surprise us in the least to find that the hydrostatic effect of a Velex round would be greater than with a regular bullet, since the explosive effect of the charge most certainly would add to the normally occurring hydrostatic shock.

In San Antonio, Texas, several police officers conducted an experiment on the police range. The medical examiner was invited and had several pointed comments concerning exploding bullets.

The .38 Special Velet load showed limited penetration in the Duxseal medium used in San Antonio PD evaluation.

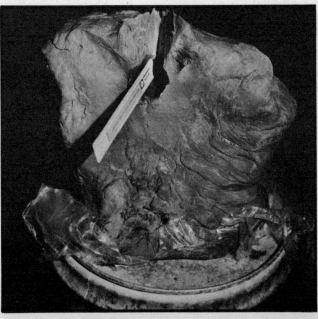

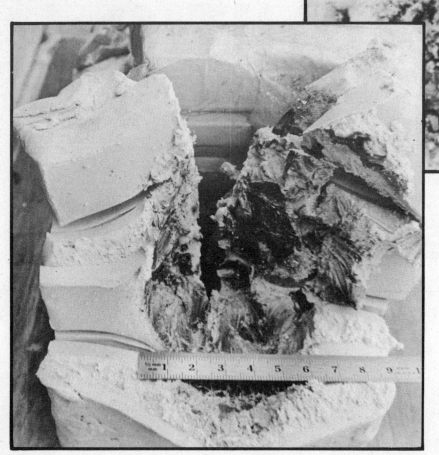

Above, a 9mmP Velet, fired into modeling clay, produced this relatively shallow hole at five feet. Dark areas are residue of burned powder charge. Left, the .45 ACP punched this 5cm (1.96'') hole in the modeling clay. Penetration was much deeper than 9mmP.

It was found that the Velet round offered a visible flash on impact with Duxseal, which was being used to explore penetration and injury potential. It left an egg-shaped cavity a uniform two inches deep.

The medical examiner expressed the thought that such a wound would look a lot like a contact wound — the muzzle pressed against the victim when fired — when in reality, he may have been shot from several yards away. After feeling the texture of the Duxseal, he stated that damage to a human body would be five times as great, adding that, "if you took a hit in the chest with it, you could forget about surgery."

The Velet rounds then were fired into quarter-inch plywood. All calibers showed a clean entrance hole and a ragged, blackened, splintered exit hole, indicating detonation after initial impact. Several times, the plywood was set ablaze, smoldering for several minutes. The 9mm and .357 magnum rounds always produced this effect, as did the .38 Special on occasion. When fired into a Second Chance armored vest, none of the bullets got through, but detonated about half way through, according to the test staff, "knocking a good dent in the Duxseal backing."

"It would be almost impossible to shoot into a human body without the projectile exploding," was the opinion of one police officer, who felt it was not suitable for police use.

He pointed out that statistics prove police officers shoot themselves accidentally five times as often as they shoot felons, "which means a lot of crippled-up officers.

"There also is the matter of officers who are killed with their own handguns. Quoting Federal Bureau of Investigation statistics, thirteen percent of all policemen killed in 1976 had their own weapon wrested from them and were shot."

Fired into a steel backstop at twenty-five yards, every bullet destroyed itself on impact, fragmenting harmlessly. No accidents resulted in firing several dozen rounds. The Velet ammo seems to be completely bore-safe. As mentioned, Velet warns that tampering with the impact fuse may be hazardous. During basement range testing, several rounds were dropped deliberately from waist level, but failed to go off.

The Velet brochure states it may be handled like any other type of ammo.

HANDGUN AMMUNITION TRENDS

Chapter 7

By Dean A. Grennell

THERE IS an organization that endeavors to preserve a reasonable semblance of uniformity and predictability in the field of ammunition for small arms. Appropriately enough, it's known as the Small Arms & Ammunition Manufacturer's Institute, customarily abbreviated to SAAMI. They specify important details that include standardized dimensions for cartridge cases and maximum allowable pressures for each given cartridge.

I'm not certain as to the exact date that SAAMI came into being but I feel it was hardly a moment too soon. In bygone years, there was more than a touch of anarchy in the matter of case dimensions, for example. About the dawn of the Fifties, when I was getting my feet wet in the burbling brook of reloading, it was all too common to find that you had to keep two or more shell holders on hand to accommodate your hoard of empty brass. This particular batch of cases had heads too large — either in thickness or diameter or perhaps both — to go into that shell holder. Another, more charitable shell holder might accept the heads of the first lot, but a second lot of brass had heads so small that they'd slip out of the larger shell holder.

And then there was the perplexity with flash holes. You'd be depriming blithely and suddenly there would be a case you couldn't pluck free of the shell holder, because its undersized flash hole had seized the depriming pin in a death grip and wrenched it loose from the little collet within the die.

Modern die sets have depriming pins that seem to run around .072-inch in diameter. My usual procedure was to set aside cases with flash holes smaller than that and give them a pass over a No. 45 drill in the drill press. A No. 45 drill reams the flash hole to right around .082-inch, thereby eliminating that problem with that case in future encounters.

Thanks to SAAMI and its dedicated workers, it's been many a year since I've encountered an epidemic of cases with undersized flash holes. Minor dimensional peculiarities still occur, of course, though of a nature less conducive to panic. For example, there is the matter of brass thickness at the neck. The .38 Colt Super is a prime offender in this respect and the many headstamps of 9mm Luger are at least one other. You work out your dies and adjustments to turn forth truly lovely reloads with some one particular batch of brass, with a just-right grip of case neck against bullet base. Suddenly, as you're seating the bullets atop the powder charges, you come to one where the bullet just goes *ploop!* and drops spang through the neck to come to rest on top of the powder.

Checking out the cause of the contretemps, you find its headstamp is that of some maker other than the source of the rest of the brass. The metal is thinner in the neck, thus the resizing die didn't bring it to an inside diameter (ID) as small as the others.

Reloading some of the old Super Vel brass from the days when they produced the stuff at Shelbyville, Indiana, can drive you slightly up the wall in this respect. At one time or another, they bought their cases from several different sources, all with the Super Vel headstamp, but hardly ever with quite the same precise dimensions. All of which brings one to two alternatives: Either throw the empty cases out — unthinkable to even a casually devout reloader — or figure out some way of sorting and identifying them. That's by way of explaining why visiting reloaders sometimes come down bemused at finding containers of .38 Special or .357 magnum brass on my loading bench labeled "Super Vel/loose" or "Super Vel/tight." I run all of them through the full-length resizing die, then sort them as I mouth-bell/deprime, according to the amount of resistance felt when the ram drags the case back out of the die.

The practice of hotrodding the humble and ubiquitous .38 Special cartridge is an ancient one, even if not especially honorable nor judicious. At some point well upstream of

It's Hard To Think Of A New Way To Improve Ammo Performance, But A Lot Of Hopefuls Keep Trying!

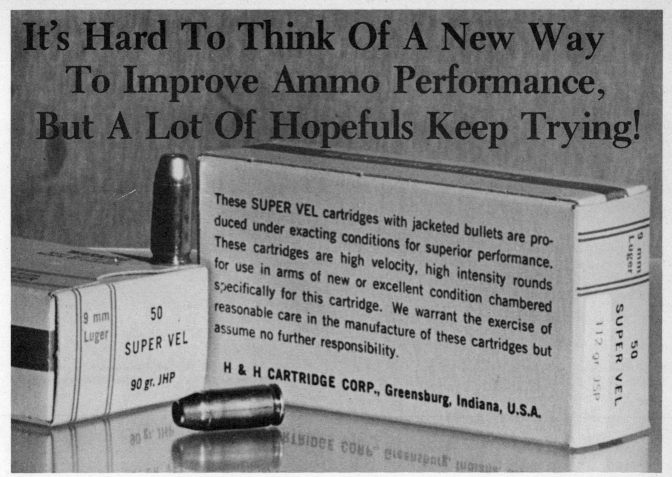

These SUPER VEL cartridges with jacketed bullets are produced under exacting conditions for superior performance. These cartridges are high velocity, high intensity rounds for use in arms of new or excellent condition chambered specifically for this cartridge. We warrant the exercise of reasonable care in the manufacture of these cartridges but assume no further responsibility.

H & H CARTRIDGE CORP., Greensburg, Indiana, U.S.A.

Super Vel ammunition currently is produced in a variety of handgun calibers at H&H Cartridge Corporation, in Greensburg Indiana, as exemplified by these loads for the 9mm Luger. Text discusses minor difficulties encountered in reloading the early Super Vel cases and techniques for avoiding problems caused by varying neck thicknesses from different case suppliers.

WWII, Smith & Wesson produced a .38 Special revolver on their large N frame, AKA their .44 frame, and termed the resulting husky handgun the .38-44 Outdoorsman. Having a comfortable mass of metal around the chambers, the .38-44 could digest comparatively hairy loads with bland insouciance; loads that would have caused grave distress and profound trauma if fired in lightweight .38 Special revolvers of the era.

The .38-44's moment in the limelight was destined to be all too brief. With the debut of the .357 magnum cartridge and guns in 1935, high-performance enthusiasts gained access to a gun in which they could fire .38 Special ammo loaded to fairly crazy pressures with few if any dire consequences. To that, I might dourly sidenote that I've rarely, if ever, encountered a .357 magnum revolver of any make or model that would group as well with any .38 Special load as would one of the better guns chambered expressly for the shorter cartridge. The .357 magnum and .38 Special are nominally identical in outside dimensions except that the .357 is .135-inch longer.

When you boot a bullet out of a .38 Special case enclosed in a .357 magnum chamber, it appears that something drastic and unfortunate happens to the bullet as it goes past that .135-inch of larger chamber before zitzing down the front of the chamber and on into the forcing cone at the rear of the barrel.

All of which is hardly Damon nor yet Pythias. The key

point is that the .38-44 Outdoorsman, during its brief salad days, spawned introduction of a somewhat more energetic cartridge of nominally .38 Special dimensions, known as the .38-44. It was the precursor of today's +P loads for the .38 Special.

Nominal SAAMI specs for the .38 Special seem to ceiling-out at right around 16,000 copper units of pressure (cup, often cited as pounds per square inch [psi] in some sources). The +P .38 Special loads seem to develop about 20,000 cup, which may seem like a relatively trifling gain. Most of the +P loads for the .38 Special carry bullets in the lighter weights such as 110 or 125 grains at listed velocities in the brackets of 1220 to 1070 fps, respectively.

The more timorous handgun makers manifest a great deal of quease regarding the use of +P loads in their output. Others — to this point — have been sanctioning such diets without overmuch visible alarm. If you want the current do/don't of the matter, query the maker of the gun in question. Books such as this one remain on sale and in use for extended intervals and the status quo before this goes to press could change within the next year or three, which is why I'm being seemingly coy about naming names and brands. It's just that I've no great yen to rock anyone's rowboat.

Thus, as we've seen, there have been efforts to upgrade performance of the .38 Special round by driving the bullets a bit faster at the expense of a moderate boost in peak

Winchester-Western's Xpediter .22 LR load packs a 29-grain hollow-point bullet that averages about 1200 fps from a 5.5-inch autoloading pistol barrel, as discussed.

CCI Stinger was the first of the current crop of extra-high velocity .22 LR loads, appearing late in 1976. Its 33-grain Penta-Point expanding bullet averages 1214 fps in handgun.

Newest of the high-performance .22 LR loads is Remington's Yellow Jacket, with 33-grain hollow-point that goes out of a 5.5-inch auto pistol barrel at average 1270 fps velocity.

pressures. The other cartridge benefiting from a similar approach is the petite but popular .22 Long Rifle (LR). The first edition of PARD devoted a chapter to reporting the measured performance parameters of typical .22 LR loads in equally typical handguns of that chambering. Within months of the printing of the first edition, the enterprising troops at Omark/CCI up in Lewiston, Idaho, had launched a new .22 LR round known as the .22 Stinger. Its case was a trifle longer than the standard and high-velocity .22 LR and its bullet was a few grains lighter and the powder charge was compounded with such craft and guile that the slugs whizzed forth at paces undreamed-of hitherto.

In late 1976/early 1977, at the time of the Stinger's appearance, I clocked its performance out of several handguns and a few typical rifles. All doubts were quickly dispelled as to its ability to scamper briskly, indeed. I timed one slightly maverick round of the stuff through a ten-inch barrel in my Thompson/Center Contender at a truly astounding 1960 fps. That shot copped the gold medal by several lengths. Out of barrels as long as twenty-eight inches, nothing else even came close. All observations indicate that somewhere around ten inches represents the optimum length for getting the ultimate erg out of the .22 LR cartridge. As barrel length increases, velocity drops off progressively.

More recently, in the early part of 1978, Winchester-Western brought forth a corresponding cartridge they called the .22 Xpediter. Like the CCI Stinger, the Xpediter case is slightly longer than conventional .22 LR cases. As a usual rule, guns with chamber dimensions made to SAAMI standard specifications handle the Stinger and Xpediter without problems. Moderate difficulties may be encountered if the two cartridges are fired in certain foreign-made guns.

Another more recent entry in the field of hot .22 LR loads is Remington's Yellow Jacket, rated by the maker to deliver 1500 fps with its 33-grain hollow-pointed bullet. Presumably, the 1500 fps velocity was obtained in a full-length rifle barrel. Six rounds of Yellow Jacket, chronographed from a Ruger Mark I autoloader with 5.5-inch barrel spanned from a low of 1254 fps to a high of 1287 fps and averaged 1270 fps. Measurements were taken with the chronograph screens placed fifteen and seventeen feet from the muzzle, so actual muzzle velocities would be a bit higher. A 33-grain bullet, at 1270 fps, carries 118 foot-pounds of energy (fpe). The case of the Yellow Jacket is the same length as conventional .22 long rifle cartridges.

Curious as comparative performance of all three .22 LR sprinter loads, I fired some of the CCI Stingers from the same bull-barreled Ruger Mark I and velocities ranged from 1189 to 1265 fps, averaging 1214. From the same gun, the W-W Xpediter loads clocked from 1147 to 1268 fps, with 1197 fps as the average. The Xpediter bullet weighs 29 grains. The Stinger bullet weighs 33 grains. The moderate variation in weight and velocity does not result in a lot of difference in net foot-pounds. The span is from a 29-grain bullet at 1147 fps (92 fpe) to a 33-grain at 1287 (121 fpe); a margin of 29 foot-pounds.

I think it's safe to say that all three cartridges are remarkably good and the soundly strategic approach is to test them in the given gun to see how they perform in comparative grouping ability. Testing all three loads through several different handguns, I find that results vary significantly from one gun to the next.

First-hand observation underscores one trenchant fact: Never be content with the accuracy performance of any .22 LR gun — handgun or rifle — until you've tried several other loads under strictly identical conditions. It's best to test them off a good, solid benchrest, using a scope if that's practicable. The important point is to eliminate the human factor insofar as possible. The net difference in grouping capability is apt to be something you'll find hard to believe.

Resist the obvious temptation to leap atop a soapbox and tell the world that Brand Y is super-great whereas Brand Z is rotten-rotten-rotten. Check the whole group of loads through a few other guns and it's highly probable that you'll find some other gun that groups stunningly with Brand Z and doesn't perform worth sour owl sweat with Brand Y. So it goes. The key fact is that different guns handle different loads with varying effect to a really astounding degree, and seldom is this so much the case as with the .22 LR cartridge.

There are just a few areas in which ammunition performance can be improved significantly. You can boost the effective velocity provided you can do so without a corresponding boost in peak pressures generated. You can enhance the average accuracy (and call it a damned good trick if you bring it off!). As the last promising field of endeavor, you can improve the effectiveness of the bullet in delivering its kinetic energy to the target at the moment of impact.

What might be termed impact response has come in for its rightful share of attention in recent times. Some fearless innovators have chosen the obvious route of fitting the bullet with a scaled-down version of a nuclear warhead in the form of percussion caps coupled with small charges of brisant materials such as black gunpowder. Just about the last word that can be applied to such a concept is original. It has continually been discovered and invented by intrepid hopefuls over the past century or so, quite possibly even longer.

Ever since the first introduction of bursting shells for use in artillery, crafty schemers have been trying to adapt the same concept to bullets for small arms. As it turns out, it's

CCI-Speer's Lawman Ammunition line includes a .45 ACP load they call the Inspector, with a 200-grain JHP bullet. It performs well on accuracy, velocity and sure functioning.

Federal's No. 45C Match load in .45 ACP carries a bullet made for them by Sierra; a 185-grain jacketed hollow cavity (JHC), also available as component for reloading.

Remington's Index 6945 load for the .45 ACP features a 185-grain JHP bullet with hexagonal cavity and lightly scored jacket nose to assure maximum expansion at impact.

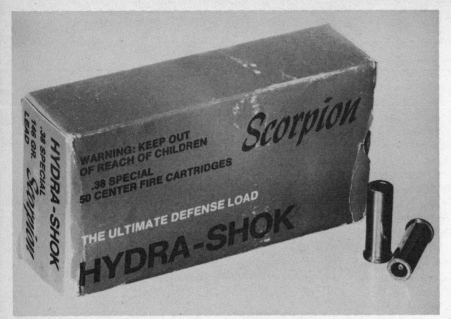

Here are two .38 Special SWC loads. Federal No. 38G has a hollow-point and W-W No. W38WCP is a solid, but is loaded to +P velocity levels.

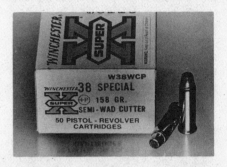

The Hydra-Shok Scorpion load in .38 Special carries a unique 146-grain hollow-point bullet with an integral central post, visible in this photo. It's designed to expand to about .6-inch, even in two-inch barrel guns.

In terms of actually delivered foot-pounds of energy (fpe), Norma's No. 19119 load, with 110-grain JHP bullet is one of the most powerful commercial loads available for the .38 Special revolvers at present.

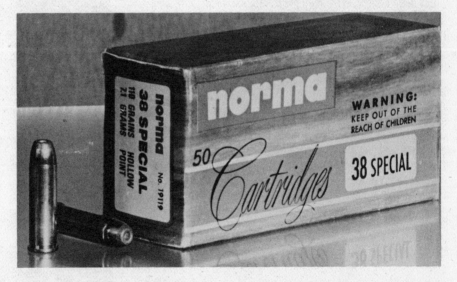

Winchester-Western No. W38S2P load, below, carries a 158-grain round-nose bullet of the full metal jacket (FMJ) pattern for applications where penetration is desired rather than expansion. Such bullets usually are favored for military use.

Grennell makes these "Scoop-Snoot" JHP bullets on his Corbin Mity-Mite bullet press. Expanded specimen is from a .38 Special fired into sand.

not all that formidable a challenge. Explosive bullets were utilized in warfare on a few recorded occasions before the Hague Conference proscribed the use of such ammunition. Contrary to popular faith, the Geneva Convention never dealt with that particular topic.

Explosive bullets, along with tracers, incendiaries, et al., are quite properly legislated against in areas where terrain conditions impose a severe fire hazard during a portion of the year. When the ground is covered with sun-parched grass and brush waiting to go up like gunpowder at the merest spark, the last thing anyone needs is someone firing bullets that can devastate thousands of acres and use up megabucks in firefighting efforts.

Less hazardous approaches remain and these have been explored intensively. Hollow-points have been around since about the day after time immemorial. Such modifications do not produce instant expansion upon initial contact but depend upon the filling of the cavity with an appropriate medium scooped from the target at the moment of impact. It is is possible to accelerate the effect by filling the nasal cavity of the bullet with a fluid and sealing it against loss en route. Water or similar liquids can be used, but common bullet grease works at least as well and is a lot easier to contain during the flight downrange.

Most reloaders have long been aware of the potential performance obtainable through the simple expedient of loading the readily obtainable hollow-base .38 wadcutter bullets into the case backwards, with cavity to the fore. If desired, the exposed cavity can be filled with bullet grease to hasten upset upon contact. The approach involves a small sacrifice of inherent accuracy, but not enough to present serious problems.

Oddly enough, no one seems to have offered such a concoction to non-reloaders via commercial outlets. The outstanding example of a comparable load is the Hydra-Shok Scorpion, currently made in .38 Special and planned for introduction in other popular calibers. The bullet used in the Scorpion resembles the familiar reversed hollow-base wadcutter but it has the added feature of a small post in the center of the cavity, presumably to add penetration as well as the splash as the front skirts expand to about caliber .60 upon impact. The effect of the Scorpion is quite salutary, even in snubnosed guns with barrels as short as two inches.

Tests indicate the Scorpion gives away little if any advantage as to accuracy. Out of any test gun at a given distance, groups with the Scorpion are on a close par with those obtainable with a good factory wadcutter target load.

In certain instances, it can be a great advantage if a load is capable of greater than average penetration. Armor-piercing is the usual term for such bullets and cartridges. The most noteworthy example of such

Here's an early example of the KTW load with a 200-grain metal piercing bullet in .38 Special. As discussed here, KTW produces comparable loads in several other calibers, restricting their sale solely to police and law enforcement agencies.

The well known Hornady bullets are available in the form of loaded ammunition from Hornady's Frontier Cartridge Division. Several bullet types are available in popular calibers and the larger sizes are sold in packages of twenty, as shown in photo.

ammunition in the current market is the KTW cartridge, produced and distributed by KTW, Incorporated, 710 Cooper-Foster Park Road/West, Lorain, Ohio 44053. The KTW loads are available in calibers .25 ACP, .30 M-1 carbine, .32 Auto, .38 Colt Super, .380 Auto, 9mm Parabellum, .38 Special, .357 magnum, .44 Special and .45 ACP. KTW restricts the sale of its ammunition exclusively to law enforcement agencies. Authorized personnel may request details as to price, delivery and penetration capabilities on departmental letterhead.

One further avenue for exploitation is that of multiple projectiles. A few years ago, one Midwestern firm was offering quad-loads for the .38 Special that would put four holes in the target per tug of the trigger, provided the shooter performed adequately. To the best of my knowledge, that particular supplier is not currently active in the same field, but the concept remains to any enterprising firm that cares to buck an unresponsive market.

Separating the projectile into four equal pieces quadruples the frontal area with no sacrifice in total kinetic energy. As noted, the Hydra-Shok Scorpion bullet expands to an average diameter of .600-inch – not quite .283 square inches against .101 square inches for the original .358-inch cross-section. Four .358-inch circles have a combined cross-section of .403 square inches, equivalent to the area of a circle having a diameter of .716-inch.

A bullet derives much of its effectiveness from the abruptness with which the energy is transmitted to the target. Given time to roll with the punch, vast amounts of foot-pounds can be absorbed without ill effect. To illustrate, a mass with the weight of an average human body, traveling at sixty miles per hour, possesses an impressively lethal number of foot-pounds (roughly 120.4 foot-pounds per pound of body weight). A passenger in an automobile traveling at that speed suffers no great

discomfort as the vehicle's brakes are applied to halt it over the course of several seconds. If the car hits a bridge abutment, the situation is tragically different.

By dividing a bullet into several pieces, the trauma effect is multiplied proportionally and the end results are accelerated to some degree, with a balancing loss in penetration capabilities. In a number of instances, reduction of penetration is regarded as a benefit, one example is in the instance of densely populated urban locales.

The projectiles employed in the Quads as made, until sometime in 1976, by Michigan Fire Rescue Equipment Corporation, 148 North Groesbeck Highway, Mt. Clemens, Michigan 48043, carried a powder charge weighing 6.5 grains in the .38 Special version, behind four bullets with a combined weight of 206 grains. The bullets had conical noses and matching indentations in the base, to nest as compactly as possible. The individual bullets averaged 51.5 grains apiece. That works out to 41 foot-pounds each at a velocity of 600 fps or 56 foot-pounds at 700 fps.

Several other possibilities have been explored for abrupt transmission of bullet energy. The Glaser Safety Slug consists of a copper alloy jacket filled with No. 12 shot coated with a silicone solution, with the open front end capped by a Teflon/Fiberglas enclosure. It is designed to travel to the target intact and disintegrate upon impact.

The Short Stop represented another attempt to achieve similar results. Its projectile was a small pancake of tough fabric, filled with fine shot and sealed at the edges. Rolled and enclosed in a plastic capsule, the resulting round could be loaded into revolvers and fired in the conventional manner. Upon leaving the muzzle, the plastic enclosure ruptured to send the little beanbag spinning flat side-foremost toward the target, guided by the centrifugal

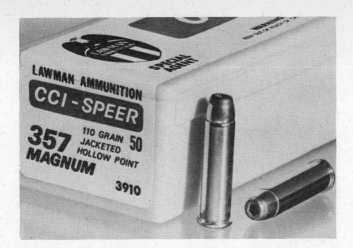

The Special Agent is Omark/CCI-Speer's designation for their .357 magnum load with a 110-grain JHP bullet that, like many of the firm's bullets, features unusual Penta-Point.

Above and below, Winchester-Western recently introduced their Silvertip hollow-point bullets as a factory load in 9mm Luger and .45 ACP. Increasingly higher prices of ammunition is the major factor causing a shift to packing twenty instead of fifty rounds/carton in heavier calibers.

The .45 Winchester magnum developed for the Wildey auto, currently is offered in the Thompson/Center Contender, as well. From the latter, it drives the 230-grain factory load bullet to velocities of around 1450 fps.

Speer no longer markets their half-jackets, but they're to be had from other sources. By swaging a No. 4 buck shot into one, bullets can be produced that serve well for loading two to a .38 Special or three in .357 magnum cartridge cases.

Speer offers shot capsules, here in .38 and .44 size, which can be filled with shot of desired size for reloading, as discussed in text.

Speer offers six-packs of factory shot loads for the .38 Special and .357 magnum (left), but produces .44 shot loads only in the magnum size, making it necessary for the .44 Special owner to reload, using the empty capsules illustrated here. In point of fact, anyone with the capability to reload can save attractive sums of money by means of homemade shot loads.

Thompson/Center Arms offers their Hot Shot capsules in both .357 and .44 diameters, with load data printed on the carton. Available in a variety of shot sizes, the Hot Shots are not readily hand-fillable. They're also available as factory loads in both .357 and .44 magnum. They must be fired from the Contender barrel with the choke device described here in order for the capsule to shred at the muzzle for release of pellets. As noted, the .44 load compares favorably with .410 shotguns.

force imparted by the rifling in the gun barrel. The Short Stop was conceived at a time when airline hijackers presented a severe enforcement problem, having been designed for maximum effect at very short distances.

Omark-CCI/Speer continues to make and market shot cartridges in .22 long rifle, .22 WMRF, .38 Special and .44 magnum, as well as empty plastic capsules in the .38/.357 and .44 diameters for use in reloading. The empty capsules can be filled with shot pellets of the desired size and sealed with the supplied base cap. The resulting projectile is handloaded in the same manner as a conventional bullet.

The .44 capsules enable the owner of a .44 Special revolver — such as the Charter Arms .44 Bulldog — to make up shot loads for use in such guns, since the shorter .44 Special chamber won't accept the .44 magnum factory load. The two rimfire shot loads from Omark have plastic shot-enclosing capsules that approximately duplicate the outer profile of conventional bullet loads in the same cartridges. The recoil effect of the rimfire shot loads is insufficient to operate the mechanism of most autoloading pistols, but the slide can be cycled manually to feed fresh cartridges out of the magazine into the chamber.

The Hot Shot capsule, made and distributed by Thompson/Center Arms as a reloading component and factory ammo in .38/.357 and .44 magnum sizes, is capable of duplicating or slightly exceeding the performance of the .410-bore shotshell, when fired from the especially designed barrels for such cartridges in the maker's Contender single-shot pistols. The Hot Shot barrels incorporate a special choke tube at the muzzle, with straight longitudinal ribs that arrest the swirling motion imparted by the normal rifling and, at the same time, shred the capsule to deliver the shot charge in a well controlled pattern.

The slightly complex approach of the T/C Hot Shot system is made necessary by federal laws forbidding the use of smoothbore barrels for handguns. It is illegal for a smoothbore to have a barrel less than eighteen inches or an overall length less than twenty-six inches. More precisely, such guns are legal but require complicated registration and the payment of a $200 transfer tax.

As a charge of shot pellets is driven up a conventionally rifled handgun barrel, it is spun to a high number of revolutions per minute (rpm) and, as a result, the pellets tend to disperse rapidly on paths tangential to the axis of the bore on leaving the muzzle. The choke tube at the muzzle of the T/C Hot Shot barrel nullifies the described effect to deliver the pellets in an effective pattern instead of the usual expanding hollow circle. If desired, the choke tube can be removed to permit the use of conventional, single-bullet ammunition in .357 or .44 magnum, depending upon the chambering of the barrel.

As suggested by the foregoing, vast ingenuity has been devoted to the quest for superior ammunition performance, leaving the field quite well cultivated. My first impulse, in closing, was to offer a couple of facetious suggestions as to further possibilities to check out. Discretion prompts me to refrain, lest someone not see the tongue in cheek. The world is not yet ready for what I had in mind, thank goodness!

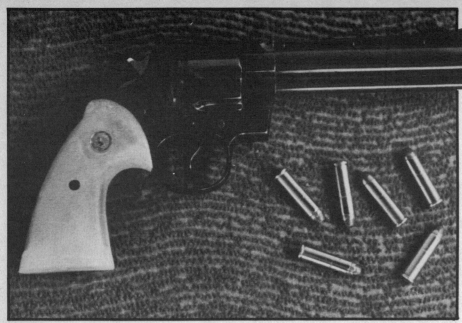

Left, this Colt Python sports a handsome set of pearl grips, cast from the original wooden set. Facing page, applying the first layer of latex mould material, as described here.

Chapter 8

A GRIPPING MATTER

You Can Fancy-Up Your Favorite Handgun At Minimal Cost

By Frank & Robert Mauro

WITH TODAY'S HIGH prices, the average handgunner thinks twice before going out and buying a fancy set of pearl grips or a set of those good-looking hand-carved wooden target models. But even the most economically minded shooter can have either one for under $1.33! And all it takes is several hours of work over two or three weekends.

It's all done with liquid plastic resin and a latex mould. The latter you make from the grips you'd like to own. Of course, these grips must be for a handgun like the one you intend to use them on and, unfortunately, this process will not work with metal grips, since metal reacts with the latex. Only wooden, plastic, nylon and the commercially produced pearl variety can be duplicated.

First you must make a mould of the original wooden grips. For this we used Mold-Tex liquid latex manufactured by American Handicrafts. That was where, incidentally, we purchased everything we needed for the project; however, similar arts and crafts shops should stock most of the materials you'll require. The Mold-Tex cost us $4.95 for a quart and ten to twenty moulds can be made from it, so you'll have more than enough to experiment with.

The pearl grips are made from several ounces of Clear Cast liquid-casting plastic; a quart is $3.95. You'll also need a quarter-ounce bottle of catalyst hardener, which is about forty-nine cents. Pearl luster, of course, is your main ingredient and runs about $1.29 for a half-ounce bottle. But you'll only need a few drops of it for each pouring, so over a dozen pearl grips can be made from a single supply.

You'll require some plaster of paris for your mould's support shell and, if you don't already have a bag lying around the workshop, a five-pound sack costs about eighty-nine cents. With this, be sure to pick up a pint of Plasta-Solve to clean your moulds and brushes. It sells for $1.69 and goes a long way.

That brings your shopping list up to $13.26, and you should have enough material to turn out about ten pairs of grips!

Start by removing the grips you intend to duplicate from the handgun. With an old toothbrush carefully clean each grip, being sure to remove any dirt particles that might be present, especially in the checkering and around the emblems. If these particles are not removed completely, they will register in the mould and decrease the detail and overall quality of your finished grips.

When you've cleaned the handgun's original grips thoroughly, polish each with furniture wax; this will create a smooth surface and facilitate removing the latex mould from them later. Next, using a drop of rubber cement, mount each grip on a small board, butt end to board. The cement can be cleaned off the grips by rubbing it away with your fingers.

Begin by applying a very thin coat of liquid latex with a

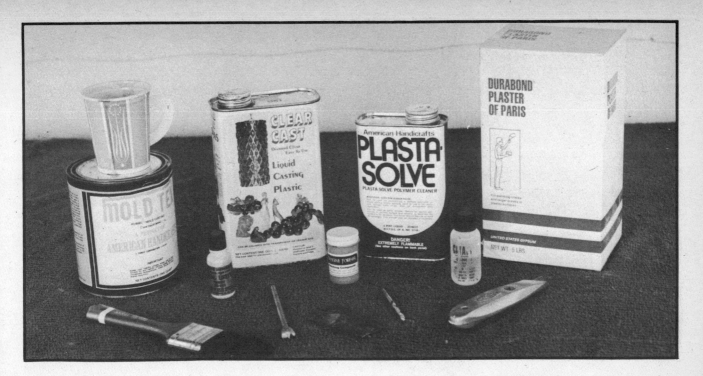

one inch to 1½-inch soft-bristle paint brush. The latex can be thinned with water — following the manufacturer's instructions. Remember, the thinner your first coat, the more detail you'll pick up from the grip you're copying. Start brushing from the top of the grip and work your way down towards the butt end. Paint an additional inch out from the bottom onto the board to provide a lip on your latex mould.

As you paint on your first coat, try not to create any tiny air bubbles, for these will end up giving your pearl grip a pitted look.

When you have covered each grip completely and painted one inch out from the butt end, allow the first coat about half an hour to dry. Then apply a second coat and, half an hour later, a third one. Wait until this coat has dried, then begin building up thicker and thicker layers of latex. Be sure to give each at least half an hour to dry and continue to apply latex until the mould is one-sixteenth to one-eighth-inch thick. Check the lip at the base of the mould to determine when you have reached this thickness. About twelve to sixteen coats should be required depending on how heavily you apply the liquid latex. Don't rush it!

When you have applied your final coat, allow three or four days for the mould to dry.

While waiting, construct a form for a plaster support shell. This can be made from cardboard and waterproof tape. Just be sure to allow at least one-inch clearance around the perimeter of your original grip. This will make the cardboard form about four inches deep. Set it aside now, until your latex mould is dry.

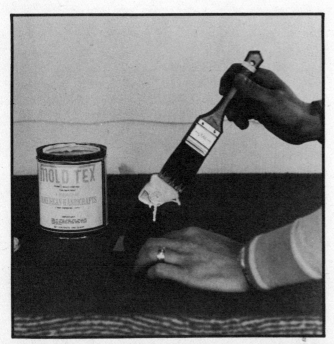

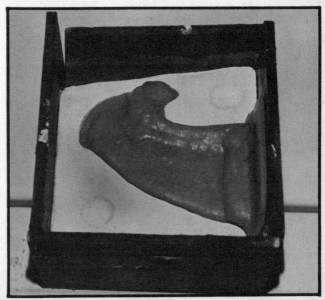

Above, bill of materials cost the author a bit over $13, with enough supplies to make about ten sets of grips. Right, the latex mould on half of supporting plaster.

Right, peeling the latex mould from the plastic after it has set and hardened. Below, pour the mixture into the mould carefully to avoid air bubbles.

After the three or four days have elapsed, do not remove the original grip from the latex mould, for it is now ready to set into the plaster support shell. Begin by applying vegetable oil to the mould. Do not use mineral oil, for this will harm the latex. The vegetable oil will prevent the plaster from adhering to the mould.

Next, mix a sufficient amount of plaster of paris to fill approximately half of the cardboard form. The plaster should be of soupy consistency, the exact amount depending on the size form your particular grip requires. Pour the plaster into the form and, since it sets rapidly, be ready to depress your vegetable oil-covered latex mould and grip into it as soon as the plaster is sufficiently leveled.

When the plaster becomes pasty, make two scores about one-quarter-inch deep in it. These will permit alignment bumps to form in the second batch of plaster when it is poured later. You then should wait about two hours for the first batch to harden before continuing.

When the plaster has set, coat the exposed latex grip and the surface of the plaster with more vegetable oil. Be sure to coat everything adequately to prevent the plaster from sticking to any surface.

When you have done this, pour the second soupy batch over the grip, entirely filling up the form. Allow another two hours for the plaster to harden, then remove the dry support shell from its cardboard form and carefully pry the shell's two halves apart.

You now remove your original grip from the latex and vulcanize the mould. Vulcanization is accomplished by simply boiling it in water for one to three hours. When you have done this, fill the latex mould with water and measure its liquid volume. You then will know just how much Clear Cast will be required to fill it later.

Before you begin casting, make sure the latex mould is completely dry and free of dirt. When certain it is, place it into one half of the plaster shell and cover it with the other half. Make sure the alignment bumps fit into their respective scores. The support shell then can be held together securely with several rubber bands.

You are now ready to mix the Clear Cast, pearl luster and catalyst materials. This can be done in a paper cup using a wooden tongue depressor to stir the mixture. Pour the required amount of Clear Cast into the cup and add ten drops of catalyst for every ounce of Clear Cast required to fill your mould. (We have discovered that less catalyst will make the grips sticky and too much will be wasteful.)

Stir gently for one minute, trying not to create any air bubbles in the mixture. If trapped internally, these tiny pinpoint bubbles will expand, while the pearl grip is hardening, and crack it.

Next add about one-half cubic centimeter of pearl luster for each grip and mix gently for fifteen seconds. Slowly pour the entire mixture into your latex mould. While doing this, tilt the plaster shell back and forth to allow any trapped air to escape. Set the support shell and mould combination down and tap it sharply a few times on each side to release any air bubbles clinging to the inner wall of the latex. Then allow at least twenty-four hours for the Clear Cast to harden.

When the exposed ends of your new grips are no longer tacky, they are ready to be removed from their respective moulds. Grasp the lip of the mould and roll it back like a stocking.

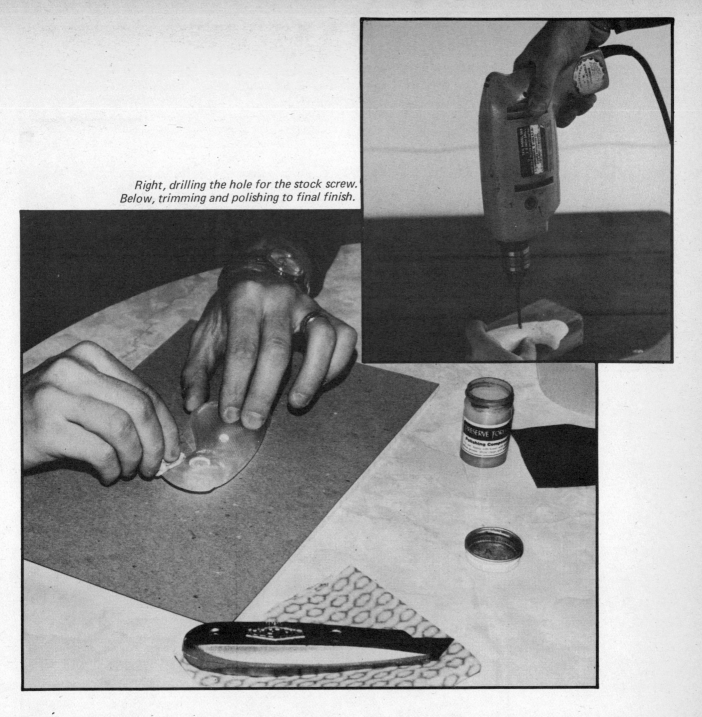

Right, drilling the hole for the stock screw. Below, trimming and polishing to final finish.

When the latex moulds are completely off, they will be inside out. This is the ideal time to clean them, as the pearl grips are set aside to dry for another day or two.

Using a little Plasta-Solve remove all Clear Cast still clinging to the moulds. After both have been thoroughly cleaned and dried, they can be turned right side out. They now are all set for another casting.

To finish the grips, drill out the mounting holes. To determine the proper bit size for this, use the hole in the original grip as a gauge. Either a wood or metal bit may be used. A variable-speed electric drill is helpful, but a single-speed electric model in a sure hand should do the job just as well.

If you intend to inset your handgun's emblem, a wood auger of the proper size can be used to cut out a mounting hole. Again, use the hole left in the original grip by the removed emblem to gauge the correct auger size.

This step completed, trim away the rough edges from your new pearl grips with a razor blade, then sand down each one with a wet piece of number 400 sandpaper.

In polishing, put a dab of toothpaste on a clean rag. Rub this vigorously against the grip until you begin to see a luster appear. At this time, switch to a polishing compound such as jeweler's rouge. With a little time and elbow grease, you will end up with an impressive-looking, high-luster pair of pearl grips. Finally, wash each in cool water. When they are dry, you can mount them.

You might try adding a drop of black opaque color (supplied by American Handicrafts) in with the pearl luster, catalyst and Clear Cast. This will give the finished grip a lustrous black and white marbelized effect. The same can be done with different colors, opaque or translucent. You might even try mixing in some metallic glitter. This looks particularly good in a crystal-clear set.

With a little time and imagination there is little limit to what you can do.

Then There Are Approaches For Those Who Don't Have Time To Cast And Whittle!

By Bob Zwirz

WHAT IS ONE man's cup of tea, in the matter of gun grips, could well be another's poison; but as there is a choice between revolvers or semi-automatic pistols, as well as dozens of variations in calibers and handgun designs, there are vast differences in both the physical charactersitics and in-use handgun requirements of the people who will own them.

Thus, it's up to each handgun shooter to carefully analyze the specific uses to which his handgun or guns will be subjected — then give serious thought to this business of choosing functional grips; grips that will best serve his particular requirements, while fitting him physically.

The point of the matter is really one of basics. Individuals who, of necessity, must carry an undercover-type handgun, be it a revolver or autoloader, normally are most interested in concealment; it's this specialized use of a compact handgun that tends to designate the style and contours of the grips that may be considered as likely choices.

As an example, when wearing a business suit or during the summer, when the occasion allows for substitution of a sports shirt worn on the outside of my trousers, ninety-nine out of a hundred times I'll be carrying a short barrel, compact sidearm, sheathed in the best designed, form-fitting holster available. The grips on such a special-purpose gun feature as little bulk as possible and

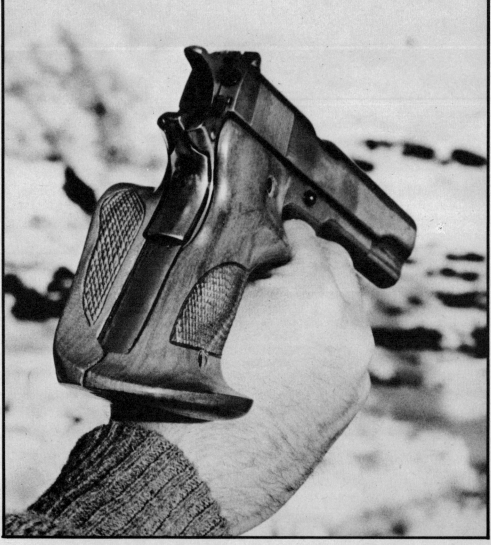

Contoured Jay Scott stocks for the Government Model auto feature generous thumb rest for right-handed shooter and support ledge for the lower edge of the palm. While not suited for concealed carrying, such grips help target scores.

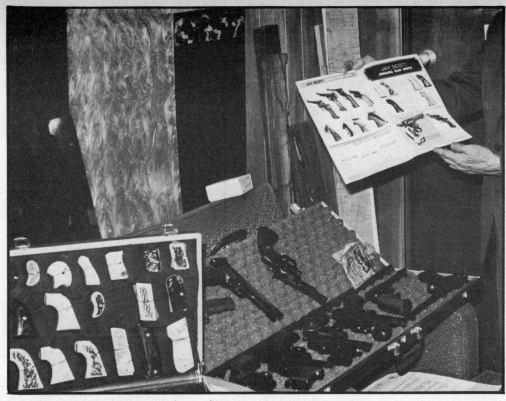

A small sampling of the bewildering variety of grips available from Jay Scott's catalog.

probably are described best as being of the standard, round butt variety. To me, it is a most important consideration that I be able to appear in public, free of any onlooker's suspicions that I am, indeed, heeled.

Over the past several years I've carried either the Charter Arms Undercover or a well-tuned Smith & Wesson Chiefs Special, both revolvers featuring two-inch barrels. Using the high velocity HP loads I prefer, I will shoot far more accurately when these handguns are equipped with either Bulldog or Gunfighter-type oversize grips. But it's just as true that they don't lay-into the belt area as smoothly as do the standard, streamlined, round grips that have proved themselves best for purposes of concealment.

It's the same business of specialization that plays so important a part in the choice of functional grips for the handgun hunter, the serious target shooter or the uniformed law enforcement officer who has come to realize the importance of equipping his service sidearm with grips that fit his hand, as well as his personal technique of "holding."

Though the basic approach of designing and producing grips for all manner of handguns correctly centers around the idea of creating functional products that will serve to better the shooter's proficiency, it isn't the sole concept. Shooters who take special pride in the appearance of their revolvers or autos are prone to give more than a passing

Just a portion of the Jay Scott reference section on handgun frame dimensions.

thought to finding grips that are handsome-to-behold, as well as designed with correct fit and functionability in mind.

Seeing as how I'm an admitted lily-gilder by nature, it isn't too surprising that I finally gave in to a long-nurtured desire to browse my way through the U.S. plant of one of the world's largest producers of handgun grips. It's the kind of place where, for the most part, if you can name it, they can show you the goods in such variation that you had better be explicit!

My personal session in this land of plain, fancy, and extraordinary grips took place at the New Jersey facilities of Jay Scott, Incorporated, while under the guidance of old master himself, Archie Lasser. Lasser, who is president of the organization, has introduced to the gun grips business that special kind of design, production and selling know-how wherein all the talents of his staff are brought into play. In fact, much of the intricate machinery for turning out and finishing this company's selection has been designed within the Jay Scott plant, then either built by them or custom manufactured to their own designs and specifications. The firm now is part of Colt Industries, incidentally.

I mentioned that the key word is "explicit," when you attempt to call the shots with Lasser. Maybe you would appreciate seeing a new grip for that favorite old Colt, S&W or you name it.

"Well," says Lasser, "would you prefer to feast your eyes on our Armarc line of polyester grips or have you set your little heart on the distinctive look of wood?"

If you would like to choose from the polyester models, all of which are laminated on a base of impregnated wood, you have the choice of black pearl, stag horn, ivory, white pearl and only Lasser and his people know what else!

By the time you've had a gander at the zebrawood, the deeply grained walnut or the mahogany, you are close to confusion. You then are queried on your preferences concerning standard style grips; Gunfighter oversize; target grips; target grips (oversize); Targeteer or High Score.

Though the above may seem a bit overdone to some skeptics, I can assure you that the possible choices available in Jay Scott's line-up of gun grips is both surprising and staggering. It is obvious the moment you walk into their inventory areas that you are looking at thousands of dollars worth of gun grips, tailored not only for our more popular, modern day handguns, but for famous old revolvers as well. This latter classification includes both top-break and solid-frame models.

Jay Scott not only had the proper grips available in the finishes noted, but can give you a choice of square or round butt.

A mathematician I'm not, but damned if I'm far wrong by stating that there are mighty close to 1100 ways a shooter can come to grips with the Jay Scott people. The obvious advantage of such a selection is that the needs or whims of most every handgun owner can be satisfied by simply browsing this company's brochure. There is

Above, zebrawood stock for Ruger Super Blackhawk shows care in matching butt grain pattern. Below, thumb rest stocks on S&W .22 auto and several other Jay Scott samples.

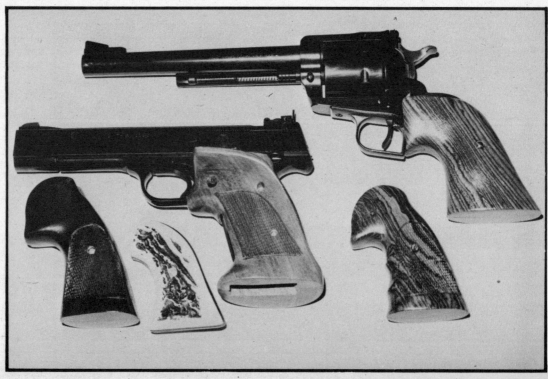

something there for everyone that includes sizes, shapes, finishes and special purpose models.

In addition, their vast array of functional grips makes it an easy matter for a gun owner to use a specific sidearm for multi-purposes; while at the plant, I picked out a custom-checkered set of target grips, with thumb rest, for a Colt .45 auto that was customized a few years ago by John Dewey.

Having tried the .45 ACP with these new grips, I can attest to the fact that my scores have improved. By simply changing grips following target shooting sessions, I have the auto back to its more compact lines, ready to use for other purposes when needed. The possibilities for those owning any of the more reliable, accurate-shooting revolvers or automatics are extensive. A favorite gun or two can be equipped with anything from target grips to oversize hunting grips, from standard replacement to special combat-type grips. A few turns of a screwdriver makes the transition a cinch.

As for the quality of the grips I carefully examined and am using now on several of my own guns, I checked laboratory reports, as well as several dozen letters from dealers and customers.

From what I judge, the impregnated wood bases render the Armarc grips virtually unbreakable. They are both resistant and impervious to water, gun oils and body acids; according to the lab report, these grips will not swell, shrink or warp, even under extremes of heat or cold. It would seem apparent that the Jay Scott organization has the same faith in their product's reliability, seeing as how each pair of Armarc gun grips comes with a lifetime guarantee!

It should be apparent that for those of us who do not have the talents of a Swiss woodcarver, there are all manner of size and type-variations to take care of our wildest whims. However, for those shooters with creative fingers, I suspect that the dozens of grip types available in an unfinished state would offer excellent opportunities for whipping up a truly personalized custom job. They come inletted and shaped, and are pre-fitted to the proper frame, ready for whittling, filing, sanding and final finishing. You can hand-rub your own creation until it shines like a diamond — if that be your delight.

I wouldn't be at all surprised to learn that out of the forty-five million handguns owned by U.S. shooters, more than a few are showing signs of oil rot, chipping or various of the other maladies that eventually attack the older, pre-Space Age gun grips. And I know for certain that there are untold numbers of handguns that would lend themselves to the multi-function grips system, at the same time making it possible for their owners to possibly better their shooting performances.

A worker at the Jay Scott plant adds finishing touches to a set of stocks for installation on a double-action revolver.

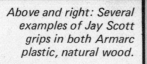

Above and right: Several examples of Jay Scott grips in both Armarc plastic, natural wood.

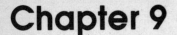

Chapter 9

A LOOK AT LEATHER

The Hundreds Of Handgun Holsters On The Market Have One Thing In Common — Design And Manufacture Depends On Skilled Hands

By Roger Combs

WALK INTO THE largest and most modern gun leather factory or into a one-man custom holster operation in somebody's garage and one thing in common is apparent immediately. It has taken and still takes the skill of the human hand to produce the best protection for pistols and revolvers; and that best protection is made of natural leather.

The variety of handgun holsters is as great as the variety of handguns. The leather must hold and protect revolvers

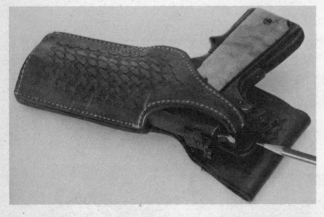

Pistol and revolver holsters offered by manufacturers in plain or basketweave, for long barrels and short. Top of the page is Bianchi's Model 50 Chapman Hi-Ride, named for champion pistol shooter, Ray Chapman. Thumb break holster, above, and long-barrel revolver holster, Model 25, by Safariland. Pencil indicates thumb break.

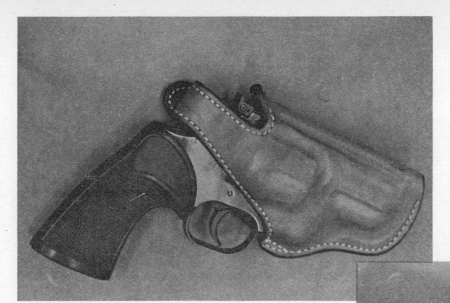

Outside and inside views of Bianchi Model 5BH, neatly handles Dan Wesson two-inch barrel revolver with Pachmayr Presentation grip. Note how rear sight is protected.

and pistols with barrels from two inches to more than twelve inches long, made from several kinds of metals and finishes, produced in many parts of the world with different shapes and sizes of stocks and grip frames. Furthermore, the holster is to be worn on the belt — left side, right side, rear; high, low, tilted, swiveled, tied down, tied up; inside the belt, outside the belt; on the leg, on the ankle; under the arm, high and low.

To add to the variety, many holsters are available in

Larger leather manufacturers cast moulds of nearly every foreign and domestic popular handgun from which holsters are designed and production checked.

several colors in the same style; black, tan, cordovan, natural and recently, camouflage finish of more than one color and pattern. The leather may be finished plain and smooth, in a basketweave or flowered pattern, or in a Clarino — black and shiny — finish. Many holsters are built with a lining of elk hide or other leather for increased durability and strength. An examination of each style produced by one of the larger manufacturers leaves the mind somewhat boggled.

No matter who is making it, the first step to constructing any holster is the design. Someone, perhaps it is the research and development director, must first obtain a sample handgun as consumer demand for the gun becomes manifest. There is more to a holster design than merely wrapping a piece of heavy leather around the gun and cutting a couple slots in the inside to slip a belt through. The primary function of the gun — backup, hunting, plinking, target shooting, law enforcement, etc. — must first be considered. Where is it to be worn? For what purpose?

Most high-quality holsters these days are moulded to shape around a sample gun — or in the case of some of the larger manufacturers — around a metal casting which was made from the gun. Given the variety, style, lengths and overall size dimensions of all the handguns on the market today, the inventory of pistol and revolver moulds on hand could be large, indeed. The cast moulds are kept on hand as long as a holster is in production to check the fit of the leather production.

Once the design has been established, production techniques must be defined for the line. True, machines are

Skilled hands, above, mould moistened leather around dummy handgun cast for design check. Raw materials for thousands of holsters are stockpiled at Bianchi's California plant, below. Hides are carefully selected.

used to stamp or cut out certain parts or pieces of the product but skilled hands are put to work at every step.

The basic raw materials of gun holsters is, of course, leather. If you've purchased a new pair of shoes, boots or belt lately, you know that the price of high-grade leather has kept pace with the rising inflation rate around the world. Because each holster is clearly visible and subject to

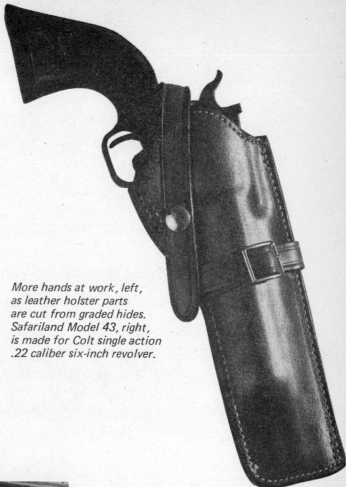

More hands at work, left, as leather holster parts are cut from graded hides. Safariland Model 43, right, is made for Colt single action .22 caliber six-inch revolver.

Above: Ruger handgun holster parts, made by Bianchi, await their call to the assembly line. Steel plate, right, helps cut out and basketweave holster body.

Thick leather holster part comes out of cutting mould, to be assembled later in production cycle.

Note basketweave pattern on portion of holster leather section above. Left, edges are dressed and smoothed on special machines.

minute examination, most holster makers buy the highest grade — meaning hides with the least flaws and of uniform, specified thickness throughout — on the market. This is one place where the practice of buying from the lowest bidder may not be the best policy. Leather is a commodity which may take as long as two years to reach the market and supply is often subject to non-controllable fluctuations such as the weather. One result of all this uncertainty is that each large or small manufacturer must stockpile an adequate supply of hides, well in advance of actual use.

Unless the holsters and belts are turned out by a one or two-person operation, another major problem to be overcome — as with any sort of manufacturing operation — is the supply of skilled help. The leather industry is of a size that most of the personnel must be trained and supervised from within the industry.

Each holster is cut, trimmed, fitted, stamped, embossed, formed, smoothed, glued, sewn, cured, dyed, oiled, checked

A comparatively small industry, employing relatively few workers, most training is done within the factory itself; new employees learn from the more experienced.

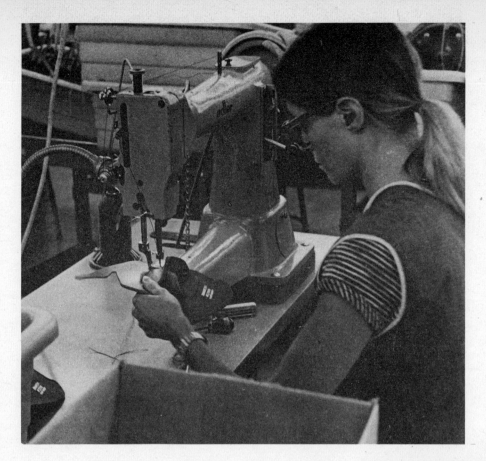

Strong, heavy-duty lock-stitching is done with massive Adler stitching machines, above. At right, champion pistol competitor Ray Chapman, checks namesake holsters.

and inspected each step of the way; mostly by hand. Holsters are then assembled, stocked, stored, packaged and shipped to the customer for delivery to the user; again, all through the use of skilled hands. When you slip your pistol or revolver into your new holster, the fit is perfect and the construction appears flawless, you know that somebody's hands and heart went into the product, not merely another production line machine.

One of the welcome developments recently introduced into the design of many holsters is a track or groove built into the holster to guide and protect the front sight blade of the handgun. In some cases, it is reinforced with another layer of leather, in others, a channel of lined plastic or metal is built into the holster.

Safariland calls their model the Safariland Sight Track, Bianchi terms their innovation a Sight Channel. By whatever name, the feature is intended to protect the front sight blade from wear and misalignment, as well as ease

Plain or fancy, large or small, most handgun holsters must be held up by something, usually a belt. Many of the larger holster manufacturers offer a wide variety of belts.

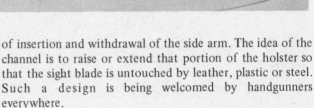

Three Bianchi models designed primarily for the law enforcement concealment customer are: Above, the Col. Charles Askins Avenger with optional safety strap, full grip clearance; Right, the Pistol Pocket for small autos; Thumb snap, below, with hammer cocked.

of insertion and withdrawal of the side arm. The idea of the channel is to raise or extend that portion of the holster so that the sight blade is untouched by leather, plastic or steel. Such a design is being welcomed by handgunners everywhere.

Lining a holster with suede or cowhide may add an ounce or two to the total weight but would seem to be well worth that slight inconvenience. Aside from cowhide leather, elk seems to be the most commonly used material for lining. The softness of the suede´nap appears to offer better protection to the gun's finish and will tend to absorb any latent moisture from the metal while the gun is holstered. The rough finish of the suede would also seem to

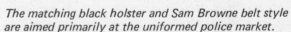

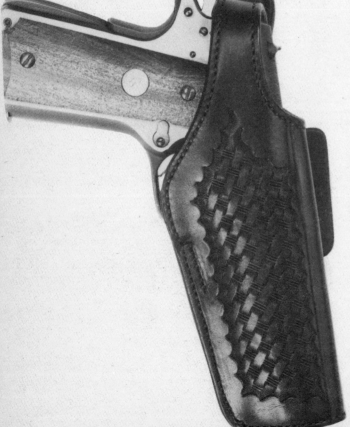

The matching black holster and Sam Browne belt style are aimed primarily at the uniformed police market.

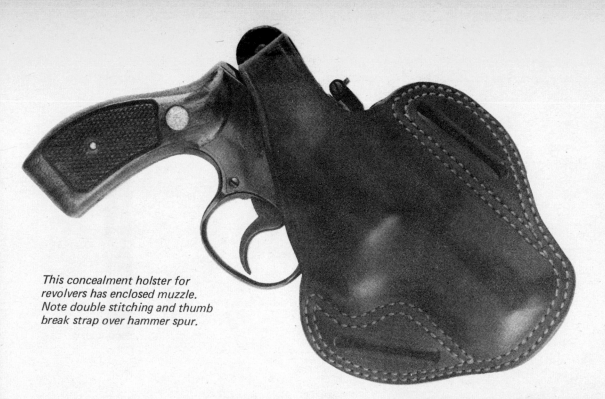

This concealment holster for revolvers has enclosed muzzle. Note double stitching and thumb break strap over hammer spur.

hold the handgun more securely during physical activity by the wearer.

The thread used to stitch together the parts of a fine holster must be strong when it is sewn and remain strong for years afterward. The jury is still out on what is the best kind of thread; linen or nylon. Safariland, for instance, uses nylon exclusively. On the other hand, Bianchi uses a number of strands of heavy, waxed linen thread on most of their models. All use a lock stitch, similar to that used on saddles. Each stitch is individually locked and should a few stitches somehow become cut or broken, the whole seam will not simply unravel and the holster fall apart. Such an

Shoulder holsters are designed for large and small autoloaders, above and left, or for revolvers, top. Rogers police models feature handcuff, ammo cases.

The largest caliber .44s as well as .45 autoloaders may be accommodated in shoulder holsters such as those manufactured by Lawman Leather, Dirty Harry model, left, and Custom Guns & Leather of Michigan, above.

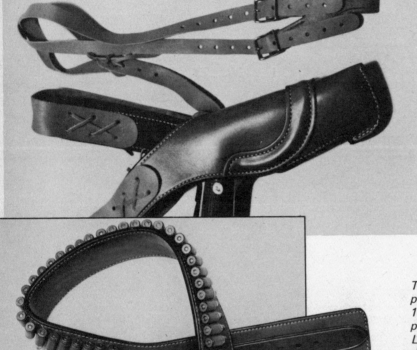

Two revolver holsters with divergent purposes in mind. The Bianchi Model 1890, left, is intended to be worn in plain sight for fast draw competition. Lawman Leather's Dirty Harry Model shoulder holster is carried concealed.

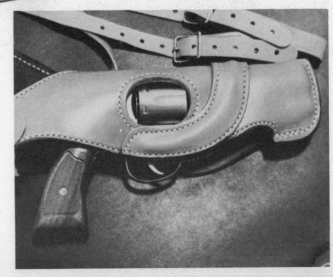

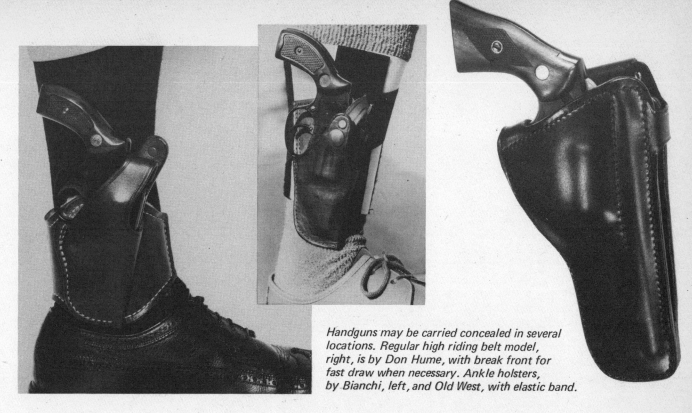

Handguns may be carried concealed in several locations. Regular high riding belt model, right, is by Don Hume, with break front for fast draw when necessary. Ankle holsters, by Bianchi, left, and Old West, with elastic band.

occurrence is unlikely at worst, anyway, but it's nice to know the insurance is there should the need arise.

There are a number of firms in the holster business who specialize in shoulder or underarm holsters. Ask the bigger companies what their best sellers are and they will tell you the shoulder holsters are their biggest movers. That the style is popular with law enforcement people for undercover or off-duty use is understandable. However,

many hunters who actually hunt with handguns or who carry a pistol or revolver as a backup have come to prefer a shoulder holster to a belt holster. Their reasons are several.

On most hunting trips, carrying a handgun on the hip may prove inconvenient if the hunt involves climbing in and out of vehicles several times a day, typical in some parts of the country. If the terrain is rough, full of boulders and heavy brush, a hip rig can get hung up. Inclement weather is

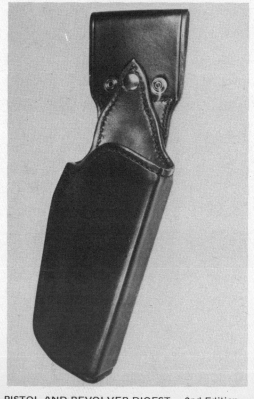

Don Hume makes the Master holster at left, designed for the serious police combat match competitor. Constable, right, is by Bucheimer-Clark, features open muzzle and thumb break safety strap.

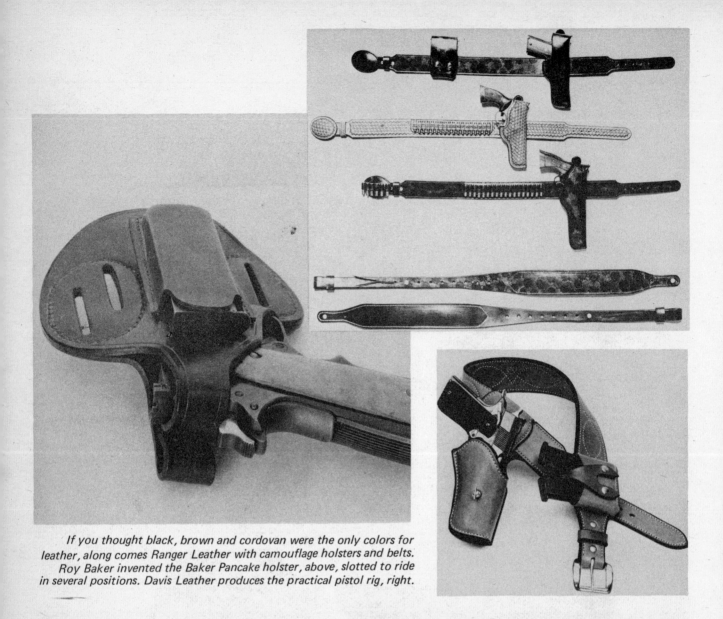

If you thought black, brown and cordovan were the only colors for leather, along comes Ranger Leather with camouflage holsters and belts. Roy Baker invented the Baker Pancake holster, above, slotted to ride in several positions. Davis Leather produces the practical pistol rig, right.

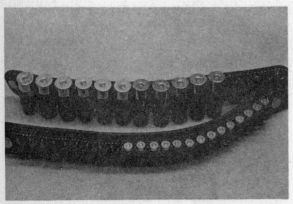

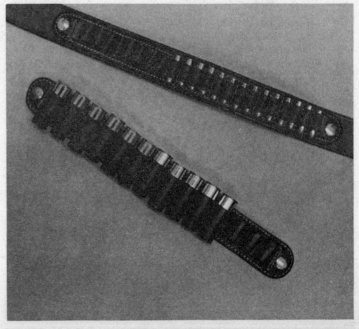

Liberty Organization's cartridge belt features interchangeable loop strips in sizes from .22 cal through 12-gauge shotgun shells. Strips are securely attached with Velcro band and heavy metal snaps.

106

This Baker Pancake design has thumb break strap, three slots.

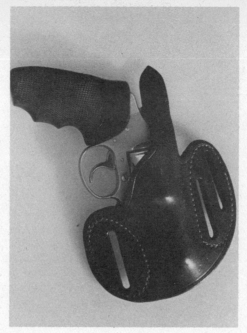

Left is Roy Baker's Pancake for small double action revolvers. Right is Safariland's concealable large auto, safety strap removed.

where the shoulder holster comes into its own, however. In rain or snow, the gun is well protected by the wearer's arm and shoulder, yet the firearm is readily accessible. For law enforcement persons and others, concealment makes the shoulder holster a necessity.

Size of the handgun to be carried would seem not to be a problem. Shoulder holsters are available for autoloaders and revolvers, single or double action, in barrel lengths from two to 8-3/8 inches. Guns as large as the 8½-inch barrel Auto Mag and the Dan Wesson with eight-inch barrel are accommodated in most factory-made and any custom-made shoulder holsters. Holster models include those which carry the gun butt up, butt down or butt forward. Some have elastic and others have steel spring reinforced breakaway

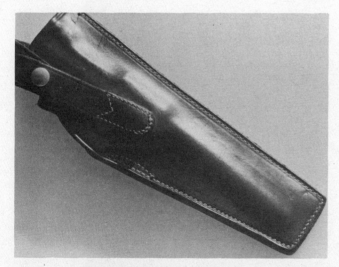

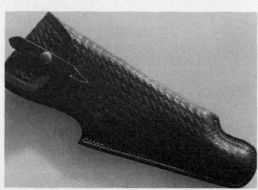

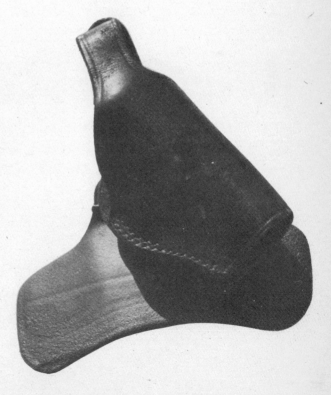

Safariland, upper left, will protect the .44 Auto Mag, scoped Contender fits into Thompson/Center holster at left, both large pistols. At other end of the scale is the Safariland paddle, adjustable for small revolvers.

Back side of Safariland's Model 43 with now-discontinued Colt .22 single action, left. Safety strap on auto holster may be over or under hammer. Bottom of page: two sides of Safariland forward cant model; Baker Auto Mag Pancake.

designs to hold the gun securely while allowing smooth, easy draw.

One firm, Lawman Leather, has built a large portion of its business selling a shoulder holster model based on a design for motion picture actor Clint Eastwood. The holster is called the "Original Dirty Harry Shoulder Holster," as worn by Eastwood in a number of the popular Dirty Harry films. The rig was designed specifically for the Smith & Wesson Model 29 .44 Magnum. The Lawman

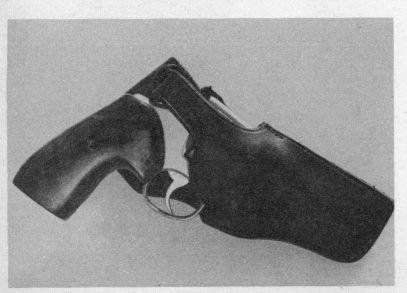

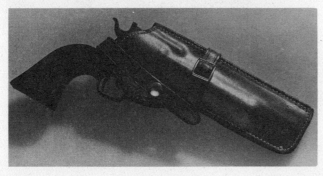

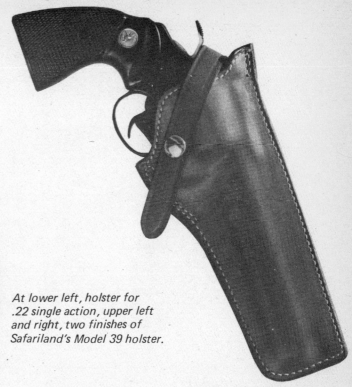

At lower left, holster for
.22 single action, upper left
and right, two finishes of
Safariland's Model 39 holster.

company has expanded the line to include Dirty Harry shoulder holsters for most revolvers and autoloaders in most barrel lengths.

Lest we forget the thing that holds our trousers up and our holsters on our hips, some mention must be made of belts. Most holster makers also make and sell leather belts in styles from plain to highly ornate and fancy. Cartridge loops of several calibers and numbers may be ordered, also. For the law enforcement buyer, belts and leather accessories such as magazine and cuff pouches, must match the color and finish of the holster. Some police departments still number the Sam Browne belt and cross strap as part of the official uniform. A prodigious amount of gear must be hung on a duty belt these days. Despite the added weight, the items may be purchased so as to all match.

Safariland is offering a different version of the traditional Sam Browne belt, which replaces the shiny, bullet-inviting buckles and snaps so easily spotted in dim light. The fastening method is Velcro. Adjustment range is unlimited and some of the weight has been eliminated. The total appearance is neater and trimmer.

An outfit called the Liberty Organization has come up with a neat idea for carrying ammunition on the belt. They have designed the loop strip to be attached through use of a

Pistol rug, left, is secure way
to transport handgun to and from
place of work/recreation. Thumb
break holster, above, is designed
for autoloaders by Safariland.

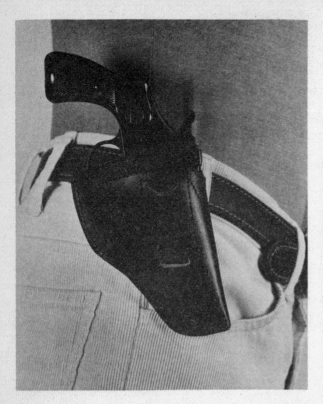

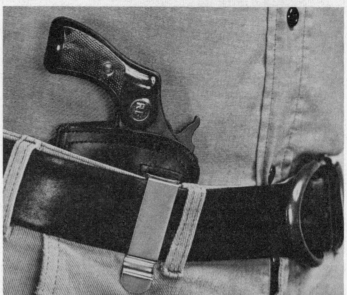

strip of Velcro fastener. The female, or pile, portion of the Velcro is permanently affixed to the rear of the belt. Onto a strip of cartridge loop leather, is the male or hook section of Velcro. Loops are available in all the popular handgun calibers from .22 to .45, as well as .410, 20 and 12-gauge shotshell sizes. Buying several cartridge strips is certainly cheaper than buying a like number of looped cartridge belts.

With the increasing participation of shooters in aspects of the sport such as practical pistol competition and

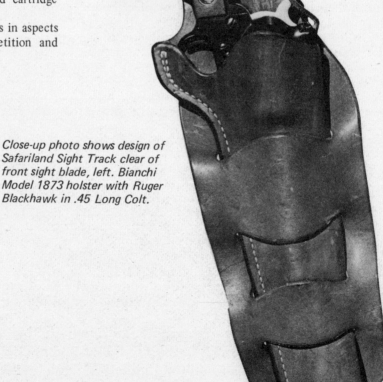

Close-up photo shows design of Safariland Sight Track clear of front sight blade, left. Bianchi Model 1873 holster with Ruger Blackhawk in .45 Long Colt.

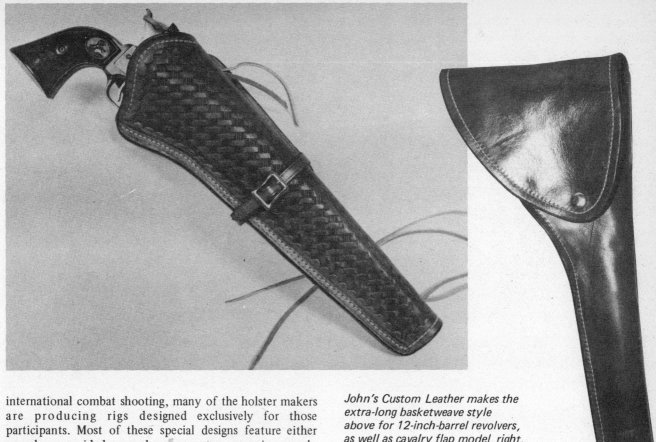

international combat shooting, many of the holster makers are producing rigs designed exclusively for those participants. Most of these special designs feature either crossdraw or sidedraw and a one or two-magazine pouch. The majority of the practical or combat pistol competition is with autoloaders such as Colt .45s, AMT Hardballers or Browning Hi Powers. The holster cradles a minimum amount of the barrel, leaving the grip clear for rapid and sure draw. Most do not include a safety strap, relying on the holster design to hold the gun in place under combat conditions.

True, powerful machines are used in the leather holster industry. Most stitching is done by heavy-duty sewing machines and the leather pieces are cut by power knives and presses. Much of the actual leather shape forming is done by hydraulic presses. But the construction, finishing and artistic creation continues to be done by skilled hands. Let's hope it never changes.

John's Custom Leather makes the extra-long basketweave style above for 12-inch-barrel revolvers, as well as cavalry flap model, right.

Heavy-weight leather belt, with or without cartridge loops, tooled to match pistol holster, by John's.

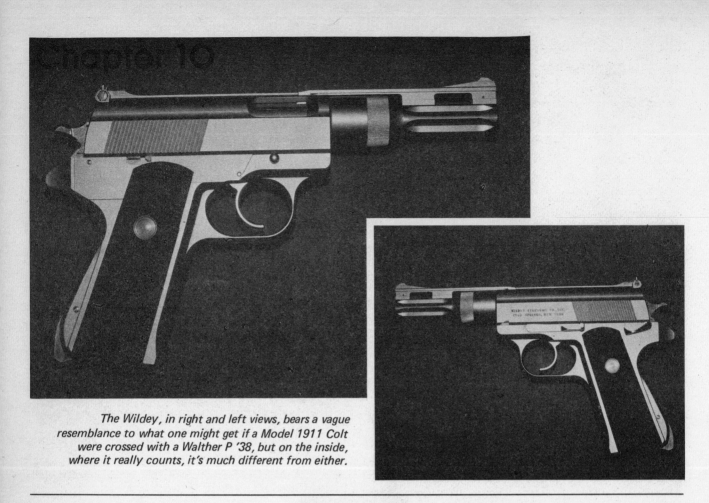

Chapter 10

The Wildey, in right and left views, bears a vague resemblance to what one might get if a Model 1911 Colt were crossed with a Walther P '38, but on the inside, where it really counts, it's much different from either.

THE WILDEY IS A FACT!

And Here Are Facts Of The Handgun And Its Ammo!

By Bob Zwirz & Dean A. Grennell

FOR MORE THAN five years there were rumors of a new, high-powered handgun in the offing. Will Moore, the father of this then unveiled innovation, was making gun shows, talking to gun writers, getting his ideas in line.

And during much of this time, there were questions throughout the industry as to whether this new design — and the cartridge to fit it — would ever see the light of day. Gun writers, in particular, were somewhat jaundiced. They

have seen them come; they have seen them go. There are plenty of guns for which a prototype was developed, but that's as far as they ever go. There just isn't the available financing.

In late 1977, Winchester-Western revealed to outdoor writers the new .45 magnum and 9mm magnum cartridges designed for the planned handgun, but even then, they asked that the assembled gun scribes not get carried away with publicizing the new rounds. Obviously, they weren't

View of the Wildey in field-stripped condition shows the considerable complexity of its unique gas-operated design system.

all that certain there would be a gun to handle the oversize cartridges.

But now the long-awaited, much discussed Wildey automatic pistol is finally in production. Thus, true magnum-powered handgun cartridges are commercially available and offered as standard for an auto pistol.

The claim is that the .45 Winchester magnum is the world's largest bore magnum pistol cartridge, the 9mm Winchester magnum the world's highest velocity commercial pistol round for an autoloading pistol.

Here's how the adjustable gas operation of this pistol works: There is a cylinder-like unit with a finely knurled ring just forward of the frame and behind the rear base of the vent rib. In the rotatable gas-metering device there are three, small, well defined holes marked High, Low, and Off. Above, in the vent rib is a detent index plunger which lines up exactly with the holes corresponding to the three markings. A slight rotation of this metering device permits peak performance with high velocity factory or handloads. Low for moderate loadings and Off when the shooter wishes to fire single rounds, using the slide manually. According to the available vital statistics of the two new caliber handguns, the chamber pressures in the Wildey pistols is up to 40,000 copper units of pressure (CUP).

It was slightly over five years ago that Will Moore displayed the decidedly ugly pistol he had seen and secured from the once hopeful designer. Along with it he had painfully few drawings which, like the gun, had not come anywhere near the point of final systems design or cosmetic

possibilities. Close tolerance studies had not even been considered. In meetings with Winchester, an unparalleled decision was made to join hands on the project; Wildey Firearms on the pistols in the two chosen calibers, Winchester on research, development and production of the long-heralded, long-awaited 9mm Winchester magnum and the .45 Winchester magnum. Theoretically, these calibers should offer substantially better ballistics than the .357 magnum and the .44 Remington magnum, normally used in revolvers.

When the pistols were stripped, it was noted that the feed ramp of the Wildey is less than half the angle of any conventional auto. This single feature should make it less of a problem for handloaders to choose from a greater number of bullet types and nose designs.

Due to design, weight and the gas system, recoil in the .45 Win mag is acceptable though not negligible; in the 9mm Win mag, recoil is practically a lark for the shooter who thinks in terms of big bore calibers.

Although Winchester came up with the factory rounds, the magnum idea and basic ballistics were thought up by Will Moore. Winchester worked from his thoughts, bringing them to a point of reality and agreed to produce them. Word has it that jacketed hollow-points which should be able to take heavy, hard-to-kill big game will be on the market possibly by the time you read this. We should also see some well thought out bullet designs and weights coming from the top names in bullet making. Several sources, including Winchester, will prepare a tested lineup

Demonstrating the ingenious grip panel fastening.

and charts of loads for those who are to mix their own brand of powerful medicine. Weight of the present 9mm Win mag bullet is 115 grains, full metal clad; .45 Win mag is 230 grain, FMC. The 9mm Win mag magazine will take fifteen rounds into its innards; the .45 Win mag can take eight rounds.

The frames are interchangeable, caliber to caliber. The difference will be in the barrels, extractors, face of the bolt and magazine dimensions.

For the foreseeable future all Wildey pistols will be produced from top quality stainless steel.

During the firing cycle the barrel never moves. You'll enjoy a higher degree of accuracy potential and that should add to trouble-free use of a wider variety of bullet designs for handloaders.

There is increased action strength with the Wildey's five locking lugs and enclosed-face rotary bolt. An ability to tolerate high pressure loads is a certainty.

Barrel lengths available are: five, six, seven, eight and ten inches. Hunting/silhouette pistols will have ten-inch barrels and will bear a higher price than standard pistols.

Rear sight is adjustable for windage and elevation to two hundred meters. This sight will have a red outline; on the special hunting/silhouette model, the front sight will have two different colored inserts, each for different range estimation. Rear sight will have a white outline (optional on standard pistol).

Weight has been established at fifty-one ounces, with the six-inch barrel.

It has a positive hammer block, magazine safety and rebounding firing pin. Grips are select German hardwood

Zwirz prepares to load up a magazine of .45 Win mag.

Recoil of the .45 WM Wildey is substantial and ear protectors are a must!

with optional target style with a ventilated rib standard on all models.

The main coil spring located in the hammer uses a superior torsion system spring that is twisted, not compressed.

Height, from magazine release to top of standard rear sight measures 5¾ inches. Inner curve of trigger to relating curve of back strap is 2¾ inches.

The gas system on the pistol is patented, while the designs of the hammer safety, the quick-detachable grips and the magazine safety are pending patents.

Accuracy of the factory-produced 9mm Win mag cartridge has proved excellent, both from benchrest and combat stances with two-hand hold. Absence of uncomfortable levels of recoil makes this an enjoyable pistol to shoot. The .45 Win mag delivers little more reaction than a standard .45 ACP. Some estimate twenty percent less than .45 handloads but this is subject to question.

Are there any negatives on the Wildey pistol? The shooter with a small hand or short fingers may have problems. The trigger-to-backstrap measurement could cause the shooter to have less control over his hand hold. In cold weather, only the tip of the trigger finger may reach the trigger, due to glove bulk.

As for the Wildey's application in law enforcement, we wonder what can be done to conceal this pistol on one's person. In a fitted suit or sports jacket, the gun is hard to hide with either a shoulder holster or one of the belt styles. It is definitely not lightweight. For a uniformed man, the gun does not feel like a feather on the belt.

Even before the Wildey got into serious production, we had had an opportunity to check out the .45 Winchester

magnum ammo.

Another New England gunmaker, Thompson/Center Arms, had added the .45 Win mag to the caliber offerings for their Contender, a single-shot pistol featuring readily interchangeable barrels.

At that time, Warren Center, the Contender's designer, noted that they had no plans to add the 9mm Win mag as an available Contender chambering for the present. The test gun came with a ten-inch bull barrel and it is an attractive bet that it will be offered in the Super 14 version — a fourteen-inch bull barrel with the new adjustable Williams rear sight — as well.

T/C's lack of interest in the 9mm Win mag is justified by the fact that they currently offer barrels in .357 magnum, .357 Herrett and .35 Remington and the envisioned demand for the 9mm Win mag does not seem encouraging.

It is logical to wonder about the justification of adding the .45 Win mag to Contender calibers that already include comparable powerhouses such as the .44 Rem mag, .41 Rem mag, .30-30 Win, .30 Herrett, .357 Herrett, .45 Long Colt and .35 Rem. Can the .45 Win mag do anything that ones just listed can't do? After the first few preliminary skirmishes with the new round, our consensus is that the new entry out of the New Haven stables is destined to be one worth considering. That's to say that the other tough kids on the cartridge block will do well to watch their laurels closely.

At first glance, the .45 Win mag resembles nothing so much as a King Size round of .45 Auto Colt Pistol (ACP), left a bit long on the vine. From base to mouth, measuring specimens on hand, it's about 1.210 inches, compared to the nominal length of 0.898-inch for the .45 ACP. For the convenience of readers accustomed to the metric system,

dimensions in inches can be converted to centimeters by multiplying them times 2.540005, or inches times 25.40005 equals millimeters; drop as many decimals as you wish.

There are a few other dimensional differences, apart from the 0.312-inch of added length. The most important difference is the fact that the head of the .45 Win mag won't quite go into most of the shell holders usually used with the .45 ACP. In shell holders nominally intended for cartridges such as the .41 mag or .30-30, it fits well enough to permit reloading, if not with ultimate precision to delight the soul of a Swiss watchmaker. We were happily surprised to discover that the .45 Win mag brass fit nicely into a shell holder on a well aged Texan turret press, vintage *circa* 1961. Accordingly, the old Texas press was laved lavishly in Break-Free and pressed into service for reloading the spent hulls.

Loading dies presented no problem in the slightest degree. It was but the work of a moment to install conventional .45 ACP dies and readjust them about 0.312-inch higher in the press. A set of Pacific Durachrome dies constituted the backbone of the system and the decapping stem assembly out of an RCBS .38 Special die

Left, Zwirz points to orifice of adjustable gas collar that permits setting gun for intensity of loads being fired in it. Below, Zwirz takes aim at a distant mark in his firing test.

Zwirz fired group at left with two-handed hold at fifty feet. Below, Wildey with Thompson/Center Contender, also in the .45 Winchester magnum size.

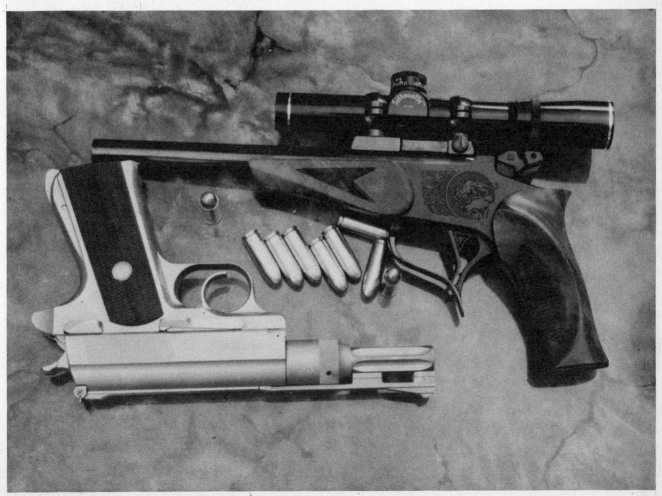

Above, designer Will Moore fires a test group from fifty yards at silhouette target. Right, closeup view of one of the early development prototypes, without barrel fluting.

was substituted for the .45 ACP decapping unit during the depriming operation, then replaced by the regular stem for expanding the neck and flaring the case mouth.

Ordinarily, there is a close rapport between producers of cartridges and firms making reloading equipment. It seems to have broken down in the instance of this case. A phone call to Buzz Huntington, of Omark/RCBS, revealed that they were still fawning for their first eyeballing of the new round. We promptly sent spent cases representing three percent of our entire stock (well, three cases) to Omark/RCBS, with compliments and best wishes. Since it was envisioned that several of the powders in the reloading tests would be in the difficult-to-ignite category, Omark/CCI-350 large pistol magnum primers were used in bringing the once-fired brass back to load-ready status in preparation for the reload test session. The primers were seated with a Lee Auto-Prime tool, using Lee Precision's No. 3 shell holder, nominally specified for the .30-30, rather than the No. 2 holder recommended for the .45 ACP.

Powder was dispensed from an RCBS Uniflow measure dating most of the way back to the Coolidge era, checked against an RCBS No. 505 powder scale of 1978 model year.

We elected to concentrate upon powders still generally available to readers as of early 1979.

Velocities of both the factory loads, with their 230-grain full metal jacketed (FMJ) bullets, and test reloads were clocked with a Speed-Meter. That's a new chronograph, with skyscreens, powered by six AA size (penlight) batteries.

On the first session, set up primarily for recycling factory fodder into spent hulls for reloading, conditions were such that it was impossible to set out the skyscreens much over three feet ahead of the Contender's welkin-shattering muzzle. That proved to be a bit too close. The readings, though impressive, were less than credible. Reviewing the supplied instructions, it was noted that the maker recommends locating the screens beyond the worst of the muzzle blast.

On the second test session, at a more convenient location, the screens were set out with the rearmost (start) unit about fifteen feet ahead of the gun muzzle. As of that time, there were no further problems. Identical rounds were fired through a second chronograph for cross-checking and through both units in tandem, with figures that agreed within entirely acceptable limits.

We have it on hearsay, from a source deemed reliable, that the Sporting Arms and Ammunition Manufacturers Institute sets a pressure limitation of 40,000 copper units of pressure (CUP) on the .45 Win mag. That puts it into roughly the same category with such rounds as the .44 Rem

Moore, with the silhouette target fired at in the tests, felt results were encouraging. Below, T/C Contender with T/C Silhouette 3X scope on Leupold mounts was used in working up the experimental reload data; it has a ten-inch bull barrel, spur extension.

mag, .44 Auto Mag Pistol (AMP) and so on. In comparison, the .45 ACP is hobbled to 18,000 cup and the .45 Auto Rim (AR) to 16,000 cup. There have been batches of load data released for use of the .45 Long Colt (LC) in sturdy guns such as the Ruger Blackhawk and the T/C Contender, boosting the performance of this usually diffident cartridge considerably.

Over the past several years, there have been occasional rumors of a massive revolver in .45 LC, with a five-shot, unfluted cylinder, a single-action (SA) design firing an oversexed version of the .45 LC at pressures sufficiently vigorous to drive a 250-grain slug out of the maw at a touch above 2000 feet per second (fps). At that weight and velocity, it works out to 2221 foot-pounds of energy (fpe). Originally, this was said to have been achieved by a crafty compounding of specified quantities of three different powders, all loaded in the same case. More recently, similar claims have been made for a homogeneous powder charge.

Right, setting up field reloading facilities for reload development session. Below, when 260-grain Speer slug leaves at 1468 fps, the commotion is notable.

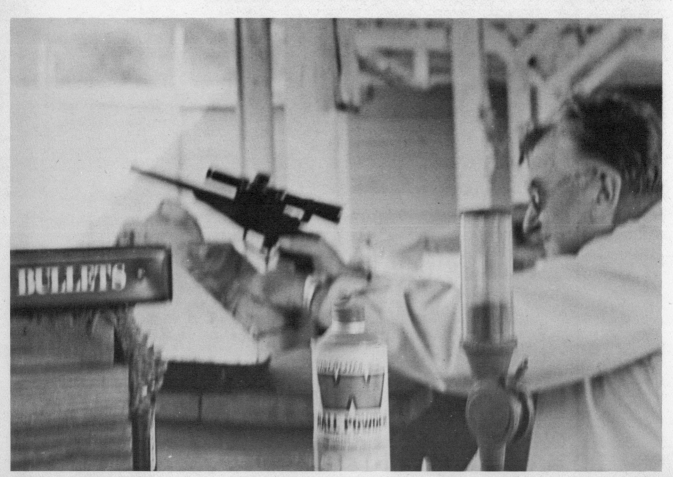

There are several existing cartridges closely comparable in size to the .45 Win mag. We compared them as to total volume by filling each with Winchester-Western No. 296 powder, level-full to the mouth and decanting the contents into the pan of the scales for weighing. The resulting figures were:

.44 AMP (CDM headstamp)	40.0 grains
.44 AMP (LC/66 - military)	39.2 grains
.44 mag (Peters headstamp)	41.1 grains
.45 LC (W-W headstamp)	44.5 grains
.45 WM (W-W headstamp)	39.3 grains

That left the .45 Win mag closely comparable in internal volume to .44 AMP cases made up from military brass such as .308 or .30/06, although the .44 AMP is 1.298 inches in case length; 0.088-inch longer than the .45 Win mag. At the same time, its jacketed bullet with customary diameter of 0.429-inch has a cross-sectional area of 0.1445453 square inches (93.255221 square millimeters) compared to the area of the 0.451-inch diameter jacketed bullets for the .45 Win mag: 0.1597285 square inches/103.05085 square millimeters.

In other words, the .45 Win mag has a bullet base area roughly ten percent greater, against which to push, maintaining peak pressures at the same levels. By reasonable expectations, it ought to be able to shade the .44 Auto Mag under identical ground rules.

NOTE CAREFULLY: We are about to enter discussion of reload test results. The cited loads were developed at personal risk and discretion. As such, the results are offered for the interest of readers, but the reload data are not intended nor suggested as recommendations for use by readers. The loads quoted here have not been tested for pressures developed. There is a distinct possibility that any or all may exceed the SAAMI maximum of 40,000 CUP. Readers are urged to wait until load data for the .45 Winchester magnum cartridge appears in manuals and handbooks. Since we have no control over methods, equipment and techniques employed in reloading by others, we cannot accept any responsibility, either expressed or implied, for events alledged to have arisen from use of data cited here, if employed by others. *You have been warned.*

First, a look at the state of the art, as represented by factory loads from Winchester-Western: Seven rounds registered velocities (taken over a two-foot distance, fifteen to seventeen feet from the muzzle) of the following figures in fps: 1437.8; 1433.6; 1458.7; 1471.6; 1457.7; 1467.3; and 1460.9 fps. That's from a low of 1433.6 (1049.88 fpe) to a high of 1471.6 (1106.2 fpe). The average velocity, for seven shots, is 1455.3714 fps; average energy for that figure, based upon a bullet weighing 230 grains, is 1082.0103 fpe.

The proliferating availability of electronic pocket calculators among the public at large makes it a little ostentatious to boil all muzzle velocities in fps down to equivalent energies in fpe. Conversion of bullet velocity and weight to equivalent kinetic energy involves a simple

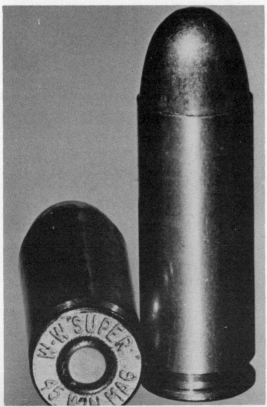

Below, .45 Win mag. factory load and right, for comparison, from top, .45 ACP; .45 WM and a loaded round of the similar .44 Auto Mag. Pistol.

tickling of calculator keys. The drill goes like this: Enter the velocity in fps; hit the "X" key, then the "equals" (=) key. Then hit the "divide" (÷) key and enter the figure of 450,240 (derived from 7000 — the number of grains in one pound — times 64.32, the gravimetric constant for this particular planet) and multiply the result times the number of grains the bullet weighs: 230 or whatever. The resulting figure is the kinetic energy of the bullet, in foot-pounds, at that particular velocity and weight. From here on in, we'll cite only weights and velocities in fps.

Reading that last paragraph back, we can see possible confusions, so let's clarify it a bit. The first step consists of squaring the velocity figure for feet per second. If it's — for example — a 230-grain bullet at 1450 fps, you start by multiplying 1450 times 1450 (i.e., squaring 1450) and the product is 2,102,500; divide that by 450,240 (= 4.6697316) and multiply the resulting quotient times 230 (bullet weight in grains). The answer should be close to 1074.0382 fpe. An associate advises me that some calculators do not square the displayed figure by hitting the X key and the = key in that order. If in doubt, follow the sequence of 1450/X/1450/= and you should end up with the correct answer.

The exploration of a new cartridge's reloading qualities is always a little spooky, at first. The object is not to get overly intrepid. We still recall developing a pioneer load for the .350 Remington magnum cartridge that sizzled a 180-grain bullet out of the muzzle at 3400 fps. Please don't write for details because they will not be divulged. Such things fall into the category of lore for which the world is not yet ready.

Thus, our first test load was diffident, indeed. It put 22.3 grains of Hercules Reloder-7 powder behind a 250-grain Hornady JHP bullet and, when triggered, it coughed it out of the muzzle at 875.6 fps. Ahead of the same charge, a 260-grain Speer JHP departed at 810.7 fps.

Shifting over to 23.7 grains of Norma's type N200 powder and crowning it with a 260-grain Speer JHP, the

velocity was 1068.9 fps. Keep in mind, please, that all of the quoted velocities are at a spacing of fifteen feet from the muzzle to the first screen. Actual muzzle velocity would be a bit higher. The quoted velocity figures are a bit conservative, but so it goes.

With a couple of reassuring test shots to the rear, some Hodgdon's H4227 powder was decanted into the hopper of the RCBS Uniflow and weighed at 21.6 grains as a starter, topped by a 185-grain Sierra JHC (jacketed hollow cavity); that one went out at 1333.3 fps. Boosting the powder charge to 23.0 grains of H4227 behind the same bullet got it to 1388.8 fps, a modest gain. The same powder charge behind a 200-grain Speer JHP dropped the instrumental velocity (at fifteen feet) to 1362.3 fps.

Boosting the charge weight of Hodgdon's H4227 to 24.5 grains sent the 185-grain Sierra JHC forth at 1448 fps and the 200-grain Speer JHP at 1456.6 fps. The same charge behind a 225-grain Speer JHP delivered 1397.6 fps. Inching up in bullet weight to the 230-grain Norma JHP, same charge, the velocity climbed to 1440.9 fps. It was at this point that the back pressure began to get the combustion boosted a little. With the powder charge held at the 24.5 grains of Hodgdon's H4227, with a 250-grain Hornady JHP bullet, the velocity was 1413.4 fps and going on to the Speer 260-grain JHP (the heaviest bullet currently available in 0.451-inch diameter), velocities held at 1392.7 fps.

One final boost of charge weight, to 25.7 grains of Hodgdon's H4227 sent the 185-grain Sierra bullet out at 1444.0 fps, the 225-grain Speer at 1424.5 fps and the 230-grain Norma JHP at 1469.5 fps. That last one, you'll note, is close to duplicating factory load performance.

At about that point, attention was transferred from Hodgdon's H4227 to other powders. There is barely zilch by way of data for the use of Winchester-Western No. 680 powder in straight-sided pistol cases. They list it for the .22 Hornet, but for little else, if anything. It seemed like a promising avenue for pioneering, but readers are warned

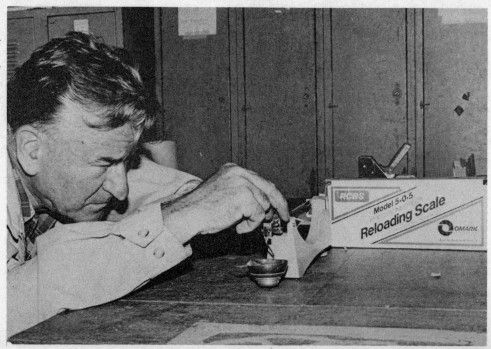

Grennell used an RCBS Model 5-0-5 scale to weigh out experimental test loads.

Left, setting up the photoscreens for the Speed-Meter chronograph. Below, .45 ACP, .45 WM, 9mmP and 9mm Win mag.

that such loads are neither sanctioned nor recommended per the foregoing.

Setting the RCBS Uniflow measure to dispense 30.7 grains of W-W No. 680, we put a 185-grain Sierra JHC out as a starter and clocked it at 1483.6 fps. Moving up to a 225-grain Speer JHP, velocity rose to 1518.6 fps. On the 185-grain Sierra, the muzzle flash was spectacular, suggesting that a lot of unburned powder was coming out of the muzzle. The same charge, behind a Hornady 230-grain round nosed FMJ churned up 1519.7 fps. The last try with that powder charge paired it to a Norma 230-grain JHP for 1546.7 fps.

Cutting the ration of W-W 680 back to 29.2 grains and ringing in the two heaviest test bullets, we got 1479.2 fps on the 250-grain Hornady JHP and 1468.4 fps on the 260-grain Speer JHP. On the heavier bullets, it appears that W-W 680 merits exploration; manual/handbook compilers, please note.

To this point, we felt we'd been neglecting the lighter bullets. As a promising pusher for such wispy wanderers, we emptied the measure and refilled it with Hercules Blue Dot powder. It proved to be the rewarding choice for the lighter pills. Gorblimey, but that stuff shoves 'em out! Our early explorations, compared to existing reference works, were badly out of line. We got down to a matter of working into a set of brackets suitable for quoting, if not recommending. If you put 18.1 grains of Blue Dot behind the 200-grain Speer JHP, it goes forth at 1558.8 fps; on the same charge, the 185-grain Sierra takes off at 1578.5 fps.

We ran some tests with W-W 296 powder and obtained results regarded as encouraging, but feel compelled to withhold the report on that one. The load data supplied by W-W for existing cartridges is adamant on one point: Listed charges for 296 must be neither increased nor reduced.

With a little more time, we would have liked to try out several other powders that seem to show promise for the .45 Win mag, including W-W's 630, Hodgdon's H110, H4198 and (possibly) H322.

The first shooting session was carried out with a T/C 3X Lobo scope topside. With the factory loads, the recoil did not seem overly dreadful. Preparing for the reload tests, we replaced the Lobo with a Fontaine Industries 3X Silhouette scope on Leupold STD mounts.

Grouping ability of the factory loads appeared to be on the general order of three inches at fifty yards and five inches at one hundred yards. Although the 230-grain FMJ slug is about as streamlined as an old Spanish galleon, its trajectory seems remarkably taut when leaving the muzzle at upward of 1400 fps. Sighted for point of aim at one hundred yards, it hit about two inches high at fifty yards. The heavier bullets, such as Hornady's 250-grain and Speer's 260-grain JHPs are certain to become favorites of a lot of shooters for this round, particularly in metallic silhouette competition. It should prove to be a ram-slammer par excellence!

TWO MODERN CLASSICS

Smith & Wesson's Models 29 And 66 Share A Mystique Which Keeps Them In Demand

By John R. Hansen, Jr.

Chapter 11

SINCE THE BEGINNING of its history, there has always been a particular firearm that was and is so unique that it becomes as highly sought after as any fine gem. An item as precious as this would most definitely have an honored home in the inventory of both the shooter and the collector.

Given contemporary tastes, needs and production capabilities of any specific time, we can find several firearms that fall into this selective group. Surely the single action Colts and various lever action Winchesters would easily be with us in this classic sense. These workhorses of guns, while fulfilling every practical application thrown their way, still maintain the charm, romance and excellence that is only found in too few examples in our day.

While this sounds like an all too hopeless situation, we are not left without two modern examples to come to the rescue. Not only are these two handguns in current production, they come from the same manufacturer. These immortal guns, sure to sound familiar to any firearms enthusiast, are the Smith & Wesson Model 29 and the Model 66.

When the shooting public is asked to comment on the Model 29 the responses are as varied as the uses for this particular revolver. As true of any gun, some people swear by them while others swear at them. However, even those who don't take the Model 29 to heart still are caught up in its mystique. I know of few other handguns that can be considered common vocabulary for the enthusiast and layman alike.

For the everyday shooter, unfamiliar with handgunning specifics, the big .44 magnum certainly paints a vivid picture. The awesome stories that go along with this gun are endless; he sees in his mind a handgun of almost immeasurable power and size. Yet this gun holds an unusual attraction, for there seems to be no higher state of the art. His opinions are a true depiction of the Model 29. His information has gotten to him in a roundabout way, but this information has left a permanent impression on our Mr. Average.

While this fellow feels generally that all guns are basically the same, the Model 29 is something totally different. Few handguns can claim that their origins and functions are completely different, spectacular and, no less important, romantic.

Many handguns are given birth on a designer's drafting board. But not many can claim that they developed out of a realization of a shooter's dream. We now introduce one of the most colorful shooting celebrities; one of the deans of modern handgunning and riflery, Elmer Keith. Elmer Keith has been a major proponent for the ideal design of the ultimate handgun. He worked with the Model 29 project from its inception, right through to its final production stages and initial test firing.

His idea for his dream gun began with his Smith & Wesson .44 Hand Ejector Model. By using heavy loads in this revolver, Keith found that his results surpassed the .45 Long Colt cartridge. Being the true explorer and enthusiast, Keith actively set out to find someone who would produce such ammunition for him on a large scale. He brought together two of the most famous firearms manufacturers in the world and presented his plan.

It was in 1953 that Elmer Keith managed to get the ball rolling on his project. Upon receiving an invitation from C.G. Peterson, of Remington Arms, Keith proceeded to the Remington plant to talk over the prospects of developing a

The writer, John R. Hansen, Jr., is a gun dealer/collector from Southport, Connecticut. Here, he's checking the trigger pull on an empty .45 Colt SA, another gun he views as classic.

hot factory loading for the .44 Special. During its initial stages, the discussion about such a cartridge met with an interesting problem. The design engineers and Keith felt that they might be running an unnecessary risk in producing this heavy load for the .44 Special. There were and still are a large number of old revolvers in that caliber. The possibility of risk to the shooter was increased through the use of these loads in these somewhat weaker or worn out revolvers.

The answer came from Elmer Keith, when he suggested that a new cartridge be developed. This would essentially be the same as the .44 Special except that the cartridge case would be .125-inch longer and would be loaded to newly proposed ballistics. By lengthening the case that .125-inch, this new cartridge could not be loaded in the older model revolvers and lessened the chance of injury to shooters.

Here was a brand new cartridge with no real home of its own. Being eager to see his dream come to fruition, Keith put the problem to Smith & Wesson. He sought out C.R. Hellstrom, who was president of Smith & Wesson from

1946-1963, and proceeded to get things in motion. Hellstrom contacted R.H. Coleman of Remington and talked over the new project. At Hellstrom's request, the new cartridge was to be called the .44 magnum.

Smith & Wesson received from Remington, in 1954, the dimensions for their .44 magnum cartridge and set to work. Shortly after receipt of the dimensions, Smith & Wesson produced four prototype revolvers to handle the new .44 magnum rounds. The fact that these guns were produced so quickly and with such enthusiasm would seem to indicate that everyone concerned was enthusiastic about this project. Having lived through many proposed new gun introductions, I can honestly say that this particular one was established with unprecedented speed. This isn't surprising when one considers who was involved in this project; two of the foremost firearms companies in the modern world and one of the all-time great promoters of the shooting sports.

To handle this special function, Smith & Wesson took four of their Model of 1950, Hand Ejector .44 Special

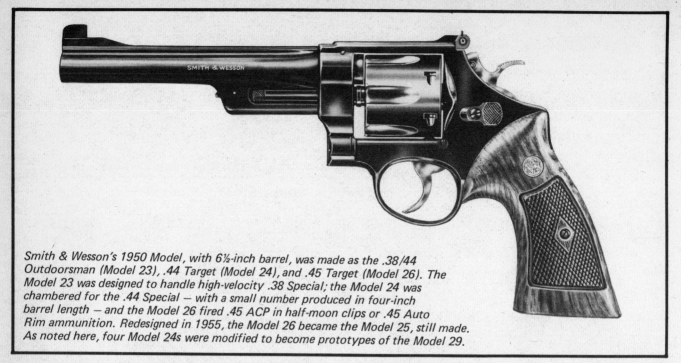

Smith & Wesson's 1950 Model, with 6½-inch barrel, was made as the .38/44 Outdoorsman (Model 23), .44 Target (Model 24), and .45 Target (Model 26). The Model 23 was designed to handle high-velocity .38 Special; the Model 24 was chambered for the .44 Special — with a small number produced in four-inch barrel length — and the Model 26 fired .45 ACP in half-moon clips or .45 Auto Rim ammunition. Redesigned in 1955, the Model 26 became the Model 25, still made. As noted here, four Model 24s were modified to become prototypes of the Model 29.

revolvers and heat treated them. Factory records have these guns listed as serial numbers S121,636; S121,637; S121,638; and S121,639. With the necessary alterations, these guns were ready for their test firing debut and were in fact the original .44 magnums. These sample guns were tested by Remington and Smith & Wesson. The results were quite favorable and one can certainly imagine both the satisfaction and excitement both companies felt toward their new project. The only recommended change was that a little more weight be put onto the gun. By increasing the diameter of the barrel and the heft of the frame, 7½ ounces were added. After testing this modified version of the .44 magnum revolver, Smith & Wesson started tooling up for full scale production of the handgun, while Remington set to work on producing sufficient ammunition to meet what was expected to be an overwhelming demand for this new combination.

In December 1955 the first Model 29 was completed and sent to R.H. Coleman of Remington, the second Model 29 was given to Major General Julian S. Hatcher and the third Model 29 was given to the man who had an idea, Elmer Keith. Few guns can claim to have had such an illustrious start on life and the romance that accompanied the Model 29 at its birth has not left it.

Why is the Model 29 such a captivating handgun? You can get a sense of the answer just by looking at and handling an example. An impression is made and a presence is felt by the shooter that this gun is different from anything that he previously has examined or shot. The gun manages to get its heroic dimensions comfortably into the hands of the shooter. Immediately, one is struck by the fact that this gun is within reach and can be mastered. It has been reported that the Model 29 has successfully accounted for most species of North American game, big and small.

A reputation such as this is very impressive and everyone wants to be a part of the club. However, the Model 29's fame isn't to be proven in the field alone. Its acceptance with competition shooters worldwide has contributed to its monumental character.

One of the faster growing handgun sports, silhouette target shooting, has been one of the areas where the Model 29 is in constant demand. It provides the all important knockdown power which is a key to this type of shooting. The Model 29 is devastatingly accurate at ranges up to two hundred meters.

For this reason, the selection of a 29 by handgun hunters becomes obvious. Its use as a hunting gun is world renowned.

Various firearms publications that I have seen throughout the world almost always have some mention of the .44 magnum. If there is one source to make the Model 29 Smith & Wesson .44 magnum a household word, it would be the American film industry. Actor Clint Eastwood, in his "Dirty Harry" motion picture series, played up the 29's character and potential to its fullest. People who had never had any previous exposure to handguns, were soon talking about this super gun, Model 29: "You know, just like the one Dirty Harry used in the movie."

This was the word in gun shops throughout the world. This was the gun to have and, in some cases, any amount would be paid to have one. In some gun shops the request list for a Model 29 in any barrel length and finish is several pages long. The demand can not be sufficiently met for this fine handgun for to do so would mean a sacrifice in production standards and that simply isn't to be the case. As it stands right now, the Model 29 has seen no cut back in its demand. In fact, people have been buying them up in attempts to make money with and from them.

The Model 29 has some other factors contributing to its mystique. It was, from its beginning, a favorite handgun of engravers. It affords the engraver ample room to create his artistry and embellish the gun. It is a gun that can rise to the artistic challenge because it is a product worthy of an engraver's efforts. It embodies all of the characteristics of a fine piece of art and for that reason serves to further the personal and intrinsic value of the gun.

Smith & Wesson chose not to rest on its laurels and leave

126

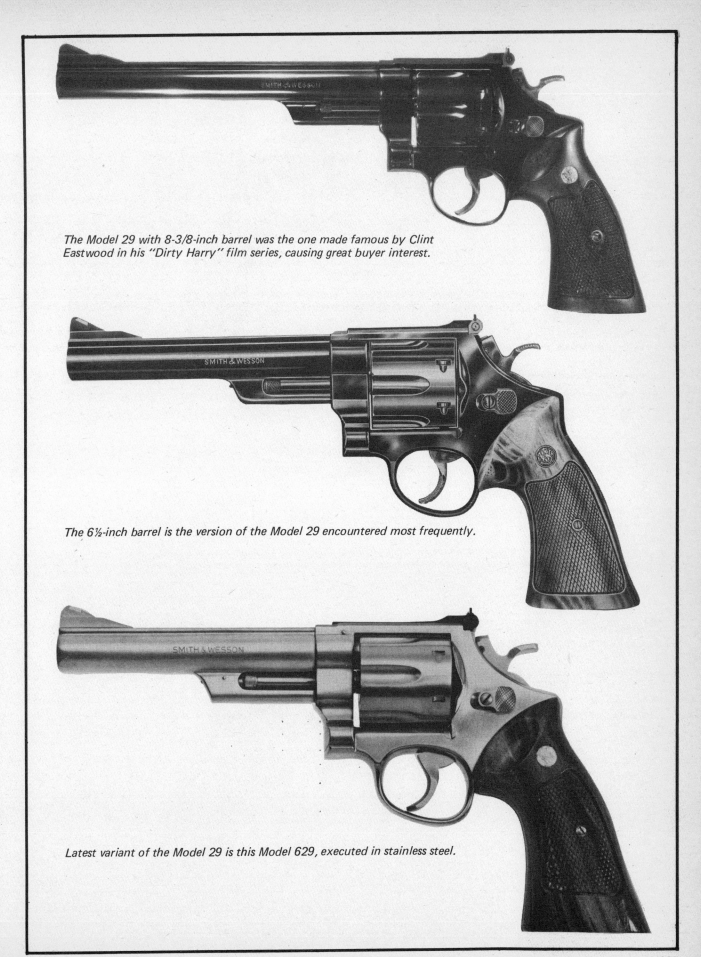

The Model 29 with 8-3/8-inch barrel was the one made famous by Clint Eastwood in his "Dirty Harry" film series, causing great buyer interest.

The 6½-inch barrel is the version of the Model 29 encountered most frequently.

Latest variant of the Model 29 is this Model 629, executed in stainless steel.

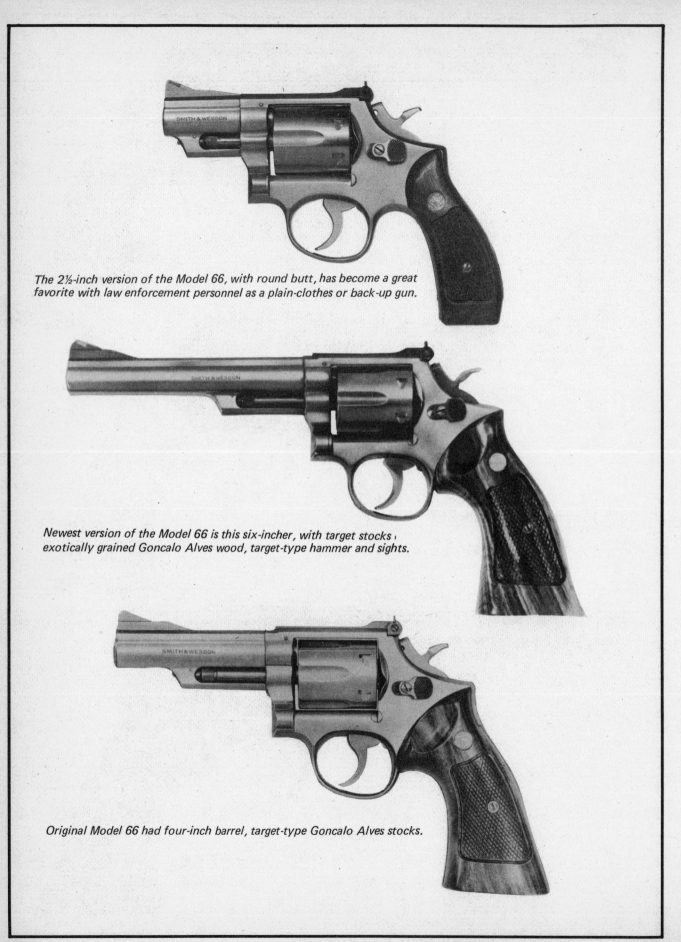

The 2½-inch version of the Model 66, with round butt, has become a great favorite with law enforcement personnel as a plain-clothes or back-up gun.

Newest version of the Model 66 is this six-incher, with target stocks exotically grained Goncalo Alves wood, target-type hammer and sights.

Original Model 66 had four-inch barrel, target-type Goncalo Alves stocks.

well enough alone. The most recent addition to the Smith & Wesson line of firearms is the new Model 629. This is the basic Model 29 in a stainless steel version.

Quoting directly from the news release on this gun: "Smith & Wesson is responding to consumer demand with a new .44 magnum revolver made of stainless steel, inside and out. The S&W Model 629 is a stainless version of the famous Model 29. The original Model 29 earned its reputation among hunting guides and others who travel remote backwoods wilderness. Alaskan guides, who could face the challenge of defending a hunter against the rage of a wounded bear, initiated the demand for the .44 magnum revolver. Now stainless steel relieves the worry of being far from proper facilities for cleaning and caring for a revolver.

"The Smith & Wesson Model 629 takes the advantages of the Model 29 .44 magnum revolver and adds the advantage of stainless steel. Being more resistant to the demands of rugged field exposure, this revolver is more likely to be ready when you need it. The Model 629 will be offered initially with a six-inch barrel. An 8-3/8-inch barrel version will be available soon thereafter. It has a target hammer and trigger and its weight is about forty-seven ounces. Other specifications are the same as for the Model 29. The front sight is the 1/8-inch S&W red ramp. The rear sight is S&W's Micrometer Click sight, adjustable for windage and elevation, with a white outline notch. A sight combination that is easier to pick out in the confusion of shaded woods. Special oversize target Goncalo Alves stocks are checkered for a sure grip. The S&W Model 629 is offered in a lined, wooden presentation case to be available October 1979. Suggested retail price is to be determined. While stainless steel resists corrosion better than blued steel, any firearm should be cleaned and oiled the same as any high quality tool."

This new Model 29, the 629, followed a progression much like another Smith & Wesson handgun, the Model 66. The gun that is responsible for the Model 66 development is the Smith & Wesson Model 19. We see in the Model 19 a beginning which was very much like the .44 magnum's. C.R. Hellstrom, while speaking to another one of modern shooting's prime movers, Bill Jordan, asked what he considered the ideal police handgun. Jordan's reply was that the gun should be of the medium frame size, a heavy, four-inch barrel with an ejector rod shroud similar to the larger frame revolvers, target grips and target sights. This new .357 caliber revolver was to be a first of its type because, up to this time, .357 handguns were built only on large frames. Hellstrom put Bill Jordan's ideas to the engineers and they proceeded to wrap a gun around his

The 2½-inch-barreled Model 19 with round butt is a blued steel counterpart of the Model 66 shown in the photo at the top of the opposite page.

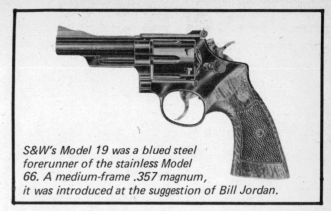

S&W's Model 19 was a blued steel forerunner of the stainless Model 66. A medium-frame .357 magnum, it was introduced at the suggestion of Bill Jordan.

suggestions. The first of these new .357 revolvers was completed in November of 1955 and the first gun of the production run was sent to Bill Jordan. As did the Model 29, the Model 19 met with with unprecedented market acceptance. Their popularity has yet to wane.

Again, Smith & Wesson was not going to rest on its fame and they set out to make the Model 19 an even finer handgun. What evolved was the Smith & Wesson Model 66. This gun is similar to the Model 19 .357 Combat Magnum, except that the 66 is made of stainless steel. Another standard of excellence was set with the creation of this handgun. Its practical applications were endless and its aesthetic appeal no less. The Model 66 is one of the most highly sought after handguns on the market today.

A good indicator of the popularity a particular firearm enjoys is the quantity of them one sees for sale, used or otherwise. Scarce few, if any, used examples are available for sale. Once a person owns a Model 66, he is unwilling to part with it. Few are the examples of this gun out for sale at retail and then never for long.

This Model 66 was the first stainless steel .357 magnum introduced to the commercial, police, and military markets. Its popularity was immediate and widespread. It had every phase of the shooting sports buzzing. A logical home for this new gun is its use as a police sidearm. Its specifications were as if tailor-made for the target shooter, hunter, as well as policeman.

The Model 66 did, in fact, become the little darling of many police departments around the country. It has become the issue revolver of the U.S. Treasury Department. These Treasury-issue Model 66s have 2½-inch barrels with a round butt frame and have the U.S. Department of Treasury seal engraved on the sideplate. Connecticut State Police devised an interesting twist to the Model 66 revolver. Their standard issue Model 66 is specially blued! They combined every possible advantage into this project because not only is the stainless perfect for the salty Connecticut waterfronts, the bluing gives the guns a non-reflective finish.

Until 1978 Smith & Wesson offered the Model 66 only in 2½ and four-inch barrel lengths. Conscious of consumer desire, they have started production on a six-inch barrel version. There is little doubt that this gun will be as popular as the Model 629 among target shooters and hunters.

While the Model 66's story is brief, it is every bit as qualified to be termed a classic. It maintains characteristics that are timeless in aesthetic appeal and practical application. The Model 29 and Model 66 are handguns that will remain in demand as long as there is the opportunity to use them.

Chapter 12

Jeff Cooper developed freestyle practical pistol shooting and helped found both API and IPSC, with a profound effect on concepts and philosophies of defensive pistolcraft today.

TO GAIN a proper perspective on the American Pistol Institute and the International Practical Shooting Confederation it is necessary to backtrack in time a bit.

The sport of freestyle practical pistol shooting, as it has come to be called, has been in existence for approximately twenty years. While many individuals have made important contributions, one man's efforts have comprised the driving force behind the developing concept of freestyle handgun shooting as it relates to competition, training, and practical defensive application on the street.

Jeff Cooper came up with the original idea of posing a varied series of challenges set up to simulate typical defensive situations, and allowing the shooter nearly complete freedom to come up with his own method of solving them.

In the mid-1950s the very idea of permitting a pistol shooter to do anything but sedately punch neat, round holes

INTERNATIONAL COMBAT SHOOTING

This Sport Is Developing Interest Around The World – And There's Even A School To Teach You How!

By Rick Miller

At the Columbia International Combat Pistol Conference in 1976, from left, Gerry Gore, of South Africa; Jeff Cooper, USA; Albert Pauckner, West Germany; and Nigel Hinton, England, discuss aspects of practical pistol shooting and benefits of organized efforts.

Dick Thomas, left, and Raul Walters in a 10-yard "leatherslap." First to score two hits out of three shots on a 10x14" steel plate wins the bout.

in paper targets was beyond belief. To allow a man nearly complete freedom to shoot two-handed, from the kneeling position, from prone — or standing on his head if he wished — and with all types of handguns competing equally, just wasn't done!

To those who tried the new sport it soon became evident that it possessed several outstanding virtues. Since equipment and technique were almost unrestricted, it quickly became apparent that some ideas worked better than others. Old and cherished ideas on defensive shooting just didn't stand up to the harsh test of open competition, where various concepts were pitted and tested one against the other.

Another thing that freestyle shooting helped to foster was innovation. While the traditional shooting sports tend to standardize and stagnate technique and equipment in the name of "fairness," freestyle practical pistol shooting tends

Jim Cirillo, left, and Dick Thomas engage in a man-to-man event identified by author Miller as the "Columbia Fumble."

to reward efficiency in both areas.

In short, if you can find a better way to get the job done, you are welcome to try. If the new idea works out, everyone present will have learned something, and the technique of modern pistolcraft will have been expanded that much more.

This is all pretty much known and accepted today, but it was not always so.

Strange as it may seem, the modern sport of freestyle practical pistol shooting got its start as an offshoot of the Western-oriented quick-draw game. Through the middle to late 1950s, quick-draw was sweeping the country. This stylized game called for single-action revolvers, blank cartridges or wax bullets, ten-gallon hats, and high-heeled boots. Quick draw was great fun, but any relationship with reality was strictly accidental.

At about this time Jeff Cooper tried to inject some meaningful realism into the exercise by promoting a number of quick-draw matches with several innovations. His matches were restricted to service-type sidearms using full-charge duty ammunition, no squib loads were allowed. Further, single-action, double-action revolvers and autoloading pistols competed on an equal footing. Matches were usually man against man, from the leather, at a range of seven yards. Inflated toy balloons or other breakable targets were used. The first man to hit his target won the bout, and usually two out of three bouts won the round. The man who shot down all comers took top honors. It was as simple as that.

The "leatherslap," as this type of match came to be called, incorporated control of a powerful handgun, speed of delivery, and short-range accuracy.

This style of contest was rather limited in scope, but Cooper was feeling his way along, and other innovations were not long in coming.

Soon Cooper's basic concept of freestyle shooting began to emerge. Matches were forthcoming that presented a wide range of challenges, anything from extreme close-range speed problems, to long-range shooting, speed reloading, use of the weak hand, friend-or-foe situations, firing at movement, and many others were injected to test the shooter. Through it all ran the same basic theme: so long as the competitor acted in a safe manner he was free to shoot

World champion Dave Westerhout of Rhodesia, right, discusses points of technique with Michael Harries, a top Class A contender in the Southwest Pistol League. Below, Westerhout tries on one of Richard Davis' Second Chance vests.

top-notch pistoleros were given free reign to try to outdo one another. The ingenious techniques that these men came up with in the process now are available to anyone with determination, perseverance, and the wit to see their value.

Over the years, the Combat Masters of the Southwest Pistol League have acquired near legendary status. They one and all have turned in shooting performances that no one would have believed, had they not been witnessed. These men, Ray Chapman, Elden Carl, Thell Reed, Jack Weaver, John Plahn, and Jeff Cooper himself, as well as Al Nichols, Leonard Knight, and Buck Toddy, all helped the sport grow with their innovative and outstanding performances. They, in turn, inspired other shooters to greater effort. Their impact on advanced technique is incalculable.

As the program caught hold and interest grew, various clubs sprang into being around Southern California. Cooper's original club, the Bear Valley Gunslingers, was the focal point for most of the early activity, and was based at Big Bear Lake, California.

After a time, it became apparent that an overseeing organization was needed to coordinate club activity, and to actively promote and protect the emerging principles of freestyle practical pistol shooting. Again in the forefront, Jeff Cooper helped organize the Southwest Combat Pistol League to that purpose. In 1963, the league was incorporated under California law as the Southwest Pistol League.

For a number of years, Cooper actively participated as a contestant in the emerging sport. In 1959 and 1960 he was the top shooter in the Bear Valley Gunslingers match program, this being comparable to winning the Southwest Pistol League championship in later years.

Even while acting in the important roles of innovator, organizer, and competitor, Cooper also was a keen observer. As freestyle shooting got off the ground and into full swing, Jeff began to make careful note of the techniques and the equipment that seemed to do the best job. As new innovations were introduced by various pistoleers, and were

any way he saw fit. Shooting technique could not be dictated, and equipment could not be restricted, so long as it was safe, practical, and fired a cartridge the size of the .38 Special or larger.

The radical new concept of uninhibited freestyle competition, coupled with a series of matches designed to simulate the conditions found in real-life defensive shooting, have revolutionized the techniques of practical pistolcraft. Shooting methods that were considered state-of-the-art fifteen years ago will not even keep you in the bottom third of a well contested match today.

All this has come to pass because a whole series of

tried, accepted, or rejected, Cooper would sift, refine, and update the overall concept of freestyle pistolcraft.

At the same time, he began to amass as much data as he could on actual street confrontations between police and law-abiding citizens on the one hand, and the creepy people on the other. Information on cartridge power, bullet shape and efficiency, what shooting techniques worked best, conditions of light, dark, range, and many other factors was compiled. Whenever a lawman or civilian versed in the new technique had occasion to trade shots with a felon, careful note was made of the end result. In short, Jeff Cooper observed and recorded the evolving concept of modern pistolcraft as it related to competitive sport shooting, and how well it worked out in the real world, where theory counts only if it works.

As this evolutionary process took place, Cooper authored a long and continuing series of articles and books designed to air the new concept of freestyle shooting, and the techniques and equipment they inspired. He has succeeded so well that clubs and leagues devoted to combat pistol shooting have sprung into being across the country and around the Free World. If you travel today to Johannesburg, South Africa; Salzburg, Austria; Vancouver, British Columbia; Salisbury, Rhodesia; Sidney, Australia; or Columbia, Missouri, you'd have little trouble finding a club devoted to freestyle practical pistol shooting, in the best Cooper tradition. At Bisley, England, the British conducted

their first official IPSC National Match in 1977. The constant flow of articles and books by Jeff Cooper all through the Sixties and Seventies is directly responsible for this proliferation of interest.

In the late Sixties, Jeff Cooper set about working up an efficient training program utilizing the new techniques and principles born of freestyle shooting. In his view, the citizens of the Free World had a deep and fundamental need for this information, and he set about finding the best method of providing it.

Cooper conducted a number of schools within the United States, Europe, and Latin America, that made these radical new concepts available to responsible citizens and organizations. This program proved so successful that, with refinements, it has been continued up to the present time.

To better provide this service, Jeff Cooper formed the American Pistol Institute in 1971. A permanent training facility was established for the API at Gunsite Ranch, near Paulden, Arizona, in 1974. Today, he is engaged in instructing aspiring shooters from all points of the Free World.

Gunsite Ranch, home of the American Pistol Institute, is situated on 120 acres of juniper-dotted hill country about twenty-five miles north of Prescott. Facilities, at this time, consist of three pistol ranges and two rifle ranges. Moving target equipment is incorporated on the basic pistol range to provide single and multiple problems for the shooter.

The Thunderbolt rig typifies holster design trends for freestyle practical pistol competition. Note that the area around grip, trigger and thumb safety is highly accessible, with dual clip pouch on opposite hip. Some units include thigh tie-down thong.

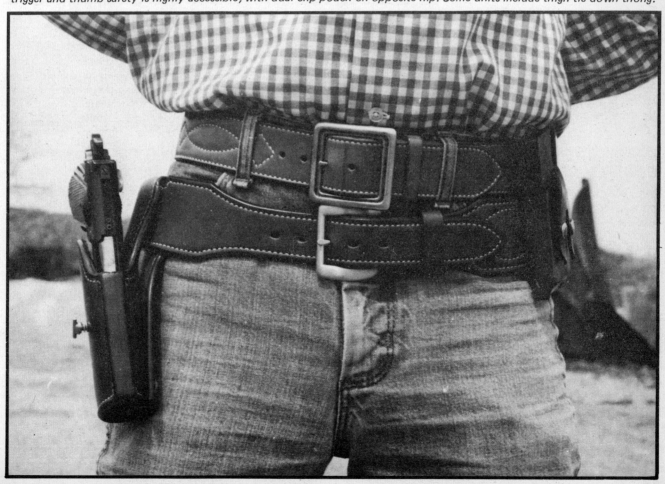

Under Cooper's watchful eye, a student tries his developing skill on 15-yard multiple targets. Right, two students compete in the "Middle Race," a graduation exercise for the basic pistol course at Gunsite facility.

An indoor reaction range, called the Fun House, can provide an almost endless variety of close-range tactical problems by use of quickly changeable interior setups, as well as low light conditions one might expect to encounter in a serious confrontation. The outdoor field reaction range teaches the student to be more observant in a natural outdoor setting, and to react properly to tactical problems at varying ranges.

There are four standard courses offered by the API. Instruction on the client's home range is also available for those groups or organizations who do not wish to travel to Arizona.

API 250 is a course designed for the beginning shooter who has little or no skill with a sidearm. This program covers all the fundamental techniques and instills the correct training habits that will lead to real proficiency. When completed, this course of instruction should turn the beginner into a competent gun handler capable of taking charge of most potentially dangerous situations. This is a five-day program, and requires about five hundred rounds of ammunition.

API 499 is an intermediate course designed to help the shooter who has mastered the fundamentals to polish and refine these skills. This course should only be considered by those well grounded in the basics. It includes night shooting, moving targets, foot work, and class time on tactics and legal seminars. Six hundred rounds of ammo are required.

For the really expert handgunner, API 599 will provide the opportunity to hone and sharpen up an already

Rick Miller, author of accompanying text, fires the weak hand phase of the table stage in the 1977 IPSC U.S. Nationals, ultimately placing ninth overall. Below, student Joe Havas fires the "Donga," an outdoor reaction course at Gunsite, as instructor watches technique and procedure.

advanced skill level. Fundamental instruction is not given, but rather individual counseling and experimentation, to fine tune the highly skilled pistolero's technique. This course also requires about six hundred rounds. In addition to instruction in the concept of modern pistolcraft, the American Pistol Institute offers courses in the practical use of the rifle and shotgun.

With Jeff Cooper's vast store of knowledge, gleaned from over twenty years' involvement in freestyle practical pistol shooting, plus combat experience in two wars, this school provides an unequaled opportunity to learn the theory and technique of modern pistolcraft. All in all, the Gunsite Ranch facility is a unique and imaginative approach to the problem of providing superior handgun training.

With interest in practical handgunning running high by the mid-1970s, it was becoming evident that some type of organization was needed to govern the sport on a worldwide basis. In many areas, well meaning people had started clubs and shooting programs that, while true to the spirit of freestyle practical shooting, actually and unknowingly violated some of the more important principles involved. This would have weakened and diverted the sport from its original goal of continuing evolution toward greater excellence in defensive shooting techniques.

A casual dinner conversation back in 1975 in Fort Collins, Colorado, swung around to this problem, and as a result, the International Practical Shooting Confederation was born.

During that conversation, Jeff Cooper, Bill French, Dick Thomas, and Ken Hackathorn discussed the current state of practical pistol shooting, and the growing need for some kind of international governing body to oversee the orderly growth of the sport on a world basis. Before the night was over, tentative plans were laid to promote the first advanced pistolcraft school in combination with a world meeting of expert pistoleros, formation of a world organization being the main goal. The place for the meeting was to be Columbia, Missouri, in May 1976.

The Columbia International Combat Pistol Conference should go down in history as one of the most important landmarks in the development of freestyle practical pistol shooting. Representatives from shooting clubs in England, Belgium, West Germany, Rhodesia, New Zealand, Japan, and South Africa, as well as a large number of U.S. shooters were in attendance. All came with the purpose of getting a viable world organization off the ground.

Jeff Cooper acted as chairman for the conference. By week's end, the basic structure of IPSC had been hammered out, the title adopted, and a course of action for the immediate future mapped out. Cooper was elected president of the new organization by unanimous vote.

The IPSC rules follow the basics set down earlier by the pioneers of freestyle shooting. Match programs must be diversified, and as realistic as possible. Equipment cannot be restricted, except that it must be practical for continuous wear, secure, and guns must be chambered for .38 Special or larger cartridges. Shooters may not be told how to shoot, except in those cases where simulated disability of an arm, such as weak hand only, is incorporated into a match.

Since control of a powerful defensive handgun is the desired goal, a scoring bonus is given to all loads that equal or surpass GI .45 ACP hardball. This is accomplished by scoring all calibers — .38, 9mm, .357, .45, et cetera — the same for hits in the kill zone of the IPSC target, but giving major calibers a one point bonus in the outer areas. Hence, a major caliber is usually scored 5, 4, 3, while a minor caliber is scored 5, 3, 2.

Following this same line of reasoning, no cartridges may be loaded down for competition. In IPSC sanctioned matches, all minor caliber loads must equal or surpass .38 Special and 9mm Parabellum duty loads on a ballistic pendulum. That means a 158-grain bullet at about 850 feet per second (fps) for the .38 Special, and a 124-grain bullet at 1100 fps for the Parabellum. In a major caliber, the load must equal or surpass .45 ACP hardball on the pendulum, or it will be classified as minor.

Holsters are quite important in IPSC competition, since almost all shooting is started from the leather with hands clear of the equipment. In the best tradition of the sport, holsters are unrestricted, except that they must retain the handgun during vigorous movement. This usually is tested by requiring the shooter to perform a slow back roll or jump over a hurdle. If the pistol stays in place you're okay; if it doesn't, you'll have to obtain a more secure rig to compete.

Holster design, while quite advanced, still is in a state of flux. Bianchi has gotten into the game with their Pistolero rig and their Chapman High-Ride cross-draw outfit is quite popular. Most of the top shooters use custom rigs by such leather workers as Milt Sparks, Gordon Davis, and Andy Anderson. The strong-side speed rig is still the most popular, but quite a few shooters have gone over to the cross-draw position. Today, the quality of design and workmanship of our leather gear is unsurpassed. The functional design is so far ahead of what was available a few short years ago that there is no comparison between the two.

As mentioned before, handguns are almost completely unrestricted also. They must be in safe operating condition, and must chamber a cartridge of .38 Special or 9mm Parabellum size or larger. All action types compete equally,

Students on the firing line in "The Square,"
the basic pistol range at Gunsite Ranch, near Paulden, Arizona.

with no handicap against the more efficient models. The Colt .45 auto is the most popular by a wide margin, and almost all of the top U.S. shooters use a modified .45 Colt 1911. This is not through prejudice, but because Old Slabside has proven to be the most efficient defensive handgun available. Remember, the shooter is free to use any handgun he chooses, and a majority of competitors wouldn't use the .45 auto if they felt another was better.

In Europe and Africa, the majority of shooters use the Browning P-35 in 9mm. This, however, is due largely to a problem of logistics. The .45 ACP pistols and ammunition are much harder to obtain in these areas, therefore the P-35 is widely used. Both the Colt 1911-A1 and the Browning P-35 are far and away the two most popular pistols for freestyle practical shooting around the world. You seldom see anyone in the winner's circle at a keenly contested match with anything else in his hand.

The first United States National Championship of IPSC was held near Denver, Colorado, in June 1977. One hundred twenty-five shooters competed from all over the U.S. Kirk Kirkham of Phoenix, Arizona, became the first IPSC national champion of the United States. The top five shooters — Kirk Kirkham, Leonard Knight, Jerry Kay, Ray Chapman, and Jerry Usher — were eligible to represent the U.S. in the upcoming world championships. At the same time all the other IPSC regions were busy selecting their teams for the world championships.

Salisbury, Rhodesia, was the site of the first International Practical Shooting Confederation world championship match. Eighty-seven shooters from many parts of the world entered this first match. When the smoke had cleared a Rhodesian, Dave Westerhout, was the new world champion. Peter Maunder of Rhodesia was second, while Raul Walters of the U.S. came in third. Ray Chapman finished sixth, Jerry Usher eighth, Ron Lerch ninth, and Leonard Knight came in tenth, all of the U.S. The Rhodesian team took top honors, while the United States team finished second.

The 1978 U.S. IPSC Nationals were held near Los Angeles, California, and the 1979 world championships were scheduled for South Africa. The International Practical Shooting Confederation appears to be solidly established and on its way to being accepted in most parts of the Free World.

Above, students scoring and pasting the camouflaged IPSC targets on the basic pistol range of Gunsite's API. Left, working on correct techniques for the roll-over-prone position.

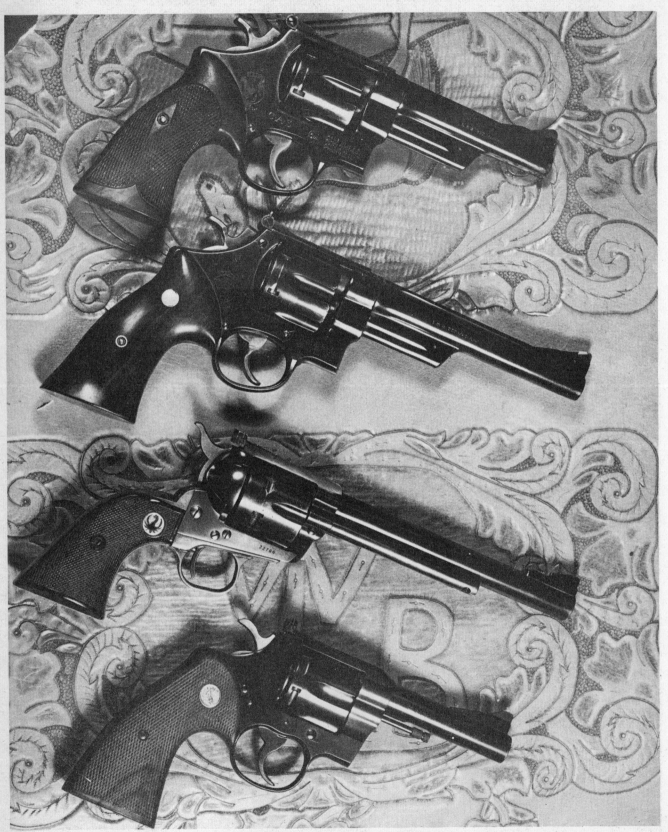

Chapter 13

FOR THE ONE-GUN MAN

By Charles A. Skelton

THE SUN WAS about to make its date with the western horizon when I spotted the young antelope buck sauntering over the crest of the Texas Panhandle hill that rippled from a rocky prairie six hundred yards to my left. It was the final day of the three-day season, and this plains goat was my last chance to lay in the winter's chili meat.

My partner and I held our breath until the buck had passed from view over the top of the brushy mound. Then I stepped on the gas of my battered pickup and headed toward the hill, careful to avoid chuck holes and gullies that would amplify the squeaks and rattles of our jitney. The wind flowed from our quarry into our faces at about twenty miles per, carrying away, we prayed, any scent or sound that would tip our approach.

Abandoning the truck about a city block from the base of the buck's hill, I began my stalk on rubber-soled feet. Climbing the steep slope without kicking loose a clattering rock was sweaty work. Sometimes one hand reached for a mesquite limb support, sometimes two. My heart thudded against my chest as I flopped to my belly and snaked the last few feet until I could look down into the grassy basin beyond. There, forty paces in front of me, grazed my buck.

Flat on my face, I rested a few seconds, recovering at least a part of my mind. Then I made my gun ready.

It wasn't necessary to roll over and unsling my rifle. Nor to remove the lens covers from the scope, nor to jack a shell into battery. I simply drew my Smith & Wesson .357 revolver from its holster at my waist and thrust its 8-3/8-inch barrel at the unsuspecting animal. Drawn up on elbows, I gripped the wrist of my shooting arm in my clenched left hand, lined up the sights on the buck's neck, and squeezed off. Result: One succulent antelope dead in his tracks.

This was not the first large game that had fallen to my handgun, nor was it the last. My Ruger .44 magnum has filled skillets with desert whitetail steaks. An earlier .357 Smith & Wesson bagged a Sonora javelina. Quail, doves, ducks, geese, bullfrogs, squirrels, opossum and bunnies by the bushel have made their delicious journeys to hungry outdoorsmen's stomachs through the good auspices of my pistols.

In the domestic line, everything from pigeons to pigs, through chickens and goats to slaughter beeves have received a humane *coup de grace* from one or the other of my holster battery.

And almost one hundred percent of my gameshooting ammunition has been handloaded. Two equally important, solid reasons cause me to load my own. First, to have purchased the number of pistol rounds I have fired in the last twenty-five years would have required the resources of a Rockefeller, and though I'm a Texan by birth and choice, no oil stocks bulge my portfolio. I ain't even got a portfolio.

The second, and even more vital motivation for fabricating my own six-gun shells is one that is not always understood or believed by non-handloaders. For any given purpose, I can make better ammunition than I can buy, with the attendant saving in scratch.

Although I own high power rifles and shotguns, my gun is the pistol. After a lifetime of versing myself in its use, I am aware of its limitations as a hunting arm. I am equally sure of its many strong advantages as a weapon of defense.

As a light, portable, fun gun it has no equal.

The one-hand lead pusher is available in a multitude of calibers, from the peashooter .22 short to the magnificent .44 magnum in factory loadings. The benchloaded, special purpose variations of its centerfire cartridges are without number. Light loads for low recoil plinking are put together by almost every handloader. Experimenters cast ultra hard, pointed slugs for maximum penetration of tough targets. Sharp-shouldered, flat-nosed bullets loaded over heavy powder charges give the hunter and home defender more knockdown potential. Hollow-pointed, soft alloyed pills expand spectacularly when zeroed in on thin skinned game.

On a recent rainy night, I sipped some good Demarara and let my thoughts flicker between my rack of oily pistols and the dying, blueflamed coals in my fireplace. What if I were so poor that I could only own one gun? What if the bomb were dropped and I had to head for the hills fast, taking one shooting iron to serve all purposes? What if my next wood fire were high in the Rockies, in a lonely cabin to which I had packed in for a long, long stay? Which gun would I choose?

The answer didn't come easy. My first thought landed on my long barreled Ruger .44 magnum. It can do almost anything. A sure killer on man or heavy game out to 150 yards, it would be the deadliest big game and defense gun in my arsenal. But the 250-grain slugs it throws really are a bit much on pot meat like squirrels and rabbits, and the mess it makes of a grouse or pigeon you wouldn't believe. Besides, its cartridges are mighty bulky, needing more powder and almost twice the lead to put together a handload than does the .38 Special or the .357. I wanted to go light.

Next to the .44 nestled my beautiful new Model 57 Smith & Wesson in the dynamic .41 magnum caliber. That was the one! Loaded up to full magnum velocities, its 210-grain bullet jazzes along at 1500 fps, making it a close rival of the .30-30 Winchester, as far as killing power goes. Its lighter loaded semi-wadcutter lead slug at about 1000 fps is a good compromise game load, too. Somewhat the same objections applying to the .44 magnum tended to rule out the .41 magnum — cases that are relatively bulky and not too widely available, plus a hearty appetite for the heavier bullets that would make harsh inroads on a dwindling supply of bullet casting alloy.

The GI, graybacked .45 automatic scowled at me from atop the two boxes of issue ammunition where it rested. It was still embarrassed from having center hit a buck jackrabbit the day before, only to watch the stringy-muscled hare do forty miles per hour to get out of range of its famous quick second shot. The old warhorse resented the fact that I refuse to handload hunting ammunition for it, and I equally resented the fact that it throws empty brass so indiscriminately into the weeds that it takes a metal detector to retrieve them.

Just a bit of the butt of my little Smith .38 Chiefs Special peeked from its hiding place. It knew it wasn't in my league. A fine companion for post-nuclear resistance and cloak and dagger work, maybe, but I'd hate to have to feed my family with it.

Next in line was my slick Smith & Wesson K-22. Maybe I had something here. For lightweight portability, plus accuracy, the .22 long rifle handgun is in the blue ribbon class. Loaded with high speed hollow points for the larger species of small game it is an adequate killer, and for defense purposes outdoes a lot of small caliber centerfire belly guns. Stuffed with high or even standard velocity solids it kills neatly on the most delicate table game, such as quail, with a minimum of tissue destruction.

There is also the consideration of the low cost and low bulk and weight of .22 ammunition. Two cartons — a thousand rounds — of the little rimfires can be comfortably packed a long way, and, carefully used, last a long time. I recall another writer, a famous rifleman as well as pistol shooter, having stated in print that if he could have only one gun it would be a .22 pistol. He outlined the above motives and more.

I reluctantly rejected the twenty-two as my sole armament for one reason — the probability of my one six-gun's having a chance at big game. If you undertake to feed yourself from day to day with a handgun, most of your meat is going to be of the small variety. But the occasional bonanza of a crack at a deer or elk, a bear or wild boar, or other large and perhaps dangerous animal, depending on your locale, will undoubtedly present itself if you hunt regularly. The use of a gun chambered for the .22 in even its most powerful loadings on such animals is the height of folly unless an extreme emergency exists. It is true that many head of big stuff has been brought to bag by the .22 rimfire. It is positive that for every large game animal so taken, thousands of others have gotten away carrying painful, senseless wounds.

I have killed hundreds of heavy beef cattle, hogs, and a few sheep and goats with the .22 pistol, but practically all of these kills were quick, merciful head shots at close range under slaughterhouse conditions. This does not qualify the

Skelton's test loads used four different bullets and three different powder charges. First four loads, from left, carry Lyman cast bullet Nos. 358156 HP, 358156 solid, 357446 HP and 358429, loaded in .357 brass with 14.5 grains of Hercules 2400 powder. Next four, bullets in same order, are loaded in .38 cases, bullets seated forward for added powder space, over 12.5 grains of 2400; last four, same order, carry 4.6 grains of now-discontinued Du Pont 5066.

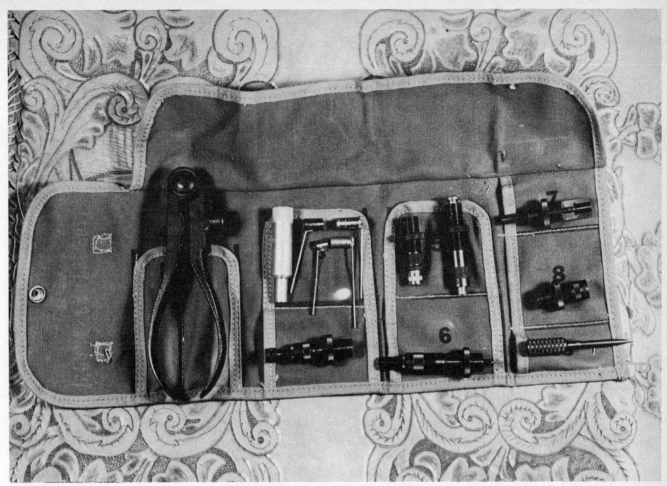

Above, Army surplus canvas parts packet accommodates entire No. 310 loading outfit, including both factory and homemade powder dippers, Kake Kutter, and screwdriver. Package rolls to about the size of a one-quart oil can. Below, supplies for a winter of judicious shooting fit into surplus musette bag with room to spare, weigh 16 pounds.

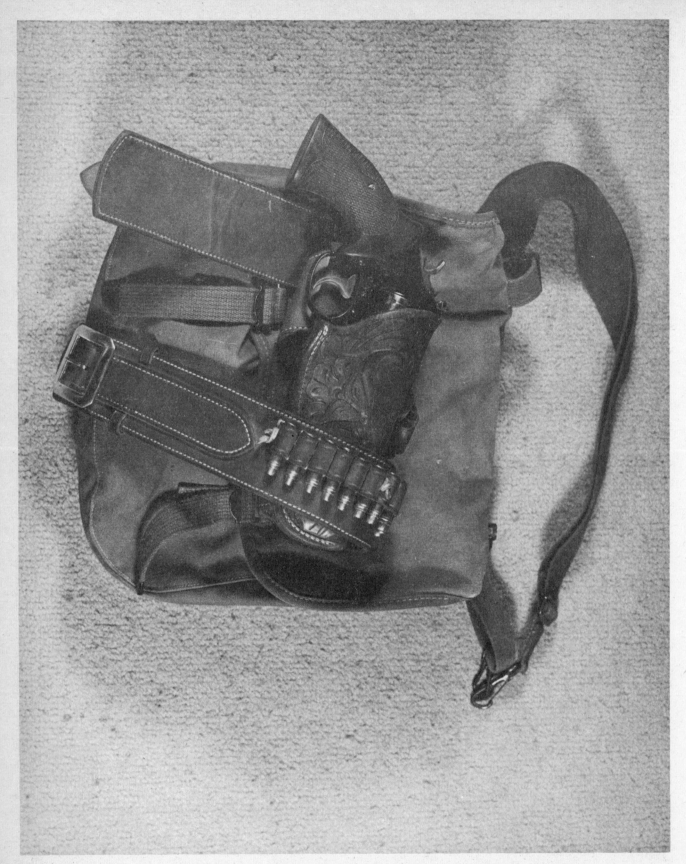

Smith & Wesson Model 27, with five-inch barrel, together with holster, cartridge belt and traveling reloader kit.

little rimfire cartridge for body-shot kills in the outdoors, and is really of little value as a basis of determining the killing power of a firearm.

This easy chair perusal of my pistol collection had been pleasant, but it lead to an inevitable conclusion. If you give me just one gun, give me a .357 magnum. I can pick from several: A Model 27 Smith & Wesson with five-inch barrel and Roper stocks, another 27 made up to match the S&W .44 magnum, with 6½-inch barrel, target stocks, wide target trigger and hammer and red insert ramp front sight. Also in my rack are a Ruger Blackhawk with 7½-inch barrel and an early Colt Three-Fifty-Seven model with four-inch barrel.

Choosing from all these fine models is difficult, but for all around use in a holster, concealed in the waistband under a coat, or riding in a car, and for just plain versatility and handiness, I'll take the five-inch Smith & Wesson as the best compromise. There are other good .357s, of course. The fine Colt New Frontier, with flat top frame and adjustable sights is a masterpiece. Their Python is one of the country's most popular double actions in this chambering, and the old Single Action Army is available with its fixed sights. Smith makes their Highway Patrolman and Combat Magnum models for a little less money than the M27. Not to be overlooked are the excellent pre-war Colt Shooting Master double action target guns, a few of which were chambered in .357, as was the fixed sight New Service.

The reasons for the one-gun man sticking with the .357 caliber are several. First, in its heavy loadings, it can and has killed the heaviest game in North America and proved itself to be notably dependable as a defense cartridge. With light .38 Special velocity loads it is probably the perfect choice as a small game sidearm, preferable even to the .22 rimfire on the medium-to-large varieties, such as rabbit, beaver, and porcupine, the latter being an exceptionally tough customer.

Light, small-game loads can be put up in the longer .357 magnum cases, and very heavy, near-magnum class rounds are quite feasible using the shorter, more common .38 Special case. Properly chosen, the same loading dies and bullet moulds will reload either hull to perfection.

Three-fifty-seven hulls are fairly easy to find these days. But here is the kicker: There is probably more empty .38 Special brass floating around the country than any other caliber. Almost every police department in the U.S. standardizes the .38 Special cartridge. It is the single most popular and populous cartridge case in the nation, and I daresay there isn't a crossroads village in the country where at least a small supply of thirty-eights can't be picked up.

Naturally, the backpacker, the woods loafer, the man trying to take the bare essentials for caring for himself and family into the high, far places cannot tote along a year's supply of loaded .357 ammunition. The bulk would be prohibitive. This leaves the natural alternative of setting up loading equipment at your home away from home.

Until that ruminative night before my fire, I hadn't considered the necessity of gathering up and hauling my old, much-used loading outfit anywhere. Mounted on a three hundred-pound bench, I have a twenty-year-old press, with approximately ten different sets of loading dies, a time tested Lyman No. 45 bullet lubricator and sizer, a powder measure, powder and bullet scales, an electric melting furnace, a whole raft of bullet moulds, a vise, and enough

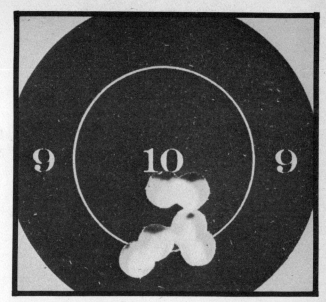

Lyman No. 358156 cast bullet, with gas check, shot this group on 14.5 grains of Hercules 2400 powder.

small tools to repair a guided missile. The corners and shelves of my loading room hold enough lead, powder, primers, cartridge cases, books of loading data, and just plain junk to keep me shooting the rest of my life. The mere idea of packing this scrap pile, even just enough of it to load for the .357, into the boondocks was laughable.

A light, compact reloader that would perform all the functions necessary to turn out top quality ammo for my six-shooter was necessary, and, to my knowledge, only one was in existence — the Lyman 310 "nutcracker" tool. I had known of this tool for years, of course, had seen hundreds, but was uninterested because of the comparatively elaborate set-up I had at home. And, frankly, I didn't believe that the simple 310 could possibly turn out ammunition that would compare with my favorite loads meticulously put together with the various precision instruments that made up my homebase loading outfit.

But compactness plus efficiency was my aim, so I ordered out what Lyman calls their "Ammunition Maker" kit in .357 caliber. What I received was a neat package containing the basic 310 tong tool, along with dies for resizing fired brass, ejecting spent primers, repriming the case, and belling the case mouth to receive a cast bullet. A die for sizing cast bullets to .357-inch diameter was also included, along with a No. 358156 mould (the excellent Thompson gas check, semi-wadcutter design) and a supply of gas checks, plus a ladle for pouring the molten bullet metal. The final items in the kit were a powder dipper marked *15.5 grains 2400,* which is a powerful, but safe load with the above bullet when loaded in .357 cases. There was even a styrofoam loading block moulded into the bottom of the packing box of the kit. This tool will reload both .357s and .38 Specials. Naturally, an instruction booklet accompanied these items, and it would certainly behoove the beginning handloader to memorize its contents before going into action. This handbook, by the way, gives some valuable information on how to use scrap metals from various sources as bullet material, as well as giving recipes for homebrew bullet lubricant.

An unusually tall stump provides a handy work surface for Skelton to try out his field reloading rig.

Thinking it over, I decided that a hollow point bullet would be a better all purpose slug than the solid 358156. The hollow point at magnum velocities is a quicker killer on big animals, and with a light powder charge developing less than 800 fps or so, won't expand, thus not destroying a lot of meat on the smaller stuff. Since I already had a fifteen-year-old 358156 hollow-point mould in my outfit, I elected to use the hollow-point version of this gas check bullet in my tests with the 310 tool.

Frankly, I didn't expect much from the dipped powder charges that are provided for with this rig. On my workshop bench I have a rather elaborate system of weighing and measuring powder charges that insures complete uniformity. Uniformity means safety as well as accuracy when stoking your empty hulls, and I simply didn't believe the little hand dipper could do the job. I was wrong.

Filling an empty cartridge box with Hercules 2400, I took in hand the shiny Lyman dipper inscribed *15.5 Gr. 2400*, scooped it heaping full of the powder and struck off the excess with a straight edge of a pocketknife. Weighed on my powder scales, the dipper's contents tipped the beam at a precise 14.5 grains. The next, and the next, and enough more dipperfuls indicated exactly the same 14.5 grains to convince me that I had been completely wrong in my distrust. The fact that the Lyman dipper threw a grain less of the slow burning 2400 than its markings indicated bothered me not at all. This is a built-in safety measure that is quite commendable. The 14.5-grain load is plenty potent with any of the 140 to 170-grain bullets, and in spite of the sameness of my dipped charges, I would never try for a maximum load with a dipper.

After several tries, I found that a fired Western .32 ACP case would dip 3.8 grains of Green Dot, which is a safe, about factory .38 velocity charge with the Thompson bullet. Since I planned to load most of my heavy loads in .38 Special cases, I needed a dipper that would deliver a less potent dollop of 2400 than the Lyman job. This was easy.

Deciding on 12.5 grains as a reasonably heavy jolt of 2400 in the .38 hull, I simply weighed out that amount of the powder on my scales and dumped it into an empty, nickel plated .38 Special cartridge and shook the case very gently — just enough to level the powder. Marking the level of the powder, I ground the case down to just above that level and attached a handle. A little final filing and

chamfering of the case neck gave me a ladle that would throw 12.5 grains of 2400 like a slot machine. (Note: Should the reader attempt making his own dippers in this fashion, they should be checked and double checked against an accurate powder scale. Strange as it seems, your .32 ACP cases could be bigger than mine!)

I had stalled as long as I could. The moment of truth had to come. Following the simple instructions, I necksized, decapped, reprimed, and belled the case necks on six .357 Remington cases. This took a lot of changing dies to bring forth just six loaded shells, but this was still the experimental phase of the game for me; later I would run shells through each phase at least a hundred at a time before changing the dies. Once adjusted and locked down, the little dies returned to the same position every time they were replaced in the tong handles.

Putting the gas checks on the bases of the 358156 bullets, I started the next, messy chore. There was a strong temptation to use my bench-mounted No. 45 bullet sizer and lubricator, but I had to learn how to do this job in the backwoods. It wasn't near the chore I had expected. Standing the gas-checked bullets on their bases in a shallow, flat-bottomed pan (it actually was an aluminum camp skillet) I melted about a cupful of bullet lube and poured it in until it came up to a level slightly above the top lubricating grooves of the bullets. Letting the pan of slugs stand until the lubricant had hardened, I used the .357 Lyman Kake Kutter to slip over each bullet, removing the excess lubricant. These were then run through the bullet sizing chamber of the nutcracker tool.

The 14.5 grain charges of 2400 were funneled into the six empty cases and the bullets seated. I had to admit the finished product of the pocket tool was as handsome as anything I had ever manufactured on my bench. But the proof was in the shooting.

No wind was blowing (a rare condition on the Texas plains) when I pinned a pistol target to the side of my haystack shooting range. Rolling up some gunny sacks for a rest, I squatted and laid my five-inch Smith over the top of a cattle sprayer. As the six rounds blasted out my old six-gun, I began to get worried. Either they were all going in the black, or they were completely off the paper at fifty feet. When the gun was empty, I opened it. Easy extraction of fired cases, primers okay, no signs of pressure. All six shots cut the same hole, about an inch and centered with my aiming point.

Later on other bullets were tried. The 358156 gas check in both solid and hollowpoint, the Lyman-Keith 358429 in solid (I had no H.P. mould for this one), and the 357446 in hollow point form, the last being ordered out as an afterthought.

I believe the 358156 gas check bullet to be the best of the lot, since in my guns it shoots without leading and is superbly accurate. I have used it for many years, and it is the slug that took the antelope described at the first of this chapter. But for the purposes of the backpacker it has drawbacks. While the tiny gas checks weigh little, they can be lost, or the supply exhausted, leaving the loader with a mould for a bullet with a shoulder at its base which renders it unsatisfactory for any but the lightest loads.

The new 357446 H.P. mould Lyman sent me is almost identical to the 358156 except that it drops a plain base bullet. Both types are almost identical in shape, the 358156 having two crimping grooves over one lubricating groove and the 357446 with one crimping groove above two lube grooves. Note that the heavy .38 loads illustrated are crimped in the center groove with each of these bullets, while the .357 cases are crimped in the top groove. In loading the Lyman-Keith 358429 in magnum cases, it is necessary to seat the bullet deep enough to crimp over the front band, keeping overall cartridge length within acceptable limits.

The hollow point cavity on the 357446 bullet is slightly larger than that of the 358156, making it a slightly lighter bullet and a faster opening one at high velocities.

When buying a hollow point mould, an extra H.P. plug can be ordered. The spare plug can be cut off just flush with the nose of the bullet cavity, thus enabling the caster to make both hollow points and solids with the same mould. Another method of using a H.P. mould for making solid bullets is to drop a steel BB shot into the mould, where it will stop up the hole through which the plug is normally inserted, and itself form the nose of the bullet.

A stop at an army surplus store got me a canvas carrying packet with enough pockets to hold all the parts of my 310 tool. The whole package folds up into a roll the size of a quart oil can. The mould and bullet ladle are wrapped separately in an old rag. These tools, along with two cannisters of powder, a powder funnel, a thousand primers, bullet lubricant, and enough premixed ingots of bullet metal for 500 bullets stash in a musette bag with lots of room left over.

As long as they are handy, I'm going to keep using my fast working bench tools. But it's comforting to reflect that a practical and workable reloading facility can be grabbed by the strap and taken afield at a moment's notice.

(Editor's note: Lyman has discontinued their "Ammunition Maker" kit based around the Lyman No. 310 tong tool, although the tong tool and die sets for it remain available. Lyman no longer offers powder dippers. The reader is referred to another chapter of this book for further details on powder dippers and compact reloading sets.)

Properly loaded and aimed from an appropriate distance, Skelton found the .357 revolver adequate for antelope.

Despite Hamilton's best efforts, he was unable to achieve adequately reliable feeding with full-wadcutter experimental loads made up by seating lead semi-wadcutter bullets in the case mouth backwards.

Chapter 14

OLD SLABSIDES NEEDS A SHOT OF TONIC

By Claud S. Hamilton

New Bullets And New Loads Are Improving The .45 Autoloader

Ed Presler and his son load lead wadcutters for the .45 testing.

THE TIME was late 1950. The place a cold, bare mountainside where the powdery snow blew mixed with dust. The mountainside was not far from the 38th Parallel in Korea.

A young field artillery lieutenant, a forward observer with a rifle company of the 19th Infantry, clawed his way toward the crest. There was almost no vegetation or cover on the bare hillsides. A feeling of strangeness prevailed in this far off land and the occasional odd, rounded flat places with the burial mounds at the center did nothing to change that feeling. He knew that this was simply the traditional rural Korean way of burying a family patriarch so that he could look down on the rice paddies that had been his in life.

Nearing the crest, our observer looked about for the highest place. That's where he'd need to dig a hole and set up his observation post to cover the company sector. Off to his right, the ridge rose slightly and there, in a clump of gnarled junipers, he spotted a small wood frame shrine. Suddenly there was movement. The now familiar quilted uniforms. He turned to yell a warning but his sergeant and the riflemen were too far. Cold fingers fumbled the draw and it seemed an eternity before he had his .45 pistol out. In the meantime, almost as in a slow motion movie, the two enemy soldiers rose from the bushes where they had been semi-hidden and started to run down the far side of the ridge. The American fired five shots at the now disappearing pair as they crossed in front of the shrine; then they were gone.

Alarmed by the shots, a platoon leader and a squad of infantry came up on the run and searched the rest of the crest. Nothing. The two must have been stragglers.

Approaching the shrine, his eye was caught by the base of an imbedded .45 bullet, one of the shots he'd fired. The bullet had not even penetrated to the depth of its base. Turning, he paced the distance back to the place from which he had fired; sixty-two yards. The lieutenant, greatly disillusioned with the .45 autoloading pistol, wondered if it would have penetrated even the quilted uniforms had he hit

Below and right, lead bullets pulled from .45 Long Colt factory loads were hollow-pointed by hand with the aid of a hollow-pointing accessory available from Goerg Enterprises, 3009 S. Laurel, Port Angeles, WA 98362.

one of those North Koreans. He carried an M-1 rifle for the balance of his time in Korea!

The .45 M1911 pistol and its ammunition, as issued, is lacking in accuracy, range and power as a defensive handgun when measured against today's standards. Back when the now famous study entitled "An Evaluation of Police Handgun Ammunition" was published in summary form, there were many howls of anger from older shooters over the low incapacitation ratings achieved by certain of the old favorite cartridges, among them the .45 ACP (Auto Colt Pistol). I make no case here for the study; it left much to be desired. But it did contain valuable data on the comparative performance of different bullets in a uniform medium of consistency similar to that of human tissue. The performance of the old .45 ACP hardball was pretty poor

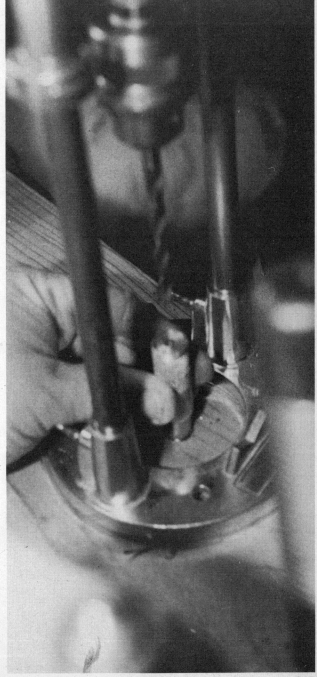

From left, one of the experimental Teflon-coated steel cases; Speer lead SWC; Speer JHP and home made lead hollow-point. The Speer SWC was loaded in reverse to try it as a full wadcutter, but didn't function well.

but then so was that of all the full metal jacketed bullets tested.

This came as no surprise to me. For as long as I can remember I have felt that the .45 ACP has enjoyed a grossly exaggerated reputation. The stories you hear about a hit anywhere on a man's arm or leg being enough to knock him down are typical and so much hogwash. Over the years I have known of many men shot with the .45. Those hit in a vital spot usually died pretty promptly but what has impressed me most has been the cleanness of most wounds and the lack of shattered bone and other side damage.

There seems, too, to be relatively little bleeding and trauma.

The thing that has bothered me the most about the as-issued .45 has been its lack of velocity. I always come away from a shoot feeling I could have done about as well throwing rocks. Ridiculous, of course, but the feeling is undeniable. I recently had an opportunity to test four pistols, two new Hardballer stainless steel .45s against two new Colt Series 70 Mk IVs. I used two new boxes of Remington and Winchester 230-grain ball ammunition. These were advertised at velocities anywhere between 815

Five loadings of commercial .45 ACP ammo, four of which were used in the tests reported here. The Norma 230-grain JHC load was omitted from the tests because it is no longer available. As reported, there was considerable variation.

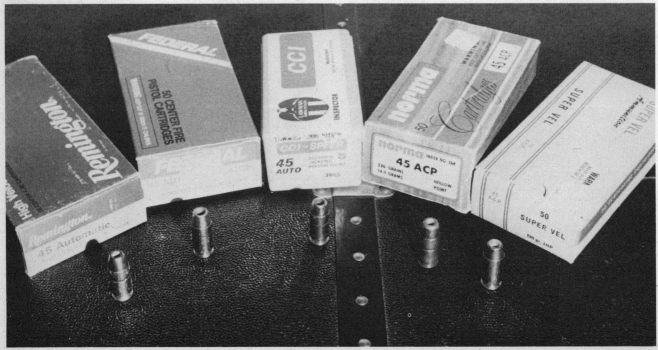

The Model 1917 revolvers, by Colt and S&W, were made before modern steels and heat-treating procedures were available. For this reason, Hamilton feels the low power standards for the .45 ACP and Auto Rim are justified, should be followed.

and 860 feet per second (fps) depending upon where you read your advertising. Now the Army field manual has always claimed a muzzle velocity of 805 fps for the service round. I was disappointed but not much surprised to find that all four new guns clocked both makes of 230-grain ammunition in the 750-770 fps range. I suspect that the .45 ACP has been SAAMI-ed like the 9mm Parabellum, the .357 and the .44 magnums have been. It would appear that someone nameless in the Sporting Arms and Ammunition Manufacturers Institute (SAAMI) has simply decided that as originally loaded, these were dangerous and has quietly slipped the accepted loadings down to "safer" levels.

Let's be fair. To begin with, we demand far more of this old cartridge-gun combination today than it was ever intended to give. We want fifty-yard target accuracy and smashing effect out to hunting ranges. These demands far exceed the original design criteria. We must understand what the military requirement was which caused the gun to be developed and for that we need to go back in time to the first decade of this century. Perhaps in this way we can better understand the factors and influences designer John Browning had to live with.

The Indian Wars were, for Army officers of the day, the longest, most violent and best remembered of our military experiences. From them, the Cavalry had emerged as The Arm of Decision. For the Cavalry, the metallic cartridge revolver had supplanted the saber as the weapon of mounted combat. The Spanish American War and the Philippine Insurrection were influences, but their importance — particularly that of the Moros — has been vastly overstated. The military requirement was a simple one; what the Army needed was an improved Cavalry weapon for mounted combat. This meant a pistol having an effective range of ten to fifteen yards, about the maximum distance at which you could expect to hit an enemy on a pitching horse while shooting from an equally unstable mount. The requirement for a pistol is easily understood, if you have ever tried to reload a revolver while at the same

time sitting a badly frightened horse. All things considered, I believe that the M1911 pistol was an excellent answer to the military requirement of the time.

The choice of a full metal jacketed (FMJ) bullet was made because such bullets tend to function more reliably through recoil operated arms. Equally compelling in that decision was the outraged hue and cry in the press of the civilized world directed at the British a few years before over the use of the so-called "Dum-Dum" bullets in India and South Africa. Suddenly, the only acceptable bullet for military use was the FMJ! How history comes full circle! Then, as now, our grandparents were urging, "If you must shoot them, shoot them just a little bit..."

Before World War I and in the years between wars, the .45 never caught on to any great degree with civilian or police shooters. Those were also days when handloading was virtually unknown and shooters who looked on a gun as something that could be improved and refined were few and far between. It was not until after World War II that real civilian interest in the .45 began to blossom and a number of police agencies began to take a hard look at the old gun. I have recently read the Colt .45 Government

Because the steel cases used as a brass conservation measure in WWII tend to stick in the chamber, causing extractor breakage, gunsmith Haywood Nelms applied a thin spray film of Teflon, effectively bypassing the breakage problem. Right, one of the Mark IV/Series '70 .45 autos used in performing the tests reported here.

Model — the civilian version of the M1911 — is the American handgun in greatest demand. This, despite the fact that any of the magnum revolver cartridges now on the market — .357, .41, .44 and perhaps the .45 Win. — will do a better job. They have so much more flexibility and can be loaded way down for finest accuracy and mild recoil or all the way up for smashing long range hunting power. Revolver function is independent of power level; not so with pistols.

One interesting thing I noted in reading through the summary report of the study on police handgun ammunition was that while the new bullets for most other calibers were discussed and evaluated, only the FMJ and the FMJ target semi-wadcutter were considered for the .45 ACP. Evidently, the testing for the study was done before the improved bullets had become available in .45. Chart (on facing page), from the study is most revealing and, I think, provides an excellent guide for use in the selection of bullets for different cartridges.

Referring to the various current handloaders' manuals and to published ballistic data in advertisements from the ammunition makers, it becomes pretty clear that what one

must work with in the .45 ACP if one hopes to improve the breed, is bullets in this general range of weights and velocities: 185-grains, 1,000 fps; 200-grains, 950 fps; 220/230-grains, 900 fps; 240/250-grains, 850 fps. These are not hard and fast figures. Different loading manuals show different velocities for the same charge. And you can usually push a properly sized lead bullet up to perhaps one hundred feet per second faster than a jacketed bullet with the same pressure level, the bullets being equal in weight.

The loading manuals tell you that the velocity levels they show as maximums are derived from the SAAMI standard of about 18,000 to 20,000 copper units of pressure (CUP) for the .45 ACP. As we shall see there are good reasons for the pressure limits they've established. For one thing, there are still in use pistols made during and

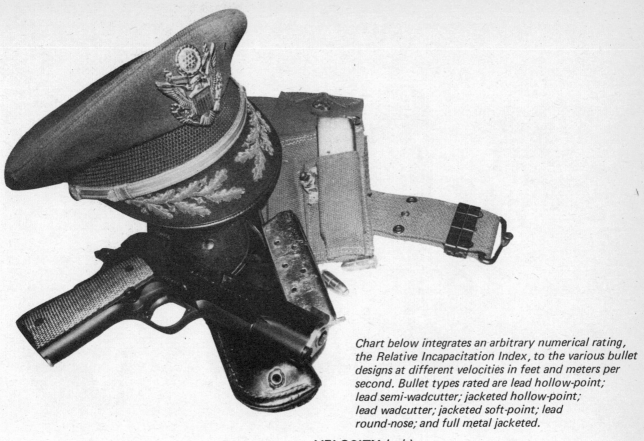

Chart below integrates an arbitrary numerical rating, the Relative Incapacitation Index, to the various bullet designs at different velocities in feet and meters per second. Bullet types rated are lead hollow-point; lead semi-wadcutter; jacketed hollow-point; lead wadcutter; jacketed soft-point; lead round-nose; and full metal jacketed.

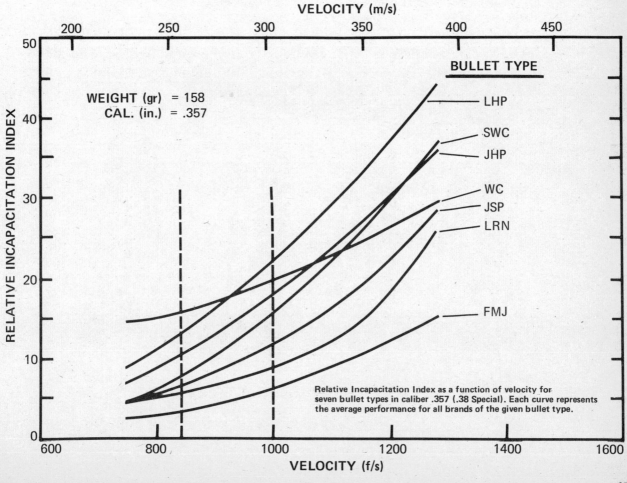

VELOCITY (m/s)

BULLET TYPE

WEIGHT (gr) = 158
CAL. (in.) = .357

- LHP
- SWC
- JHP
- WC
- JSP
- LRN
- FMJ

Relative Incapacitation Index as a function of velocity for seven bullet types in caliber .357 (.38 Special). Each curve represents the average performance for all brands of the given bullet type.

RELATIVE INCAPACITATION INDEX

VELOCITY (f/s)

Above, from left: Handloads tested were 200-grain Speer lead SWC; 250-grain Speer lead SWC; 230-grain home-made lead hollow-point; and 200-grain Speer JHP. Below, from left: The four commercial loads tested, together with recovered bullets, are Super Vel, Federal, CCI-Speer and Remington. Reloading data and further details are given in the text.

before World War I, plus many 1917 Army revolvers of both Colt and Smith & Wesson manufacture, all of which were put together before modern steels and heat treatment procedures were available. There is also the Achilles' Heel of the M1911 design, that small portion of the bottom, rear of the chamber, machined out to form part of the loading ramp. That small cut leaves a small portion of the cartridge case not fully supported. At that point, the case alone bears the entire pressure in the cartridge. In modern guns the cut has been reduced in size and modern ammunition cases are made with thick brass at the base so that this weakness has been minimized. It is well, however, to keep in mind that it is there.

It becomes evident that the choice of the best defense bullets vary. At the lower end of the velocity range — 850 fps — the leading choices would be: Lead wadcutter; lead hollow point; jacketed hollow point; lead semi-wadcutter.

As the velocity gets up toward 1,000 fps the order changes to: Lead hollow point; jacketed hollow point; lead wadcutter; lead semi-wadcutter.

Commercial loads for the .45 ACP that I find available all seem to be limited to the jacketed hollow point (JHP) design. This would seem to be a wise selection since it combines the functional advantages of the jacketed bullet with the number two choice at the upper velocity limits. To fit in with this I note that all the bullets offered range in the 185-200-grain weights where the higher velocities are easier to achieve.

To see just how much improvement has been achieved in the defense capability of the .45 ACP I first chronographed four brands of new JHP ammunition, then tested them for performance in a meat-and-bone target. My target was not uniform at all but neither is the human target. I put mine together with layers of lambs' ribs at front and rear to simulate a rib cage then filled in the space between with softer meat. I believe the end result was a target having about the meat and bone content of an average to small man at the chest level. To trap bullets without added deformation I used a plastic garbage can of standard size tightly packed with polyester pillows.

Ammunition	Velocity (fps)	Retained Weight (grains)	Expansion	Remarks
Remington 185-gr JHP, Lot LE07N	896	183.5	No expansion; bullet undamaged	Penetrated 4 pillows
Federal 185-gr JHP, Lot 25A8081	977	185	Mouth opened to bullet diameter only	Penetrated 4 pillows
CCI-Speer 200-gr JHP, Lot Unknown	917	186.7	Mushroomed uniformly to a maximum diameter of .716-inch	Penetrated 2 pillows
Super Vel 190-gr JHP, Lot GC15209	1026	172.3	Mushroomed to a maximum diameter of .708-inch	Found at bottom of third pillow

There were no malfunctions with any of this ammunition.

Evidently, the .45 ACP loaded with new JHP bullets can be a great deal more effective as a defense load but not always. If jacketed hollow point bullets are used, a great

deal seems to depend upon their quality and obviously some of the makers have found the secret and some haven't. Frankly, I was surprised to find that any of the factory JHPs performed well at .45 ACP velocities.

Keeping in mind the relative performance, I wondered if better defense results might not be obtained with heavier, lead bullets. I experimented with some true lead wadcutters made by seating a Speer 200-grain lead semi-wadcutter (LSWC) loaded base forward. This makes a shorter cartridge than the standard and I found that even with a magazine modified by gunsmith friend Haywood Nelms, I could not get more than about sixty percent reliability in feeding. With some regret, I gave up on the true wadcutter.

Next I developed a series of four handloads to try each of the best choice bullets in the .45 ACP velocity range other than the lead wadcutter: Lead semi-wadcutters, hollow points and JHPs. I selected CCI—Speer's 200-grain semi-wadcutter, a marvelously accurate lead bullet I enjoy shooting in the Gold Cup National Match Pistol. Next I decided on CCI-Speer's enormous 250-grain lead semi-wadcutter with which I had had no previous experience. CCI-Speer's 200-grain JHP came next and, for a lead hollow point, I found that I'd have to make my own. I used lead round nose bullets taken right from Remington loads for the .45 Colt and reduced them to weigh 230-grains by drilling a cavity in the nose.

Shopping about among the various loading manuals, I settled upon two loads for the four bullets: For the lighter 200-grain bullets, 11.2 grains of Blue Dot; for the 230 and 250-grain bullets, 7.3 grains of Herco. For some reason I had always thought of Herco as a powder of limited value and that being mostly in 9mm. I don't think that way anymore!

My bullets were loaded in the usual fashion. I did enjoy one advantage in that I had just received a fine new RCBS taper crimper for the .45 ACP and it proved to be worth its weight in gold, giving good, tight, uniform crimps without changing headspacing. I seated all the lead semi-wadcutters so that no full diameter bullet metal extended beyond the case. I know if I don't do this, my pistol will often not quite close and lock up after a shot. My lead hollow points, being made from the old .45 Colt round nosed bullet, were very close in shape to the .45 ACP hardball bullet.

I admit to having had some misgivings about how the lead bullets would work through my pistol and about what sort of a leading problem they might cause. These are not light loads by any stretch of the imagination and the .45 ACP velocities are right in the range where leading begins to become a serious concern. Altogether, I fired a hundred or more rounds in chronographing and meat testing, about a third of which were lead, I did not experience any leading problem even at rather high velocities and I attribute this in large part to a new product called Break-Free with which I cleaned my gun before the test. This is a combination lubricant, cleanser and penetrant and it does a truly amazing job.

In my shoot I had three malfunctions, all with lead bullets. In one case I failed to seat a semi-wadcutter deeply enough and the gun failed to close completely and lock up. The other two both happened with the large Speer 250-grain semi-wadcutter and were classic stovepipes. The empty case didn't quite get out of the way during ejection and caught above the next one below as it was trying to get

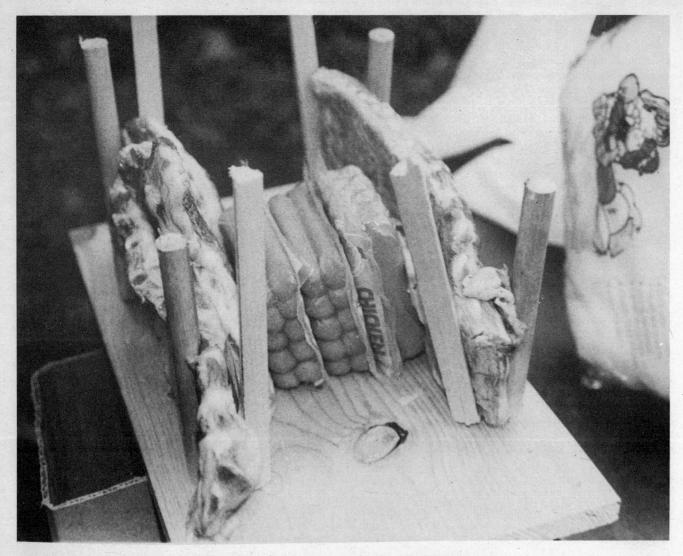

Above, Hamilton's unpatented thorax-simulating analog, with layers of lamb ribs at front and back, with plies of frankfurters in between. Left, the system for trapping bullets without any further deformation after going through the meat consisted of polyester fiber in plastic trash barrel. It worked most of the time, with one exception noted.

Hamilton checks pistol after firing the experimental hot loads. No damage was apparent, but the excessive amount of pounding was readily sensed by the hand of the shooter.

into the chamber. I don't know how to explain that. Usually a stovepipe results from lack of recoil power; that load may lack a lot of things but power isn't one of them!

Ammunition	Velocity (fps)	Retained Weight (grains)	Recovered Bullet	Remarks
220-gr CCI-Speer lead SWC, 10.2 gr Blue Dot	983	70	Only fragments were found; does not hold together at this velocity	Penetrated 1½ pillows
250-gr CCI-Speer lead SWC, 7.3 gr Herco	975	246.6	Nose flattened slightly; no other deformation. Hard lead bullet.	Penetrated target, all pillows, can and several fiber boards.
230-gr lead hollow point, 7.3 gr Herco	1042	214.6	Classic mushroom to maximum diameter of .834-inch	Penetrated 3½ pillows
200-gr CCI-Speer JHP, 10.2 gr Blue Dot	937	182.5	Expanded nicely to .741-inch	Penetrated 1½ pillows

Before going on, let me call your attention to the fact that these are all maximum or near maximum loads. Your gun and mine are different, so work up to them from the low side should you wish to try them. I got no pressure signs but that doesn't mean that you won't.

On balance, I would give the nod to my 230-grain lead hollow point load as topping the commercial ones from a defensive point of view. While I like my lead hollow point and had no feeding problems with it, I doubt that others would find it as reliable a feeder as I did. Soft lead noses will catch on anything rough that may be in the way; they are perverse that way.

I said that my loads were maximum or near maximum and gave the usual warning about approaching them with care. You may ask, just what is a maximum load? The .45 ACP is an excellent cartridge to use as a basis for discussion on this point. There are a number of pistols and revolvers today chambered for it; several new ones introduced recently. What is a safe maximum load for a sixty-year-old Smith & Wesson Model 1917 Army revolver with a non-

heat-treated cylinder is certainly not as great as what would be safe in a new Colt Series 70 Mk IV Government Model pistol. I suspect that the Smith & Wesson Model 25, 1955 .45 Target revolver can safely handle loads that go well beyond what ought to be fed to the Colt. The makers of ammunition and the authors of the loading manuals have no control over the gun in which their loads may be used and so they must hold pressures down to where they are safe in the weakest one of the group.

Just to show what can be done with the M1911 Government Model if it is new and in excellent condition, remember that the .45 ACP is the only American small arms cartridge ever loaded with steel cases; at least it is the only one known to me. This was done toward the end of WWII as an expedient to save scarce brass. These were anodized or treated with some sort of very effective wash because they stood up well against corrosion and there are quantities of them still available and in use. If a shooter must rely upon a .45 pistol as a hunting arm and must have more power than the loads I developed, these can be made up with reasonable safety using steel cases for added strength at the weak point in the bottom of the chamber.

There was always one problem with the steel cases. Not having the elasticity of brass, they tend to expand in the chamber on firing and stick there causing broken extractors.

I mentioned to gunsmith Haywood Nelms my interest in trying some heavy loads in my Government Model using steel cases and my concern about extractor damage. He recently read that the Air Force had a problem with cases freezing in the 20mm Vulcan gun at high altitudes and that they had solved it by Teflon coating their ammunition. He recommended that I try the same thing and I did.

I secured thirty steel cases in good condition which he and I degreased and sprayed with Teflon. After they were thoroughly dry I loaded these with the only jacketed hollow point bullet I had available, the CCI-Speer 200-grain and seated this ahead of a load fifteen percent heavier than the maximum shown in most loading manuals. I am not going to relate what the load was because I do not want some hasty reader to glance through this, pick it out and try it out! I would never use such a load in ordinary brass cases under any circumstances. The load gave me a consistent 1100 fps and the Teflon proved to be the answer. There were no malfunctions and no stuck cases. Although I did not note any signs of high pressure, this load is too heavy for my pistol and causes definite pounding and wear. I use a Bar-Sto stainless steel buffer in place of the recoil spring guide but that wasn't enough; heavier springs are needed.

My point is that a good, new Government Model or M1911 in excellent condition can take pressure levels a little higher than those shown in the manuals, if one must use it to hunt. I still consider it a poor choice for that compared to any of the modern magnum revolvers available.

In loading for the Government Model or M1911 pistol I recommend that you stick to the loads listed in the most recent loading manuals or to good factory-loaded ammunition. After my testing there is no question in my mind that the .45 ACP has been vastly improved in effectiveness as a defense gun. Well thought out handloads can make it even better.

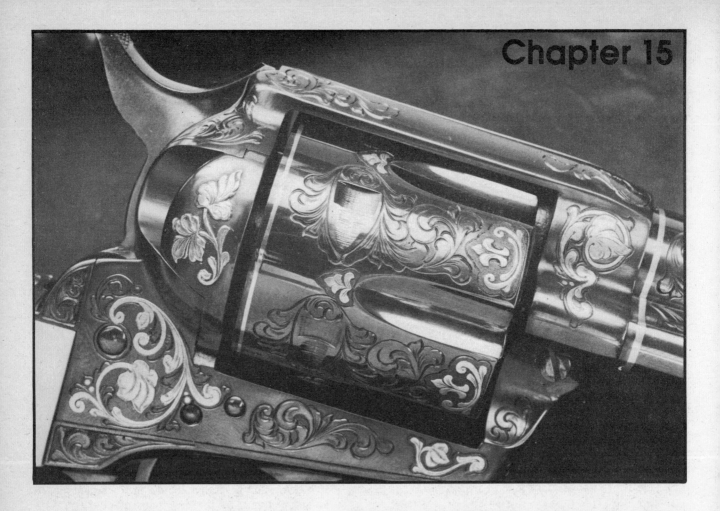

Chapter 15

COLT'S CUSTOM GUN SHOP

S AMUEL COLT was not only a discerning gun enthusiast and firearms inventor, but a masterful showman as well. In *The Book of Colt Engraving,* R.L. Wilson points out that it was Sam Colt who first came to realize the prestige attached to one of his handguns, when customized and tastefully decorated for its owner.

As gunmaker and showman "he hired that period's leading engravers, ordering for himself, the general public and for the giants of finance, industry, the military and royalty, what are recognized as the finest handguns made in 19th Century America. The unique tradition of custom and deluxe firearms was a highlight of Samuel Colt's unparalleled contribution to gunmaking.

"From Colt's death in 1862 into modern times, the firm he founded has added to its achievements in the field of custom firearms. The Colonel's successors, too, shared an appreciation of quality, history and the uniqueness inherent with the products marked with the name Colt. A few of the best known clients who took pride in their custom Colts included Buffalo Bill Cody, Bat Masterson, George Armstrong Custer, U.S. Grant, John J. Pershing and Douglas MacArthur, the artists Frederic Remington and George Catlin, Western stars Tom Mix, Chuck Connors and John Wayne; and several Presidents of the United States...."

From the time of World War I into the 1960s, the continuing requests for custom Colt arms could be handled only partially due to a lack of skilled craftsmen. However, during the past fifteen or more years requests have continued to rise. Who can look at Teddy Roosevelt's presentation piece — a museum-preserved, fully customized Patterson longarm — or General George Patton's much-publicized pearl-handled Colts, without wishing that similar treasures could be available to them?

Colt Firearms is fortunate that a new era in America has

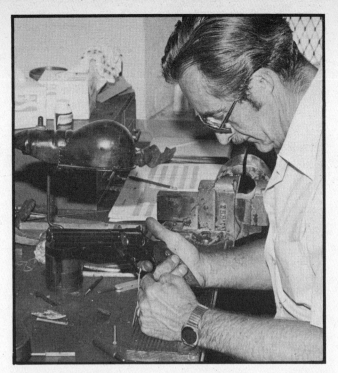

Functional excellence gets its share of attention, along with esthetic appeal at the Colt Custom Gun Shop. Earl Giggey, above, specializes in fine-tuning the Colt Python.

brought forth a new breed of individuals who earnestly work toward becoming the almost extinct craftsmen and artisans that once were much in evidence. The course is long and difficult, but a growing number of men and women are developing excellence in custom hand-checkering, engraving, inlaying, and even highly artistic and realistic wood carving of the type associated with the master German and Austrian stock carvers of the past.

It has not been easy for those responsible for the Colt Custom Gun Shop to find and relocate the number of skilled engravers required. They have turned up several young men who have come a long way in expertise and now wish to work under men who can teach them the tricks of their crafts, and help them reach the degree of skill they wish to achieve.

Eventual growth of the custom department lies with such men as Stan Newman, Walt Gleason and Al De John. All are dedicated to the Colt tradition and all totally involved in the custom gun shop's end product: guns of top quality bearing the unmistakable mark of the custom craftsman. They have produced some unbelievable works of art, including the Bicentennial gold-inlaid and engraved dragoon sold by Colt at the record auction price of $55,000. Nor can one ignore the $49,500 Tiffany-gripped single-action or the privately commissioned Philadelphia Bicentennial single-action Armies.

Such magnificent show guns are not the daily projects in the Colt Custom Gun Shop. The price gamut runs from a low of about $329 to $514 for class A engraving; this treatment covers approximately one-fourth of the gun. If

By Bob Zwirz

This Assemblage Of Artisans Can Produce As Much Custom Gun Work As Your Bank Account Can Stand!

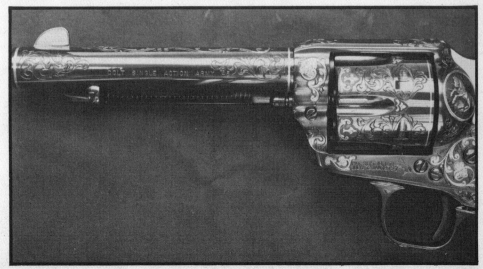

A Colt single-action Army revolver that has been elaborately engraved and inlaid with gold in Colt shop.

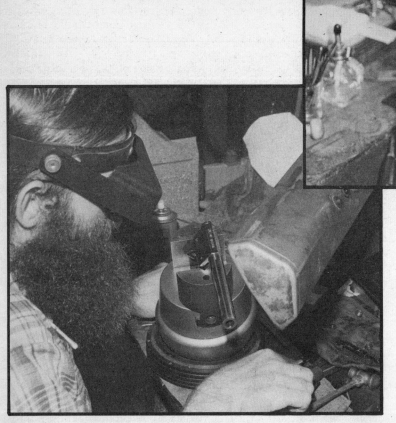

A Custom Edition of the legendary Colt 3d Model Dragoon percussion revolver is seen taking shape here, with a close-in view of its engraving.

you happen to have up to $993, or even $671, you can skip grades B and C and move right into the D class. Prices show this variation, since one gun can be quite unlike another, particularly in size. A fair example is the difference between a flat-side autoloader and a Colt Peacemaker with all its curves and rounded surfaces. Naturally, the auto presents less time-consuming workmanship and application of the craftsman's tools.

Standard work of this nature can be ordered through your Colt dealer, but the work commissioned is in addition to the price of the gun. It can be a Colt you have owned and cherished or a new gun you have purchased specifically for customizing or even for hand-finishing the ultimate Colt.

Earl Giggey, a long-time Colt employee, is the master of the special service department for obtaining a custom tuned action. This delicate work is offered on Colt Python models. The result is an extremely smooth, light, steady double-action trigger pull through modification and super hand-honing of the internal mechanism.

The double-action pull will measure an average of 7½ pounds or less, with the single action pull also reduced to an average of 2½ to 2¾ pounds. Custom-tuned actions may be ordered without single action and are performed only by a Colt master gunsmith. Giggey will spend a good 2½ hours on each gun. Only then is he certain he has his tuning down to perfection.

His department also can install an Elliason rear sight.

Installation of this rear sight with a Patridge front sight is another Python option.

Another item I like is their barrel and bushing kit. The Colt Mk. IV/Series '70 barrel and spring-loaded bushing for placement in Government Model Series autos enhances gun value and assures consistent alignment for lifelong accuracy

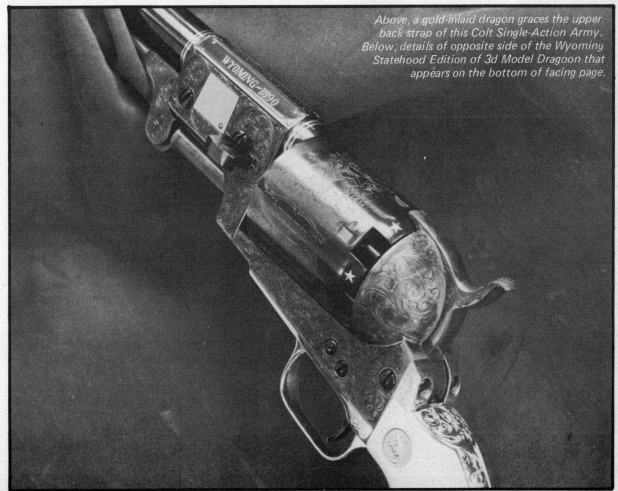

Above, a gold-inlaid dragon graces the upper back strap of this Colt Single-Action Army. Below, details of opposite side of the Wyoming Statehood Edition of 3d Model Dragoon that appears on the bottom of facing page.

Right, a Colt craftsman polishes a revolver frame. Below and opposite page, the ornate Colt with Tiffany grip auctioned for $49,500.

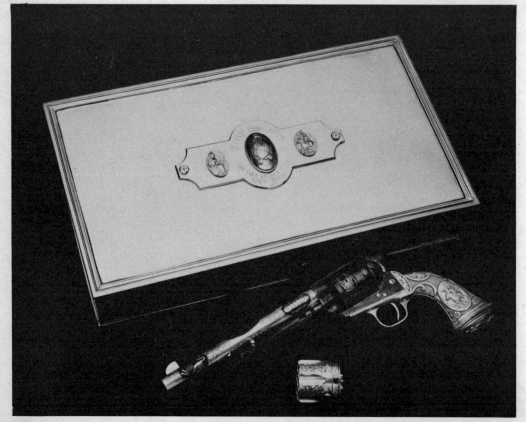

and precision. You also can look forward to refinishing, reconditioning, ambidextrous safeties, caliber conversions and barrel conversions as additional services.

If you would like matched pairs of autos or revolvers, a beautifully engraved Colt/Sauer (one of four grades), or custom grips that would please a prince, the shop can comply with your desires. Even a Colt belt buckle to match your grips is in the cards as is a fantastic line of super-custom bolo ties. The latter is the creation and work of the multi-talented Earl Giggey.

A draft for $3 will bring you a beautifully illustrated custom shop catalog. This is a must for those who desire the finest or an original motif of engraving with the ultimate Colt touch. You can create your own engraving designs, wildlife or historically significant inlays, grip design/material and decoration. In this catalog, you'll find line drawings on which you can sketch scenes, your name, foliated patterns and practically anything your heart desires. This is assuming, of course, that your purse can stand the strain!

Once your wishes are known to Colt, an estimate will be prepared, with possible suggestions and comments included for your consideration. Assuming agreement, you then will be informed of the estimated date of the project's completion.

By 1985, Colt looks to have the largest custom staff in the world. Much sooner, photoengraving will be added to their list of custom options. One of the country's law enforcement units has ordered a Special Edition, with photoengraving, for a number of commercial 1911A1 autos.

With this project, an Ohio historical gun and a Wyoming custom edition of the 1890 Colt Third Model Dragoon, things are humming. This Wyoming black powder gun is a statehood edition. The volume of orders already coming into Colt's Custom Shop is far in excess of all expectations, and continues to grow in scope each month.

Men like master engravers Bob Burt, Leonard Francolini, Daniel Goodwin, Bryson J. Gwinnell and Steven Kamyk have begun the new era for Colt with style. With Earl Giggey's talent, patience and self-demanding attitude concerning the revolvers on which he works, it's no wonder word of the special services and other options is spreading among members of the gun fraternity.

If you require further information, write to Colt Firearms, c/o Custom Gun Shop, 150 Huyshope Avenue, Hartford, Connecticut 06102.

Above, Bryson Gwinnell engraves a custom hammer unit.

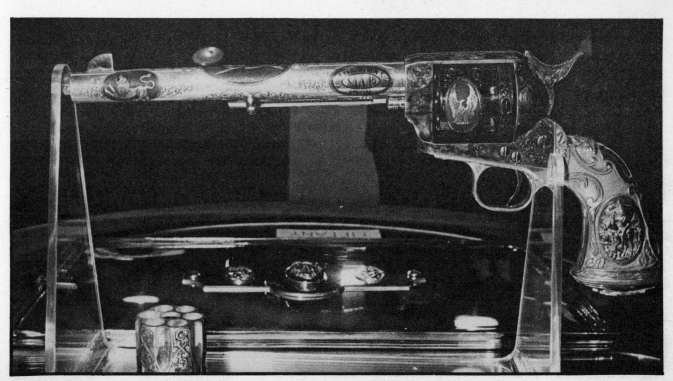

Chapter 16

Gunsmith Heywood Nelms test-fires one of the S&W Combat Masterpieces off the sandbags.

WHY REVOLVERS DON'T SHOOT ALIKE By Claud Hamilton

Some Semi-Scientific Investigations Offer Reasons For The Differences!

Some revolvers become sprung or warped in the vulnerable and critical area of the crane. Usual cause is dropping the cylinder open abruptly or snapping it shut in the manner so widely favored by bad-hats on television. This causes cylinder misalignment, degrades accuracy and may cause bullet shaving and other problems.

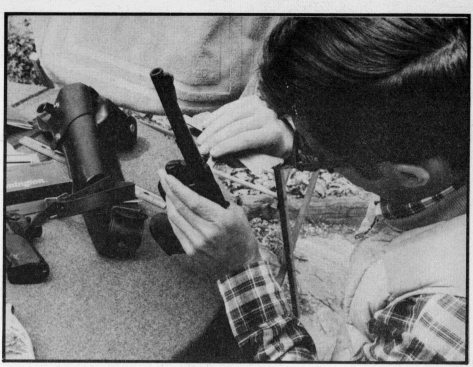

Nelms used a set of feeler gauges to check the cylinder gaps on the test revolvers.

MOST EXPERIENCED shooters will tell you that each individual revolver seems to have preferences for certain brands and loads of ammunition with which it tends to give best accuracy. Rarely will any two revolvers of identical make, model and barrel length give the same muzzle velocity with the same ammunition. If you've any doubt of this, I recommend that you glance over pages 348 to 350 of Speer's loading manual, number nine. Speer presents the results of chronograph tests with dozens of revolvers, all caliber .357 magnum using several different loads. The spread in velocity between guns of the same barrel length is impressive and sometimes exceeds 200 feet per second (fps).

Revolvers are more complex instruments than most of us realize. To illustrate what I mean, several years ago at the Speer plant, engineers undertook to discover how pressures vary in revolver chambers and why. The late William M. Caldwell, a distinguished young engineer, did most of the work and here is the essence of what he learned:

At the moment of firing, the base of a revolver bullet begins to move forward before the remainder of the bullet. In the ample throat of the usual .38 Special or .357 chamber — .358 to .360-inch — this causes it to upset to a larger diameter.

At the moment of peak pressure in the revolver, there is no gap; the bullet is crossing over it and sealing it! It then takes from 3000 to 4000 pounds per square inch (psi) of pressure to swage the bullet back down to groove diameter so that it may enter the barrel.

As soon as the bullet clears the gap, pressure drops off rapidly. The rate of pressure loss is twice that of a solid handgun barrel of the same length and the peak pressure is notably higher in the revolver due to the swaging action described. Pressure does not, however, fall off to zero in either the solid or the revolver barrel before the bullet leaves the muzzle.

Caldwell found that factors which seem to influence pressure include:

Bullet diameter: Undersize bullets generate lower pressures, but without any great loss in velocity.

Bullet length: Long, heavy bullets require more time to accelerate from rest and tend to upset more in the chamber throat.

Bullet seating depth: The deeper the bullet is seated the longer it takes in the chamber throat and to cross the gap and the higher the pressure will be, all other things being equal.

Caldwell indicated that smaller, lighter bullets which are swaged less tend to better maintain their structural integrity and give better accuracy as a result.

The Speer research Caldwell performed was conducted with a Smith & Wesson Model 27 .357 magnum revolver in which the original cylinder had been replaced. A special cylinder having but one chamber was constructed so that a transducer could be mounted in its side to measure pressure.

For years I've known of the wide velocity variations between apparently identical revolvers and wished that we might know more about the causes of this. I would also like to know more about the important matter of individual gun preference for certain batches of ammunition. The more deeply I probe into this murky question the more convinced I become that there is no one, simple explanation. I think the Speer research certainly supports this. When we do find a definitive answer, I believe that it will turn out to be a complex combination of factors including such things as tiny variations in finished barrel diameter, lengths and sizes of chamber throats in individual cylinders, bullet size, weight and length, and seating depth, as well as the more obvious barrel gap spacing.

Over the years I have handled many revolvers and noted that there was a difference among them in the tightness of the barrel to cylinder fit detectable even with the naked

Right, William Caldwell, Speer researcher, pointed out that bullet length, weight, diameter and seating depth affect pressure. Below, firing across chronograph.

eye. While some of this is attributable to wear, some of it is due to factory fitting. Gunsmiths tell me that they seek a fitting of about .003-inch as a compromise. A close fit is desired but there is a tendency to build up combustion residue and bullet metal shavings at the gap. If the gap is much under .003-inch, at least in some guns, this build-up can eventually interfere with cylinder rotation and cause jams.

Logic tells us that the larger the gap, the greater will be the loss in pressure per unit of time. Thus, all other things being equal, revolvers with larger barrel gaps should develop lower velocities than identical models that are more tightly fitted. To prove this, I looked over a selection of revolvers, with this result:

REVOLVER	GAP
Smith & Wesson K-38 Masterpiece .38 Special	.008
Smith & Wesson Combat Masterpiece No. 1	.002
Smith & Wesson Combat Masterpiece No. 2	.005
Smith & Wesson Chiefs Special	.006
Colt Detective Special No. 1	.002
Colt Detective Special No. 2	.006
Smith & Wesson Model 28 .357 Magnum	.008
Smith & Wesson Model 19	.003
Colt New Service .45 Colt	.0015

These guns are all virtually new. Although there is a great variation in their actual ages, none have been fired more than a few dozen rounds. The Colt New Service hasn't been made since World War II and this particular example, in mint condition, was one of the last made.

To make any sort of a meaningful test, I needed at least two guns of identical model and barrel length to compare. Fortunately, I had two pairs to compare which promised to make the results all the more interesting. Keeping in mind the things that Caldwell had discovered at Speer I decided to use both light and heavy bullets of differing types to see what results they might give.

Make	Caliber	Bullet	Lot
Super Vel (Old)	.38 Special	110 grain JHP	B115602
Speer +P	.38 Special	125 grain JHP	410032
Winchester Super X +P	.38 Special	158 grain LHP	4858LH2
Federal	.38 Special	158 grain LRN	18B-6224

The shooting was done at the Fairfax Rod & Gun Club near Manassas, Virginia, on a dull, overcast day with rain a constant threat. For some reason, my chronograph thrives on such weather and gives its best results against a leaden sky. This shoot proved no exception, and here were the average velocities achieved by each gun for each of the different loads:

Ammo	Guns (Muzzle velocity in feet per second)			
	S&W No. 1	S&W No. 2	Colt No. 1	Colt No. 2
Super Vel 110 JHP	1179	1178	1101	1080
Speer 125 JHP	1045	1022	978	951
Winchester 158 LHP	859	923	774	633
Federal 158 LRN	841	867	717	642

This Super Vel load proved to be hot for factory ammunition, resulting in flattened primers and difficult extraction in all four guns. Even though both the Winchester and the Speer ammunition is marked +P neither seemed particularly powerful and there were no pressure signs. The Federal people apparently used kapok or something similar as a filler in their load; the chronograph was covered with fine bits of brown matter after the shoot.

Note that the four-inch barrel Combat Masterpieces varied by only one foot per second with the lightest bullet although their barrel gaps varied by .003-inch. With the heavy, lead bullets the situation was reversed and the gun with the larger gap gave higher velocities with two brands of ammunition. For the Colts, the situation looked more clear cut: The tighter gun gave higher velocities consistently and the difference became greater as bullet weight was increased. This fact seemed to give me a hint that more than one factor was involved. On a hunch I measured the chamber throats of the two revolvers and while gun number one mikes a consistent .358-inch, number two goes .360 all the way around.

I think what happens with the two Colts is obvious. Not only is there a greater pressure loss from the larger barrel gap of number two gun, the longer, heavier lead bullets also upset more seriously in its large throat and require more swaging to get them down to barrel diameter. This combination of factors explains why the difference is greater with the heavier bullets.

The Smith & Wessons pose a different problem. With them the situation reverses: The tighter gun does better with the light, jacketed bullets while the gun with the wider gap excels with the heavy, lead bullets. I thought immediately of the throat problem and measured each gun with care. There is some small variance, but it is small indeed and both can be said to have .358 throats smoothly and uniformly cut.

For a time I was left without an explanation for this peculiar performance until I remembered one thing different about these two guns I had almost forgotten. Gun number two with the larger barrel gap is much the older of the two, not in terms of shooting but in actual age. Number two was made during the early 1950s while the other gun was made in the late 1960s. The difference is that the barrel of gun number two had been hand lapped by a gunsmith, back when it was new, as a means of showing in detail how barrel lapping is done. That mirror smooth barrel, probably just a hair larger in internal dimensions, explains what happened. With light bullets the reduced barrel friction of the lapped barrel was nearly enough to offset the effect of the greater barrel gap. With heavier bullets it proved to be more than enough. Caldwell found that undersized bullets offered much less resistance and achieved greater velocities. A slightly oversize and super smooth barrel ought to do the same.

I had confirmed my original premise. Larger barrel gaps allow gas to escape faster after the bullet passes but the velocities different revolvers of identical model produce isn't just a matter of barrel gap. It involves much more; at least the factors Bill Caldwell mentioned: Throat size, bullet size, length, weight and seating depth, barrel dimensions and the width of the barrel gap.

Comparison testing involved this pair of Colt Detective Specials and S&W Combat Masterpieces.

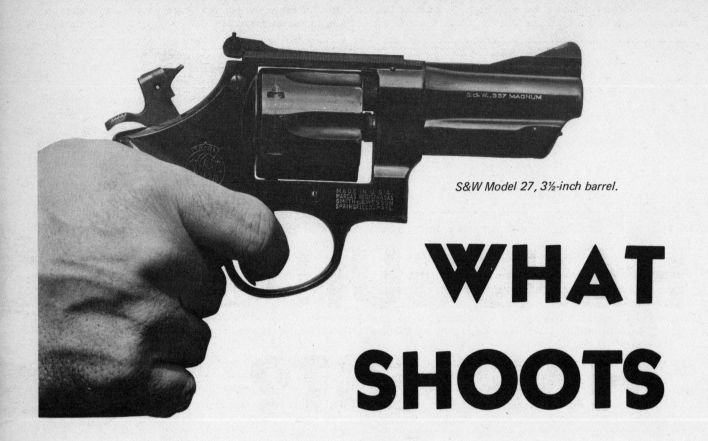

S&W Model 27, 3½-inch barrel.

WHAT SHOOTS

There's Foundation

To The Old Wives' Tale —

Up To A Point

Colt Trooper Mk III, 4-inch barrel.

HANDGUN HARDEST?

Chapter 17

By Claud Hamilton

HOW MANY TIMES over the years have you heard some elder authority say, that "Colt .38s shoot harder (to higher velocities) than Smith & Wessons — their barrels are bored tighter"?

I've run into it a lot and for many years the idea formed a part of the legendary framework of handgunning as I knew it. It wasn't something to be doubted or challenged; it simply was accepted as wisdom from the past.

Recently, a young friend who is a member of Texas' San Antonio Police Department mentioned casually in a letter the fact that he and the departmental armorer had confirmed this old saying after chronographing literally hundreds of Colt and Smith & Wesson service revolvers. This one started me thinking. Of course, it is a well-known fact that Colt and Smith & Wesson never have made their .38 Special barrels to the same internal dimensions. W.H.B. Smith in *The Book of Pistols and Revolvers* lists them as Colt, lands .347 plus or minus .001, grooves .346-.3472; Smith & Wesson, lands .354 plus or minus .001, grooves .355-.3572. Thus, the average Smith & Wesson barrel will be somewhat larger in the groove diameter than the average Colt.

While mulling over what my young friend had said, I bought a copy of Speer's fine No. 9 Loading Manual. Since I'm relatively new to handloading, I put in more time than most would reading through the manual, and thus came upon the remarkable data on page 350.

Speer presents these to show the tremendous variations in muzzle velocity given by apparently identical revolvers in

Making partially-jacketed bullets with Corbin swaging dies in an RCBS Rock Chucker loading press, as described here

Bullet fired from S&W Combat Masterpiece .38 Special shows engraving of the barrel's five lands and grooves.

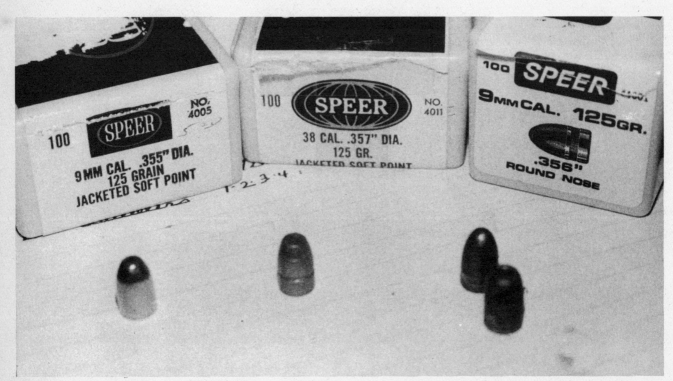

Bullets used in Hamilton's tests, as reported here, included .355 Speer JSP, .357 125-grain JSP and lead swaged to HP.

GUN	BULLET	LOAD 1 (UNIQUE)	LOAD 2 (BLUE DOT)
Colt Diamondback	Speer 125-grain JSP .355	790	858
	Speer 125-grain JSP .357	753	832
	Speer 125-grain LRN .356	805	901
	Swaged 125-grain LHP .357	838	927
Smith & Wesson Combat Masterpiece	Speer 125-grain JSP .355	755	801
	Speer 125-grain JSP .357	818	902
	Speer 125-grain LRN .356	802	881
	Swaged 125-grain LHP .357	773	850

Minor problem in checking bore/groove diameters out of S&W barrel is that one is always opposite the other.

Chart gives details of results obtained in Hamilton's tests.

.357 Magnum caliber. Using three different Speer loads, the case is certainly well made. Something else soon began to be evident to me, however, as I looked over Speer's figures: on average, the Smith & Wesson revolvers — of which there were quite a few — seemed to outshoot the Colts in terms of muzzle velocity! Granted, I am mixing calibers here, but the .357 Magnum and .38 Special use identical barrel and bullet dimensions, so the comparison is valid.

This revelation led me to go back and rethink what we all know about barrel-bullet dimensions in general. How well I remember peashooters in which the pea was grossly undersize for my tube, and I got massive gas leak and low velocities. On the other hand, grossly oversize projectiles being forced through a tube do one of two things, generally: they swage down to size, if you're lucky; cause a detonation, if you're not.

I found I wanted to know more about how bullets perform that are very close to barrel dimensions, and the influences of "tight" and "loose" barrels.

On the basis of the evidence I had so far, I formed a theory. Checking with my San Antonio police department friend, I confirmed my suspicion that all their testing had been done with lead service loads. And, from Speer's report, all their testing was done with their jacketed bullets.

All of this seemed to make sense. Lead is notoriously soft and malleable, and lead bullets usually are lubricated, as well. It made sense that, in a tight barrel, these qualities would make for a better gas seal and higher velocity. Jacketed bullets, on the other hand, are much harder and

offer great resistance to engraving by the lands, and great friction in passing through the bore. A looser barrel, which imposed less violent swaging requirements upon a jacketed bullet, logically ought to give higher velocities as long as a good gas seal is maintained. Or so it seemed to me.

I was aware that my premise was an oversimplification. Although I have no way of measuring their influence, I am positive that certain other factors enter importantly into the problem: tightness of crimp, for one; length of the bullet bearing surface for another. Jacket and lead hardness, seating depth and the nature of the powder used, I'm sure, all play a role. For example, we know that there are certain powders that do not burn efficiently or deliver their full energy unless they are constrained by heavy bullets very tightly crimped in place. However, I suspect that all these factors tend to be more important with high-pressure rifle calibers, and I felt I was able to test my theory in a way that would minimize their influence.

I have a Smith & Wesson Model 15 Combat Masterpiece which has a four-inch barrel and is a good example of a service revolver, except for its adjustable sights. I'd use this gun to test my theory by firing through it bullets of identical weight but different diameters, then measure the resulting velocities. Running through the stock of bullets on my loading bench, I found the following which seemed to suit my purpose well indeed: Speer 125-grain JSP .355 (9mm Parabellum); and the Speer 125-grain JSP .357 (.38 Special). Then I found a lead bullet which allowed me to check the characteristics of the two bullet materials. This

Hornady lead SWC bullets have novel knurled base to hold the lubricant in place. They are also packed 100 to box.

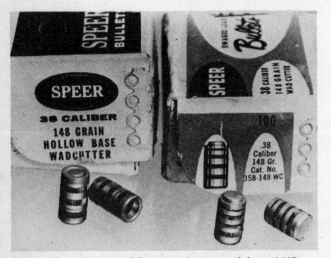

Two well-aged boxes of Speer wadcutters, plain and HB.

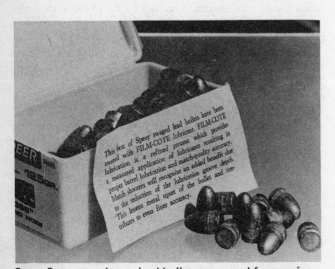

Speer 9mm round nose lead bullets were used for swaging to hollow-point configuration by Hamilton in his tests.

was a Speer 125-grain lead round nose made for the 9mm Parabellum. Using Dave Corbin's .357 swaging dies, I was able to make up from this bullet a 125-grain lead hollow point in .357 diameter. This gave me just what I wanted; both lead and jacketed bullets in nominal .38 Special caliber, .357, and both lead and jacketed bullets that were slightly undersize at .356 and .355, respectively.

Now all that remained was to obtain a Colt four-inch .38 Special, then to slug both barrels and see how they compared. A friend kindly lent me a new Diamondback which proved to be a most pleasant revolver to handle. Carefully, I drove .358-inch wadcutters through both barrels using a small mallet and wood dowel of near barrel diameter. The Colt, with its six-groove barrel, proved easy, but I had to get the help of a gunsmith friend to come up with the five-groove Smith measurements: *Colt Diamondback .38 Special, lands .346; grooves .354. Smith & Wesson Combat Masterpiece, lands .347; grooves .357.*

Since I wanted to avoid any possible leading which might distort the result, I shopped through the loading

Carefully computed undercharge of powder left this bullet lodged near the muzzle of the S&W Combat Masterpiece, to be carefully driven back out for bore measurements.

manuals to find a pair of light loads that offered promise of uniformity. I settled on 5.0 grains of Unique and 7.0 grains of Blue Dot, both well down the line from top pressures, and put up twenty-five rounds of each load with each of the four bullets. Using new Winchester-Western brass and CCI 500 primers, I took special care to weigh each individual charge. A time-consuming process, but I felt it worthwhile for the sake of uniformity. I also was careful to get the seating depth uniform and to apply the most even crimp possible.

Bright and early one morning, I loaded chronograph, guns, targets and ammunition and headed for the range.

I use a small, portable chronograph known as the Model 500D, which is made by Bob Medaris' Chronograph Specialists (Box 309, Mira Loma, California 92704). It is simplicity itself, consisting of two black box sky screens, a master readout box and a small switch, used to recycle the screens. As you fire over the slits of the sky screen boxes, you trip photoelectric cells. No printed paper screens are required, which speeds the operation. You can fire as fast as you can record your readings and tap the recycle switch!

Before starting the shoot, I sat down to think through just what data I ought to get if my theory was correct.

First, of course, the Colt ought to show up best with lead bullets, and the larger .357 bullet probably should lead the pack, because of its malleability and tendency to form a good gas seal with minimum friction resistance in the bore.

The Smith & Wesson ought to shine with the jacketed bullets, especially the small diameter .355 JSP made for the Luger, since minimum swaging and barrel-to-bullet contact seems to promote best velocities with the harder, jacketed bullets.

As to which should come out on top overall, I had no idea. I felt that the lead bullets probably would have an edge, however.

After carefully averaging readings, the results are reflected in the accompanying chart.

Obviously, these were not hot loads, and I had no leading problem whatever.

Mulling over the data collected from the averages, it looked as though this particular pair of guns had pretty well confirmed my theory. I emphasize "with this particular pair of guns," because I feel another pair of the same two types might give nearly opposite results! I can emphasize the point the Speer people made in Manual No. 9 (page 350), that no two identical guns perform alike; that there can be some really spectacular differences.

There was one fly in the ointment, however. My Combat Masterpiece hadn't handled that small jacketed bullet as it ought to have with either load tried. By all rights, that bullet should have shown the highest velocities of the lot, but it came in dead last. At first, I put this down to one or two really bad rounds that pushed the averages to the low side, so I shot five more rounds on each load as a check. That resulted in a disagreeable surprise: this time I got 751 and 793, respectively.

Generally, I was satisfied that my theory was correct, but the problem of that .355 jacketed bullet bothered me. Then I had a stroke of luck. I remembered some old Super .38 bullets I had pulled six months or so ago to make up some .38 ACP reduced loads for a friend. I seemed to remember being surprised that these FMJ bullets miked

.356. A search of the loading bench located them and confirmed my recollection. I carefully made up twenty-five of these using load one, and a couple of days later was able to fit in a trip to the range for just long enough to chronograph these .356 bullets through both guns. Through the Colt they averaged 750 fps; about what I'd expected. But through the Smith & Wesson, they gave me 842 fps, better than any of the 125-grain bullets originally shot, and these were 130 grains in weight!

I believe I understand what happened. The relationship of bullet material and bullet diameter to the barrel is a subtle one. What happened with the Smith & Wesson, I am sure, was that diameter .355 is just too small for that gun to form a good gas seal. By slightly increasing the diameter to .356 — just .001-inch — the change is dramatic! Going beyond that to .357 still gives good velocity, but the increasing resistance and friction begin to take their toll.

So, do Colt .38s, in fact, "shoot harder" than Smith & Wessons? Yes and no. I think it's clear, though, that tighter barrels tend to handle lead bullets more efficiently, and looser ones do the same thing for jackets.

The important thing to remember is that every gun is different; unlike even the next one to come off the factory production line. Also, it's worth noting that minute differences in diameter seem to make pronounced differences in bullet performance. I suspect this may tend to show up more with Smith & Wessons in .38 Special caliber because the depth of the grooves is significantly greater, and groove depth has quite a bearing upon swaging and the effectiveness of the gas seal achieved.

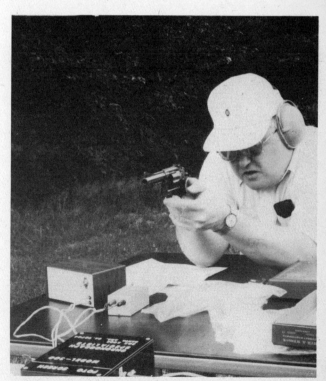

Hamilton, firing S&W test gun over his chronograph.

The Historic Town Of Temecula, California,
Will House Famous Western Firearms Memorabilia

Colt .45 revolver owned by John Selman reposes on a photo of the gunman who killed John Wesley Hardin and twenty other men. It was stolen from Selman's body after he was killed by George Scarborough, about April 5, 1896, at El Paso.

Chapter 18

JOHN BIANCHI'S FRONTIER MUSEUM

By Jack Lewis

GUNS HAVE PLAYED a leading role in the life of John Bianchi. As a manufacturer of leather goods, he is a recognized figure in the international firearms and law enforcement industry. Bianchi, who appeared with Paul Newman in the film, "Buffalo Bill and the Indians," is about to launch his most audacious gun-related enterprise, the Bianchi Frontier Museum which he hopes one day will become the Smithsonian of the American West. Core of the museum will be the 40-year-old Bianchi's growing collection of historic American firearms totalling nearly 125 revolvers, rifles and shotguns.

Bianchi parlayed a home garage business into a multi-million dollar, worldwide industry selling more than 3000 different styles of gun belts, holsters and other accessories to lawmen and sport shooters. He is not awed in the least by his new role as an American museumologist.

"This is an old dream," he says, puffing on a fat cigar and sitting behind a massive desk in the corporate offices of his sprawling Temecula, California, factory. "It's one I have held since I was a kid."

Bianchi took his first real step toward building the Frontier Museum, as it is legally named, seven years ago when he seriously began collecting historic firearms with the acquisition — for $20,000 — of a Colt Single Action Army .45 revolver owned and once carried by Marshal Wyatt Earp. It is a rather plain-looking piece. So plain, you wonder if the flamboyant Earp would own up to it.

"No doubt as to its authenticity," explains Ron Graham, owner of the Antique & Classic Arms Gallery in Yorba Linda, California. Graham has settled into Bianchi's boardroom-turned-mini-museum to appraise and catalog for display the leatherman's gun collection. To make his point, Graham produces correspondence between Earp and Fred Dodge, chief special officer for Wells Fargo & Company, from whose family collection the Earp Colt was obtained. The gun appraisal expert quickly explains the homeliness of the firearm. "Guns were to Westerners like tools are to a farmer and men such as Earp had many of them," he asserts.

The Earp gun, most expensive in the collection, is in character with Bianchi's sense of history. "I look for guns that show character, guns that have good honest use and those with a story to tell," he says. Bianchi demands authenticity and has collected considerable files on all the arms in his collection.

Gun appraiser Graham, pointing to prizes in the Bianchi display cabinets that purportedly belonged to Pat Garrett, Pancho Villa, John Wesley Hardin, the James Brothers, Heck Thomas, Judge Roy Bean, and John Clum, who was Indian agent, mayor of Tombstone, Arizona, and editor of the famed frontier newspaper, the Epitaph, explains that historically documenting a gun is a tedious, time-consuming process that is difficult and dicey at best.

"It takes a long time, much browsing and diligent research to authenticate who owned a gun, when and why he carried it, and how he may have used it," Graham says. "More often, the value of the gun is determined by the notoriety and public popular opinion — not the true importance — of the owner," he asserts. "The notoriety is determined largely by popular image of the gunfighter or Western figure which often is fiction or pure legend created by novels, movies and television," Graham adds.

"A revolver with worn finish or rust with no claim to notoriety or alleged history might be worth $400; with a good finish, perhaps $4000; with an historically proven and popularly-known owner, it can be worth $40,000," continues Graham. The gun appraiser says he does not personally favor this form of evaluating the worth of arms.

"How can you compare the importance of a figure such as Clum to Earp or Harry K. Street?" asks Graham, indicating he classified the latter two as mere tinhorns when compared to Clum.

The Bianchi collection did not happen overnight. It has been a labor of more than a decade and a half.

The Pancho Villa gun was obtained from one Fred Harvey in Encinitas, California, in 1952. Harvey had spent some two years with Villa and recognized the gun, when it turned up in the hands of a trader. He obtained it, adding it

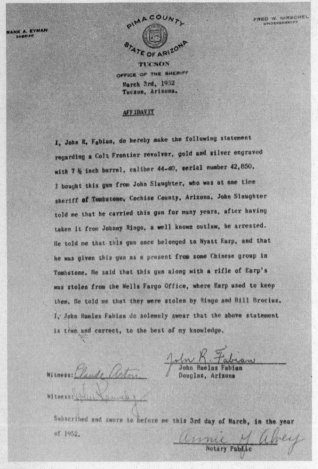

Guns in the growing Bianchi collection are exhibited under glass, with accompanying plaques giving pertinent details regarding their noted or notorious former owners and the particulars of their careers during turbulent frontier days.

Above and below, two sworn and notarized affidavits that identify a .44-40 Colt, serial No. 42850, as one stolen from Wyatt Earp by Johnny Ringo and later recovered by Slaughter, "after quite a battle," with Ringo and Bill Brocius.

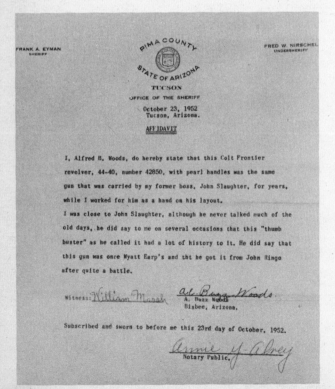

to his own collection. It was singular in that it was made for a Captain Gillett of the Texas Rangers and has a Texas Ranger stamp in the metal. Just how it came into the possession of the Mexican revolutionary is open to question. In addition to grips of walrus tusk ivory, the gun also has a copper-plated cylinder.

The firearms originally owned by Captain Fred J. Dodge, a special agent for Wells Fargo & Company for more than forty years, were offered for auction by the son of the agent. Included in the original collection were a Stevens 10-gauge double-barrel shotgun No. 927, used by Wyatt Earp when he killed the outlaw, Curley Bill. According to Fred J. Dodge, Jr., this same shotgun was used by U.S. Marshal Heck Thomas in killing outlaw Bill Doolin. A Colt Single Action revolver, No. 69562, also is verified as having belonged to Wyatt Earp. A Burgess folding shotgun, No. 3033, was used and carried by Captain Dodge on the thousands of miles he traveled as a special agent for the freight company.

The collection was split up and it was not until 1973 that Bianchi was able to purchase the Wyatt Earp pistol for $20,000. The Stevens 10-gauge was purchased at the same auction by a Texas man for $10,000.

Included in the Bianchi collection is a Colt .45 Single Action originally owned by Judge Roy Bean, the legendary Law West of the Pecos. Bianchi obtained this gun also in

This Colt single-action, serial No. 69562, is fully documented as having once been owned and operated by Wyatt Earp during his law enforcement career. From the collection of Captain Fred W. Dodge, it appears that it must have served its owner faithfully because Earp was one of the rare gunmen of that era who died of natural causes at an advanced age.

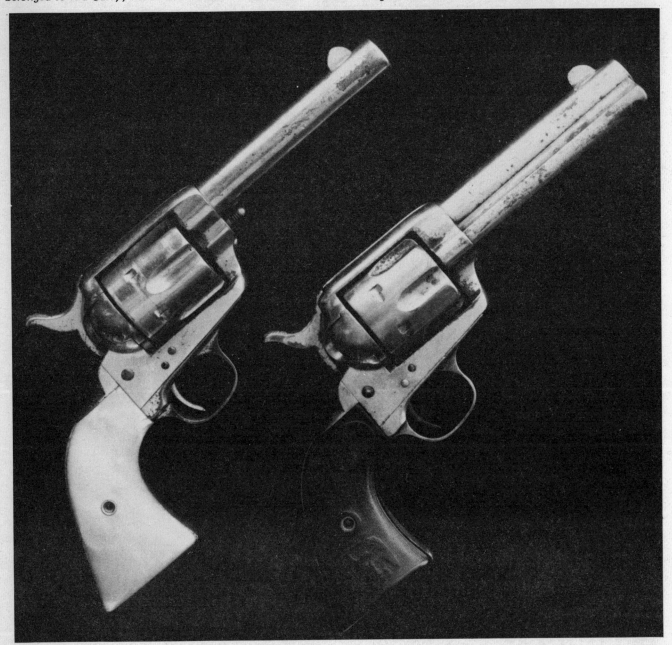

Harry K. Street's gun is the pearl-handled Sheriff's Model at left. Lacking the customary ejector rod, it was necessary to extract spent cases with the aid of a stick or similar means. Gun at right, with stocks of gutta percha belonged to Kid Curry, one of the members of the Hole In The Wall Gang in that distant and lawless point in history.

1973. The trail of authentication shows that the gun was acquired from the State Treasury Office in Austin, Texas, in 1919 by a Captain E.B. Averill. Texas authorities had confiscated this gun, along with other real and personal property of the late Judge Roy Bean "for non-payment of fines collected in his official capacity as judge." This gun was examined by the late Cole Agee, the noted gun engraver, at Fort Worth, Texas, in 1947. Agee identified the engraving as the work of a Mexican engraver, Sergio Moreno, who worked in San Antonio, Texas, in about 1885.

The revolver was identified, according to documentation, "as belonging to Judge Bean by his daughter, Zulema Bean Voss, of New Orleans, Louisiana, in 1947. She stated that the gun was sent to her father by the

British stage actress, Lily Langtry." Bean's distant infatuation with Miss Langtry, of course, has been the subject of many a story and legend, although it has been more or less established that the two never actually met.

This particular single action carries serial number 8054 and has a 4¾-inch barrel, nickel finish and is scroll-engraved, with the words, *Judge Roy Bean, Law West Of The Pecos,* as well as numerous early Texas cattle brands, including XIT, the King ranch, Snake River, Little & Little and the Rocking Chair marks. The gun has one-piece ivory grips.

Authentication of some of the guns has been more simple than with others, of course. For example, a Colt .44/40 single action that belonged to John P. Clum, founder of the *Tombstone Epitaph,* was obtained from

John Clum, posing in the center of group at left, was the founder of Tombstone, Arizona's pioneer newspaper, the Tombstone Epitaph. Quite possibly, he is wearing the same belt, gun and holster shown in the lower photo, although the holster visible in the photo is what we'd term a right-hand type worn for crossdraw and the one in the lower photo is a left-hand pattern.

Clum's long-barreled Colt, web cartridge belt and badly worn holster are depicted in a contemporary photo from the Bianchi collection. Buckle has a bear's-head emblem.

Carol Kingsland Clum Vachon, grandson of the frontier figure. Included with the gun with its 7½-inch barrel and walnut grips — serial number 72157 — was a black left-hand holster and a tan web cartridge belt that Clum owned until his death in 1931.

Clum was Indian agent at the San Carlos Apache Reservation from 1874 to 1877 and was instrumental in the capture of Geronimo. A friend and supporter of Wyatt Earp, he was elected Tombstone's first mayor in 1881.

Included in the Bianchi collection is a .41 Colt, serial number 68837, which had been the property of John Wesley Hardin. It is listed in the inventory of property received for probate, the document being on file in the records of El Paso County, Texas. This particular handgun had remained in the Hardin family until 1970, when it was obtained by Robert E. McNellis of El Paso. Bianchi obtained it in 1975.

Hardin was said to have killed forty-one men during his reign as a gunfighter. Later imprisoned, he studied law and became a lawyer in El Paso upon release. He was shot in the back in a local saloon.

From Jarvis Powers Garrett, son of the late Pat Garrett, the Bianchi collection obtained a Hopkins & Allen XL double action revolver in .32 rimfire. Bearing the serial number 3164, the gun has a blued and case-hardened finish and the barrel is engraved *PATRICK FLOYD GARRETT*. The gun has black rubber grips and a 2¾-inch barrel.

For those who don't make the connection, Garrett was the slayer of Billy the Kid. He was sheriff of Lincoln County, New Mexico, in 1881, and was murdered near Las Cruces, New Mexico, in 1908.

Bianchi now has more than thirty-five wax figures representing noteworthy characters of Western Frontier days. William F. "Buffalo Bill" Cody is the subject of the figure above. All of the figures are rendered full lifesize and finished to the finest possible detail, based upon photographs. When possible, authentic period costumes are used.

Wax figure at left, wearing hat, is Jesse James. The one of Tom McClury, right, will take a place in the OK Corral diorama.

Another gun that was authenticated with ease was a .38 New Navy Model double action Colt that belonged to lawman Heck Thomas. The gun bears the serial number 130541 and has a six-inch barrel, with the printed name, *Heck Thomas*, scratched inside the grip.

The gun had been given to Earl W. Thomas, the son of Heck Thomas. The former died in January 1973, at the age of 87. The gun had been passed to Claude Miller, then 71, a nephew, who sold it to the Bianchi interests in 1974.

Heck Thomas, a famous marshal in Oklahoma Indian Territory, is said to be the first frontier lawman to take a scientific approach to crime. He was the inspiration for the *Heck Ramsey* television series, which starred Richard Boone.

Obtained for the Temecula museum in 1973 was a Remington single action .44 revolver with a 7½-inch barrel that was authenticated as having been the property of Frank James. Also included with the Model 1875 handgun — serial number 5116 — was a left-handed holster and a cartridge belt that the famed outlaw brother owned, according to a statement handwritten by Frank James on September 8, 1903.

The gun was surrendered by Frank James to Governor T.T. Crittenden at Jefferson City, Missouri, on October 5, 1882.

Another Frank James gun — a single-action Colt Bisley Model — also is in the Bianchi collection. In .32-20 caliber with a 5½-inch barrel and black rubber Colt grips, this gun bears serial number 304918 and was used by James as a "prop gun" when he and Cole Younger starred as "The Wild West Out-Laws of the James Gang" with the Cole Shows in 1909-10.

Charles Frohne of Parsons, Kansas, obtained the gun from James in 1910 at Corsicana, Texas, after James and Younger decided to quit the show. In his last years, Frank James was a ticket taker in a theater in St. Louis, which shows he didn't desert show business totally.

Frohne sold the gun in 1959 to Illinois collector George Virgines, who in turn, sold it to the Bianchi collection.

To date there is one noted lawman not represented in the collection: Bat Masterson. But this lack may be by design.

Upon retiring from law enforcement, Masterson went to New York and became a sports writer on the long defunct New York *World*. He is reputed to have purchased numerous guns from local hock shops, carved notches in the grips, then sold them to anyone who had the price for a Masterson gun.

As Graham documents, Bianchi is busy putting his latest dream together, piece by piece. He says he intends to produce an animated and dynamic museum which will entertain and enthrall the visitor.

The museum building itself, which he plans to construct on freeway-fronting property adjacent to his seven-acre plant site about two miles outside historic little Temecula, "will be Spanish-style architecture, roomy, bright and airy within." Architect for the project, Ron Stevens, did much of the design of Disneyland in Anaheim, California. Bianchi says he plans to have the first unit of the museum, a 5000-square-foot building. He plans to build a number of

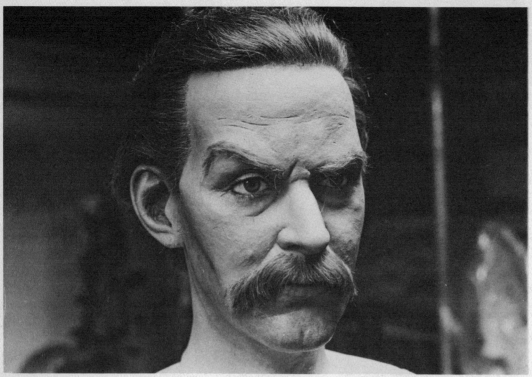
The legendary "Doc" Holliday, dentist turned gunfighter, also will be placed in full-scale re-creation of OK Corral battle.

One of the few originals from Bianchi's collection of wax figures from the modern era is John Wayne, who has been costumed in same style as seen in one of his late films.

The famed Mexican revolutionary general, Francisco "Pancho" Villa (1877-1923) is depicted as he appeared at the zenith of his tempestuous career, bandoliers and all.

No wax in this one! The flesh-and-blood Bianchi holds a trophy made up in July 1975 to commemorate production of the one-millionth Bianchi holster: Several acres of hide!

other buildings at the same time and will use them for commercial purposes until each is needed to expand the Frontier Museum.

"I want this to be a true museum in every sense," states Bianchi, who plans to develop a research facility and reference library as an integral part of the complex. The Frontier Museum will not be a commercial enterprise, avows Bianchi, and any admission charge will be only enough to maintain and expand the museum. He estimates that he will have spent $1 million from his own pocket.

"Since I want the best for the museum, I am getting the best," asserts Bianchi, launching into a description of far-flung activities presently under way. "I have the last living craftsman who worked for Wells Fargo restoring two stage coaches — an Abbott & Downing Concord Coach, and a mud coach — in Northern California," he explains. "The latter looks like a wagon with seats and the Concord is the one you see in the Western movies."

Bianchi also has commissioned Henry Alvarez, whom he describes as "this country's finest wax-figure artist," to create fifty replicas of individuals who have made Western history. Several of these wax figures, including Geronimo, Wild Bill Hickock, Frank James, Wyatt Earp, Bill Cody and Billy the Kid, have already arrived at the Temecula plant and are stashed in lofts and storerooms where they are being authentically attired in arduously collected clothing and artifacts.

"Authentic Western clothing and accessories are not easy to find and we end up making most of the costumes which involves some prodigious research work," Bianchi explains.

He plans to stage the wax figures in dramatic scenes. One such exhibit will involve the Gunfight at the O.K. Corral. "With absolute authenticity," — Bianchi has Western historian John Gilchrease researching the event — "we are going to create, at eye level, that gun battle. The viewer will be given every dimension and will be able to walk in and out of the scene, looking down gun barrels and seeing the event as it actually happened," Bianchi explains. This exhibit, as many of the others, will also feature sound effects, he says.

For presentation of the stage coaches, Bianchi is having four stage horses mounted. "These were unusual animals," he says, "and were probably a crossbreed of the Morgan and the Mustang although I am not absolutely certain of that." Bianchi is also having a Nineteenth Century cavalry horse mounted for a scene showing an Army officer capturing Geronimo, the Apache chief.

He is designing wall-hanging displays which incorporate artifacts, photography and artwork. In one such case, Bianchi has installed the hemp noose used to hang Black Jack Ketchum, with contemporary photographs of the hanging in which the force of the fall tore the outlaw's head from his body. It is an arresting display.

Bianchi's chief assistant in his museum venture and his in-house curator is Frank Boyer, a native of nearby Hemet and formerly a retail chain store executive. Boyer says the museum also will house an impressive collection of Bianchi custom belts and holsters which include three leather and silver commemorative models valued at $15,000, $20,000 and $25,000 each. One, called the Buffalo Bill matched holster set, was worn in the aforementioned movie by Paul Newman, who recruited the versatile Bianchi to play a cavalry officer when he took the equipment to the scene of filming in Calgary, Canada.

The manufacturer-become-museumologist has converted virtually every available empty space, including his spacious, paneled boardroom, in his modern, seven-year-old plant into a work area for the museum. Along a wall adjacent to the employees' lunchroom stands a handsome, sculptured, floor-to-ceiling, wall-to-wall authentic cherry wood Western bar that Bianchi found in Kansas and resurrected.

Just a few feet from the assembly and packaging areas, where many of Bianchi's two hundred employees work, is a diorama re-creation of the town of Temecula as it appeared in the Nineteenth Century. The diorama, which shows many of the community's still-standing and well-preserved historic buildings, reflects Bianchi's interest in his adopted community.

"Temecula is a town time passed by and we have an opportunity to preserve much of its history and that long-ago flavor and feel," says Bianchi who, in his boosterism, recently became president of the Temecula Historical Society and a director of the local Chamber of Commerce. He sees the historical restoration work in Temecula and his Frontier Museum as mutually complementary and is leading an effort to preserve the city's many historic buildings which reach back to the period when Temecula was a crossroads in California and an important byway of the Western immigration.

"This community has a long and colorful history," he explains. It was an Indian village, a Spanish outpost, a wagon stop, stagecoach station, railroad town, agricultural center and is now a fast-developing, modern California community of residential, commercial and light industrial activity. Bianchi hopes to make it a tourist center, too.

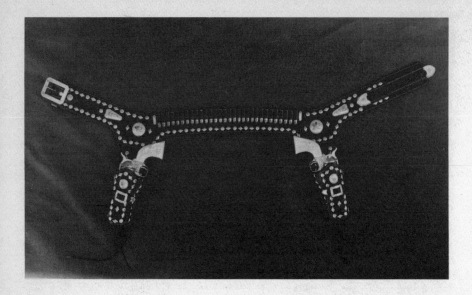

Display includes sample of the more elaborate and ornate work from the Bianchi shop, such as this twin rig.

Highly engraved Colt, with stocks of checked ivory, was once the property of Judge Roy Bean, the self-styled Law West of the Pecos. It's said to have been a gift to Bean from British actress Lily Langtry; they were mutual fans, although they never happened to meet each other.

This rather startling specimen from the Bianchi collection was made up as a factory display gun for display at shows.

A holographic memo displayed with this single-action Remington revolver affirms that the pistol, scabbard, belt and cartridges were owned and carried by Frank James and given to Dr. A.H. Corkwright, "...during his lifetime and just before I surrendered. Frank James."

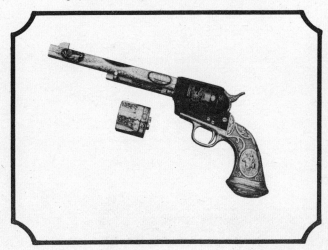

Probably the revolver least likely to be used for driving a staple into a fence post is this Tiffany Colt, with intricately hand-chased grips of sterling silver and spare cylinder.

Not too many years ago, John Bianchi was an officer on the Monrovia, California, police department, making holsters in his garage during off-duty hours. Today, he's the head of one of the largest holster factories and spends available free time bringing his dream museum to reality.

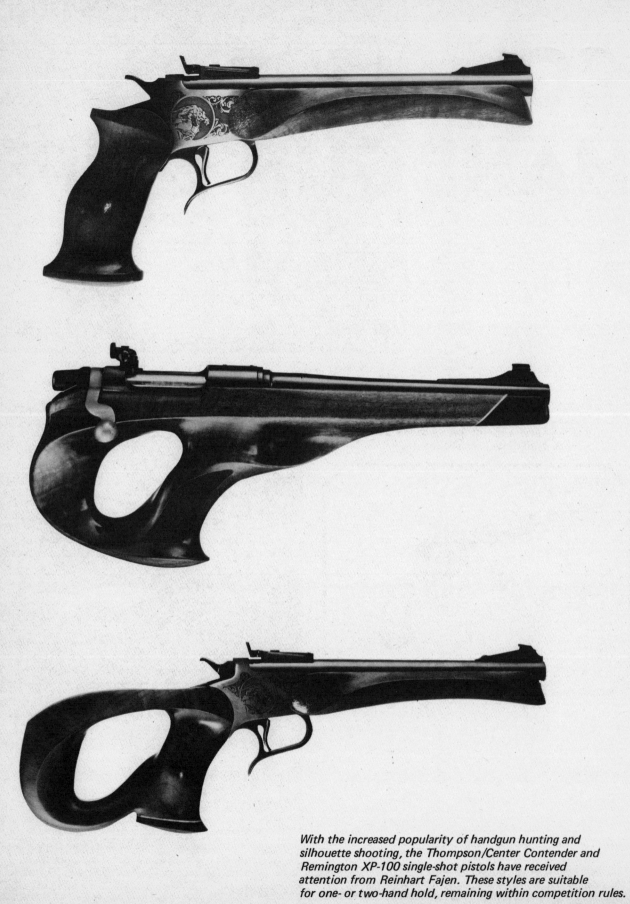

With the increased popularity of handgun hunting and silhouette shooting, the Thompson/Center Contender and Remington XP-100 single-shot pistols have received attention from Reinhart Fajen. These styles are suitable for one- or two-hand hold, remaining within competition rules.

Chapter 19

COMMERCIAL HANDGUN GRIPS

Quick And Easy Handgun Customizing Merely By Changing Your Grip!

By Roger Combs

WHAT DOES it cost to have a handgun customized? The answer is limited only by the number of dollars in the budget. There may not be any actual limit; only a practical limit to the number of things one may do to a handgun and still have it operating. At any rate, a gun owner may spend upwards of a thousand dollars on customizing and be forced to wait up to three years for some of the top, over-committed gunsmiths of the country to finish the job.

Most of us would find that much time and money unacceptable. At the same time, most of us would like to do some sort of customizing work on our favorite handguns to the point that they don't look like every other one produced. Furthermore, customizing may be more than merely an ego trip to cause one to stand out in a crowd. Any given pistol or revolver may or may not correctly fit the hand that holds it. Changing the factory grip may be a necessity for optimum utilization.

Putting some sort of new grip on your favorite handgun is easy, fast and inexpensive, yet it seems to be something that a lot of handgunners overlook. Prices on good wooden stock blanks — the kinds which allow the shooter to form and finish a grip to exactly fit his own hand — start as low as eight or nine dollars. Other wood or plastic revolver grips will vary from $12 to $15, on up to $100 for a carefully selected walnut or maple stock, specially designed to take the added recoil of a powerful, modified XP-100 metallic silhouette shooting pistol. Both ends of that scale are rather specialized products; you may not have the requisite skill/time/inclination to fashion your own pistol grips and you may not be into silhouette shooting. For most of us, owners of a well-known brand pistol or revolver, a new set of grips will put only a mild dent in the checking account to the tune of $15 to $30; reasonable, indeed.

While there may be some exceptions somewhere, most all the replacement grips on the market today are manufactured and sold to the consumer already inletted to fit the particular handgun for which they were designed. Installation of a replacement grip, then, is rapid and simple. It is merely a matter of unscrewing one or two screws from the gun, removing the factory grip or grips, slipping on the new one and replacing the screws. Those steps must be qualified in some cases to allow for minor model gun-to-gun differences, but that is basically all there is to customizing a gun with a new grip.

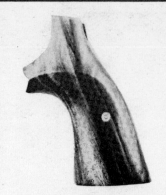

J.L. Galef offers replacement grips for target use on Colt, Smith & Wesson and Ruger.

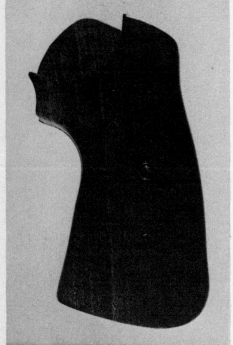

Schiermeier of Idaho offers replacement stocks for most popular American handguns, ready to install with a screwdriver, left and below. Inletted walnut blanks, above, for the Contender, are available for under $7.

Another Galef style is combat round-bottom grip of imported Philippine bolong, oiled wood.

Combat square-bottom style replacement grips by Galef.

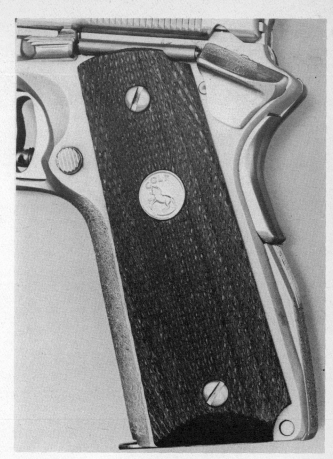

Personal taste is the final judge as to the relative beauty of a replacement grip such as the tiger-stripe Oregon myrtle by Paul Holguin at left, or the checkered grip retained on the customized autoloading pistol at right.

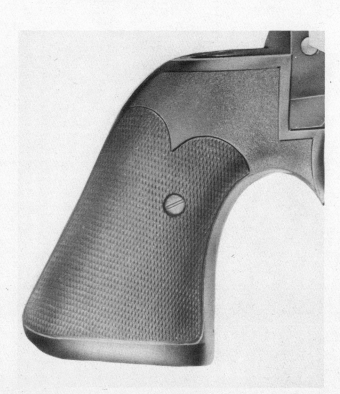

Pachmayr's hard-rubber replacement grips for the Ruger Super Blackhawk are of one piece but open like clam shell, enclosing the frame in a smooth backstrap.

Changing or replacing the grip is simple enough but what kind of a grip should we choose? Aye, there's the rub. Before we can answer that question, we must ask another or two. Why do we want to change the grip and what purpose will the handgun serve?

It is probably an oversimplification to state it this way but if the only purpose of replacing the grip is cosmetic, all we should have to do is look at the products available for the gun in question and pick out the one that looks the best. Of course, nothing is that simple.

Different designs of handgun grips facilitate different functions for the hand and the gun. Does the shooter participate in weekly practical pistol combat matches or merely the semi-annual get-together at the local range? Are the usual targets paper bull's-eyes, metal silhouettes or discarded tin cans in the desert? Is the shooter engaged in law enforcement work with the gun concealed for eight or ten hours a day? Perhaps the gun in question is an eight-inch-barreled Dan Wesson used for hunting big game throughout the North American continent. Use defines form.

Again, there is the size of the hand(s) to be considered. There are big hands and small hands; long fingers and short fingers. The Dan Wesson .357 Magnum revolver, for instance, is normally sold with a standard checkered zebrawood target grip. As far as I know, the thing is designed for the Jolly Green Giant. I don't consider my hands as particularly small but there is no way I can safely handle the gun with that grip on it. To reach the trigger, I

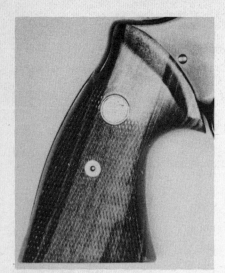

Sile oversize, checkered-walnut grip on J-frame MK III Colt.

For serious target work, the Sile auto-pistol checkered grip with thumbrest, adjustable heel rest.

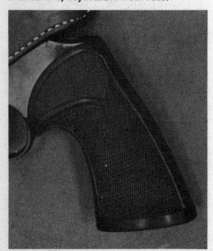

Two-inch Dan Wesson, Pachmayr grip and Bianchi holster make ideal concealment combination.

Fuzzy Farrant produces checkered ebony grips for S&W K-38.

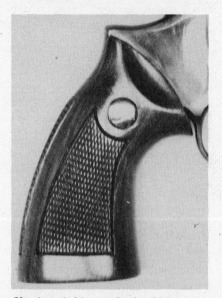

Checkered side-panel grips from Sile help control High Standard and Dan Wesson Revolvers.

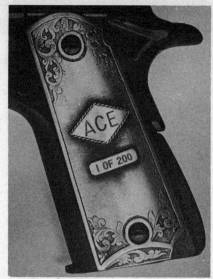

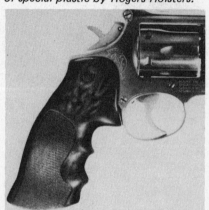

Sid Bell makes grips for Colt Ace rimfire, above, of traditional pewter, while replacement grip for S&W Combat Masterpiece, below, is made of special plastic by Rogers Holsters.

Smith & Wesson centerfire automatics benefit from Sile full target replacement grip.

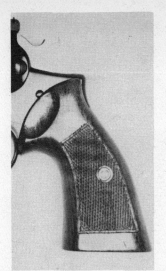
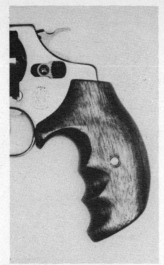

Two additional Sile grips for Ruger Security Six, new-model backstrap, left, and S&W J-frame round butt.

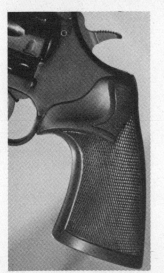

Pachmayr offers large and small hand grips for Dan Wesson. Skip-line checkering, right, is by Herrett.

All Ruger Security-Six models will accept Sile's checkered-walnut grip, completely covering grip frame.

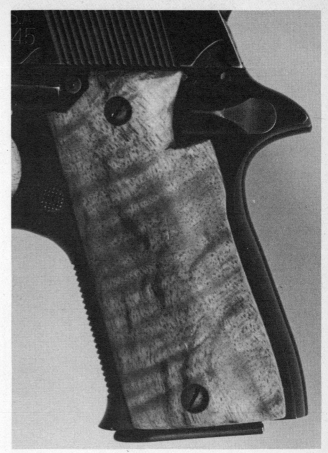

Paul Holguin produces beautiful replacement stocks of Oregon myrtle for Star Model PD .45 autoloader.

had to slip the stock to my left in the right hand until all the recoil was being taken up on the lower part of my right thumb instead of the heel of the hand where most of the padding is.

There are several remedies for this situation. The Dan Wesson people offer a couple of alternatives: With the requisite time and skill, one may fashion a customized grip using the Dan Wesson inletted walnut wood blank. That may be more work than most of us bargain for but if the stock doesn't fit the hand properly after carving, we have no one to blame but ourselves. The company also offers such interchangeable grips as their oversize target model, plain or checkered; a combat style and a Sacramento style. The latter two are smaller and faster to draw from a holster.

The other possibility for the small-handed individual who owns a large-gripped revolver is to attack the problem from a slightly different angle, going to Pachmayr Neoprene rubber grips. Most models of popular American guns, such as Smith & Wesson, Colt, Ruger, Dan Wesson and Charter Arms, plus the Italian Astra .357 may be grip-exchanged with Pachmayrs. Most of those models are further available in large or small size grips. There are some shooters who do not care for the appearance of any kind of grips except wood on their handguns. Others find no objection to the black, checkered rubber appearance and enjoy the positive feel and comfort provided by the Pachmayr Presentation grips. The replacement grips sell for under thirteen bucks. For the auto pistol shooter, grips for some Colts, Brownings, Smith & Wessons and Walthers are

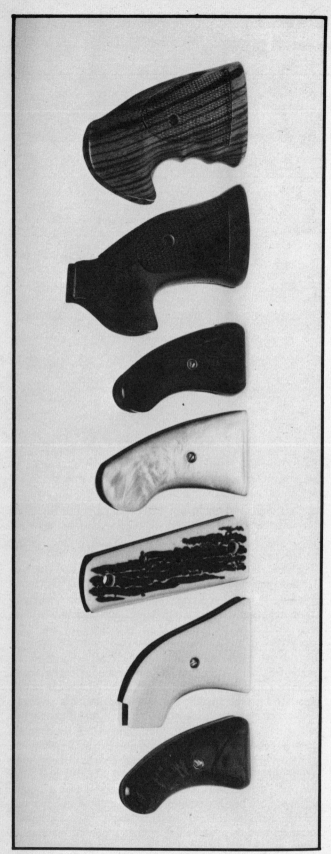

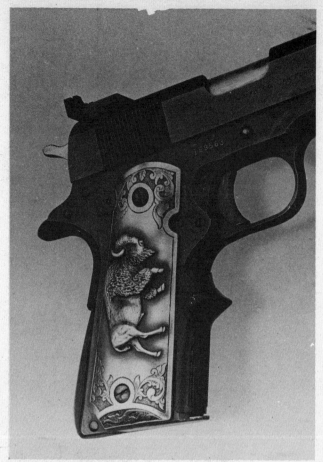

Artist Sid Bell displays his talent carving pewter figures for Colt auto-pistol replacement grips.

Heavy-frame magnums may need grip with extra checkering, as at upper left. Sile's smooth rosewood replaces Colt M1911 issue grips.

Jay Scott grips, an operation of Colt Firearms, makes replacement grips for various pistols and revolvers of several materials. A polyester-laminate material called Armarc is used for first five grips from bottom; checkered walnut next; checkered zebrawood on finger-groove model.

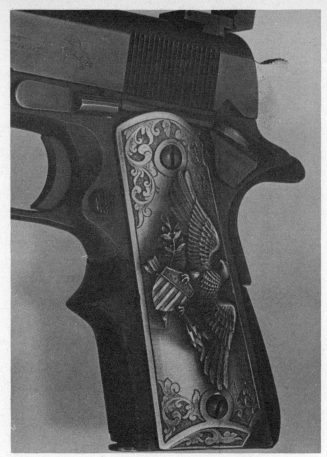

American eagle design in pewter, by artist Sid Bell, enhances and customizes any automatic-pistol grip.

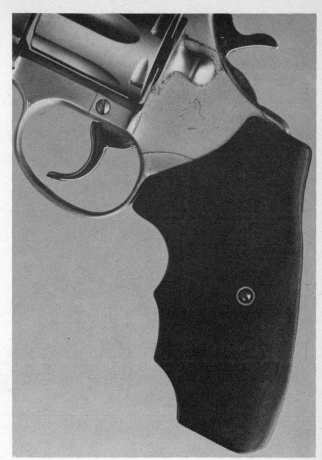

Colt Detective Spl. restocked with Fuzzy Farrant ebony.

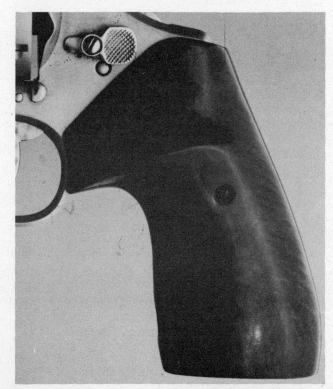

Jordan Trooper model by Herrett, carved from fancy walnut, replaces stocks on Smith & Wesson Model 1917.

marketed, although they only come in one size. Pachmayr grips are popular with the law enforcement buyer, as well as the hunter and target shooter.

The styles, materials and gun models produced by the Jay Scott people of Colt Firearms are discussed elsewhere in this book and need not be repeated here. The Jay Scott people make replacement grips for more guns than merely Colt and their catalog would indicate one of the most varied choices of styles, colors and functional grips anywhere.

Some stock and grip makers tend to specialize in certain handgun makes or functions. Steve Herrett, in Idaho, makes carefully-designed grips for many handguns but may be best known for his Controller model for the Thompson/Center Contender single-shot pistol.

Also up in Idaho and also producing some fine replacement stocks for the Contender, is Ted Schiermeier. He has gone a step further than merely producing hand-filling stocks for the Contender, Smith & Wesson, Colt and single-action Ruger. He has introduced some laser engraving into the wood.

The appearance of the laser engraving is striking, indeed. Schiermeier describes the process, using an invisible beam of laser light, as heating selected portions of the wood to a high temperature, hot enough to literally vaporize the wood. He says the individual wood cells are actually cross-sectioned without damage and very little, if any, charring is visible. Clearly, this is a case of a replacement

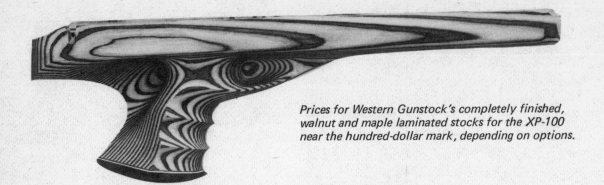

Prices for Western Gunstock's completely finished, walnut and maple laminated stocks for the XP-100 near the hundred-dollar mark, depending on options.

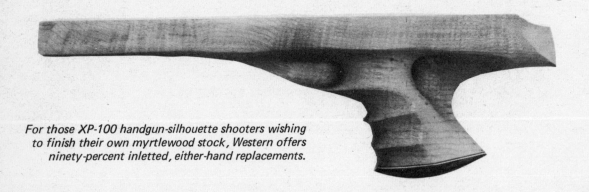

For those XP-100 handgun-silhouette shooters wishing to finish their own myrtlewood stock, Western offers ninety-percent inletted, either-hand replacements.

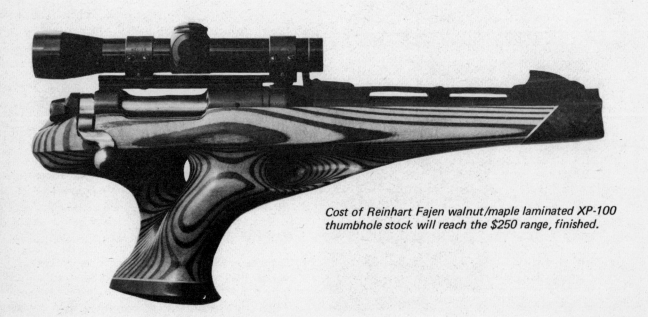

Cost of Reinhart Fajen walnut/maple laminated XP-100 thumbhole stock will reach the $250 range, finished.

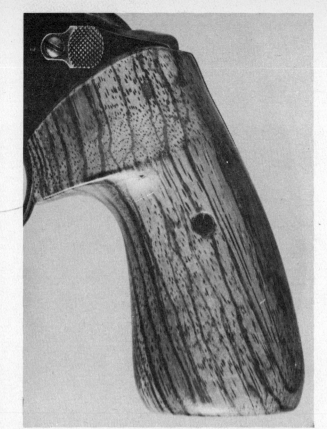

Herrett's Combat Masterpiece zebrawood Jordan Trooper.

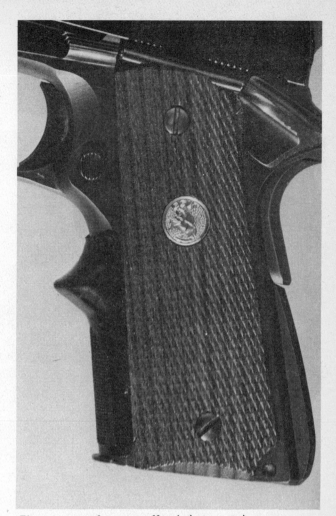

Firearms manufacturers offer their own replacement grips at times, such as this fancy, walnut set by Colt.

Philippine monkeypod wood is the raw material for this Colt Python replacement stock by D & J Exotic Grips.

stock which has both functional and cosmetic advantages for the shooter.

Somewhere near the top of the price scale for factory-made handgun replacement stocks are the ones offered by Western Gunstock of walnut and maple for the Remington XP-100 and Wichita actions. Models are available for right or left-hand shooting, in different densities and weights for hunting, varminting and metallic silhouette target shooting. Western offers a number of options/styles with prices nearing a hundred dollars at this time.

Other well-known stockmakers, such as Fajen who is better-known for his rifle stocks, produce some beautiful replacements with which to hang on to the XP-100 or Contender.

It makes no sense to invest any dollars at all in a new set of grips for your favorite handgun if there is no improvement in the gun, either in appearance or function, or both. If the revolver or pistol in question is satisfactory just as it comes out of the factory box and if it shoots just the way the owner expects it to, there is no more to be said. But if some customizing is in order, for whatever reason, examine the many styles of replacement grips on the market today. There is sure to be one or two which will fit your needs to provide you with an easy and inexpensive customizing job for your pistol or revolver.

Fajen's Sidewinder stock is offered in the thumbhole and thumbrest configurations. Both are mounted under Remington XP-100. Styles are available for the Wichita pistol and Shilen BP action. Banana-forend shape is designed for silhouette prone-shooting.

Herrett makes this Controller replacement stock for the Thompson/Center Contender large-caliber handguns.

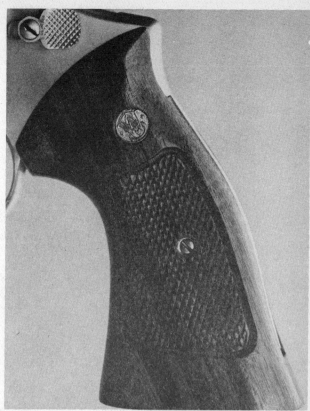

Smith & Wesson makes its own replacement stocks for medium-frame revolvers of exotic Goncala alves wood.

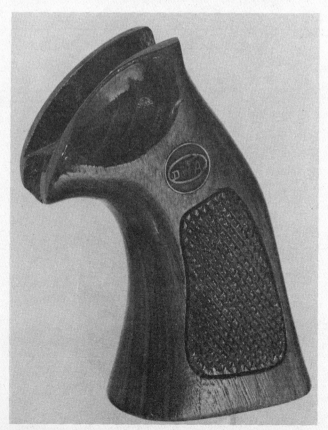

Checkered walnut, oversize target-model grip for Dan Wesson, is easily interchanged by one screw.

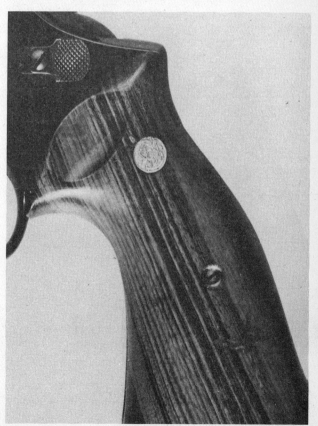

This S&W factory stock for target work is of zebrawood.

HANDGUN COLLECTING

Chapter 20

By John R. Hansen, Jr.

Generalized Or Specialized —
Pistols And Revolvers Become
Collector Items For Many Reasons

ANYONE WHO HAS been around guns for any time has heard the term "collectors' item" used in the description of a certain firearm. I have talked with gun people with many different interests and have been surprised at times to find out what the term meant to some. For example, while attending a large gun show on the east coast, I met a fellow who was displaying a rather extensive collection of Smith & Wessons. This fellow had one of everything that the factory had produced starting from the early 1950s to present.

His collection included blue and nickel models that gave choice of finish, plus the unusual factory two-toned models; a mix of blue and nickel parts. I spoke with this fellow for some time, although I must admit that he did most of the talking. He informed me of the number of gunshops visited and phone calls involved in obtaining such an extensive collection. When I stepped over to the next display, I overheard another fellow who was wearing an exhibitor's badge proclaim to his friend that the Smith & Wessons were not collectors' items but were production guns and should not have been allowed in the show.

Later I found out that this fellow collected pre-war Colt single actions. Now, at the time they were being made, the Colt SAAs were also production guns. Was this fellow correct in thinking that the current Smith & Wessons were not collectors' items while his Colts were? Is a Smith & Wesson five-screw .44 magnum any less of a collectors' item than a Colt SAA .38 Special with British proofs? The answer is yes to some and no to others.

Let us examine some of the factors that might make a gun a collectors' item. First is availability. The fewer items produced the harder they are to obtain. In the case of the .44 magnum Smith & Wesson versus the Colt SAA, the Smith & Wesson is easier to obtain but certainly cannot be called readily available.

Another factor affecting desirability is quality. Here both the Smith & Wesson and the Colt are about the same, although some might argue the point.

Also to be considered is appreciation of value. The British-proofed Colt is already worth big money and is constantly increasing in value. The Smith & Wesson .44 magnum now commands a premium price and will probably appreciate more as time goes on.

One curious category that warrants mentioning is the White Elephant; a gun that was introduced by a maker that never sold well enough to warrant keeping in production. A classic example of this is the Ruger Hawkeye. I am sure that William B. Ruger wishes to forget about this gun from the sales point of view but just show a mint example to a member of the Ruger Collectors Association and watch him reach for his billfold. Ruger produced several thousand of these guns before they were discontinued and they were sold for less than $100 new. Today, each commands over $500. In review we find that our example Smith & Wesson .44 magnum and Colt SAA conform to much the same criteria, making them both collectors' items.

Gun collectors have diversified interests, collecting odd and common brands, rare and routine specimens. There are some who specialize in only one model and others who collect whatever they fancy at the time. Which method is the best for you?

The type of collection that excites me the most is the one containing a variety of guns. I recently found a collection owned by a person who collected guns for more than thirty years. When first asked what type of guns he had he replied, some Lugers, Colts, Smiths, and maybe a Ruger or two. I went to his home to have a look. There was a first year of production Colt Official Police in .22 Long Rifle, a somewhat well-used Ruger .44 Flat Top, several Lugers and some 1930s vintage Smith & Wessons.

After the financial details were taken care of I asked the fellow how he came by so many good guns. The collector said he had originally collected Lugers but after a time found out there were too many variations. He sold or traded most of them off for guns that seemed to be well made and good looking. Although some of the guns were made in the latter part of the 1960s, each one could be considered a collectors' item because of scarcity, low serial numbers or because they conformed to some of the earlier-mentioned criteria.

Deciding what to collect, the individual should pick a type of gun that personally appeals to him, whether it be one type of handgun, or handguns in general.

One does not have to be wealthy to acquire a quality collection. For example; Sturm, Ruger, a firearms company that is only about thirty years old, has made and distributed quality products since its inception. Good

The S&W Model 29 at the top and the Colt Single-Action Army revolver both are highly prized by collectors.

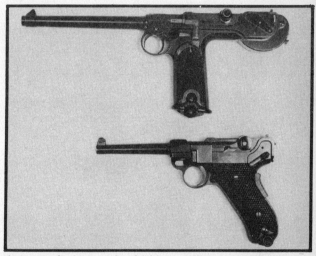

Luger at the bottom is a highly modified, streamlined and improved version of the original Borchardt, at top.

From top, Model 1900 Luger, Model of 1906 and Model of 1908. Note the dished toggle knobs on the Model 1900.

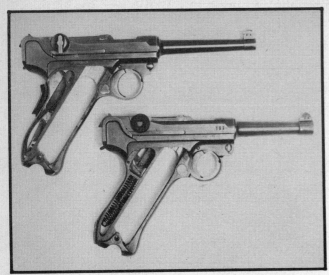

Upper gun is Luger Model 1900 with S-type mainspring and anti-bounce latch. Later Lugers are found with the coil-type mainspring and no latch in the toggle mechanism.

The "Broomhandle" Mauser Military Model is considered one of the most important developments in firearms design and it paved the way for modern military semi-automatics.

discontinued Rugers may still be found on dealer's shelves at reasonable prices. Several good collectable Rugers may be had for the same price that a fair condition Broomhandle Mauser would bring. Before starting to collect, research your choices before making a decision. It may not be wise to start collecting a model only to find later that more than three hundred variations are needed to complete your collection.

One of the most collected handguns today is the Luger, or Parabellum, as it is known in Europe. The Luger is a refinement of the Borchardt pistol, brainchild of Hugo Borchardt. Georg Luger was responsible for streamlining the design, eliminating much of the Borchardt's bulk.

Variations of the Luger can be broadly broken down into three basic categories: 1900 Old Model; 1906 New Model; and the 1908 New Model, the most common.

The 1900 is equipped with a grip safety, leaf-type mainspring, dished toggles and an anti-bounce latch. The 1906 is equipped with the grip safety but deletes the leaf-type mainspring in favor of a coil spring, and uses a different design toggle, frame, and receiver. On this model the anti-bounce latch was also deleted. The 1908 has the new type machining of toggle frame and receiver as the 1906 but does away with the grip safety in favor of a thumb safety. The thumb safety was common to all models. The two calibers encountered in versions of the Luger pistol are 7.65mm and 9mm.

Lugers were produced from 1900 through WW II, although dropped as the standard German military handgun in 1938. The Luger was also a contender for the standard U.S. military handgun but lost out to the Model 1911 Colt autoloader. Lugers were manufactured by several makers, the most prolific of these being DWM of Berlin.

The Luger pistol is probably one of the most aesthetically pleasing handguns of its day. From the military point of view, however, it is one of the worst. To quote a friend, "a Luger is a jam waiting to happen." The

design is sensitive to dirt and needs full-power ammunition to function properly, due to the deficient toggle lock mechanism. The Luger is also expensive to produce, requiring hundreds of machining operations and careful hand-fitting. No general gun collection should be without a Luger.

No listing of collectors' guns would be complete without mention of the Mauser Model 1896, or as it is better known, the Broomhandle. Futuristic in looks and ungainly to handle, the Broomhandle Mauser was perhaps one of the most significant designs ever produced. The Mauser pistol design paved the way for other semi-automatic pistols of the future. It proved that a self-loading pistol was practical for military purposes.

The Broomhandle was a commercial success, as demonstrated by its production for almost forty years, during which Mauser produced more than a million units. There are sixty or more variations of this gun and the collector is well advised to obtain several good reference books on the subject.

Mauser produced a holster/buttstock assembly for the Broomhandle which, when installed, transformed it into a carbine. When the gun was not in use, the rear portion of the buttstock could be hinged open and the gun slipped inside for neat storage. One of the more interesting variations of this gun was the *Schnellfeuer* (Machine Pistol). Somewhat useless for sporting purposes, the full automatic capability did, however, add a new dimension of versatility from the military's point of view.

As with all semi-automatic pistols, the development of the Mauser had to await the introduction of smokeless powder which would allow high velocity and clean operation. Found in 9mm Parabellum (Luger) and 7.63mm, the Broomhandle is one of the collectors' most prized semi-auto handguns.

When introduced in 1929 by the German firm of Walther, the Model PP (Police Pistol) was an overnight

Ruger's Hawkeye appeared in 1963. A novel turn-block design, it was a single-shot, chambered for the then-new .256 Winchester magnum cartridge. It turned out to be a design whose time had not yet come and it was dropped after a few years. Selling for less than $100 when new, Hawkeyes now bring $500 or more among collectors.

success. Until that time, Walther had been producing a small line of vest-pocket pistols of single-action design. The PP was a radical departure from many of its predecessors. Here was a design that could be safely carried fully loaded, yet could be fired quickly by pulling straight through on its unique trigger as with a double action revolver.

Walther's new safety system was also a departure from what was considered usual at the time. If the gun was not cocked when the safety was applied, the gun could not fire as the safety prevented full movement of the trigger. Should the gun be cocked and then have the safety applied, the hammer would automatically drop onto a solid piece of steel that blocked the firing pin. It works so well that it has been copied repeatedly by present-day manufacturers.

In 1931, Walther produced the Model PPK (Police Pistol Kriminal), an abbreviated version of the PP. The PPK was intended to be used as a pocket pistol, while the PP was considered a holster arm. The PPK retained all of the features of its brother and was equally as successful. Both guns were produced in .22 long rifle, .25 ACP, .32 ACP and .380 Automatic. The .25 Automatic version is considered the rarest because there were fewer produced in that caliber.

The Walther PP and the PPK are still being produced and sold. The PPK can no longer be imported into the United States because of the Gun Control Act of 1968, although any of the guns imported before the law's passage are still seen on the market.

Colt Firearms was founded in 1836 and, to date, is responsible for the production of millions of quality firearms for sporting, military and law enforcement purposes. Some of the most noteworthy Colts are the Single Action Army, the Model 1911 and 1911A1 Government Model pistol.

The Colt Single Action Army was introduced in 1873 and became a favorite of cowboys, sheriffs and outlaws alike. The pre-war SAAs are a wonder to behold: Faultless case color hardening, rich bluing, with meticulous detail given to fitting. While SAAs did have a tendency to break certain parts, they were easy to repair in the field and could generally be made to function. The most common caliber is the .45 Colt, although the .44-40 Winchester Center Fire was the most-fired cartridge in the Wild West. Today the collector must look long and hard to find a precious, mint pre-war example of this arm and once found the price it may fetch looks more like a telephone number than a retail figure.

The Colt .45 Government Model has been the standard U.S. military issue handgun since its adoption in 1911, when it beat out the Luger and Savage pistols in a severe series of tests. The 1911 stayed the same from the time of adoption until June of 1926, when the military decided to iron out deficiencies noted in the gun. The new model was modified and re-designated the Model 1911A1. The M1911A1 modification includes an arched mainspring housing to help eliminate the tendency of the gun to point low; extending the tang of the grip safety to eliminate hammer bite; shortening the trigger length and adding cuts in the frame behind the trigger to accommodate an average-size hand; improving the sights; and changing the internal barrel dimension.

Colt also produced a great number of double-action revolvers worthy of collecting. Fourteen different models alone are listed in the 1939 edition of the Stoeger catalog.

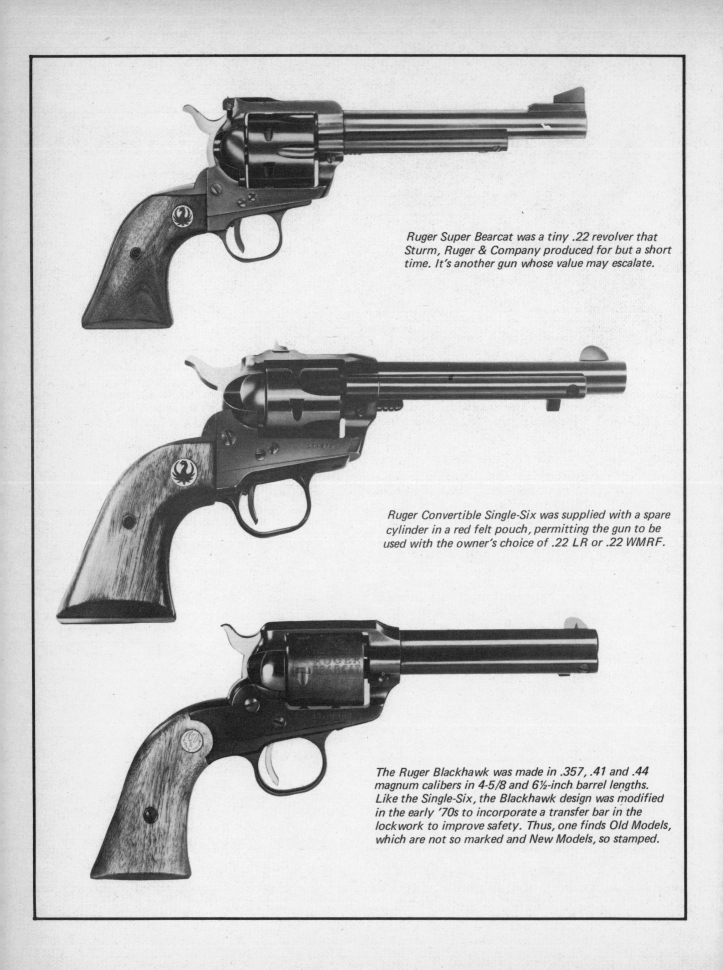

Ruger Super Bearcat was a tiny .22 revolver that Sturm, Ruger & Company produced for but a short time. It's another gun whose value may escalate.

Ruger Convertible Single-Six was supplied with a spare cylinder in a red felt pouch, permitting the gun to be used with the owner's choice of .22 LR or .22 WMRF.

The Ruger Blackhawk was made in .357, .41 and .44 magnum calibers in 4-5/8 and 6½-inch barrel lengths. Like the Single-Six, the Blackhawk design was modified in the early '70s to incorporate a transfer bar in the lockwork to improve safety. Thus, one finds Old Models, which are not so marked and New Models, so stamped.

Ready interchangeability of parts makes it a real challenge to collect an authentic specimen of the Model 1911 Colt such as the one shown here. The numerous variations of the basic M1911 design make it an interesting field for the collector who wishes to specialize. Right, the Walther Model PPK/S is another example of a gun with collector interest potential.

Colt's quality probably peaked in the 1930s even though they still produce some of the finest guns in the world.

The relative newcomer into the world of quality handguns for the collector is Sturm, Ruger and Company, founded in 1949 by William B. Ruger. The firm's first gun was the Standard Auto. It was and is a best buy for the money. Later came the single action revolvers which the company was able to sell reasonably because of their development of investment-casting manufacturing methods. Using this process, much of the expensive machining operations are eliminated and a quality product still results. Ruger produces .22s, .357s, .41s and .44 magnums that many feel are among the nicest handling and dependable single actions made.

Some of the collectable Rugers are the early Standard Autos, the aluminum cylinder Single-Six .22s, the flat gate Single-Six, the flat top .357 and .44 magnums and the Hawkeye single shot. Now that Ruger has introduced the new improved model Single-Six and Blackhawk series, almost any old model may be considered collectable. I do not include the Ruger Bearcats because they are still around in fairly great quantities.

No discussion of collectors' handguns would be complete without mentioning Smith & Wesson. Smith & Wesson has always been one of the finest producers of hand-held firearms in the world. A distinct characteristic of older S&Ws is the total lack of tool marks and superb polish and blue. Smith & Wesson is responsible for giving the world .357, .41 and .44 magnums. When introduced in 1935, the .357 magnum created quite a stir among hand-gunners. The gun was massive, and the bullet boasted a muzzle velocity of 1,512 feet per second, then the most powerful production handgun in the world. The original .357 sold for about $60 new and I doubt it could be duplicated for ten times that today because of the hand work involved. Handgunners are a hearty breed and when S&W produced the .44 magnum in the mid-1950s, American shooters could not get enough of them.

Current production Smith & Wesson Model 29s command a premium price. The older four- and five-screw .44 magnums are every bit as nice as the earlier .357s and the collector may expect to pay a stiff premium if one is found.

WHAT EVER HAPPENED TO

After A Two-Year Gap, The Auto Mag Is Again

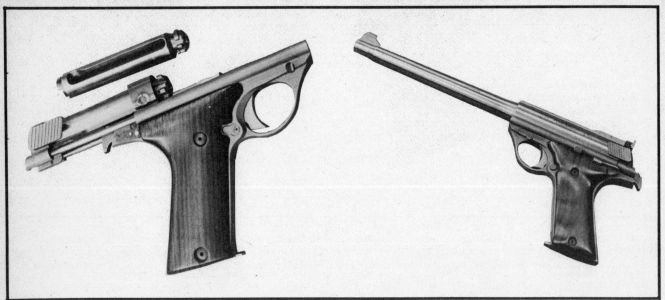

The Model B Auto Mag features a solid bolt shown installed on frame at left; heavier Silhouette barrels, 8½ or 10½ inches long.

By Roger Combs

OWNING AND SHOOTING an Auto Mag pistol is a lot like owning and driving an expensive hot rod or fine sports car. It's a lot of fun, it gives you all kinds of prestige, it attracts attention but after a few hundred rounds, you have to take it down and tune it up. Those, more or less, are the words of one Harry W. Sanford, designer and manufacturer of the Auto Mag pistol.

"The Auto Mag is a hot rod. I just got tired of making it, along about 1977," said Sanford. "We've made some changes and improvements to the gun and will make about five hundred more 'Model B' pistols. When all the parts are used up, that will be it. I don't plan to make any more Auto Mags."

The Model B is basically the same gun that appeared on the handgunning scene in the late 1960s, except that the six-lug locking bolt is solid metal, versus the slotted model originally produced. The solid bolt, says Sanford, makes the gun function better, and is stronger and more reliable overall. The gun with the solid bolt is a definite improvement over the old model, he claims.

Owners of original model Auto Mags need not despair nor go out and purchase an entire Model B to receive the benefits of the newer bolt configuration. The new model bolt will interchange into the older guns although some machining and welding is required to exchange bolts. Cost of the modification, including the new bolt is $250 from Arcadia Machine & Tool Company, 11666 McBean Drive, El Monte, California 91732.

The second modification from old to new model is a heavier barrel for metallic silhouette shooting. The Model B may be fitted with the newer barrel, as ordered, or any one of the original Auto Mags may accept the 8½-inch or 10½-inch stainless steel barrel. The new barrels are marked "Silhouette" on the side. As of the present Sanford is not planning to produce any other barrel lengths for the Model B. Original Auto Mags had barrels of 6½ inches but the owner or prospective buyer of either model will have to look elsewhere to obtain a barrel of that length. Sanford says he has no intentions of producing the shorter barrels.

When conceived, the Auto Mag was intended primarily

Chapter 21

THE AUTO MAG ?

In Production — But The Numbers Are Limited!

Developer and manufacturer of the Auto Mag, Harry Sanford, right, displays new model of successful pistol, to retail for about $1,000.

Barrel locking/unlocking latch is located on forward edge of trigger guard, magazine latch to rear of trigger guard, safety to rear and above grip; hold-open assembly in center.

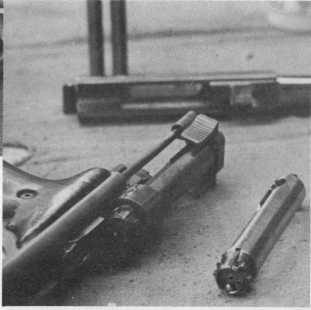

Original model Auto Mag was marketed with channeled out bolt, right. Pistol functions better with solid core. Auto Mag features six locking lug bolt.

Early in 1974, plans were announced that the manufacture of Auto Mags would be taken over by High Standard. Early production High Standard Auto Mag with vented rib is shown above. Left, old and new models must be partially disassembled in order to reach trigger adjustment screws.

Acceptable accuracy load for older model .44 AMP calls for 20.0 grains of Hercules 2400, behind 240-grain Sierra JHP bullet.

Ammunition for the .357 AMP, left is necked down from original .44 AMP.

Alloy used by Auto Mag proved so tough, few pistols were engraved.

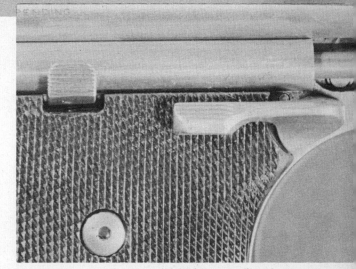

Creditable group measures 1.1 inches, top, fired from 25 yards. Loading consisted of 20.0 grains of 2400 powder over 240-grain Sierra bullet. Hold-open latch was not included in first Sanford design, now standard.

for the long-range handgun hunter. Handgun metallic silhouette shooting had not gained wide acceptance in the United States until more than a decade later. However, the Auto Mag itself was instrumental in the introduction of the sport, first in Arizona, in September 1975.

The first national match of handguns against steel silhouettes was the many-month project of Lee Jurras, an early Auto Mag enthusiast and official of the Club de Auto Mag Internationale, Incorporated. The club sponsored the 1975 match, called the 1st National Handgun Metallic Silhouette Championships, held at Three Points range, near Tucson, Arizona. The original plan was to restrict handguns used in competition to the Auto Mag in its various calibers but as things progressed and as the match was shot, fourteen of the forty-six shooters who participated used Auto Mags. Six competitors used .357 Auto Mags, seven shot .44s and one fired a .41 Auto Mag pistol. These figures

compare with twelve shooters using Model 29 Smith & Wesson revolvers chambered in .44 magnum and eight using the Ruger .44 magnum. Popularity of all of these guns for silhouette shooting has not diminished one bit.

The course of fire in that first national handgun silhouette match was basically the same as that which is being used in the sport today. One shot, two courses are fired at each silhouette; a perfect score would be forty points. Chickens are shot at fifty meters, javelina at one hundred meters, turkeys are set out 150 meters from the firing line and rams are placed at two hundred meters. With its tight grouping and flat trajectory, the Auto Mag was then and continues to be a popular choice for the thousands of handgun silhouette competitors in North America. Attend any large handgun silhouette match in the country today and there are sure to be several Auto Mags in evidence.

As further tribute to the popularity of silhouette

shooting since the introduction of the original Auto Mag, Sanford is offering what he calls a silhouette sight as an option to the Model B. The silhouette sight allows the shooter of metallic targets to pre-sight-in the gun at the normal ranges — fifty meters, one hundred meters, 150 meters and two hundred meters — from the targets. With the turn of a small screw, the gun sight may be set for any pre-selected range. Adjustments are within the sight itself, with a camming arrangement permitting rapid, precise sight settings without the usual click or mark counting for different distances. The gun, according to Sanford, should be a winner on the handgun metallic silhouette circuit.

Old and new model Auto Mags are known for their accuracy and relatively mild felt recoil. During some early testing of the gun, all groups fired at a starting twenty-five yards were well within silhouette-size limits. They also proved to be so at one hundred yards. There is no question as to the accuracy of Auto Mags in competition.

Most shooters find the recoil noticeably less than that felt when firing a revolver with .44 magnum, factory or reloaded ammunition. Many say the jolt is no tougher than that from a .45 ACP hardball pistol. The action of the autoloader is meant to reduce the velocities, but at the same time, less powder is needed to gain the same velocities as in a revolver, because of the lack of gas leakage from the gap between cylinder and barrel.

The trigger pull on most Auto Mags is crisp and even and

is fully adjustable with two Allen screw stops positioned inside the frame. Having the trigger adjustment in this location means one has to remove the barrel assembly to adjust the trigger. This is a bit inconvenient and some may prefer it located externally.

Removal and replacement of any Auto Mag barrel, to reach the trigger adjustment screws or for any other good reason, is the simplest of tasks. With the magazine removed from the pistol, the cocking piece is pulled fully to the rear and the hold-open thumb piece is pressed. The hold-open thumb piece is located forward of the safety lever, on the gun's left side as viewed from the rear. The hold-open is levered manually upward to engage the bolt and lock it and the cocking piece in the rear position.

A barrel latch is located also on the gun's left side, just above and forward of the leading edge of the trigger guard. Serrated, the latch swings down approximately ninety degrees to unlock the barrel. Then the barrel and extension assembly slide forward and off the pistol frame. One merely reverses the procedure to return the same or another barrel to the frame.

Trigger adjustment is done with the barrel removed, using the Allen 5/64-inch hex-head wrench, as mentioned. Sanford cautions the buyer to fire his Auto Mag enough times to become familiar with the factory settings before attempting any trigger adjustments. The trigger-play adjustment screw is located in the top of the frame

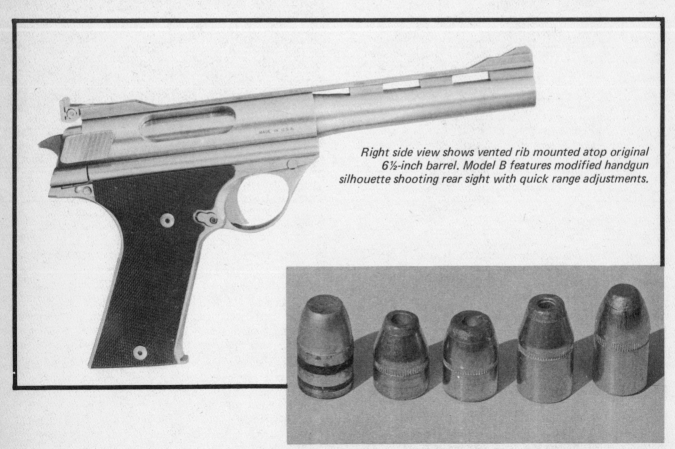

Right side view shows vented rib mounted atop original 6½-inch barrel. Model B features modified handgun silhouette shooting rear sight with quick range adjustments.

Tested .44 AMP bullets include, from left, Lyman cast No. 429434; 180-grain Super Vel; 200-grain Speer; 240-grain Sierra and 265-grain Hornady bullet. Results are in text.

Original Auto Mags were sold with padded carrying case, below. Hex-wrench for rear sight adjustment, shown right. Old and new models are easily field stripped, below right.

Fitted, padded case, above, featured space for spare magazine, lubricant and provision for ammunition container.

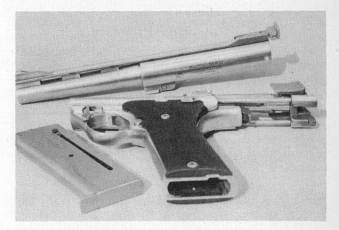

Bolt face, above, reveals six locking lugs, extractor and rod-type ejector, unchanged from earlier models. From left, .30/06 Springfield, .308 Winchester ammo, with empty and loaded .44 Auto Mag Pistol cartridges.

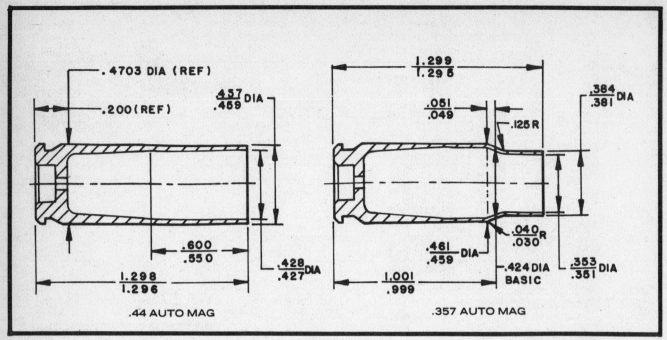

The .357 Auto Mag cartridge is formed by running the .44 AMP cartridge into a .357 AMP sizing die, as described in text.

immediately above the trigger. The barrel and extension assembly must be removed from the frame in order to gain access to the adjustment screws, as described above. Sanford cautions that insufficient play may make the pistol action inoperative after firing one cartridge. Counter-clockwise rotation increases trigger play. Excessive play, according to the manufacturer, is not conducive to accurate shooting.

The trigger overtravel adjustment screw is located in the center of the trigger and may be adjusted without pistol disassembly. Clockwise rotation decreases trigger overtravel. Again, Sanford warns that insufficient trigger overtravel may make it impossible to fire the Auto Mag. Counterclockwise rotation of the screw increases trigger overtravel. Accuracy will be adversely affected by excessive trigger overtravel.

The barrel, rib, if any, receiver and sights are all one assembly. Removal and replacement of the unit should not interfere with accuracy. A shooter may have several barrels; in the original 6½-inch length or the Model B 8½ or 10½-inch configuration. Or barrels chambered in .357, .41 or .44 Auto Mag Pistol may be equally facilitated on one frame. Sanford contends that once each barrel is sighted-in individually, none would change the point of bullet impact, no matter how many times they are changed.

The head of the rotary bolt shrouds the cartridge base completely and features a rod-type ejector on the left side of the bolt face. This is true for the old and the new models. The bolt itself is supported by a ring extending upward from the rear of the frame. The bolt is inserted from the rear through the ring. A cross bolt is placed through the ring and a longitudinal slot in the bolt acts as a bolt stop.

Attached to the rear of the bolt is a wing-shaped affair with serrations on each side. Beneath this are two rods, one

on either side of the frame, extending from the tube-shaped parts on the frame that house the recoil springs. The rods act as guides and are attached to the bolt.

The frames are investment cast of stainless steel alloy containing titanium. The alloy is extremely tough and durable but difficult to machine. Engraving an Auto Mag takes special skills and special tools, as many have found. It can be engraved, but not easily.

The first factory loads for the Auto Mag were on the market in the mid-1970s. This ammunition was produced in Mexico with a headstamp of CDM over .44 AUTO MAG. It was available in 240-grain jacketed hollow point in .44 Auto Mag only. Then, as now, cases for the .357 AMP may be formed by a single pass into the full-length resizing die of that caliber, as available from RCBS. It should be noted that large-pistol primers are recommended for reloading either the .44 or .357 AMP, not large-rifle primers.

Norma-Precision offers .44 AMP factory loaded ammunition and cases for the reloader. Norma (Lansing, New York 14882) is producing a 240-grain load with jacketed power cavity bullet (Index No. 11105) together with .44 AMP unprimed cases (Index No. 21102). The loaded ammo blasts out of the standard-length Auto Mag barrel at 1350 feet per second (fps) for 975 foot-pounds of energy (fpe). It sells for a bit over $27 per box of fifty. The unprimed brass is $13.30 per fifty and bulk lots of brass are available through holders of a federal firearms license only.

The .44 AMP brass is easily converted to .357 AMP or .41 Jurras Mag Pistol (JMP) by means of a pass into the full-length resizing die of the intended caliber. As with all the other Norma cases and ammunition, the .44 AMP is Boxer-primed and readily reloaded with primers and equipment in normal supply.

For those shooters of the Auto Mag who are reloaders, we asked Dean A. Grennell, Managing Editor of *Gun World*

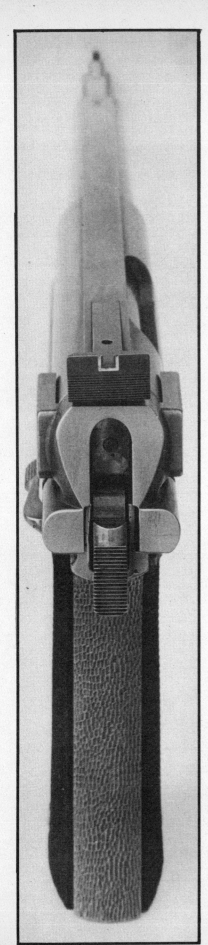

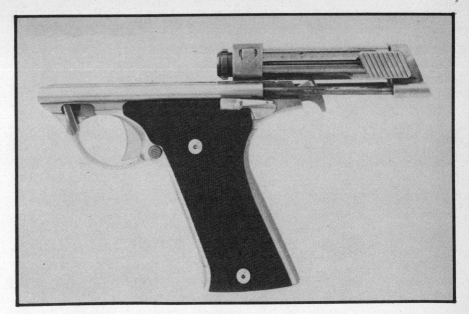

Breech assembly rides rearward on two guide rods. This view is of older Auto Mag model, identified by absence of hold-open assembly.

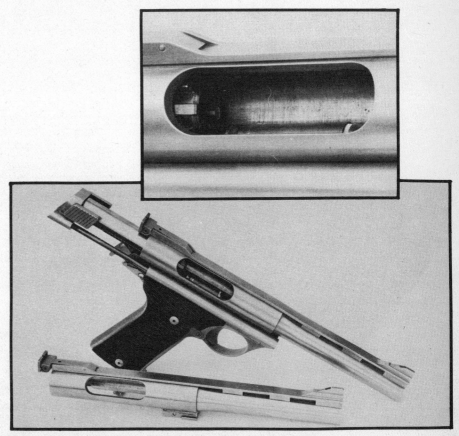

Top: View through right-side ejection port in receiver shows ejector rod and cartridge-enclosing bolt face. Gun barrels of varying lengths and chamberings may be swiftly interchanged without disturbing strike of bullets. New barrels fit old frames.

Earlier Auto Mags had stippled frame; newer models are serrated. All have exposed hammer, light recoil.

Magazine and co-editor of this volume, to provide some preliminary loading data. Here is the report:

Loading procedures are fairly routine and straight-forward. Auto Mag recommends the use of large-pistol primers. You may find that these will bottom out well below the surface of the case head, as they are slightly less thick than large-rifle types. This does not seem to pose any significant problem, ignition being totally reliable in the tests. Possibly, large-rifle primers could be used, but there would not seem to be any obvious advantage in so doing.

Length over all (LOA) must be adjusted to assure positive feeding from the box-type magazine. This will vary, according to the nose profile of the bullet being used. In general, the various types of jacketed soft point and hollow point bullets have cannelures for crimping when used with revolvers. If the case neck is brought to the center of this cannelure, the LOA should be correct. Note that the .44 AMP is given a gentle taper-crimp. It should not be roll-crimped in the same manner as the .44 Rem mag because, as with the .45 ACP, the loaded round headspaces by contact between the case mouth and a ledge at the front of the chamber.

In the tests, Grennell used a flat bullet seating punch and seated all loads to a LOA of 1.610 inches, finding that this worked well with all bullets used.

Factory data supplied by Auto Mag, specifies use of the CCI-350, magnum-type, large-pistol primer. Grennell used this same primer throughout all of the tests.

Supplementary data was worked up by use of the load-ready, unprimed brass supplied by Auto Mag, after conducting tests which showed that cases made from military brass by means of Eagle dies functioned fully as well. Cases were primed with CCI-350s, chamfered inside the mouths and taken to the test range with a press, scales, powder measure and supply of assorted bullets and powders. This permitted the desirable process of starting low and working up cautiously, as conditions seemed to warrant. A T333 Avtron chronograph was hooked to a photo-screen box by Chronograph Specialists — offering the two-fold advantage of being able to save considerable time

by recycling at the push of a button, besides being able to chronograph and fire groups on target simultaneously. Firing was by use of the adjustable iron sights (well, stainless steel sights, to be precise) off of a sandbag rest on the bench.

There seems little profit in devoting extensive discussion to group sizes obtained, beyond noting that several were quite gratifying. As is common with bolt action rifles, groups expanded or shrank as the charge weight of powder was varied behind any given bullet. It is highly probable that another individual Auto Mag might "go to sleep" and group its tightest with a load up or down a grain or three of powder from those which gave best groups in the test gun.

For what it's worth, 20.0 grains of Hercules 2400, behind the 240-grain Sierra JHC bullet, grouped astoundingly well. The first three shots, at twenty-five yards, all went into one hole. Center to center spread, as well as it could be measured, was less than .025-inch — with the fourth and fifth shots about .322-inch between centers, but ending with a maximum spread of 1.100 inches for all five.

Gathering some white chips of claybird and placing them on the dusty bank of the range backstop showed that it was immensely capable from a two-handed, standing hold at one hundred yards. It was common to either hit the chip or land the big slugs so closely that it went flying in the ensuing ruckus. It was rare for the radius to exceed an area equal to the vitals of a deer or steel pig at that distance.

Dean Grennell spot-checked several of the combinations listed in the factory-supplied load data, finding that the chronograph agreed within the natural minor variations. In fact, it came out considerably closer than most such data when attempting to verify it.

Grennell branched off to explore some of the bullets and powders not covered in the dope from Auto Mag. He had brought along the remnants of a box of the 265-grain JSPs made by Hornady for use in the .444 Marlin, wanting to see how these might perform in the big silver pistol. Seated to the same 1.610-inch LOA, they fed and fired flawlessly. He obtained peak velocity with this bullet on a rousing 18.0 grains of Alcan AL-8 powder; 1315 fps, about 1015 fpe.

Which is hardly a moment too soon to ring in the

Norma-Precision offers .44 AMP factory-loaded ammunition as well as empty cases for reloading, described in text.

Earlier factory ammo was available only from Mexico.

familiar refrain: Approach all maximum listed loads with caution in any individual handgun. Reduce charge weights if the loads are to be fired in extremely high temperatures; ambient temperature for the tests, by the way, was 97 degrees F. Since the writer and the publisher have no control over techniques and materials used in reloading, they cannot and do not accept any liability, expressed or implied, for events arising from the use of data listed here.

Running the 18.0 grains of AL-8 down the weight scale of bullets, a 240-grain Sierra went 1367 fps; a 200-grain Speer went 1297; and a 180-grain Sierra went 1367 fps.

Hodgdon's H4198 — virtually identical to D4198 — proved a bit too slow-burning to be efficient in the 6½-inch

barrel with this cartridge. A charge of 23.0 grains was as much as could be compressed behind the bullet at the requisite LOA and a 240-grain Speer bullet went to 1064 fps while a 200-grain Speer barely hit 1015 fps.

Norma's N-200, being denser, permitted a charge weight of 26.5 grains and gave 1152 fps with a 180-grain Sierra, 1173 fps with a 200-grain Speer and 1210 fps with a 240-grain Speer.

The load which grouped well — 20.0 grains of 2400 with Sierra's 240-grain JHC — clocked 1261, 1270, 1261, 1267 and 1239 fps; remarkably consistent uniformity. Raising the charge weight to 21.0 grains of 2400, same bullet, gave

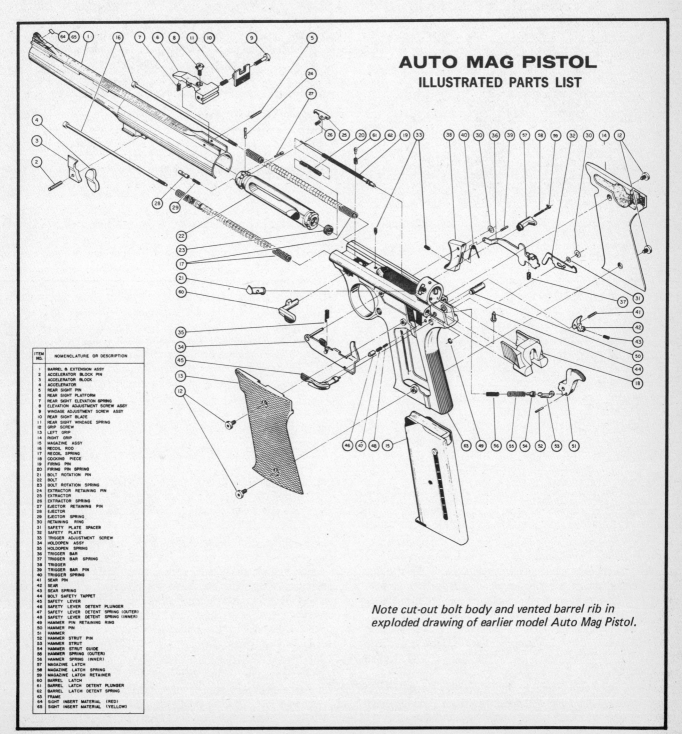

AUTO MAG PISTOL
ILLUSTRATED PARTS LIST

ITEM NO.	NOMENCLATURE OR DESCRIPTION
1	BARREL & EXTENSION ASSY
2	ACCELERATOR BLOCK PIN
3	ACCELERATOR BLOCK
4	ACCELERATOR
5	REAR SIGHT PIN
6	REAR SIGHT PLATFORM
7	REAR SIGHT ELEVATION SPRING
8	ELEVATION ADJUSTMENT SCREW ASSY
9	WINDAGE ADJUSTMENT SCREW ASSY
10	REAR SIGHT BLADE
11	REAR SIGHT WINDAGE SPRING
12	GRIP SCREW
13	LEFT GRIP
14	RIGHT GRIP
15	MAGAZINE ASSY
16	RECOIL ROD
17	RECOIL SPRING
18	COCKING PIECE
19	FIRING PIN
20	FIRING PIN SPRING
21	BOLT ROTATION PIN
22	BOLT
23	BOLT ROTATION SPRING
24	EXTRACTOR RETAINING PIN
25	EXTRACTOR
26	EXTRACTOR SPRING
27	EJECTOR RETAINING PIN
28	EJECTOR
29	EJECTOR SPRING
30	RETAINING RING
31	SAFETY PLATE SPACER
32	SAFETY PLATE
33	TRIGGER ADJUSTMENT SCREW
34	HOLDOPEN ASSY
35	HOLDOPEN SPRING
36	TRIGGER BAR
37	TRIGGER BAR SPRING
38	TRIGGER
39	TRIGGER BAR PIN
40	TRIGGER SPRING
41	SEAR PIN
42	SEAR
43	SEAR SPRING
44	BOLT SAFETY TAPPET
45	SAFETY LEVER
46	SAFETY LEVER DETENT PLUNGER
47	SAFETY LEVER DETENT SPRING (OUTER)
48	SAFETY LEVER DETENT SPRING (INNER)
49	HAMMER PIN RETAINING RING
50	HAMMER PIN
51	HAMMER
52	HAMMER STRUT PIN
53	HAMMER STRUT
54	HAMMER STRUT GUIDE
55	HAMMER SPRING (OUTER)
56	HAMMER SPRING (INNER)
57	MAGAZINE LATCH
58	MAGAZINE LATCH SPRING
59	MAGAZINE LATCH RETAINER
60	BARREL LATCH
61	BARREL LATCH DETENT PLUNGER
62	BARREL LATCH DETENT SPRING
63	FRAME
64	SIGHT INSERT MATERIAL (RED)
65	SIGHT INSERT MATERIAL (YELLOW)

Note cut-out bolt body and vented barrel rib in exploded drawing of earlier model Auto Mag Pistol.

The Auto Mag Pistol, itself, helped bring about the introduction of handgun metallic silhouette shooting to the United States from its neighbor to the south. Pistol offers the necessary knock-down power to flatten heavy steel ram silhouettes at 200-meter range.

1390, 1367, 1375, 1386 and 1381 fps; still excellent uniformity. But the group expanded to 2.572 inches, from the previous 1.100 with the lighter charge, although four of the hits were within 1.250 inches.

The foregoing example points up an important difference between the .44 AMP and the .44 Rem mag when fired in revolvers: Absence of a gap between barrel and cylinder means no pressure loss at this point. As a result, you tend to match the revolver velocity with substantially less powder.

Switching back to the 265-grain Hornady, 16.0 grains of 2400 gave 993 fps and worked the action, as did 17.0 grains of 2400 at 1091 fps and 18.5 grains of 2400 at 1213 fps. There were no obvious pressure signs at this point, but the base of the bullet was commencing to compress the powder and experience has shown that 2400 tends to lose velocity as you begin to compress the charge.

Wanting to try some cast bullets, Grennell selected Lyman's number 429434 gas-check design as one which duplicated the nose profile of the jacketed bullets closely. Cast in straight linotype alloy, this bullet weighed 215 grains and 18.5 grains of 2400 gave it a comfortable and effective 1226 fps of velocity, with flawless functioning through the action. Groups averaged around the two-inch mark at twenty-five yards — acceptable and probably capable of improvement through trial-and-error research. This cast bullet design — listed under the caliber .44-40 in the Lyman charts — has given highly satisfactory results in several revolvers and rifles chambered for the .44 Special and .44 Rem mag, according to Grennell.

One powder not listed in the Auto Mag load data was Hodgdon's H110, a number which has given good results in .41 and .44 Rem mag loadings. With 21.0 grains of H110

behind it, the 240-grain Sierra JHC slid out at a sizzling 1414 fps, with good uniformity and accuracy.

Staying with H110 and switching to the 180-grain Sierra JHC, 24.0 grains of H110 gave 1447 fps; 27.5 grains of H110 went 1569 fps; 28.3 grains delivered 1618 fps and one final boost to 28.8 grains of H110 screamed through the screens at a howling 1748 fps.

By way of comparison, Speer's Number 9 manual gives data on the 200-grain JHP bullet, using a Ruger Super Blackhawk in .44 Remington magnum in its 7½-inch barrel at 1490 fps ahead of 27.0 grains of H110. While by no means a precise correlation, it appears the gapless barrel of the Auto Mag extracts greater power from comparable loads.

All in all, the .44 AMP checks out as a reloader's dream-cartridge; beefy and tough in the head, since the parent brass is built to withstand the hairiest of rifle pressures; locked into the chamber with full support at the time of firing by a rotary bolt design featuring six locking lugs.

Lee Jurras prefers Winchester-Western's 296 powder for the .44 AMP and the loads listed should be regarded as the maximum and approached with caution. Velocities quoted are from a 6½-inch barrel, of the older model. With the Sierra 180-grain JHC bullet, 32.0 grains of 296 for 1885 fps and 1421 fpe; with the Sierra 240-grain JHC bullet, 26.0 grains of 296 for 1750 fps and 1632 fpe; with the 265-grain Hornady JSP bullet, 24.0 grains of 296 for 1480 fps and 1289 fpe.

The .357 Auto Mag Pistol (AMP) cartridge is derived from the .44 AMP that, in turn, was derived from the .308 Winchester or .30/06 Springfield rifle brass. If formed from rifle brass, some amount of inside neck-reaming will be

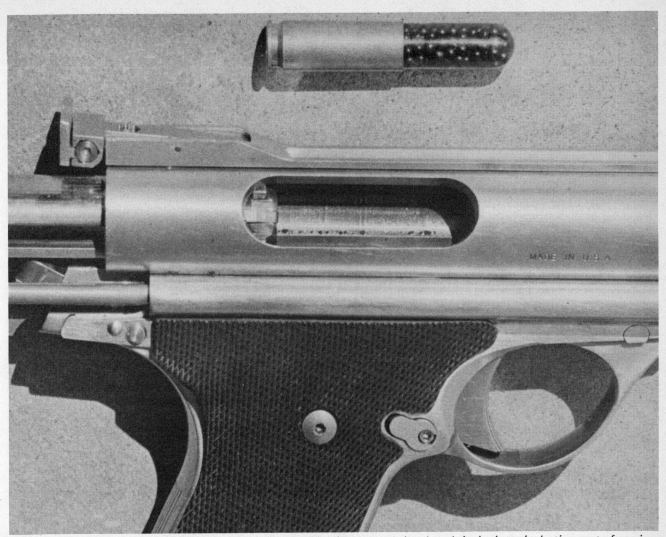

Shot capsule load by Thompson/Center can be loaded in .44 AMP case and chambered singly through ejection port of receiver.

The .44 AMP loading, case-forming and reaming dies, were earlier available from Eagle Products. RCBS is now source for reloaders' Auto Mag supplies, equipment.

necessary. Forming and reloading dies are available from RCBS, Incorporated, Box 1919, Oroville, California 95965, together with instructions for the various operations.

When starting out with .44 AMP brass from Norma, all that is necessary is to apply a bit of resizing lube to the case and run it up into the regular full-length resizing die of the regular reloading die set.

The Speer No. 9 Manual provides the most comprehensive listing of load data for the .357 AMP that is available. Some amount of judgment is needed for effective employment of this data, however. Dean Grennell has had reports from Auto Mag fans that the Speer data, both for the .44 AMP as well as the .357 AMP, may not provide sufficient power to function the action of all guns reliably. As noted in the Speer book, however, they encountered some amount of problems from pierced primers in working up to the levels they list. A change to large rifle primers might help to offset the pierced primers, but this tends to result in failures to ignite.

In Grennell's .357 Auto Mag, a highly satisfactory load consists of 24.5 grains of W-W 296 powder behind the 140-grain Speer JHP bullet. They list 23.5 grains as maximum (1793 fps). Grennell says his barrel carries the Maxi-Mount plus an M8-2X Leupold scope and the added weight on the recoiling parts makes for occasional failures to feed. In another iron-sighted .357 Auto Mag, 24.0 grains of 296 functions perfectly, although 23.5 grains doesn't quite make it. Grennell has not chronographed these loads from local guns, but assume they're getting a touch over 1800 fps, which should be good for upward of 1000 foot-pounds. What impresses him is the load's ability to dot off clusters of holes spanning about one inch at fifty yards.

Needless to say, as with any high-energy handgun, effective ear protection is absolutely mandatory with any of the Auto Mag cartridges. Apart from that, recoil is amazingly mild, being even more gentle if the barrel has been Mag-na-ported.

The .41 Jurras Mag Pistol (JMP) cartridge was developed by Lee Jurras (Drawer F, Hagerman, New Mexico 88232).

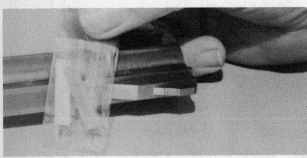

Left: Strips of self-adhesive reflective material, in choice of red or yellow, were furnished for use on rear surface of front sight blade. Improvements in design and production of Auto Mag have been hallmark of pistol's history since introduction in late 1960s.

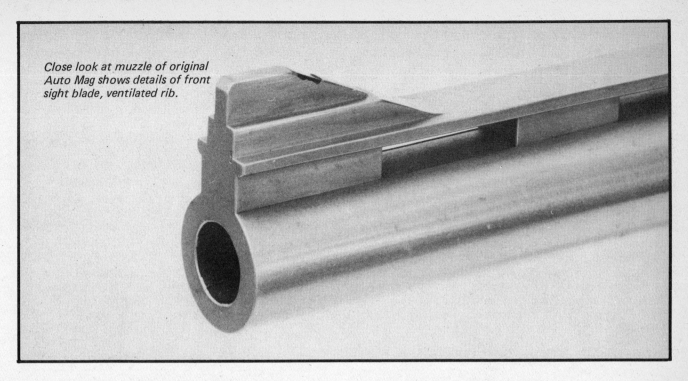

Close look at muzzle of original Auto Mag shows details of front sight blade, ventilated rib.

It is formed by running a .44 AMP case up into the full-length resizing die of the regular reloading die set. Bullets for it are the .410-inch size used in the .41 Magnum.

Not too many of these guns are in service. The barrel extensions can be interchanged in the Auto Mag receiver in the same manner as barrel extensions for the .357 AMP and .44 AMP.

Jurras notes that he has just one load for this cartridge and it works so well he has quit looking for others. It consists of the 170-grain jacketed hollow cavity (JHC) Sierra bullet, with 31.0 grains of Winchester-Western 296 powder. Velocity is 1900 fps and muzzle energy is 1363 fpe. The accuracy of this load in a well-tuned Auto Mag is outstanding, with occasional five-shot groups at one hundred yards clustering close to the one-inch mark. That is with the M8-2X Leupold scope carried in Jim Herringshaw's Maxi-Mount.

Accuracy on that level requires considerable skill in the reloading, plus careful adjustment of the full-length resizing die. Headspace — the dimension between shoulder and case head that regulates the fit of the cartridge within the chamber — must be controlled precisely, so that the action just barely closes reliably in feeding. Since the shoulder is quite shallow, this consideration — important on any bottlenecked case — is exceptionally critical with the .41 JMP. Feeding reliability, says Jurras, is better than with the .44 AMP and about the same as the .357 AMP. Loading die sets are available through RCBS.

Judging from the continuing popularity of the original-design Auto Mags and the growing sport of handgun metallic silhouette shooting, Harry Sanford will be swamped with requests to build more Auto Mags, Model B, or any other model developed. The Auto Mag is distributed and sold through authorized, licensed dealers. While the one-thousand-dollar price tag may seem a bit steep, keep in mind that the original models were on the market at less than $300 in the early 1970s. That price seemed a bit steep then, too.

AUTO MAG LOADING DATA

BULLET	POWDER	VELOCITY (fps)
180-gr. Super Vel	24.0 gr Olin 630-P	1653
	25.0 gr.	1687
	26.0 gr.	1751
	19.0 gr. Norma 1020	1295
	20.0-gr.	1482
	21.0 gr.	1605
	25.0 gr. Hercules 2400	1596
	26.0 gr.	1659
200-gr. Speer	18.0 gr. Norma 1020	1402
	19.0 gr.	1525
	20.0 gr.	1585
	22.0 gr. Olin 630-P	1570
	23.0 gr.	1624
	24.0 gr.	1680
	22.0 gr. Du Pont 4227	1255
	23.0 gr.	1303
	24.0 gr.	1375
	22.0 gr. Hercules 2400	1485
	23.0 gr.	1561
	24.0 gr.	1574
240-gr. Speer	8.0 gr. Hercules Unique	980
	10.0 gr.	1230
	12.0 gr.	1346
	17.0 gr. Olin 630-P	1259
	18.0 gr.	1319
	19.0 gr.	1384
	20.0 gr.	1428
	18.0 gr. Hercules 2400	1252
	20.0 gr.	1378
	21.0 gr.	1435
	22.0 gr.	1479
	15.0 gr. Norma 1020	1245
	16.0 gr.	1329

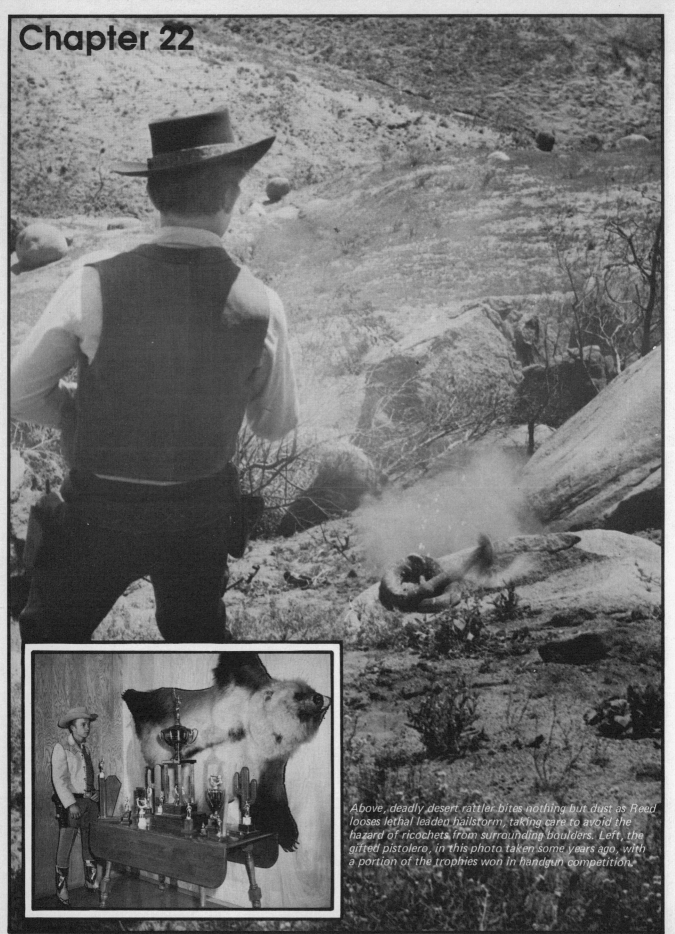

Chapter 22

Above, deadly desert rattler bites nothing but dust as Reed looses lethal leaden hailstorm, taking care to avoid the hazard of ricochets from surrounding boulders. Left, the gifted pistolero, in this photo taken some years ago, with a portion of the trophies won in handgun competition.

For his serpent safari, Reed packed along an assortment of twelve handguns, proving equally adept with all of them. The smaller derringer carries .38 Special shot cartridges.

BATTLE FOR A RATTLE

Techniques For Handgunning Rattlesnakes Are Simple — Once You Find The Reptile Den!

By Jack Lewis

A BRIGHT-FACED young man, Thell Reed, Jr., didn't exactly cut his teeth on a sixgun, but has been shooting against expert handgunners almost from the time he was able to level the muzzle at the age of 7.

Today, he is considered one of the fastest and most accurate handgun shots in the world, handling a Single Action .45 with the speed that would make even most Double Action shooters turn in their gunbelts if forced to compete against him.

Not only has he won most of the combat shooting events in the Western states, but he has made the professional rodeo circuit as an exhibition shooter. Touring Japan with Casey Tibbs, he doubled as trick shooter and bronc rider, adding to his personal laurels. During a tour with the U.S. Marine Corps, he taught gun handling to recruits.

Reed has killed deer and javelina with his sixguns, and has proven himself far above average with a rifle and shotgun. In his first try at trap shooting, he broke

forty-eight of fifty birds, a showing that many oldtimers would give their favorite tube guns to achieve on a regular basis.

But there is a difference in watching anyone fire at a silhouette target in a combat shoot and seeing him in action in the field. With this thought in mind, we originated a Southern California rattlesnake hunt.

The snake hunt was set for 3 a.m. on a Sunday morning, with Thell Reed Jr. guiding us to a spot at the desert's edge near Corona, California. Reed had hunted the area before, it turned out, and knew where to find snakes. We arrived upon the scene, an area of sand and rocks – a beautiful endless beach, with no ocean – just as the sun was coming up.

First off, Reed set up several wooden target frames as he wanted to check his personal armory before clambering into the rocks after his slithering quarry. This took a little time, since Reed never does things by halves and had brought along an even dozen handguns. Included were seven Single Action Colts; a .45 automatic; a .44 magnum; a

The Pacific rattlesnake, Crotalus lucifer, *grows to an average length of about six feet and should be treated with all available caution and respect; avoided, if possible. Left, Reed practices from the hip with SA .45 Colt.*

derringer of modern manufacture in .38 Special, plus an assortment of Smith & Wessons in .45 and .38 Special.

After rattling off some two hundred rounds at the paper targets and determining that all was in order, Reed allowed us to carry the derringer model for the sake of the personal self-confidence. Reed had prepared some special loads for this little hideout gun. The cases were loaded with 3.5 grains of Bullseye powder with a cardboard disc pressed down to hold the powder in tight, then another disc, measuring one-sixteenth of an inch was dropped in over this. The case then was filled up with No. 9 shot and covered with a couple of one-thirty-second-inch discs. The case finally was given a slight crimp and glue was added and allowed to harden as a final precaution.

Reed, who averages five hundred rounds per week just in practice, long ago learned that reloading was the answer for this kind of fodder consumption, so he reloads for all of his guns, using Star reloading tools. Rather than swaging bullets for his gang of forty-fives, he uses cast bullets, turning them out en masse in a gang mould, then lubricating and sizing them. Fully realizing that to keep in top form he must practice, he works out his favorite guns some three times per week.

This is one reason he wasn't too concerned with the idea of running into multiple rattlesnakes there in the Southern California desert.

How do you stalk a rattlesnake? It is obvious you don't crawl among the rocks on your belly. Coming face to face with one of these venomous creatures in the prone position could prove fatal. Instead, the answer is to creep around amongst the rocks, standing straight up. If one could levitate a bit, it would prove even safer, but a pair of heavy boots usually is enough to stop the fangs of even the largest

Above, rattler lurks in the shade of overhanging rocks. Left, keeping well out of striking reach, Reed prods quarry with dead stick. Below, another rattler about to retire.

Reed took care to aim for the heads, assuring instant incapacitation of the deadly fangs and poison sacs, with the added advantage of not ruining the skins. The larger rattlesnakes can strike with sufficient force to break a man's leg. Below, the M27 Smith & Wesson in .357 magnum has more than ample penetration capability, as demonstrated by the exit hole on this sun-toughened log.

SNAKE BITE TREATMENT

Anyone traveling in areas inhabited by poisonous snakes should carry a snake bite kit consisting of a piece of rubber tubing, a razor blade and a rubber suction cup. There are a number of commerical varieties put out by Cutter Laboratories, Johnson & Johnson and others. When struck by a poisonous snake, swelling starts almost immediately, there is intense pain and the victim suffers shock. First, make the patient lie down and remain quiet. Give first aid treatment for shock as well as for the bite. For shock, be sure the victim's feet are raised and keep him from becoming cold. From the snake bite kit, tie the rubber tube about the limb about two inches above the fang marks; between the bite and the heart, and work fast! If you have no tubing, you can use a handkerchief or bit of rope to cut off the blood flow. Open the fang marks with shallow cuts, using the razor blade or the sharp point of a knife which has been burned for sterilization. Start suction to remove the poison from the wound, using suction cups if you have them. Or you may use your lips, spitting out the poisoned blood and rinsing the mouth with water. But do not use this system if you have had a tooth pulled recently or have a sore in your mouth! If the swelling moves up the arm or leg, keep the constriction ahead of the swelling. Make more shallow cuts, no more than an eighth-inch deep and twice that in length, continuing the treatment. Be careful not to cut an artery and make cuts parallel to the limb. Treatment should be continued as the patient is being transported to a doctor. Should you be by yourself when bitten, do not panic and run as this only forces the poison through the blood stream that much more rapidly. Instead, remain quiet and apply the type of treatment just described, moving only after you are certain you have removed as much of the poison as possible.

Between snake-sniping sessions, Reed keeps hand and eye in tune by practicing hip shots at empty tin cans from suitable distance. Such shooting is not recommended for the less expert shooter, due to the danger of ricochets from rocks.

snake. However, there are other problems: If a six-foot rattler strikes and hits your leg just right, the force of the strike with the snake's weight behind it is like being hit by a sledge hammer. This can result in a broken leg. There are such cases on record!

And in this supposed desert paradise — where the horizon is free of smog; where the sagebrush offers up its fragrance; where there are soft purple shadows at sundown — there are six-foot rattlesnakes. The den mothers are as friendly as a pit boss in Las Vegas.

Reed had chosen the area well, and had done some plain and fancy snake shooting here before as evidenced by the rattlesnake band gracing his broad-brimmed hat. In fact, it wasn't long before we had reached the nervous state: Rattlesnakes — most of them big and well fed — were in obvious evidence.

As the sun rose, bearing down bright and hot, some of the reptiles had slithered from their dens and had started to sun themselves upon the smooth rocks that littered the area. And that was when the slaughter began in a reptilian rhapsody.

Reed spotted a sizable rattler perched on a rock some five yards distant and promptly drew, shooting from the hip. The head promptly disappeared, while its former owner began thrashing about wildly, rattles still popping in ominous threat in this frenzy of death, as the offender departed for that Great Snake Pit in the Sky.

For this type of shooting, the youthful sharpshooter was using a pair of Colt Single Actions with handloaded bullets in 225-grain weight. The cases were loaded with 9.0 grains of Hercules' Unique powder. This combination is reported to afford a muzzle velocity of approximately nine hundred feet per second, maintaining a speed at a hundred yards of 786 fps. At close range — needless to say, perhaps — there is

plenty of power to down almost anything that can be found on the North American continent in the way of game, let alone a snake.

The youthful Californian began shooting at anything that moved. By coincidence, all of these targets happened to be rattlesnakes. By design, rather than coincidence, all of Reed's shots neatly severed the reptiles' heads.

"Why always aim for the head?" we asked innocently. Reed looked mildly amused.

"I don't want to louse up the skins," he replied.

It has been scientifically reported that snakes have no sense of hearing and that they respond instead to vibrations created by sound. Whatever the reason, the initial shots created panic among the den of rattlesnakes.

In a few minutes, there seemed to be snakes all around us, and Reed was having a field day, firing almost as rapidly as he could reload from his belt loops. The shoot went on for more than two hours, but it must be pointed out that Reed made a point of choosing his shots. In the heavy rocks, shooting a heavy .45 slug that might ricochet off a boulder can be dangerous.

During part of this, Reed switched from his favored Single Actions to the Smith & Wesson .38 Specials, proving just as deadly with these firearms. He also used a .45 Service automatic in a specially built holster, showing his dexterity with this oft maligned hunk of iron, ultimately switching to the .44 magnum.

When the snakes finally had retreated into their dens, the hunters set about skinning out the larger snakes, several of which measured six feet or so in length. When it was over and the snake skins had been rolled up, Reed glanced about at the remains, then up at the buzzards that were circling overhead, waiting to pick at the litter. "What a waste," Reed murmured. "Down in Florida, they can rattlesnake meat. It brings high prices in some markets."

Chapter 23

MAKE YOUR OWN HANDGUN CASE

By Dean A. Grennell

Use This Simplified Basic

Approach For Building

Cases To Fill Any Need

This case employs a novel system to secure the scoped Ruger Mark I. A 7/8" hole was drilled lengthwise through a block, which then was slit to form the barrel cradle. A short section of 1" wooden dowel was glued to provide support at the rear. Above, case for Behlert-customized K-38 provides space for Lee Precision reloading kit, or ammo box, if preferred.

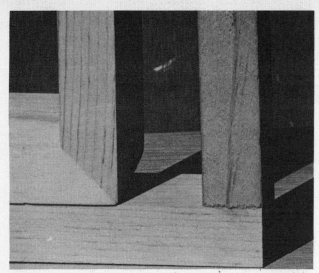

Upper joint is mitered to a 45-degree angle for improved strength and appearance. Lower joint is an example of the simpler butt-glued approach. Text discusses both types.

A CUSTOM GUN CASE makes a thoroughly useful accessory for a favorite firearm. Today's market offers a good variety of ready-made cases, excellent in manufacture and moderate in cost. I have several such factory jobs, use them often and appreciate them considerably. By making your own cases, you can save a bit of money (provided you charge the construction time off to recreation), but, more importantly, you end up with exactly the kind of case you had in mind and its features are limited solely by your imagination, ingenuity and building skill. As a generality, the more cases you make, the better they get. The discussion at hand will endeavor to show you the easy approaches and help you avoid some of the lurking pitfalls.

Currently, I'm winding up seventeen grateful years of

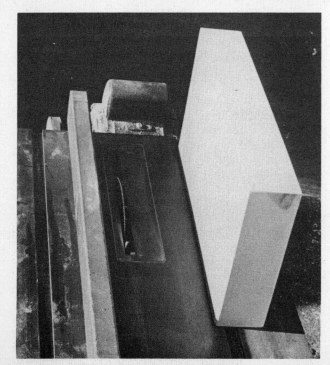

partnership with a modest table saw, an Atlas by make. I suppose that should have dictated that I call him Chuck or Charley, in memory of the world's most famous eighty-seven-pound weakling, but, in a mood of classic whimsy, I christened him Euripides, instead. When it comes to building things such as gun cases, a table saw is indeed useful. A radial arm saw would work at least as well, I'm sure and one of the little electric hand saws — either the rotary type commonly called a SkilSaw or the reciprocating saber saw — can be used with good effect. In a pinch, one can make do with a handsaw and lots of elbow grease.

One thing about the table saw shown in the accompanying photos should be noted: Somewhere along the seventeen years, I lost track of its blade guard. I do not recommend removing the blade guard from your saw. Power saws must be treated with vast amounts of cautious respect, at all times. Euripides has yet to get in his first bite, probably because I'm scared green of that whirring blade. I've gotten nicked countless times by hand tools, doubtless because I'm not as frightened of them.

As to materials for construction, you can use plywood, natural wood or synthetic materials such as particle board or masonite. The last two are the least satisfactory for the purpose, particularly if you rely upon glue as the sole bonding agent. I've made several cases of masonite and have had to spend a lot of time regluing opened joints. The glue holds just fine; it's the material that gives way. As a wood-butcher over many years, I have to note that today's market does not seem to offer the choice materials of yesteryear. It's hard to find plywood anymore of the quality that used to be available, often with attractive outer veneers of walnut, birch or oak. The natural or solid woods tend to have lots of knots, or cost an arm plus a leg; sometimes both.

Solid woods usually occur in thicknesses of at least 0.75-inch, the nominal "one-inch" boards; seldom thinner. For building gun cases, that's a bit heavier than you want or need. With an eight-inch blade, my table saw has a maximum cut depth of 2.225 inches. Sometimes, I cut 0.75-inch boards into strips about 2.2 inches wide, stand them on edge against the rip fence and slit them into a pair

The case at left has been assembled as a complete unit and is about to be separated against the rip fence of the table saw. Lower photo shows the two halves after cutting. Since the blade guard must be removed, great caution is required. If preferred, a saber saw can be used instead.

After completing the outer shell of the BK-38 case, pine strips were slit on the table saw to about 3/16" thickness, mitered at the corners and glued to the inside surfaces of the lower portion, as shown. This provides a stronger joint that is much better suited to keep dust and foreign matter out of the case's contents. Text discusses staining techniques for color match.

of thinner planks, not quite three-eighths, due to the loss of wood in cutting. Such home-sawyered boards work well for the front, back and sides of a pistol case. If desired, a series of such pieces could be glued edge-to-edge to form the top and bottom segments. So far, I've not gotten that dedicated.

In putting the pieces together, you've a choice between butt joints and mitered joints. In the latter, both edges are beveled to an angle of forty-five degrees and, when glued, no exposed end grain shows. The width of the glued joint is increased usefully in the process, too. For example, if the stock is .375-inch thick, the mitered joint has a width of 0.530-inch (Thanks, Pythagoras!). With half-inch stock, the miter is 0.707-inch in width, and so on.

If you also miter the top and bottom edges of the side pieces as you go along and cut matching bevels around the top and bottom, they drop neatly (it's to be hoped) into place, leaving no exposed edges showing at all. The resulting case presents a highly attractive appearance.

The secret of getting everything to fit, without unsightly gaps, lies in measuring, laying out the lines and cutting them with all possible precision. A long time ago, I swore off using carpenter's squares. I'm prepared to believe that, somewhere in the world, there are carpenter's squares made to an exact ninety-degree right angle. It's just that I've never seen one, thus far. I use a drafting T-square and forty-five degree triangle, both of adequate quality and recommend them heartily. Usually, I do my measuring with a meter-stick passed out by a local lumber yard. It has yard and inch graduations on one side and centimeters/millimeters on the other. The latter are highly addictive, I've found, for precise measurement and layout. Instead of courting brain fever by trying to count off and juggle thirty-seconds and sixty-fourths, just whack to the nearest millimeter, or fraction thereof, as desired.

An old patternmaker once told me a couple tricks of his exacting trade that I've found highly helpful. The first was his iron-clad rule: "Measure it twice, then cut it once." The second item was the gimmick of folding a sheet of sandpaper into thirds, rough-side out, top and bottom. That provides a helpful purchase for your fingertips, so that you can hand-finish with wondrous effect. When one strip of sandpaper wears out, just bring the fresh side outermost and use it up, too. As with so many things, it's so darned obvious, once it's pointed out.

Most hardware stores carry adjustable corner clamps, currently going at around five or six bucks apiece. I started out with two, years ago, finally building up the supply to eight. I use them on the larger projects, such as gun cabinets or book cases. The advantage in having so many is that you can assemble the entire four sides, with a clamp on each of the eight corners, to hold everything in perfect alignment as the glue dries and hardens. For something as small as the typical handgun case, however, the hardware corner clamps are much too big and clumsy.

My solution to the dilemma was to take a couple of pieces of scrap one-inch pine, miter the mating ends, and glue them into a small angle, with the two arms about three inches wide and five inches long. After the glue dried, I checked them with the drafting triangle and found them dead-on, within acceptable tolerances. I had used two of the regular corner clamps to hold the first wooden angle bracket. After it checked out ninety degrees on the nose, I

Spring clamps hold the liner strips in place as the glue sets up to complete BK-38 case shown on opposite page.

Case for the Behlert K-38 was fully mitered on all mating edges. The sides were assembled first. Here, the top and bottom pieces are held in place by a series of C-clamps, with strips of scrap wood between clamp jaws and case to prevent marring surface.

Thin plywoods and veneers are useful for gun case construction, but correct blade choice is important to assure cuts that are clean and free of splinters. Hollow-ground blades, such as this one from Black & Decker, work exceptionally well.

used the new wooden angle to make a second one.

I keep a dispenser box of waxed paper in the shop and tear off a narrow strip, folding it to form the corner and put it against both inner surfaces of the wooden angle. That keeps oozing glue from sticking the workpiece to the bracket. I use a pair of small spring clamps to hold the new pieces against the waxed-paper-covered angle bracket as the glue sets up. With the first angle, I made the second and, with both of those, the third and fourth.

The resulting angle brackets are used for holding the sides of the cases in alignment as the glue sets. As a final check, after clamping them into place with both spring clamps on one side, the edges of the two workpieces are gauged against a surface believed to be flat and true.

Usually, I use the milled cast iron top of the table saw for the purpose. You know the corner is going together at ninety degrees, but if the front goes a little up as the end goes a little down, you can still encounter problems. The described procedure is intended to prevent that particular bogey, and it works.

The usual procedure is to join the front and one side, then the back and other side, setting them aside for the glue to harden. My favorite glue for such purposes is Elmer's Professional Carpenter's Wood Glue, or Titebond, both of which are of the aliphatic resin formulation, light cream-yellow in color. It's pertinent to point out that such glue needs an ambient temperature of sixty-five degrees F, or better; preferably, quite a bit better. At sixty-five, it

Power sanders, such as this Black & Decker belt sander, can save a lot of time and effort in final finish phases. Alternatively, discs of sandpaper can be used in swiveling Swirl-away head with electric drill.

Watco Danish oil finish, topped by same maker's satin wax, provides a finish that is attractive and resistant to minor wear and damage. Another good approach is the G-96 preparation for sealing and filling, topped by polyurethane spray.

takes a long time for the joint to develop useful strength; below that, forget it. In the cooler times of the year, if there's sunlight, I'm inclined to put such clamped-up assemblies into the old Buick in the driveway. It has black upholstery and, with all the windows up, it serves as a superb solar-powered drying oven. In a pinch, on a cloudy day, I've borrowed the oven of my wife's kitchen range for a quick setup on the smaller assemblies, boosting the inside temperature to one hundred degrees F. or so. When all Southern California is ninety-plus, I have no problem!

The point is, most glues, including the admirable aliphatic resin jobs, need warmth to work their useful magic. If you neglect that, the pieces tend to come apart on you.

If you've no choice but to cut the pieces with a hand saw or inexpensive saber saw, dictating butt-glued joints instead of mitered ones, the described procedures still will work just as well. You may wish to let the top and bottom edges of the sides remain square instead of beveled, adding the upper and lower coverings and letting the edges show. If you go that route, cut the top and bottom a wee mite generous and let it project all around by a sixty-fourth or so. Then, when the whole box has set up, you can sand down the excess so that it's dead-flush with the front and side surfaces. Sandpaper, cleverly employed, can mask a multitude of sins and never forget it!

Once the front/back/sides frame is together, cut the pieces for the top and bottom, apply glue and clamp them into place with C-clamps. Put small pieces of wood scrap between the case and the clamp jaws to prevent marring of the surface. Keep a bucket of water and an old towel, or paper towels handy to remove the glue from your fingertips after spreading it over the mating surfaces in a thin, uniform

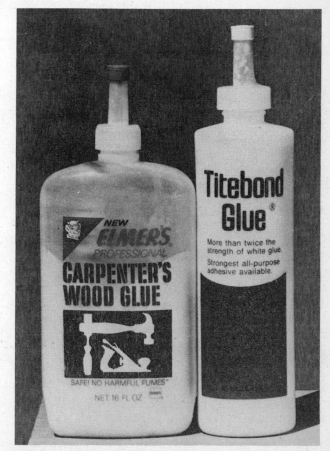

Two good choices in glue: Both are of the aliphatic resin formulation. Properly used and cured, these produce joints that are actually stronger than most woods in use.

A useful trick of the patternmaker's trade consists of folding a full sheet of sandpaper into thirds, providing a much better surface to keep the fingertips from slipping as the paper is used in final finishing phases.

As mentioned in the text, this pistol case was built by Grennell several years ago, from oak veneer plywood. An unusual but remarkably handy design feature is the receptacle for spent center-fire cases, with slide at bottom to empty it out.

Case above was constructed entirely of a lightweight, three-ply material called Ramin, resembling Philippine mahogany in general texture and color. By employing mitered joints at all mating edges, as described here, the completed case shows no exposed end-grain at any point, contributing to handsome overall appearance and providing added strength at same time.

coating. Just because a little glue is good, a lot of glue is no better. If you get too lavish, you get a lot of oozing, especially under the pressure of the C-clamps. Clean up any visible excess glue with water and a damp rag. Once you let it set up, it gives problems later when you apply the final finishes.

The discussed procedure, to this point, has been directed toward the production of a solid box, with all six sides glued more or less neatly into place. On just a few rare occasions, I've built things of this sort by the approach of making the lower half and then making a top to fit it, or vice versa. Take my word, it's vastly easier and simpler to build it as a closed box and then separate the halves by cutting them apart with a saw. Even if you build the separate halves with a precision a micrometer might envy, the grain won't match.

With a table saw available, it's a fairly simple matter to set the rip fence and cut the sides all around to separate top from bottom. If your saw has a blade guard, you'll have to remove it for this operation. Crank the blade down so that the cutting edge projects just a smidge above the thickness of the stock used for the sides. Make the cuts across the

two ends first. Then cut either the front or the back, followed by the other. The fourth and final cut is the hardest to control. Try to keep bottom and top aligned by fingertip pressure against both, but keep the fingers out of the blade's reach! I always seem to end up about 1/128-inch out of register on the final pass and have to true it up by careful sanding.

Frankly, I don't know how you'd go about separating the halves with a radial arm saw. It's easy enough with a saber saw and you're not even restricted to straight-line cuts with that.

Once you get the halves separated and the edges trued-up with sandpaper, use some scrap stock and a couple of C-clamps to realign the top and bottom as you install the hinges on the back and the fastening catches on the front. Position the hinges, mark the screw holes on the wood with a well-sharpened pencil, prick a starting hole in the center of the mark with a scratch awl and seat the screws; much the same procedure applies for the holding catches up front.

The research for the discussion at hand afforded a solid excuse to build a carrying case for my combat-customized

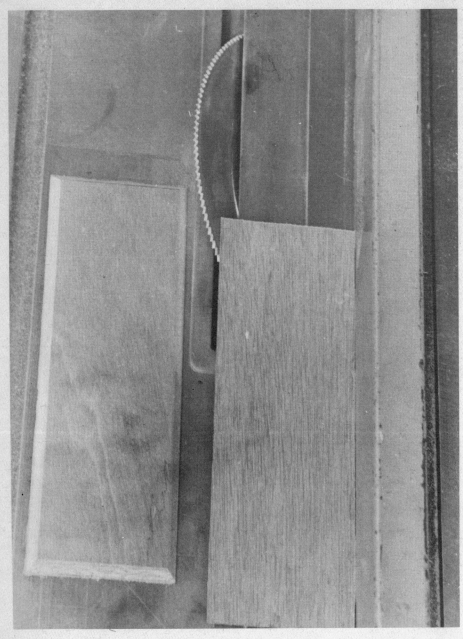

Here are two end-pieces of Ramin plywood in the process of being mitered around all four edges. The short cuts were made with the saw's sliding miter gauge or crosscut guide. The long cuts are made against the rip fence, as shown with the piece at right. A completed end-piece is at left. In actual practice, the blade guard should be left in place, not removed and lost, as this one was!

S&W K-38 out of Austin Behlert's shop. I've been lugging the BK-38 about in a Safariland pistol rug because holsters for such guns just do not seem to be available in the marketplace. True, I could build my own holster. I've done it before. In fact, I've an old garbage-grade holster for the Ruger Super Blackhawk that more or less fits the BK-38, with 1.5 inches of spare space at the muzzle. But the BK-38, long since, has carved a niche for itself as one of my favorite handguns of all time. Feed it right, do your part and it'll clip dimes at seventy-five feet, every time; definitely my kind of hawglaig!

I built the BK-38 case out of sides of clear white pine, slit to a thickness of 8mm and mitered. Top and bottom edges were mitered to accept top and bottom plates of a material the Nail Apron lumber yard calls Ramin and sells for $7.99 for a four-by-eight-foot hunk. It's a three-ply plywood, measuring 0.2118 inches in thickness and it resembles Philippine mahogany in color and general appearance. I reconciled the color of the Ramin and pine by mixing my own stain, dissolving burnt sienna artist's oil pigment in turpentine. That was a tactical goof. It took three days to bake it dry in the sun-heated Buick and nearly a fortnight to air the turpentine stench out of the car. Next time, I'll use lighter fluid as the solvent because it evaporates faster.

The improvised stain did, however, perform a good job of making the colors of the unrelated woods match. It all came out a rich golden brown. The grain doesn't match, of course, but it's not at all that obvious. I finished it with Watco Danish oil, followed by a few well-rubbed coats of Watco natural satin wax.

After assembling the BK-38 case, I added an inner liner around front/back/sides of slit pine about 0.125-inch in thickness, extending about 0.25-inch above the upper edge of the bottom portion. That provides a solid closure and helps to keep out dust and debris. I like the net effect. It almost begins to look as if a professional had made it.

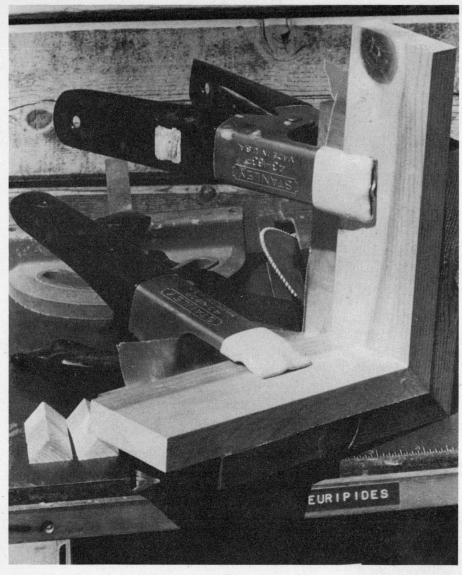

As described, a pair of corner clamps were used to glue up the first brace, followed by a check with draftsman's triangle to verify its angle as a true 90 degrees. With the first corner brace made, it was a simple matter to use it for production of additional braces from scrap wood. Note the layer of waxed paper between the two braces to prevent oozing glue from sticking them together. In the photo below, one of the homemade corner braces is shown in use to align mitered sections of plywood. As discussed, the left edge should project beyond the corner brace so that alignment of end and side can be checked against a flat surface in setting up.

The quick, neat and easy approach to finishing the wood is to use some of the spray finishes such as G96 Filler Sealer, followed by G96 Stock Finish. Applied according to directions, the G96 duo results in a smooth, handsome finish. The crafty approach is to apply the full-course finish before you cut the top and bottom halves apart. Then it is all in place as you install the hinges and catches, with no need to worry about spraying around them or masking them off. It's just a matter of "working smarter, instead of harder."

The discussion, to this point, brings us to a flat case — the sort termed a presentation case — with hinges at the back, snap catches at the front, looking nice on the outside. It remains to provide the interior furniture that will hold the gun in place and provide storage for the desired accessories, including ammunition, if you wish. Much of that is up to your personal taste, of which I've sharply limited cognizance. Several approaches are possible. I'll suggest a few.

The quick/easy approach is to plan upon installing sheets of sponge plastic foam in both the top and bottom halves. That has the useful advantage of leaving the case usable for any gun that fits within its dimensions. The padding is

Here's a further departure from the presentation-type case. Constructed of nominal one-inch (actual ¾" thickness) stock, the ends/top/bottom were mitered and the two sides were butt-glued in place, then beveled on the table saw. This case is intended to serve as a handy tote-box, carrying a pair of medium-sized handguns in holsters from the storage place to the shooting or hunting site. The integral handle was made from small scrap pieces. If desired, two screws can be driven from underneath the cover, up into the handle to add security and peace of mind. Case has one catch and one hinge at rear.

available from numerous local suppliers in a variety of thicknesses. It's easy to chop it to size on a paper cutter, if one is available. Lacking that, a sharp knife or razor blade against a metal straight-edge will serve almost as well. You can fasten it to the wood by means of the spray adhesive used for attaching sanding discs, readily available from local suppliers. Take great care in initial positioning because, once it grabs, it doesn't let go easily!

The first case was made up for the scoped High Standard Victor; another gun for which no holster exists at present, to the best of my knowledge. I'm working on that problem, too, but don't hold your breath. The Victor case has a layer of

sponge plastic foam on the bottom, covered with a piece of red felt, with another piece of red felt held to the inside of the top by sanding-disc spray adhesive. It works, but I've a visceral hunch that a better solution exists, somewhere.

For the scoped bull-barrel Ruger Mark I, I came up with an approach I find more pleasing. A rough check of the barrel diameter showed it to be close to seven-eighths-inch. That's 0.875-inch and, if you must split hairs, the barrel mikes 0.8689-inch, give or take the odd furlong. I put an 0.875-inch bit in the drill press and bored a hole 3-5/8 inches deep, lengthwise of the grain, in a piece of nominal two-inch stock. I then dressed it down on the table saw to make a segment with a semicircular groove, situated it in the bottom of the case and glued it in place.

That gave a pleasantly solid anchoring place for the barrel. Just a bit of trial checking showed that the curving area at the rear of the Ruger grip was the same radius as a one-inch circle. I cut a short segment off of a length of one-inch dowel, put the Ruger down in the case with its barrel in the channel and snubbed the piece of one-inch dowel up against the curved portion of the grip, marked it and glued it in place, with the gun itself serving as a positioning fixture.

It worked out remarkably well. Empirical approaches often do, I've noted. The Ruger now snicks home in its fitted case with a faint "thock" and, once in place, you can't even coax up a rattle by shaking the case with the lid closed.

As your fancy may suggest, you can go on to provide facilities for storage of cleaning rods, bore solvent, patches, whatever you desire. The sky is hardly the limit when you're working up the carrying case for one particular gun. Include space for one of the little reloading kits, plus components? Why not?

I still have a gun case around the place, built twenty-some years ago along the lines of the traditional handgun case for packing three or four handguns to the range or to a match. It incorporates a feature I still appreciate, one I've never seen before nor since. It has a receptacle for spent brass. Just raise the lid and dump in all

Case on facing page, after being separated with a saber saw. Two lines are laid out on sides and a French curve template was used to form the transition for cutting. Although the ¾'' wood thickness adds weight, it also provides a comfortably ample amount of wood to hold the screws that secure the hinge at the back and the suitcase bolt catch at the front.

A length of surgical rubber tubing has been stretched and knotted around the two halves to keep them aligned while the hinge and catch are being positioned and installed.

the expended hulls. When you get back to the reloading bench, pull the slide at the bottom of the chute and the cases drop neatly into whatever container you choose to provide. For the reloader, it's a first-cabin approach. Oftentimes, I've wondered why no one else ever thought to build a gun case like that. If the idea turns you on, you can build one for yourself. The details are all given here.

The basic *modus operandi* is applicable for constructing any manner of carrying case. It's by no means limited to cases for handguns. The same approach works for rifle cases, shotgun cases, camera cases, you name it. As noted early in the discussion, there are a lot of good ready-made cases on the market. If you have a need for something special, it can be made to materialize by the procedures described.

After positioning the hinge, circles are marked with a pencil and centers drilled with holes to receive the brass screws. The screwdriver is another homemade production, ground on a special holding jig from B-Square, Fort Worth, Texas.

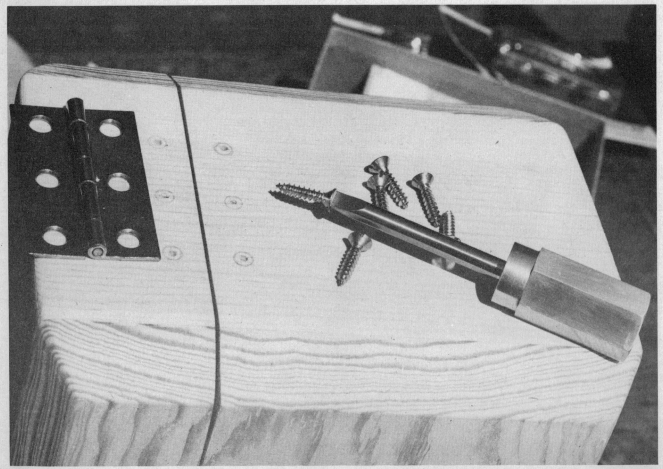

Small pieces of clear pine scrap have been cut to oversized dimensions and glued under pressure of spring clamps, Later, after setting up, handle was cut on table saw to the shape shown on page 232.

Completed case provides a convenient and unobtrusive way to transport handguns, complete with holsters, ammo and so on.

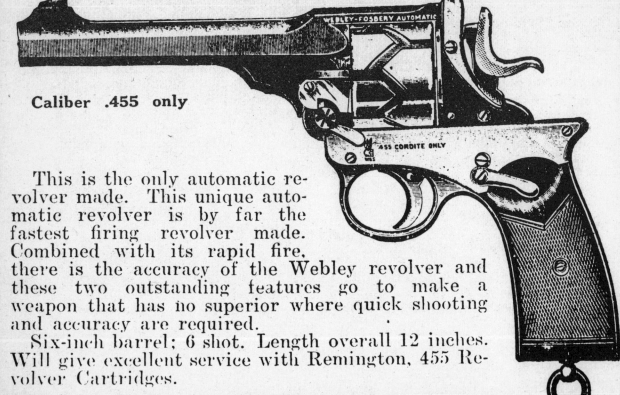

WEBLEY "FOSBERY" AUTOMATIC REVOLVER

Caliber .455 only

This is the only automatic revolver made. This unique automatic revolver is by far the fastest firing revolver made. Combined with its rapid fire, there is the accuracy of the Webley revolver and these two outstanding features go to make a weapon that has no superior where quick shooting and accuracy are required.

Six-inch barrel; 6 shot. Length overall 12 inches. Will give excellent service with Remington, 455 Revolver Cartridges.

A British design, the Webley-Fosbery was made from 1901 through 1915, usually as the 6" .455 type shown in this listing from a 1935 Stoeger's catalog. A few were made in .38 caliber, with 8-round cylinders.

THE WEIRD, UNLIKELY AND EXOTIC

Chapter 24
By Dean A. Grennell

THE ERA FROM late 1941 through well past 1946 was notable for the sparsity of many types of consumer goods, among other things. Guns, ammunition, cameras, film and many similarly desirable wares were almost impossible to obtain. Thus it came to pass that a staff sergeant named — well, we'll call him Harry Colby, out of courtesy — chanced to come into possession of an entire fifty-round box of standard velocity .22 long rifle cartridges, to his vast delight.

The problem was that he didn't have a firearm capable of setting off the .22 LR round. That might have stymied most people, but not SSgt. Colby, who was as ingenious as he was intrepid. He had a certain primitive flair with tools and was a freehand scrounger of vast capability.

I encountered the world's first Colby .22 target pistol after it had passed well beyond the stage of being just a gleam in its designer's eye. By the time I saw it, the thing was completed; in all its grotesque and ghastly glory. The most charitable thing I can think of to say about it is that it was memorable; yes, unforgettable — that, too.

Colby had started out with a one-half-inch diameter bolt, about six inches in length. He procured a 7/32-inch drill bit, perhaps four inches in total length, checked a chart of decimal equivalents and found that the hole it bored was supposed to be about .2188-inch in diameter. That's not terribly far from the bore diameter of a typical .22 rimfire barrel.

There was, of course, the perplexing matter of how to drill a 7/32-inch hole down through the center of a six-inch barrel-to-be when your drill had a working depth of only a trifle over three inches. Undaunted, Colby chucked the bolt — having beheaded the bolt with a hacksaw — into a lathe, put his drill in the chuck on the right-hand end of the lathe, drilled in as far as he could reach, then reversed the bolt in the headstock chuck and went in from the other end. To his delight, the holes met in the middle.

Well, it should be noted, they more or less met in the middle. There was perhaps 1/16-inch or so of abrupt linear misalignment at the juncture point, but to Colby's chill blue scrutiny, it didn't appear to make all that much difference.

The chamber diameter for a .22 LR wants to be around .223-inch, so he worried out a chamber of sorts by running a No. 2 drill into the proper end to a depth of .602-inch or so and then managed to cut enough clearance to accept the rim and found that one of his cartridges fitted, after a fashion.

Given a chambered barrel, the rest of the construction project went forward in much the same progression of dubious expedients. He crafted a receiver out of scrap steel stock, with hacksaw and files, mounting the barrel so that it

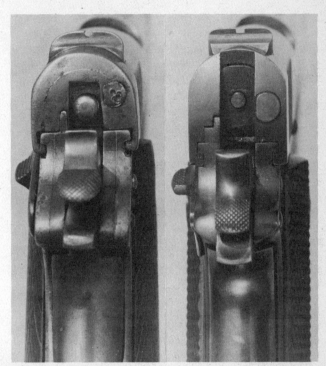

Pistol at left was laboriously handmade by a Viet Cong about 1961. Here it's compared with a standard military Model 1911 Colt autoloader to show similarities, changes.

broke at the breech in the manner of an inexpensive break-action shotgun. His firing pin was patterned after the striker of a Springfield rifle, more or less, and his lockwork was even more roundabout and tortuous than that of a Luger. The trigger pull was worse than any Luger I've encountered to date and that is praising with faint damns.

The stocks were whittled from the wood off the end of an orange crate — that being the era of wooden packing crates — and stained a sort of Venetian red with some barn paint Colby happened to find. The stove bolts that held the stocks in place tended to remind the viewer of Frankenstein's Monster.

I referred to the resulting artifact as the Colby target pistol and I'm prepared to defend the designation. You could hit a target with it, provided you selected a large enough target and fired from a suitably intimate distance. Since the bore was totally innocent of any vestige of rifling, to say nothing of the abrupt do-si-do effect at the point where the bored holes barely met, the brutally mutilated bullets emerged from the muzzle keyholing in a beserk fandango. Their resulting trajectories were not quite as

Cong-built replica is at left, next to contemporary Colt. Note the visible juncture between component parts of the barrel bushing and the casual fit of barrel and bushing.

Much of the VC pistol seems to have been formed by bending heavy sheet metal and brazing the edges, as here.

Internal parts of the VC pistol (upper), compared to Colt. Note the absence of locking lugs on top of copy barrel! Forming the recoil spring by hand must've been hard.

predictable as the next number coming up on a roulette wheel.

I regret that I cannot supply a photo of the remarkable Colby target pistol and its gifted creator. As noted, cameras and film were unobtainable at the time, too. Lest you be tempted to follow in his pioneering footsteps, be it noted that the amateur construction of firearms is unlawful unless covered by appropriate federal licenses, permits and so on. As all the described events took place in the Summer of 1945, I trust that SSgt. Colby is protected by the statute of limitations, several times over. I've changed his name for this account in hopes his craftsmanship has improved over the years, wishing to spare him possible embarrassment.

My reason for bringing up the Colby pistol is to say that, even if the unlikely gadget had survived down to the present moment, its intrinsic value would not be much beyond the price of an equal weight of scrap iron. The gun collector's rule of thumb covering such matters is that junk is junk and it stays junk forever.

The Colby target pistol was unique, in the most shimmering sense of the word. Forgive a personal whim-wham, please? In my book, something is unique or it's not unique. Phrasings such as "very unique," "nearly unique," or "slightly unique" set my purist's gorge afloat. Unique means that there is only one of the items under discussion. If there are more than one, try "scarce," instead of unique.

At some point in the waning months of 1968, MSgt. John P. Wilson, of the 5th Special Forces Group — one of the campaigners who wore the Green Beret in that singular conflict centered around Vietnam — dropped by the office to show me a really singular handgun.

The gun in question was a reasonably accurate facsimile of the Colt, caliber .45 ACP Government Model autoloading pistol, Model 1911, redundantly familiar to most readers of these pages. It was remarkable in view of the painfully obvious fact that it was handmade.

According to Wilson, a total of five handmade copies of the M1911 were turned out by a remarkably gifted Viet Cong craftsman, sometime during 1961. Communist arms shipments to the area commenced shortly after that, eliminating the need for such extravagant displays of dedicated ingenuity. Wilson said the maker of the Colt replicas was said to have used up a full month of dedicated work for the completion of each of his pistols.

At that time and place, handmade handguns were not terribly uncommon. Most of them were on an approximate par with SSgt. Colby's masterpiece, with the expedient of bending a piece of sheet steel around a mandrel and brazing the seam as the common approach to barrel production. Most such barrels were left innocent of any trace of rifling, producing parameters of accuracy readily imagined.

The VC-built .45 auto, singularly enough, had a barrel that appeared to have been bored from a length of solid steel rod and, for good measure, it was also rifled.

Here, the maker departed from his working model to the extent of giving the copy right-hand rifling instead of the left-hand rifling traditionally employed at the Colt factory.

Examining the jungle armsmaker's effort, I couldn't help feeling solidly impressed. I like to think I have a moderate amount of expertise when it comes to extemporizing artifacts and I even had a modest shop full of rudimentary

Another comparison of matching areas shows a number of resemblances and departures. The safety catch on the VC copy (above) was non-functional, as can be noted by the fact that there is no corresponding notch on the lower surface of the slide into which it can move if pushed upward. Serrations at rear of slide appear to have been executed with careful taps on a cold chisel. As noted in the text, the grip safety, like the thumb safety, was movable but purely cosmetic in effect.

Right-hand views of copy (top) and original Colt illustrate the swayback effect of the VC gun's slide, caused by violent recoil due to the absence of locking lugs. For the sake of the sharp-eyed readers about to write and point out that the Colt has a M1911A1 slide on an M1911 receiver (as apparent by lack of crescent-shaped cuts behind trigger guard) it should be explained that this is Grennell's pet .45, "Old Loudmouf," also depicted wearing a Redfield scope on the inside front cover! It has been retrofitted to approximately 90% Model 1911A1 configurations and customized with a Bar-Sto stainless barrel.

machine tools, quite possibly excelling those at the disposal of the copy gun's creator. But if anyone were to come along and press me for a deadline against which I could come up with a functional replica of a Model 1911, entirely handmade on the premises, you can feel assured that I would not be inclined to promise delivery in one month's time.

I suppose there must be a collector specializing in the Colt M1911 in its infinitely varied attributes, who'd be glad to give MSgt. Wilson a few hundred dollars to become the owner of his copy of one of the jungle munition maker's five specimens. By any standard, it is an example of a piece of work into which a human poured a great deal of devoted and concentrated effort.

Wilson said it was tested with GI hardball ammo and it functioned surprisingly well, from the standpoint of setting off one round and putting a fresh one into the chamber and ready to go. Despite the meticulous attention to providing rifling, its intrinsic accuracy left a great deal to be desired. Its grip safety moved in the usual manner, but did not interrupt the firing sequence, if left undepressed. The function of the thumb safety was quite casual, also.

Lacking, too, were the mating locking lugs on the top of the barrel and undersurface of the slide. The captured gun worked on straight blowback, giving it still another claim to

intrinsic rarity. Oddly enough, the pivoting barrel link is retained; only the locking lugs are missing.

The captured gun came complete with a leather holster sporting a pouch that carried a spare magazine. Like the rest of the gun, the magazines were handmade, and painfully so. A standard GI magazine would not fit or function in the gun. Apparently, the gun was fired extensively, utilizing GI hardball ammo from various underground sources. It would appear that the contraband fodder was a touch overly vigorous for the gun's handcrafted gizzardry. When the slide is in full recoil, its lower extension comes to a stop against a surface in the receiver. The hammering impact of countless shots had warped the front of the slide upward, giving the gun an absurd, sway-backed appearance without greatly impairing its deadly effectiveness.

In an earlier day, the Pathan tribesmen of Northern India used to whip forth remarkably efficient replicas of British military ordnance, using foot-powered lathes and similarly primitive facilities. Given a pilot model against which to copy, the more craftily resourceful humans can do astoundingly well. Thinking up the original is the challenge that requires a John Moses Browning or his gifted equivalent.

I have visited the facilities of the Los Angeles Police

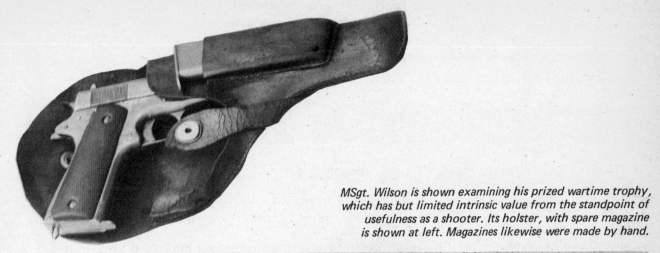

MSgt. Wilson is shown examining his prized wartime trophy, which has but limited intrinsic value from the standpoint of usefulness as a shooter. Its holster, with spare magazine is shown at left. Magazines likewise were made by hand.

Here's a close look at the maker's stamp on the manually actuated .22 pistol. It appears to say S.G. Hall & Co, with no clue as to their base of operations. Letter spacing has possible interpretation as Schall, but the cross-bar of the G makes it the more likely interpretation.

Department's Scientific Investigation Division — Crime Lab, as it's often termed — and viewed their display of captured street weapons; the LAPD's equivalent of Scotland Yard's Black Museum. The output of the intrepid Vietnamese pistolsmith would put just about all of them to sheepish shame, objectively speaking. Though I by no means share the maker's political viewpoint, I'd have to give him a lifted headgear for demonstrating that, if one wants something ardently enough, the word "can't" just is not to be found in the dictionary.

Elsewhere in this book, there is a discussion of the Semmerling Model LM-4 pistol, a manually-actuated repeater for the .45 ACP cartridge. The basic principle dates well back in time. There once was a .22 LR repeater called the Fiala, with a casual resemblance to the Colt Woodsman pistol of pre-WWII days. The Woodsman was an autoloader,

but the Fiala wasn't, making a sharp departure from their superficial resemblance.

I've encountered just one Fiala in a lifetime principally devoted to an interest in firearms generally and handguns particularly. The one I saw reposed in the display of a pawnshop in Wichita Falls, Texas, about August of 1943. I looked it over, cursorially, at the time but, because all my then-available funds were needed for living purposes, I passed it by.

The Fiala is well enough enshrined in the genre to have been mentioned in a few of the more exhaustive works on handguns. I can't provide a photo of the Fiala I saw because, as noted, cameras and film were one of the things without which we were getting along, about that time.

What I can — and do — provide are photos of yet another unlikely manually actuated repeater. I encountered

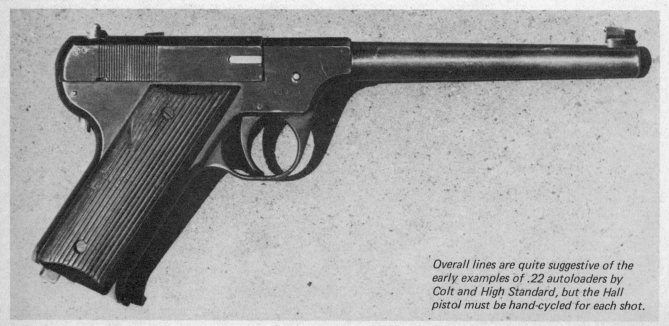

Overall lines are quite suggestive of the early examples of .22 autoloaders by Colt and High Standard, but the Hall pistol must be hand-cycled for each shot.

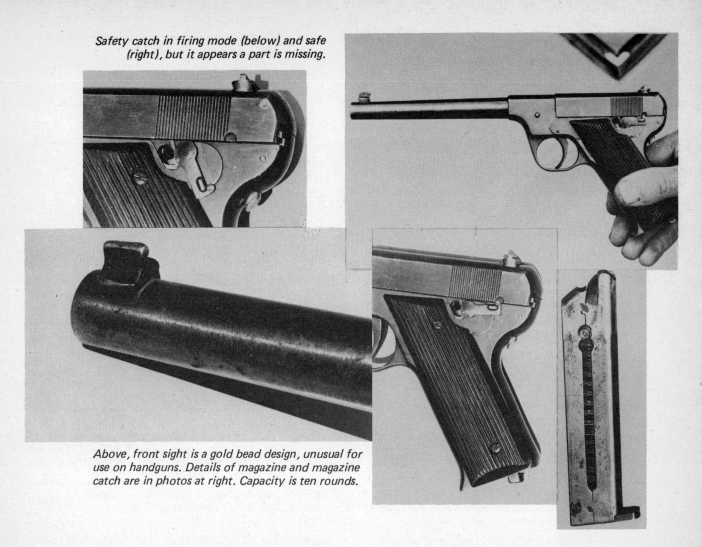

Safety catch in firing mode (below) and safe (right), but it appears a part is missing.

Above, front sight is a gold bead design, unusual for use on handguns. Details of magazine and magazine catch are in photos at right. Capacity is ten rounds.

it in the hands of a collector, in Central California, up in the mid-'70s, by which time I had reacquired ownership of a competent camera and had film in yardly abundance.

That's the good news. The bad news is that I'm not absolutely certain as to what to call it. The maker's name is stamped on the gun and I photographed it with a damned good lens and all the craft and guile I could command. I also scrutinized the name with a keen-eyed jeweler's loupe.

It seems to say: S.G. HALL.

The S.G. Hall, like the Fiala, appears to be reasonably well conceived and executed. In fact, like the Fiala, it has so much family likeness to the Colt Woodsman and the earlier High Standard .22 LR autos that it's faintly mystifying why the maker didn't just produce it as an autoloader and let it go at that.

To this particular point, we've been discussing handgunly artifacts that were either unique or, at least verging reasonably close to that ephemeral status. There was only one Colby target pistol, in all of the time since the dawn of creation, yet I wouldn't offer pocket change for clear title to it. There were, I'm told, five of the VC M1911 surrogates and I suppose, in a flush and feckless moment, I might offer $300 for one, though the mint has not yet printed enough money to hire me to fire a round through one. We've mentioned the Fiala and the S.G. Hall and if you've got one or the other, don't bother writing me for a bid.

In my purely subjective book, handguns or any other form of artillery are for shooting at something and coming as close as possible to hitting it. The late Col. Townsend Whelen phrased it so well I can't hope to improve upon the viewpoint: "Only accurate guns are interesting."

I care very little whether a given gun is unique or not unique. If it isn't impressively accurate, I'd begrudge it rack room. It could be engraved from pintle to gudgeon, in exquisite delicacy, but if it doesn't shoot well, I for one don't want it kicking about underfoot. It can be studded with diamonds, even fire opals, and inlaid with praseodymium in baroque glory; but if it groups loosely, I've no faintest interest in it. I am prepared to be proportional and pragmatical about it. I've a Thompson/Center Contender in .22 Hornet that nips dimes at fifty yards and I love it dearly. I've a Smith & Wesson Model 57, serial No. 237,700, from the days before Bangor Punta bought the operation, that terrorizes silver dollars instead of dimes from the same distance. I cherish it at least as cordially, because each of its holes represents a lot more foot-pounds.

And now, having laid it all out, let us talk for just a bit about a rare, scarce and precious firearm that I had the privilege of firing once, that I never hope to own, for which I'd be happy to put multiple mortgages upon the old homestead and do any other crafty thing I can think of to

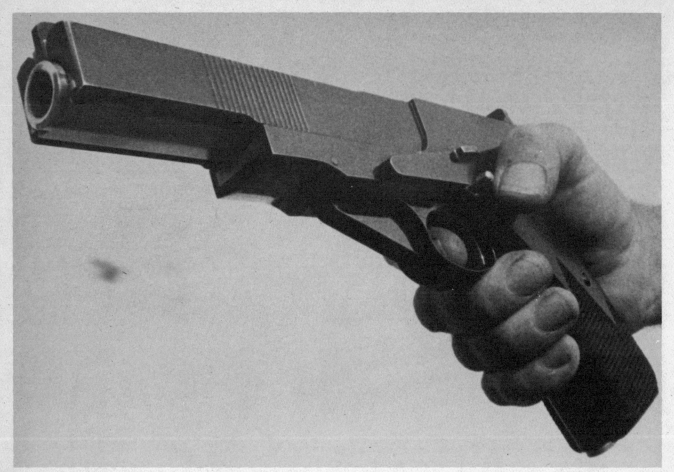

Photographed with a wide angle lens, the Wilson looks like a huge production, but its actual proportions were nicely balanced. Note vertical finger-grip serrations near the front of the slide, which telescopes inside top of receiver.

raise the asking price. I know it's not going to happen, but — since it costs little — let's talk about it, hmm?

Coincidentally enough, a name crops back up into the discussion: Wilson. Not the MSgt. John P. Wilson who owned the Viet Cong .45 replica, but another: George A. Wilson. This George Wilson designed a gun called the Wilson .45 and built three of them, all told. The one I encountered, back in the waning months of 1966, was serial No. 1. It was owned by a man named Larry Neth, residing in the Southern California area at the time. Later, he put Wilson No. 1 into a safe deposit box and went off to Saudi Arabia on a work contract. I've not heard from him in the past five or six years and I hope all continues to go well with him.

Readers who have collided with my prose before this may have noted that I've a strong predilection for .45 autos in general and the basic design known as the Model 1911 or M1911A1 in particular. Even in its primal form, I think it's an admirable hunk of ordnance, which seems to infuriate some readers out of all reason, although they carefully omit addresses on wrathfully protesting letters, by way of sparing themselves explanatory discussions. So it goes.

The Wilson .45 was designed and built to handle the .45 ACP cartridge and that is roughly tantamount to saying that a Ferrari Dino handles gasoline. In fact, putting it all into graspably picturable terms, the Wilson .45 is to the typical Model 1911 as the Model 1911 might be compared

to the Colby target pistol. Certainly, the Wilson is to the best of the M1911s as the latter would be to the Viet Cong copy of the M1911.

There are Model 1911s and, at the same time, there are other Model 1911s. I am the happy and adoring owner of a few outstanding examples of the 1911 breed, and I cherish them fittingly. But, having once fired a Wilson .45, I'd have to concede that I'd swap any and every gun I own to get my covetous hands upon any one of the three Wilsons presumed to still be in existence. I'd toss a bit of cash on the side, if need be.

The Wilson was immediately noteworthy by the fact that it rode remarkably low in the shooting hand. The central axis of its 6-1/16-inch barrel was almost precisely aligned with the supporting juncture of the thumb and palm of the shooting hand. Like the lower barrel of the Remington Model 3200 over/under shotgun, the arrangement decreed that recoil thrusts were almost precisely in line with resisting efforts.

When you fired the Wilson, the whole gun came back with the hand a little, but the muzzle didn't flip upward to any detectable degree. The slide was up front, surrounding the barrel that was fixed to the receiver. The front sight was integral to the barrel at the muzzle. The rear sight was a non-adjustable bridge mounted on the receiver that was integral to the barrel and front sight. The maker had done

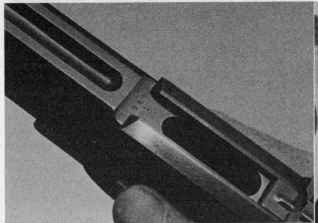

Above, right and below, views of the top of the Wilson .45, showing the ejection port in top of slide, the remarkably easy-to-memorize serial number and the sheet metal cover that extends back over shooter's hand during cycle. After firing, the cover can be pushed forward to protect the port area until next shot. Note fixed front/rear sights.

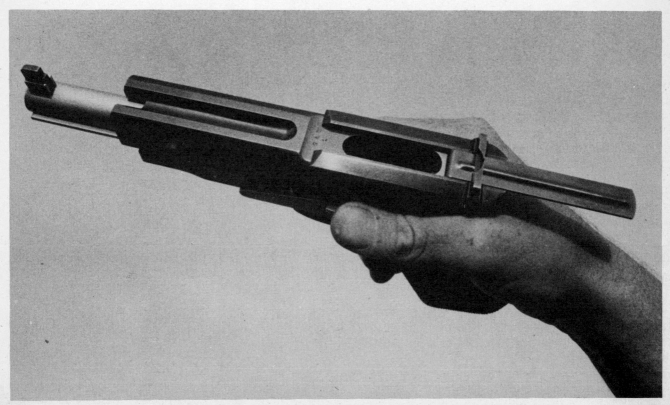

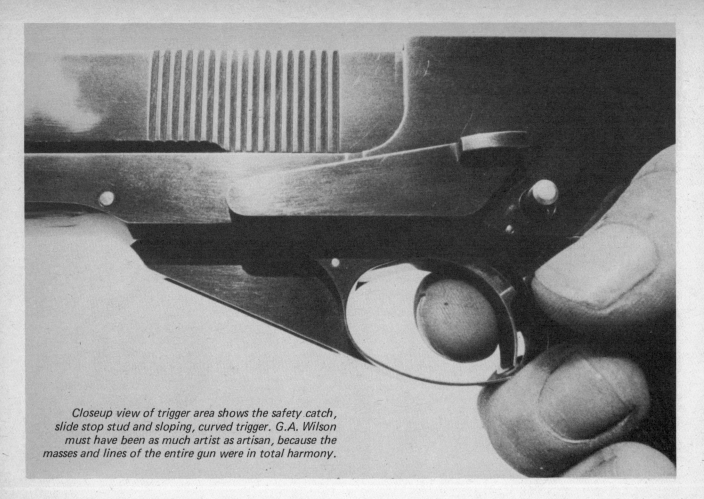

Closeup view of trigger area shows the safety catch, slide stop stud and sloping, curved trigger. G.A. Wilson must have been as much artist as artisan, because the masses and lines of the entire gun were in total harmony.

his homework well, because point of aim and point of impact, at twenty-five yards, coincided quite closely.

According to Neth, the details of the basic design work occupied Wilson for approximately three years and Neth has no details as to how much longer it took the designer to bring the concept into ferrous existence. Neth had heard that, if Wilson had been paid at his normal hourly scale of the time, the design and completion of the first gun would have run up a tab slightly in excess of $18,000. Those are pre-1966 dollars and the reader is invited to reconcile the cost figure with current inflationary spirals.

The slide of the Wilson .45 telescopes inside the receiver and nothing but a sheet metal cover over the ejection port comes back over the shooter's hand. That, among other things, permits the lowering of the barrel for the straight-rearward thrust that nullifies muzzle flip.

In line with all its other attributes, the Wilson .45 boasted a trigger that let off at precisely ½-ounce above the usual 3½-pound minimum figure and did so with the crispness of a snapping icicle. Actually, it felt even lighter, because the trigger was a broad, sveltely rounded affair that snuggled against the finger and just seemed motionless until the firing pin suddenly dropped, with no slightest apparent disturbance of the sight picture, if viewed across an empty chamber.

At the time, Neth had worked out the details of a load his gun favored: 3.6 grains of Bullseye behind the No. 130 Hensley & Gibbs semi-wadcutter bullet in nickel-plated Remington cases with a CCI-300 primer to set it off. Out of a machine rest, that load kept all hits well inside a .452-inch center-to-center dispersion at twenty-five yards; less than the diameter of the bullet itself!

Standing and firing some of Neth's tailored loads out of his pride and joy, back in the waning days of 1966, I had no great difficulty in keeping all hits nipping chunks out of the ten-ring. Just a few of the wilder fliers nipped hunks from the nine-ring, but bit enough from the center circle to keep on counting as tens.

Usually, I fire test guns off the sandbag rest, to eliminate human error. I have not the slightest delusion about my personal marksmanship ability. I regard it as depressingly mediocre. For just one time, in the past many years, I encountered a gun that can accompany me up to the firing line with no need for sandbags. Let any other pistoleer equip themselves with any gun they wish (except, of course, one of the other two Wilsons!), and let me have No. GAW-1, and I'm prepared to be well content with my track record.

How much is a gun like that worth? The question can only be answered with another question. How much is it worth to be able to feel serene confidence that you and your gun can take on and outpoint any other handgunner apt to come along, provided he/she doesn't have another Wilson .45?

It's been a long discussion, but it seems to boil down to this: How much it's worth depends upon how well it shoots. To a group of would-be buyers not quite so berserkly intent upon competitive excellence, it could make a difference if it looks good. If it doesn't look good, nor shoot well, you would appear to have a Colby target pistol, sturdily worth its weight in pot metal.

We close translating a trio of Latin phrases. *Caveat emptor* means let the buyer beware. *Caveat vendor* means let the seller beware. *Caveat lector* means let the reader beware. In any event, tread warily!

Chapter 25

GUNS OF THE GUNFIGHTERS

There Is Great Question As To Just How Good Some Were, But There Is More Authentication On The Handguns They Used!

By E.B. Mann

SPEAK OF Western gunmen in any company and the odds are that the first name mentioned will be Wild Bill Hickok. Not James Butler Hickok; many people don't know him, but everybody knows "Wild Bill." He invented the name himself, and it was a great invention.

One of the next names mentioned will be Billy the Kid; another, Bat Masterson; another, Wyatt Earp; and sooner or later, John Wesley Hardin. They are, in point of fame at least, The Big Five of the legend.

It would be easy to name a few others: Sam Bass, Clay Allison, Bass Outlaw, King Fisher, Bill Breakenridge, Oliver

Lee, Bill Longley, Frank Hamer, Dallas Stoudenmire, Doc Holliday, Ben Thompson, John Selman, Tom Horn, Jeff Milton, even Pat Garrett.

And if the talk continues, sooner or later these questions will be asked: Who was the fastest on the draw? Who killed the most men? What guns did they use?

You won't find all the answers to those questions in these pages. Some of them can't be answered. And if you are contemptuous of such words as "alleged," better just forget it. Western society was not as cluttered with records and recordkeepers as we are today, and most of what we know about the old gunmen is hearsay. The serious

Gun owned by William S. Hart, said to have been taken from Billy the Kid at the time of his capture at Stinking Spring. The front sight is missing and the name "Billy" is scratched on the back strap. Its caliber is not known to the writer, but the serial number — 0361 — is clearly visible on the cylinder in this photo. That dates it as produced in 1874.

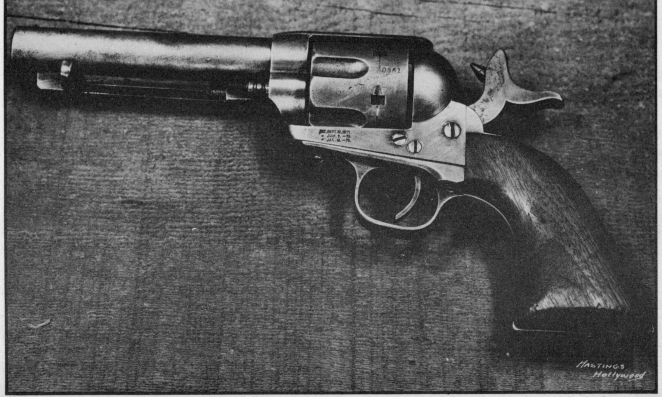

researcher finds a smattering of documentable facts, if he digs with care and patience, but most of what he finds is hearsay testimony. Much of it is so colored with wide-eyed eulogy on the one hand, or bitter denunciation on the other, that one can only weigh one against the other and draw his own conclusions. I've been doing both (research and weighing) for half a century, but you probably will disagree with me — and why shouldn't you? But what I state as facts are documentable. I only wish that there were more of them.

Western Americana addicts will note that I have not mentioned the James Brothers (Jesse and Frank), nor the Daltons (Emmett, Bob, Grattan, and Bill), nor the Youngers (Bob, Cole, Jim, and John), nor The Hole in the Wall gang (Butch Cassidy, The Sundance Kid, et al.), nor Joaquin Murieta (or Murietta) who, if one credits him with all the killings charged against him, would be, if not the champion of the Western killers, at least a top contender.

James Butler "Wild Bill" Hickok enjoys a remarkable reputation, some indeterminate portion of which may be justified, as E.B. Mann discusses in accompanying text.

The photo often published over "Billy the Kid" captions was usually reversed, giving rise to the myth that he was left-handed. Microscopic examination of the rifle proved otherwise. Artist's rendering above is a better likeness.

Not because they were outlaws (so were many of the men I have named), and not because they did not fight with guns (they did), but for some reason I find difficult to define, these do not seem to me to fit the pattern of the Western gunfighter legend. If you choose to include them, have at it!

Let's take the first question first: Who was "The Fastest Gun in the West"? This one is easy: Nobody knows!

There were no timing devices then to tell how fast those men could draw, fire and put a bullet into a target. The only way this could have been tested would have been by face-to-face shoot-outs — and that didn't happen; at least not between the ones we list among the great ones. True, there were meetings — at least two — of what could be called confrontations; as between Hickok and Hardin, or between Milton and Hardin. But in neither of those cases was a shot fired! Why not is an enigma within an enigma. True, several of the so-called greats (Hickok, Hardin, Billy the Kid, for examples) were killed by other gunmen or would-be gunmen, but not under what could be called competitive conditions. True, many of the greats killed other gunmen; but were the losers great?

So far as I know, the first scientific study of handgun speed and accuracy with split-second timers was the lifetime work of Ed McGivern. He and his cohorts devised and built electric timing devices that could record in tenths of a second the time in which a gun could be drawn and fired to hit a target, or how fast a series of shots could be fired. He tested all kinds of guns (even, at my request, a WWII Walther P-38 double-action autoloader). But his favorites were Smith & Wesson double-action revolvers. He tried all types of holsters, all kinds of carrying positions. When his results were first published, nobody believed them

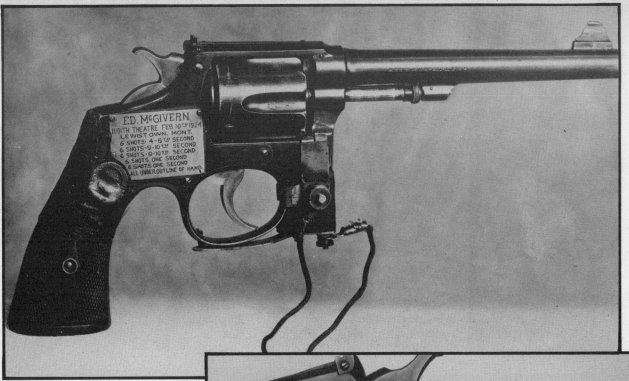

Smith & Wesson caliber .38 Special M&P Target Model, Serial 286600, used by Ed McGivern for rapid-fire exhibitions, as attested by witnessed marker plates.

— including Smith & Wesson, who thought Mac's double-action shooting was faster than the guns could operate. (They later built a machine that would operate their revolvers far faster than McGivern did.) But when Mac duplicated his reported times on Smith & Wesson's own timers, the company accepted that as proof and used his name and records in their advertising.

Would you believe five shots out of a double-action revolver in three-fifths of a second or less?

Would you believe five shots into a 5½x7-inch tin can thrown into the air, shooting double-action?

Would you believe fanning five shots from a Colt Single Action in times ranging from 1.4 down to 1.1 seconds, groups within the spread of a man's hand, at a range of twelve to eighteen feet? (But McGivern said fanning was not practical for combat; too risky.)

Would you believe hitting dimes tossed into the air, shooting a double-action revolver, scoring thirty-nine out of forty hits — once a straight run of thirty-one hits?

There are men living today who have (probably, on sophisticated electronic timers) equaled or surpassed McGivern's quick-draw records; but I know of no man, ever, who could do all the things Mac did, as well as he did them. I said to him once, "You could have killed any one of the old-timers!" But he said, "On the contrary, any one of them would have killed me. I might beat them on targets, but I lack the prime ingredient of a gunfighter — the willingness to kill. I would hesitate; they wouldn't."

How fast was Hickok? Well, he was fast enough to outlive a goodly number of men who wanted him dead! Some really tall tales have been told about his gun skills. One reports him shooting the heels off the boots of three (or five?) men running away from him across the Springfield, Missouri, town square. Many have told of his planting five (or was it ten?) bullets inside the "O" in a sign above the Market Square in Kansas City. One writer says the "O" was "about two feet in diameter," and that the range was "between 325 and 350 feet." That's a far piece for rapid-fire handgun shooting — and of course, the tellers of the story insist that "the shots were fired so fast they could hardly be counted."

What guns did he use? Name any gun current in Hickok's time and you can probably find testimony that he used it. Few writers have failed to mention the pair of white-handled revolvers which became a Hickok trademark. These are variously described as: (1) engraved ivory-handled .36 caliber Navys; (2) by Robert S. Kane (described as a firearms expert) in an article in June 1906, *Outdoor Life,* as "beautifully silver-plated S.A. .44 Colts." Kane also said that Hickok also had "a pair of Remingtons of the same caliber.

The gun with which Hickok killed Tutt in Springfield, Missouri, was described as a .44 caliber Colt Dragoon, and as a .32 caliber rimfire Smith & Wesson No. 2 Army. George Ward Nichols, in the famous story on which Hickok's fame was built, quoted Hickok as saying he was wearing "a pair of Colt Navys."

But we have only begun. Hickok is said to have worn, concealed in secret pockets inside his vest, a pair of .41 caliber Williamson derringers. Yet another hide-out gun, a small Sharps four-barreled pistol, is said to have been buried with Hickok. It was later displayed in Deadwood, Dakota Territory, where Hickok was killed.

Joseph Rosa, in his book, *They Call Him Wild Bill,* cites conflicting testimony that Hickok, in Deadwood, carried "a pair of .38 Colt revolvers converted from .36 cap-and-ball to cartridge," and from another source, that Hickok's guns were ".44 Army revolvers." Rosa also says, "the .32 Smith & Wesson tip-up Number 2 Army was a hide-out weapon."

How many men did Hickok kill? In his days as a lawman, a dozen or maybe fourteen killings can be fairly well authenticated. This would not include his tallies during the Civil War or during the Indian campaigns.

My own research in Springfield, Missouri, and elsewhere would indicate that Hickok, serving as a civilian scout for Union forces during the bloody guerrilla fighting in those Arkansas and Missouri hills, may very well have added at least another dozen — maybe twice that number — during that four-year period.

Rosa says Hickok "on his death-bed, is alleged to have claimed thirty-six 'notches.'" Skeptical though I am of Hickok's veracity, death-bed or not, I would not call that an unreasonable figure. I am even tempted to wonder how many others Hickok failed to include on behalf of his reputation. He was a deadly man, well endowed with McGivern's prime ingredient, "the willingness to kill." And he was a monumental liar, as must be apparent to anyone who reads, first, Hickok's own story of his desperate, single-handed battle with "the notorious McCandlass gang" at Rock Creek Station, Nebraska Territory, published by George Ward Nichols in the February 1867 issue of *Harper's Magazine,* and the Nebraska Historical Society's documented study of that incident published book-length in the April-June 1927 issue of *Nebraska Historical Magazine.* There was no such thing as a "notorious McCandlass Gang" (the name was McCanles); three men were killed, not ten or more as Hickok claimed; the fight was anything but heroic. Nichols didn't even get Hickok's name right; called him "Hitchcock" — which doesn't speak too highly of Nichol's journalistic integrity!

Almost as much has been written about Wyatt Earp and Billy the Kid as about Hickok. I have read it all, written some of it. Not as much has been written about Bat Masterson, but his nickname is catchy, his character as

Unique among the legendary gunfighters, Wyatt Earp — here shown at age 80 — survived to die of natural causes.

portrayed on television was colorful, and millions identify him as "that dude with the cane."

But it is my opinion that none of these belong in the Big Five we have listed; certainly not in point of numbers of men killed. I could name half a dozen or more men from the list mentioned in my early paragraph, each of whom killed as many or more men as all three of these combined.

Billy the Kid, according to the legend, killed twenty-one men, one for each year of his life. Again, I've read nearly everything written about him, have twenty-odd Billy-the-Kid books and dozens of lesser writings about him in my library, have done as much personal research about him as most of those writers — and I can't credit Billy with half that many killings. Give him two (Bell and Ollinger) in his escape from the Lincoln County courthouse; one (Bob Beckwith) dead and two (McKinney and Pearce) wounded as Bill ran, two guns blazing, across the twenty-foot back courtyard of the burning McSween house in Lincoln.

True, Billy was involved, *with others,* in several more fatalities. Billy was good with guns, so it is probable that his bullets played a part in the deaths. But individual killings? The tale of his beguiling a young stranger into letting him handle his gun, turning the cylinder to bring an empty chamber under the hammer, then killing its owner, is utterly undocumented. Add two, maybe three, possibles to the three above and you have extended the list to its limits.

Billy's fame comes partly from the nickname hung upon him, partly from Pat Garrett's (ghost-written) book, *The Authentic Life Of Billy the Kid,* in which Garrett painted Billy larger than life to improve his own image, and from the dozens of dime-novel fictions written about him.

I see Billy as a boy much like other boys, boyishly loyal to his friends (many nice people liked him), boyishly reckless, a small-time cattle thief after the Lincoln County War — small-time too on any real list of gunfighters.

I have seen a number of guns alleged to have belonged to him; read of others. There is a Winchester .44-40 M-1873 rifle Garrett is said to have found among Billy's belongings; a Whitneyville 10-gauge shotgun said to have belonged to Bob Ollinger, the gun with which Billy killed Ollinger from the window of the Lincoln County Courthouse; and a Colt .44-40 Single Action Army, Serial Number 0361, said to have been taken from Billy at the time of his capture at Stinking Spring. This gun has "Billy" engraved on its backstrap and is from the collection of the early Western movie star, William S. Hart.

There also is Pat Garrett's claim that Billy had in his hand a Colt .41 caliber Thunderer (the double-action Lightning Model) when Billy came into Pete Maxwell's dark

Right, William B. "Bat" Masterson, when he was sheriff of Ford County, Kansas. Below, the nickel-plated, caliber .45 LC Colt S.A., serial 112737, ordered by Masterson from the factory in 1885.

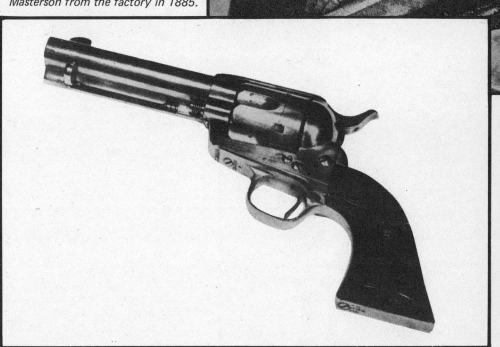

bedroom. Garrett identified the gun as "a self-cocker" (i.e., double action) and fired two shots, killing the intruder. I have personally wondered how Garrett could so well identify a specific gun in that darkness — and why Billy would have this new, vastly different model after a lifetime familiarity with single actions. But then a good many people in New Mexico wonder who the boy was that Garrett killed that night, are smilingly certain that it wasn't Billy. Just another of a thousand points in question in the gunfighter legends.

Wyatt Earp is another whose fame far exceeds his record. But unlike some, I have great respect for Earp, both as a man and as a gunman. He is, so far as I know, the only man in the whole long gallery of gunfighters who used his gun more often than not as a club, belting a man down with it, then arresting him rather than killing him. He was good with guns; frequently demonstrated his skills before admiring audiences in the belief that a reputation thus earned might help him avoid later shootings. His character and his work as a lawman are matters of documented fact, even in towns in which his detractors have said he never served. He killed some men; without digging back through a plethora of reference material I would say that to give him ten would include several probables or possibles. But he was a miracle man in one sense: he lived to a ripe old age, died of natural causes, and no bullet ever touched him.

One of the greater controversies about Earp concerns the long-barreled Buntline Special he is said to have carried. He said so; so did Bat Masterson and others. But Colt records have been searched unsuccessfully for the five guns Ned Buntline, fictioneer and hero-maker, is said to have given to five famous Western lawmen. Many have said that the guns never existed. Colt did make long-barreled revolvers; would add length to Peacemaker barrels for a dollar an inch, special order. I have always leaned to the belief that Earp did have, and did carry, a Buntline Special, since I never could see why he, and others, should lie about it. What was

there to gain? But I can't prove it, and the controversy continues.

Bat Masterson was a colorful character, a gunman good enough to impress such men as Earp, Ben Thompson, Luke Short, and others. His list of killings is brief, although he wore the star in such active arenas as Dodge City, Kansas (then described by a contemporary writer as "The Beautiful, Bibulous Babylon of the Frontier") and as a deputy United States marshal.

He was a participant in the famous "Fight at the Adobe Walls" between buffalo hunters (of which Bat was one) and a considerable force of Indians, so it can be assumed that he was entitled to some Indian "notches". But he, like Earp and Billy the Kid, achieved fame much beyond his due as a

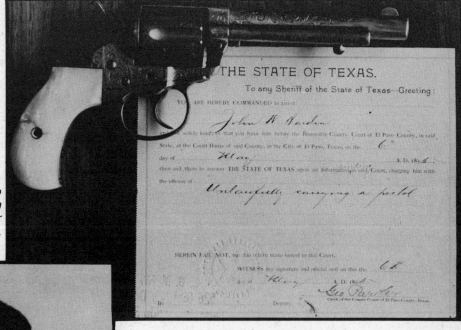

Below, John Wesley Hardin (photo copyright by N.H. Rose). Right, a warrant for Hardin's arrest, together with his .41 Colt, No. 73728 Lightning. (Photo by Robert McNellis.)

killer, probably of the nickname, Bat, which all can remember.

Masterson is one of the few whose guns — as least some of them — are documentable. In October 1879, while still a Dodge City lawman, Bat ordered direct from Colt a .45 Single Action Army with pearl stocks, silver plating, and his name, W.B. Masterson, engraved on the backstrap. This was the first of a total of eight guns which Masterson ordered from Colt's factory. They were all Single Actions, barrel lengths ranging from 4¾ to 7½ inches, all but one of them nickel or silver finish, five of them with rubber grips, one with pearl, and one with ivory. All are traceable in Colt's records, and one of them sold, in 1976, for $36,000 to a private collector. There are probably others gathering dust somewhere, and if you can find one that jibes with Colt's records, you will have a prize.

Gun collectors know how difficult it is to authenticate a specific gun to the ownership of "personage." Factory records can be checked to discover whether or not the gun could have been owned by the person in question; letters and other testimony can be provided; but it is rare indeed that such ownerships can be proved by hard, official documentation — as in the case of the Masterson revolver, and is the case with some of the guns of John Wesley Hardin.

It has always surprised me that Hardin is nearly always

Left/top, Hardin's .44-40 S&W D.A., serial 352; the gun taken from his body. Left/lower, Colt .41 LC No. 73728, found among his possessions. Below, Hardin's S.A. Army Colt in .45 LC, bearing serial 126680. Left photo, Robert McNellis; lower photo, University of Oklahoma Library.

the last named, if he is named at all, in discussions of the old Western gunmen. Less has been written about him than about Hickok, or Earp, or Billy the Kid, in spite of the fact that Hardin wrote his own biography and that it was published following his death. Despite the tendency of all self-biographers to write to their own advantage, Hardin wrote with a rather remarkable restraint, providing names-dates-places detail which has made it possible for his doings to be documented far better than can be done in other cases.

Hardin was the son of an itinerant preacher. Born in Texas in 1853, named after "the father of Methodism'" he grew to manhood in one of the bloodiest arenas of post-Civil War Reconstruction. Thousands of Texas veterans, refusing surrender, returned from war to find their properties, their towns, their local and state police, in the hands of former slaves, backed by black soldiery and black officials in their quest for wealth and power.

Wes and his older brother, Joe, grew up with guns, became dead shots as hunters, providing the family with meat. Wes was the extrovert, a frequent participant in schoolyard fights — a standard exercise for preachers' sons, as I well know, since I was one. A good student, he even taught school briefly at one point in his career.

Wes killed his first man in November 1868, six months short of his sixteenth birthday. The man was black, and Wes' father sent the boy away from home to escape the black vengeance he knew would come. But Wes, pursued by a part-white and part-black posse, met them head on, killing three men: two white, one black. Suddenly, the boy was a local hero, fighting a hated regime — a heady role for a teenager.

It went on from there. The Texas State Police, mostly black, had 2870 names on its published list of wanted men, and Hardin's name was soon near the top of that list. His price was "$800, Dead or Alive." Before the end of his seventeenth year, Hardin had killed twelve men.

Hardin tried repeatedly to follow the advice of family and friends that he should get out of Texas. He rode with a

trail herd to Kansas, to Abilene, where a man named Hickok was Mister Law. On the way north Wes killed six men, maybe seven. One, maybe two, were Indians who attacked the herd; five were members of another trail crew. In that melee, an eye-witness reported, "Wes shot down five armed and shooting men in about a minute. With either or both hands, that boy can handle pistols faster than a frog can lick flies!"

The meeting with Hickok is so much a part of both men's legends that it must be retold, though I can add nothing to it but conjecture. Hardin wrote: "Wild Bill pulled his pistol and said, 'Take those pistols off! I arrest you!' I said all right and pulled them out of the scabbards, but when he reached for them I reversed them and whirled them over on him with the muzzles in his face. I told him to put his pistol up, which he did." Whereupon, in Hardin's version, Hickok complimented him on his dexterity and promised to be his friend.

I find it difficult to believe that two men as willing to kill as these two provenly were could play out that scene without bloodshed. The spin Hardin describes was well known; a show-off stunt akin to the gun-spinning feats of the modern Hollywood gunslicks. Hardin, in an ill-advised instant of youthful cockiness, might have tried it; but Hickok knew the trick, would have recognized it at the first quiver of the boy's hands, could not have known that Hardin would not shoot. His gun was drawn; had he acted in way consistent with his record, he would have used it.

It is utterly inconsistent, too, in my opinion, that Hickok would offer friendship to a man who had made him the butt of any such horseplay. Hickok's reputation was his stock in trade, and any humiliation such as this would have galled him. But miracles do happen. Maybe it was like another gunfighter put it when asked why he did not make use of an opportunity to kill Wyatt Earp: "Yeah, I could've killed him; but he'd have killed me as he went down — and I didn't feel like dying that morning!"

Be that as it may, apparently Hardin himself placed little faith in Hickok's promise of friendship; he left Abilene within hours. A few days later, in another town, he killed another man.

Finding no peace in Kansas, Hardin returned to Texas, married, engaged successfully in buying and selling horses and cattle, killed more men, moved finally to Florida under the name of J.H. Swain.

But the Texas price for Hardin was now "$3000 — Dead or Alive," and when Hardin one day boarded a Florida train whose other passengers were mostly men seeking a share of that bounty, he was snowed under, shackled, and taken back to Texas, tried, convicted of murder for killing a man who had first shot him in the back, and sentenced to twenty-five years in prison. He served fifteen, his term shortened for good behavior. But they were bitter years. His wife died, and his brother and two cousins were victims of a lynch mob. There was not much to go back to.

Hardin "read law" in prison and, after abortive efforts elsewhere, "hung up his shingle" in El Paso. It was a poor choice of environment. El Paso, in those years, was a mecca for gunfighters, gamblers, and men to whom Hardin's record was a challenge.

But this was a different Hardin. Gone was the old youthful flamboyance, the old quick willingness for fight or frolic. Gone too were the old single actions; they would not have suited his new clothing, his new image. He bought different guns. But, except for endless practice before a

mirror in his room, he never used them, never killed another man, never so much as fired a shot in anger after he stepped out of prison.

On August 19, 1895, as Hardin stood with his back to the door in the Acme Saloon in El Paso, John Selman Sr. came through that door, fired one shot into the back of Hardin's head, two more into the arm and body as Hardin fell. Hardin was 42 years old.

How fast was he? "Faster than a frog can lick flies" is colorful but not definitive. El Paso Police Chief Jeff Milton, himself a gun-swift, said Hardin was the fastest he ever saw. (Nevertheless, Milton once challenged Hardin, called him a liar. Hardin admitted the lie, did not draw — a thing utterly uncharacteristic of the pre-prison Hardin.) I think that his record shows a higher percentage of wins over men already shooting at him, or men met in even shoot-outs, than can be proved any other gunman, and on that basis I rank him Number One. But that is only one man's opinion.

How many men did Hardin kill? Researchers are pretty generally agreed on forty, plus from two to five possibles.

According to Hardin's own writing, the guns of his pre-prison days were Colt Single Actions. He may have owned a number of them, though none (to my knowledge) have been specifically identified — unless the one found among his possessions after his death was a carry-over from the old days. But the guns he owned and wore in El Paso are specifically identified by police and court records, backed by Colt's records and dealer affidavits. The list is as follows:

The gun taken from Hardin's body in the Acme Saloon was a Smith & Wesson .44 caliber double-action revolver, serial number 352. Listed among his possessions after his death were: one Colt .41 pistol, serial number 68837; one Colt .38 pistol, white handle, serial number 84304; one Colt .45 pistol, serial number 126680; and one Colt .41 pistol, white handle, serial number 73728.

As I wrote of Hardin some years ago, "He was a man of his times, neither better nor worse than many; only quicker." It would be a fitting epitaph for many of the old Western gunmen. May they rest in peace.

John Selman (right), about 1878: He was killed by George Scarborough in 1896. Below, upper gun (No. 36693) is the one Selman carried the night he was killed. Lower gun (No. 141805) is the one he used to kill John W. Hardin. Credits: University of Oklahoma Library and R. McNellis.

BERNARDELLI MODEL 100 PISTOL
Caliber: 22 LR only, 10-shot magazine.
Barrel: 5.9".
Weight: 37¾ oz. **Length:** 9" over-all.
Stocks: Checkered walnut with thumbrest.
Sights: Fixed front, rear adj. for w. and e.
Features: Target barrel weight included. Heavy sighting rib with interchangeable front sight. Accessories include cleaning equipment and assembly tools, case. Imported from Italy by Interarms.
Price: **$285.00**

BERETTA MODEL 76 PISTOL
Caliber: 22 LR, 10-shot magazine.
Barrel: 6".
Weight: 33 ozs. (empty). **Length:** 8.8" over-all.
Stocks: Checkered plastic.
Sights: Interchangable blade front (3 widths), rear is fully adj. for w. and e.
Features: Built-in, fixed counterweight, raised, matted slide rib, factory adjusted trigger pull from 3 lbs. 5 ozs. to 3 lbs. 12 ozs. Thumb safety. Blue-black finish. Wood grips available at extra cost. Introduced 1977. Imported by Beretta Arms Co.
Price: **$245.00**
Price: With wood grips **$268.00**

CVA/UNIQUE D.E.S. 69 TARGET PISTOL
Caliber: 22 LR.
Barrel: 5.91".
Weight: Approx. 35 oz. **Length:** 10.63" over-all.
Stocks: French walnut target style with thumbrest and adjustable shelf; hand checkered panels.
Sights: Ramp front, micro. adj. rear mounted on frame; 8.66" sight radius.
Features: Meets U.I.T. standards. Comes in a fitted hard case with spare magazine, barrel weight, cleaning rod, tools, proof certificate, test target and two year guarantee. Fully adjustable trigger; dry firing safety device. Imported from France by Solersport.
Price: Right-hand **$570.63**
Price: Left-hand **$600.63**

COLT GOLD CUP NAT'L MATCH MK IV Series 70
Caliber: 45 ACP, 7-shot magazine.
Barrel: 5", with new design bushing.
Length: 8⅜". **Weight:** 38½ oz.
Stocks: Checkered walnut, gold plated medallion.
Sights: Ramp-style front, Colt-Elliason rear adj. for w. and e., sight radius 6¾".
Features: Arched or flat housing; wide, grooved trigger with adj. stop; ribbed-top slide, hand fitted, with improved ejection port.
Price: Colt Royal Blue **$370.95**

DOMINO MODEL SP-602 MATCH PISTOL
Caliber: 22 LR, 5-shot.
Barrel: 5.5".
Weight: 41 oz. **Length:** 11.02" over-all.
Stocks: Full target stocks; adjustable, one-piece. Left hand style avail.
Sights: Match. Blade front, open notch rear fully adj. for w. and e. Sight radius is 8.66".
Features: Line of sight is only $^{11}/_{32}$" above centerline of bore; magazine is inserted from top; adjustable and removable trigger mechanism; single lever takedown. Full 5 year warranty. Imported from Italy by Mandall Shooting Supplies.
Price: **$799.50**

DOMINO O.P. 601 MATCH PISTOL
Similar to S.P. 602 except has different match stocks with adj. palm shelf, 22 Short only, weighs 40 oz., 5.6" bbl., has gas ports through top of barrel and slide to reduce recoil, slightly different trigger and sear mechanisms.
Price: **$799.50**

HANDGUNS—TARGET AUTOLOADERS

SIG/HAMMERLI P-240 TARGET PISTOL
Caliber: 32 S&W Long.
Barrel: 6".
Weight: 4¼ oz. **Length:** 10" over-all.
Stocks: Walnut, target style, unfinished.
Sights: Match sights; ⅛" undercut front, ⅛" notch micro rear click adj. for w. and e.
Features: Semi-automatic, recoil operated; meets I.S.U. and N.R.A. specs for Center Fire Pistol competition; double pull trigger adj. from 2 lbs., 15 ozs. to 3 lbs., 9 ozs.; trigger stop. Comes with extra magazine, special screwdriver, carrying case. From Mandall Shooting Supplies.
Price: $1,295.00
Price: 22 cal. conversion unit ....$ 750.00

SIG P-210-1 AUTO PISTOL
Caliber: 22 LR, 7.65mm or 9mm P., 8-shot magazine.
Barrel: 4¾".
Weight: 31¾ oz. (9mm) **Length:** 8½" over-all.
Stocks: Checkered walnut.
Sights: Blade front, rear adjustable for windage.
Features: Lanyard loop; polished finish. Conversion unit for 22 LR available. Imported by Mandall Shooting Supplies.
Price: P-210-1 ....$1,295.00
Price: 22 Cal. Conversion unit ....$ 650.00

SIG P-210-6 AUTO PISTOL
Caliber: 9mm Para., 8-shot magazine.
Barrel: 4¾".
Weight: 37 oz. **Length:** 8½" over-all.
Stocks: Checkered black plastic.
Sights: Blade front, micro. adj. rear for w. & e.
Features: Adjustable trigger stop; ribbed front stap; sandblasted finish. Conversion unit for 22 LR consists of barrel, recoil spring, slide and magazine. Imported by Mandall Shooting Supplies.
Price: P-210-6 ....$1,295.00
Price: 22 Cal. Conversion unit ....$ 650.00

SMITH & WESSON 22 AUTO PISTOL Model 41
Caliber: 22 LR or 22 S, 10-shot clip.
Barrel: 7⅜", sight radius 9⁵⁄₁₆" (7⅜" bbl.).
Length: 12", incl. detachable muzzle brake, (7⅜" bbl. only).
Weight: 43½ oz. (7⅜" bbl.)
Stocks: Checkered walnut with thumbrest, usable with either hand.
Features: ⅜" wide, grooved trigger with adj. stop; wgts. available to make pistol up to 59 oz.
Sights: Front, ⅛" Patridge undercut; micro click rear adj. for w. and e.
Price: S&W Bright Blue, satin matted bbl., either caliber $252.00

SMITH & WESSON 22 MATCH HEAVY BARREL M-41
Caliber: 22 LR, 10-shot clip.
Barrel: 5½" heavy, without muzzle brake. Sight radius, 8".
Length: 9". **Weight:** 44½ oz.
Stocks: Checkered walnut with modified thumbrest, usable with either hand.
Features: ⅜" wide, grooved trigger; adj. trigger stop.
Sights: ⅛" Patridge on ramp base. S&W micro click rear, adj. for w. and e.
Price: S&W Bright Blue, satin matted top area $252.00

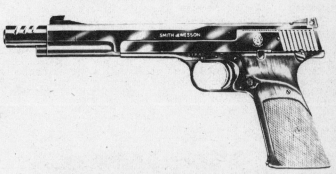

SMITH & WESSON 38 MASTER Model 52 AUTO
Caliber: 38 Special (for Mid-range W.C. with flush-seated bullet only). 5-shot magazine.
Barrel: 5".
Length: 8⅝". **Weight:** 41 oz. with empty magazine.
Stocks: Checkered walnut.
Sights: ⅛" Partidge front, S&W micro click rear adj. for w. and e.
Features: Top sighting surfaces matte finished. Locked breech, moving barrel system; checked for 10-ring groups at 50 yards. Coin-adj. sight screws. Dry firing permissible if manual safety on.
Price: S&W Bright Blue $411.50

HAMMERLI MODEL 230 RAPID FIRE PISTOL
Caliber: 22 S.
Barrel: 6.3", 6-groove.
Weight: 43.8 oz. **Length:** 11.6".
Stocks: Walnut. Standard grip w/o thumbrest (230-1), 230-2 has adj. grip.
Sights: Match type sights. Sight radius 9.9". Micro rear, click adj. Interchangeable front sight blade.
Features: Semi-automatic. Recoil-operated, 6-shot clip. Gas escape in front of chamber to eliminate muzzle jump. Fully adj. trigger from 5¼ oz. to 10½ oz. with three different lengths available. Designed for International 25 meter Silhouette Program. Mandall Shooting Supplies, importer.
Price: Model 230-1 . . . . **$979.00**
Price: Model 230-2 . . . . **$995.00**

HAMMERLI STANDARD, MODELS 208 & 211
Caliber: 22 LR.
Barrel: 5.9", 6-groove.
Weight: 37.6 oz. (45 oz. with extra heavy barrel weight). **Length:** 10".
Stocks: Walnut. Adj. palm rest (208), 211 has thumbrest grip.
Sights: Match sights. fully adj. for w. and e. (click adj.). Interchangeable front and rear blades.
Features: Semi-automatic, recoil operated. 8-shot clip. Slide stop. Fully adj. trigger (2¼ lbs. and 3 lbs.). Extra barrel weight available. Mandall Shooting Supplies, importer.
Price: Model 208, approx. **$995.00** Model 211 approx. **$979.00**

HI-STANDARD SUPERMATIC CITATION MILITARY
Caliber: 22 LR, 10-shot magazine.
Barrel: 5½" bull, 7¼" fluted.
Length: 9¾" (5½" bbl.). **Weight:** 46 oz.
Stocks: Checkered walnut with thumbrest, right or left.
Sights: Undercut ramp front; frame mounted rear, click adj.
Features: Adjustable trigger pull; over-travel trigger adjustment; double acting safety; rebounding firing pin; military style grip; stippled front- and backstraps; positive magazine latch.
Price: 5½" barrel **$222.25**
Price: 7¼" barrel **$236.25**

HI-STANDARD SUPERMATIC TROPHY MILITARY
Caliber: 22 LR, 10-shot magazine.
Barrel: 5½" heavy, 7¼" fluted.
Length: 9¾" (5½" bbl.). **Weight:** 44½ oz.
Stocks: Checkered walnut with thumbrest, right or left.
Features: Grip duplicates feel of military 45; positive action mag. latch; front- and backstraps stippled. Trigger adj. for pull, over-travel.
Sights: Undercut ramp front; frame mounted rear, click adj.
Price: 5½" barrel **$236.25**
Price: 7¼" barrel **$251.00**

HI-STANDARD VICTOR
Caliber: 22 LR, 10-shot magazine.
Barrel: 4½", 5½".
Length: 8¾" (4½" bbl.). **Weight:** 43½ oz. (4½" bbl., vent. rib), 46 oz. (5½" bbl., vent. rib).
Stocks: Checkered walnut.
Sights: Undercut ramp front, rib mounted click adj. rear.
Features: Vent. rib, interchangeable barrel, 2 - 2¼ lb. trigger pull, blue finish, back and front straps stippled.
Price: Either bbl. length **$270.50**

RUGER Mark 1 TARGET MODEL AUTO PISTOL
Caliber: 22 LR only, 9-shot magazine.
Barrel: 6⅞" or 5½" bull barrel (6-groove, 14" twist).
Length: 10⅞" (6⅞" bbl.). **Weight:** 42 oz. with 6⅞" bbl.
Stocks: Checkered hard rubber.
Features: Rear sight mounted on receiver, does not move with slide; wide, grooved trigger.
Sights: ⅛" blade front, micro click rear, adjustable for w. and e. Sight radius 9⅜" (with 6⅞" bbl.).
Price: Blued, either barrel length **$118.00**

HANDGUNS—TARGET AUTOLOADERS

WALTHER GSP MATCH PISTOL
Caliber: 22 LR, 32 S&W wadcutter (GSP-C), 5-shot.
Barrel: 5¾".
Weight: 44.8 oz. (22 LR), 49.4 oz. (32). **Length:** 11.8" over-all.
Stock: Walnut, special hand-fitting design.
Sights: Fixed front, rear adj. for w. & e.
Features: Available with either 2.2 lb. (1000 gm) or 3 lb. (1360 gm) trigger. Spare mag., bbl. weight, tools supplied in Match Pistol Kit. Imported from Germany by Interarms.
Price: GSP .... $ 990.00
Price: GSP-C $1,180.00
Price: 22 LR conversion unit for GSP-C .... $ 690.00
Price: 22 Short conversion unit for GSP-C .... $ 650.00

WALTHER OSP RAPID-FIRE PISTOL
Similar to Model GSP except 22 Short only, stock has adj. free-style hand rest.
Price: **$990.00**

HANDGUNS—TARGET REVOLVERS

COLT PYTHON REVOLVER
Caliber: 357 Magnum (handles all 38 Spec.), 6 shot.
Barrel: 2½", 4" or 6", with ventilated rib.
Length: 9¼"(4" bbl.). **Weight:** 38 oz. (4" bbl.).
Stocks: Checkered walnut, target type.
Sights: ⅛" ramp front, adj. notch rear.
Features: Ventilated rib; grooved, crisp trigger; swing-out cylinder; target hammer.
Price: Colt Blue .... **$422.95**   Nickeled **$435.95**

SMITH & WESSON MASTERPIECE TARGET MODELS

Model: K-22 (M17).	K-22 (M48).
Caliber: 22 LR, 6 shot.	22 RF Magnum, 6 shot.
Barrel: 6", 8⅜".	4", 6" or 8⅜"
Length: 11⅛" (6" bbl.).	11⅛" (6" bbl.).
Weight: 38½ oz. (6" bbl.).	39 oz.(6" bbl.).
Model: K-32 (M16). (Illus.)	K-38 (M14).
Caliber: 32 S&W Long, 6 shot.	38 S&W Special, 6 shot.
Barrel: 6".	6", 8⅜".
Length: 11⅛".	11⅛". (6" bbl.)
Weight: 38½ oz. (loaded).	38½ oz. (6", loaded).

Features: All Masterpiece models have: checkered walnut, Magna stocks; grooved tang and trigger; ⅛" Patridge front sight, micro. adj. rear sights. Swing out cylinder revolver. For 8⅜" barrel add **$9.00**.
Price: Blued, all calibers M-17, 6" bbl. $181.00
Price: Blued, all calibers M-48, 4", 6" bbl. $209.00

SMITH & WESSON 1955 Model 25, 45 TARGET
Caliber: 45 ACP and 45 AR, 6 shot.
Barrel: 6½" (heavy target type).
Length: 11⅞". **Weight:** 45 oz.
Stocks: Checkered walnut target.
Sights: ⅛" Patridge front, micro click rear, adjustable for w. and e.
Features: Tangs and trigger grooved; target trigger and hammer standard, checkered target hammer. Swing-out cylinder revolver. Price includes presentation case.
Price: Blued $331.50

SMITH & WESSON COMBAT MASTERPIECE
Caliber: 38 Special (M15) or 22 LR (M18), 6 shot.
Barrel: 2" (M15) 4" (M18)
Length: 9⅛" (4" bbl.). **Weight:** Loaded, 22 36½ oz, 38 30 oz.
Stocks: Checkered walnut, Magna. Grooved tangs and trigger.
Sights: Front, ⅛" Baugham Quick Draw on ramp, micro click rear, adjustable for w. and e.
Price: Blued, M-15 .... $149.50
Price: Nickel M-15 .... $161.00
Price: Blued, M-18 .... $181.00

Smith & Wesson Accessories
Target hammers with low, broad, deeply-checkered spur, and wide-swaged, grooved target trigger. For all frame sizes, **$7.42** (target hammers not available for small frames). Target stocks: for large-frame guns, **$14.25** to **$16.00**; for med.-frame guns, **$12.00** to **$14.50**; for small-frame guns, **$10.75** to **$14.00**. These prices applicable only when specified on original order.
As separately-ordered parts: target hammers (**$15.75**) and triggers, **$13.55**; stocks, **$15.13-$26.40**.

Consult our Directory pages for the location of firms mentioned.

TAURUS MODEL 86 TARGET MASTER REVOLVER
Caliber: 38 Spec., 6-shot.
Barrel: 6″ only.
Weight: 41 oz. **Length:** 11¼″ over-all.
Stocks: Over size target-type, checkered Brazilian walnut.
Sights: Patridge front, micro. click rear adj. for w. and e.
Features: Blue finish with non-reflective finish on barrel. Imported from Brazil by International Distributors.
Price: About **$149.00**
Price: Model 96 Scout Master, same except in 22 cal., about **$149.00**

HANDGUNS—AUTOLOADERS, SERVICE & SPORT

AMT 45 ACP HARDBALLER
Caliber: 45 ACP.
Barrel: 5″.
Weight: 39 oz. **Length:** 8½″ over-all.
Stocks: Checkered walnut.
Sights: Adjustable combat-type.
Features: Extended combat safety, serrated matte slide rib, loaded chamber indicator, long grip safety, beveled magazine well, grooved front and back straps, adjustable target trigger, custom-fitted barrel bushing. All stainless steel. From AMT.
Price: **$450.00**
Price: 45 Skipper (same as above except 1″ shorter) **$450.00**

AMT COMBAT GOVERNMENT
Caliber: 45 ACP.
Barrel: 5″.
Weight: 38 oz. **Length:** 8½″ over-all.
Stocks: Checkered walnut, diamond pattern.
Sights: Combat-style, fixed.
Features: All stainless steel; extended combat safety, loaded chamber indicator, beveled magazine well, adjustable target-type trigger, custom-fitted barrel bushing, flat mainspring housing. From AMT.
Price: **$395.00**

ASTRA CONSTABLE AUTO PISTOL
Caliber: 22 LR, 10-shot; 32 ACP, 8-shot; and 380 ACP, 7-shot.
Barrel: 3½″.
Weight: 26 oz.
Stocks: Moulded plastic.
Sights: Adj. rear.
Features: Double action, quick no-tool takedown, non-glare rib on slide. 380 available in blue or chrome finish. Imported from Spain by Interarms.
Price: Blue **$205.00**
Price: Chrome **$220.00**

BAUER AUTOMATIC PISTOL
Caliber: 25 ACP, 6-shot.
Barrel: 2-1/8'' (25 ACP).
Weight: 10 oz. **Length:** 4'' (25 ACP).
Stocks: Plastic pearl or checkered walnut.
Sights: Recessed, fixed.
Features: Stainless steel construction, positive manual safety, magazine safety.
Price: Satin stainless steel, 25ACP **$104.85**

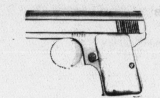

BERETTA MODEL 70S PISTOL
Caliber: 22 LR, 380 ACP.
Barrel: 3.5''.
Weight: 23 ozs. (Steel) **Length:** 6.5'' over-all.
Stocks: Checkered black plastic.
Sights: Fixed front and rear.
Features: Steel frame in 32 and 380, light alloy in 22 (wgt. 18 ozs.). Safety lever blocks hammer. Side lever indicates empty magazine. Magazine capacity is 8 rounds (22), 7 rounds in 380. Introduced 1977. Imported by Beretta Arms Co.
Price: **$198.00**

BERETTA MODEL 81/84 DA PISTOLS
Caliber: 32 ACP (12-shot magazine), 380 ACP (13-shot magazine)
Barrel: 3¾''.
Weight: About 23 oz. **Length:** 6½'' over-all.
Stocks: Smooth black plastic (wood optional at extra cost $20.00)
Sights: Fixed front and rear.
Features: Double action, quick take-down, convenient magazine release. Introduced 1977. Imported by Beretta Arms. Co.
Price: M-81 (32 ACP) **$285.00**
Price: M-84 (380 ACP) **$285.00**

BERETTA MODEL 92 DA PISTOL
Caliber: 9mm Parabellum (15-shot magazine).
Barrel: 4.92''.
Weight: 33½ ozs. **Length:** 8.54'' over-all.
Stocks: Smooth black plastic.
Sights: Blade front, rear adj. for w.
Features: Double-action. Extractor acts as chamber loaded indicator, inertia firing pin. Finished in blue-black. Introduced 1977. Imported by Beretta Arms Co.
Price: **$398.00**
Price: With wood grips **$425.00**

BERNARDELLI MODEL 80 AUTO PISTOL
Caliber: 22 LR (10-shot); 32 ACP (8-shot); 380 ACP (7-shot).
Barrel: 3½''.
Weight: 26½ oz. **Length:** 6½'' over-all.
Stocks: Checkered plastic with thumbrest.
Sights: Ramp front, white outline rear adj. for w. & e.
Features: Hammer block slide safety; loaded chamber indicator; dual recoil buffer springs; serrated trigger; inertia type firing pin. Imported from Italy by Interarms.
Price: Model 80 .... **$163.00**

Bernardelli Model 100 Target Pistol
Similar to Model 80 except has 5.9'' barrel and barrel weight; heavy sighting rib; checkered walnut thumbrest grips; 22 LR only (10-shot). Comes with case, cleaning equipment and tools. **$285.00**

BROWNING BDA AUTO PISTOL
Caliber: 45 ACP only (7-shot).
Barrel: 4^{13}/32".
Weight: 29 ozs. (9mm) **Length:** 7^{25}/32." over-all.
Stocks: Checkered black plastic
Sights: Blade front, drift adj. rear of w.
Features: Double action. De-cocking lever permits lowering hammer onto locked firing pin. Squared combat-type trigger guard. Slide stays open after last shot. Introduced 1977. Imported by Browning.
Price: 45 ACP **$349.95**

BROWNING BDA-380 D/A AUTO PISTOL
Caliber: 380 ACP, 12-shot magazine.
Barrel: 3^{13}/16".
Weight: 23 ozs. **Length:** 6¾" over-all.
Stocks: Smooth walnut with inset Browning medallion.
Sights: Blade front, rear drift-adj. for w.
Features: Combination safety and de-cocking lever will automatically lower a cocked hammer to half-cock and can be operated by right or left-hand shooters. Inertia firing pin. Introduced 1978.
Price: **$262.50**

BROWNING HI-POWER 9mm AUTOMATIC PISTOL
Caliber: 9mm Parabellum (Luger), 13-shot magazine.
Barrel: 4^{21}/32 inches.
Length: 7¾" over-all. **Weight:** 32 oz.
Stocks: Walnut, hand checkered.
Sights: ⅛" blade front; rear screw-adj. for w. and e. Also available with fixed rear (drift-adj. for w.).
Features: External hammer with half-cock safety and thumb safeties. A blow on the hammer cannot discharge a cartridge; cannot be fired with magazine removed. Fixed rear sight model available.
Price: Fixed sight model **$359.95**
Price: 9mm with rear sight adj. for w. and e. **$389.95**

Browning Renaissance Hi-Power 9mm Auto
Same as Browning Hi-Power 9mm Auto except: fully engraved, chrome plated, Narcolac pearl grips, with deluxe walnut case.
Price: With adj. sights **$1,400.00**
Price: With fixed sights **$1,450.00**

BROWNING CHALLENGER II AUTO PISTOL
Caliber: 22 LR, 10-shot magazine.
Barrel: 6¾".
Weight: 38 oz. **Length:** 10⅞" over-all.
Stocks: Smooth impregnated hardwood.
Sights: ⅛" blade front on ramp, rear screw adj. for e., drift adj. for w.
Features: All steel, blue finish. Wedge locking system prevents action from loosening. Wide gold-plated trigger; action hold-open. Standard grade only. From Browning.
Price: **$169.95**

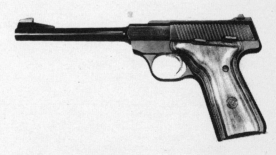

COLT SERVICE MODEL ACE
Caliber: 22 LR, 10-shot magazine.
Barrel: 5".
Weight: 42 ozs. **Length:** 8⅜" over-all.
Stocks: Checkered walnut.
Sights: Blade front, fully adjustable rear.
Features: The 22-cal. version of the Government Model auto. Based on the Service Model Ace last produced in 1945. Patented floating chamber. Original Ace Markings rolled on left side of slide. Introduced 1978.
Price: Blue only **$292.95**

COLT COMMANDER AUTO PISTOL
Caliber: 45 ACP, 7 shot; 38 Super Auto, 9 shot; 9mm Luger, 9 shot.
Barrel: 4¼".
Length: 8". **Weight:** 36 oz.
Stocks: Sandblasted walnut.
Sights: Fixed, glare-proofed blade front, square notch rear.
Features: Grooved trigger and hammer spur; arched housing; grip and thumb safeties.
Price: Blued $276.95

Colt Lightweight Combat Commander
Same as Commander except high strength aluminum alloy frame, wood panel grips, weight 27 oz. 45 ACP only.
Price: Blue $268.95

Colt Conversion Unit
Permits the 45 and 38 Super Automatic pistols to use the economical 22 LR cartridge. No tools needed. Adjustable rear sight; 10-shot magazine. Designed to give recoil effect of the larger calibers. Not adaptable to Commander models. Blue finish $143.95

COLT GOV'T MODEL MK IV/SERIES 70
Caliber: 9mm, 38 Super, 45 ACP, 7-shot.
Barrel: 5".
Weight: 40 oz. **Length:** 8⅜" over-all.
Stocks: Sandblasted walnut panels.
Sights: Ramp front, fixed square notch rear.
Features: Grip and thumb safeties, grooved trigger. Accurizor barrel and bushing. Blue finish or nickel in 45 only.
Price: Blue $276.95
Price: Nickel $292.95

DETONICS 45 PISTOL
Caliber: 45 ACP, 6-shot clip.
Barrel: 3¼" (2½" of which is rifled).
Weight: 29 ozs. (empty). **Length:** 6¾" over-all, 4½" high.
Stocks: Checkered walnut.
Sights: Combat type, fixed (adj. sights available).
Features: Has a self-adjusting cone barrel centering system, beveled magazine inlet, "full clip" indicator in base of magazine; standard 7-shot (or more) clip can be used. Throated barrel and polished feed ramp. Introduced 1977. From Detonics.
Price: Blue $444.77
Price: Nickel $473.48
Price: Hard chrome $487.04
Price: Polished blue with adj. sights $493.60

ERMA KGP22 AUTO PISTOL
Caliber: 22 LR, 8-shot magazine.
Barrel: 4".
Weight: 29 ozs. **Length:** 7¾" over-all.
Stocks: Checkered plastic.
Sights: Fixed.
Features: Has toggle action similar to original "Luger" pistol. Slide stays open after last shot. Imported from West Germany by Excam. Introduced 1978.
Price: $178.00

ERMA KGP32, KGP38 AUTO PISTOLS
Caliber: 32 ACP (6-shot), 380 ACP (5-shot).
Barrel: 4".
Weight: 22½ ozs. **Length:** 7⅜" over-all.
Stocks: Checkered plastic. Wood optional.
Sights: Fixed.
Features: Toggle action similar to original "Luger" pistol. Slide stays open after last shot. Has magazine and sear disconnect safety systems. Imported from West Germany by Excam. Introduced 1978.
Price: Plastic grips $183.00

IVER JOHNSON MODEL X300 PONY
Caliber: 380 ACP, 6-shot magazine.
Barrel: 3".
Weight: 20 oz. **Length:** 6" over-all.
Stocks: Checkered walnut.
Sights: Blade front, rear adj. for w.
Features: Loaded chamber indicator, all steel construction. Inertia firing pin. Thumb safety locks hammer. No magazine safety. Lanyard ring. From Iver Johnson's.
Price: Blue $170.00
Price: Nickel $180.25
Price: Military (matte finish) $170.00

F.I.E. TITAN II E32, E380 PISTOLS
Caliber: 32 ACP, 380 ACP, 6-shot magazine.
Barrel: 3-7/8".
Weight: 25¾ ozs. **Length:** 4" over-all.
Stocks: Checkered nylon, thumbrest-type.
Sights: Fixed.
Features: Magazine disconnector, firing pin block. Standard slide safety. Available in blue or chrone. Introduced 1978. From F.I.E. Corp.
Price: 32, blue $99.95
Price: 32, chrome $99.95
Price: 380, blue $109.95
Price: 380, chrome $114.95

F.I.E. TITAN 25 PISTOL
Caliber: 25 ACP, 6-shot magazine.
Barrel: 2⁷/₁₆".
Length: 4⅝" over-all. **Weight:** 12 oz.
Stocks: Checkered nylon.
Sights: Fixed.
Features: External hammer; fast simple takedown. Made in U.S.A. by F.I.E. Corp.
Price: Blued . . . . $49.95   Chromed: $59.95

F.I.E. "THE BEST" A27B AUTO PISTOL
Caliber: 25 ACP, 6-shot magazine.
Barrel: 2½".
Weight: 13 ozs. **Length:** 4⅜" over-all.
Stocks: Checkered walnut.
Sights: Fixed.
Features: All steel construction. Has thumb and magazine safeties, exposed hammer. Blue finish only. Introduced 1978. From F.I.E. Corp.
Price: $109.95

FTL 22 AUTO NINE PISTOL
Caliber: 22 LR, 8-shot magazine.
Barrel: 2¼", 6-groove rifling.
Weight: 8¼ oz. **Length:** 4⅜" over-all.
Stocks: Checkered plastic.
Sights: U-notch in slide.
Features: Alloy frame, rest is ordnance steel. Has barrel support sleeve bushing for better accuracy. Finish is matte hard chrome. Introduced 1978. From FTL Marketing.
Price: $159.95

HAWES/SIG-SAUER D.A AUTO PISTOL
Caliber: 9mm, 38 Super or 45 ACP, (9-shot in 9mm, 7 in 45).
Barrel: 4⅜".
Weight: 28¼ oz. (9mm). **Length:** 7¾" over-all.
Stocks: Checkered walnut.
Sights: Blade front, drift adj. rear for w.
Features: Double action. De-cocking lever permits lowering hammer onto locked firing pin. Squared combat-type trigger guard. Slide stays open after last shot. Imported by Hawes Firearms.
Price: $349.95

HAWES/SIG-SAUER P-230 D.A. PISTOL
Caliber: 32 ACP (8-shot), 380 ACP, 9mm Police (7 shot).
Barrel: 3¾".
Weight: 16¼ oz. (32), 16 oz. (380), 18¾ oz. (9mm Police) **Length:** 6½" over-all.
Stocks: One piece black plastic.
Sights: Blade front, rear adj. for w.
Features: Double action. Same basic design as P-220. (9mm, 38 Super, 45 ACP). Blowback operation, stationary barrel. Introduced 1977. Imported by Hawes.
Price: 32 or 380 . . . . $299.95
Price: 9mm Police $349.95

HK P9S DOUBLE ACTION AUTO PISTOL

Caliber: 9mm Para., 9-shot magazine.
Barrel: 4".
Weight: 33½ oz. **Length:** 5½" over-all.
Stocks: Checkered black plastic.
Sights: Open combat type.
Features: Double action; polygonal rifling; sliding roller lock action with stationary barrel. Loaded chamber and cocking indicators; un-cocking lever relaxes springs. Imported from Germany by Heckler & Koch, Inc.
Price: P-9S combat model $384.00
Price: P-9S Target Model $436.00
Price: P-9/P-9S Competition Model (similar to Target except comes with wrap around match grips, bbl. weight, 4" & 5½" bbl. $599.00

HECKLER & KOCH P9S DOUBLE ACTION 45

Caliber: 45 ACP, 7-shot magazine.
Barrel: 4¹/₃₂".
Weight: 32½ oz. **Length:** 7½" over-all.
Stocks: Checkered black plastic.
Sights: Open, combat type.
Features: Double action; polygonal rifling; delayed roller-locked bolt system. Imported by Heckler & Koch, Inc.
Price: $384.00
Price: With adj. trigger, trigger stop, adj. rear sight $436.00
Price: 8" hunting barrel ....$ 87.00

HECKLER & KOCH VP '7OZ DOUBLE ACTION AUTO

Caliber: 9mm Para., 18-shot magazine
Barrel: 4½".
Weight: 32½ oz. **Length:** 8" over-all.
Stocks: Black stippled plastic.
Sights: Ramp front, channeled slide rear.
Features: Recoil operated, double action. Only 4 moving parts. Double column magazine. Imported by Heckler & Koch, Inc.
Price: $268.00

HECKLER & KOCH HK-4 DOUBLE ACTION PISTOL

Caliber: 22 LR, 25 ACP, 32 ACP, 380 ACP, 8-shot magazine (7 in 380).
Barrel: 3¹¹/₃₂".
Weight: 16½ oz. **Length:** 6³/₁₆" over-all.
Stocks: Black checkered plastic.
Sights: Fixed blade front, rear notched drift-adj. for w.
Features: Gun comes with all parts to shoot above four calibers; polygonal (hexagon) rifling; matte black finish. Imported by Heckler & Koch, Inc.
Price: HK-4 380 with 22 conversion kit $285.00
Price: HK-4 in 380 only $265.00
Price: HK-4 in four cals. $340.00
Price: Conversion units 22, 25 or 32 cal., each ....$ 68.00

HIGH STANDARD SPORT-KING AUTO PISTOL

Caliber: 22 LR, 10-shot.
Barrel: 4½" or 6¾".
Weight: 39 oz. (4½" bbl.). **Length:** 9" over-all (4½" bbl.).
Stocks: Checkered walnut.
Sights: Blade front, fixed rear.
Features: Takedown barrel. Blue only. Military frame.
Price: Either bbl. length, blue finish $148.75

HI-STANDARD SHARPSHOOTER AUTO PISTOL

Caliber: 22 LR, 10-shot magazine.
Barrel: 5½".
Length: 9" over-all. **Weight:** 45 oz.
Stocks: Checkered walnut.
Sights: Fixed, ramp front, square notch rear adj. for w. & e.
Features: Military frame. Wide, scored trigger; new hammer-sear design. Slide lock, push-button take down.
Price: Blued $179.50

Consult our Directory pages for the location of firms mentioned.

LLAMA XI AUTO PISTOL

Caliber: 9mm Para.
Barrel: 5".
Weight: 38 oz. **Length:** 8½".
Stocks: Moulded plastic.
Sights: Fixed front, adj. rear.
Features: Also available with engraved, chrome engraved or gold damascened finish at extra cost. Imported from Spain by Stoeger Industries.
Price: $249.95

L.E.S P-18 AUTO PISTOL

Caliber: 9mm Parabellum, 18-shot magazine.
Barrel: 5½", stationary; polygonal rifling.
Weight: About 36 oz.
Stocks: Checkered resin.
Sights: Post front, V-notch rear drift adj. for w.
Features: Gas-assisted action; all stainless steel; inertia firing pin. Made in U.S.A. Both single and double action models offered, in two finish grades. From L.E.S.
Price: Std. D.A. (matte finish) $299.95
Price: Deluxe D.A. (polished) $389.95
Price: Combat D.A. $309.95
Price: Std. S.A. (matte finish) $279.95
Price: Combat S.A. $289.95
Price: Deluxe S.A. (polished) $369.95

LLAMA MODELS XV, XA, IIIA AUTO PISTOLS
Caliber: 22 LR, 32 ACP and 380.
Barrel: 3¹¹/₁₆″.
Weight: 23 oz. **Length:** 6½″.
Stocks: Checkered plastic, thumb rest.
Sights: Fixed front, adj. notch rear.
Features: Ventilated rib, manual and grip safeties. Model XV is 22 LR, Model XA is 32 ACP, and Model IIIA is 380. Models XA and IIIA have loaded indicator; IIIA is locked breech. Imported from Spain by Stoeger Industries.
Price: **$182.95**

LLAMA MODELS VIII, IXA AUTO PISTOLS
Caliber: Super 38 (M. VIII), 45 ACP (M. IXA).
Barrel: 5″.
Weight: 30 oz. **Length:** 8½″.
Stocks: Checkered walnut.
Sights: Fixed.
Features: Grip and manual safeties, ventilated rib. Engraved, chrome engraved or gold damascened finish available at extra cost. Imported from Spain by Stoeger Industries.
Price: **$249.95**

MKE MODEL TPK AUTO PISTOL
Caliber: 32 ACP, 8-shot; 380, 7-shot.
Barrel: 4″.
Weight: 23 oz. **Length:** 6½″.
Stocks: Checkered black plastic.
Sights: Fixed front, adj. notch rear.
Features: Double action with exposed hammer; safety blocks firing pin and drops hammer. Chamber loaded indicator pin. Imported from Turkey by Firearms Center.
Price: **$259.95**

MAUSER HSc "ONE OF FIVE THOUSAND" PISTOL
Caliber: 32 ACP, 380 ACP, 7-shot.
Barrel: 3¾″.
Weight: 23 oz. **Length:** 6.05″.
Stocks: Checkered walnut.
Sights: Fixed.
Features: Double action, manual and magazine safeties. Matted non-glare sight channel. Inertia firing pin. Comes in fitted case with extra magazine, bore brush, test target. Final HSc production. Imported from Germany by Interarms.
Price: Bright blue only **$275.00**

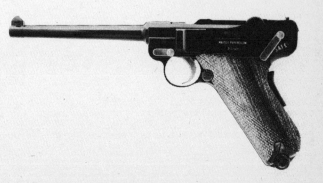

MAUSER PARABELLUM SWISS MODEL PISTOL
Caliber: 30 Luger, 9mm Para., 8-shot.
Barrel: 4″ (9mm), 6″ (30 Luger).
Weight: 32 oz. **Length:** 8.66″ (4″ bbl.).
Stocks: Checkered walnut.
Sights: Fixed.
Features: Manual and grip safeties, American eagle over chamber and Mauser banner on toggle. Final production—guns offered until supply exhausted. Imported from Germany by Interarms.
Price: **$625.00**

RG 26 AUTO PISTOL

Caliber: 25 ACP, 6-shot magazine.
Barrel: 2½".
Weight: 12 ozs. **Length:** 4¾" over-all.
Stocks: Checkered plastic.
Sights: Fixed.
Features: Blue finish. Thumb safety. Imported by RG Industries.
Price: $45.00

RAVEN P-25 AUTO PISTOL

Caliber: 25 ACP.
Barrel: 3".
Weight: 12 oz.
Stocks: Smooth walnut or Pearl-O-Lite.
Sights: Ramped front, fixed rear.
Features: Available in blue, nickel or satin nickel finish. From EMF Co.
Price: $55.95

RUGER STANDARD MODEL AUTO PISTOL

Caliber: 22 LR, 9-shot magazine.
Barrel: 4¾" or 6".
Length: 8¾" (4¾" bbl.). **Weight:** 36 oz. (4¾" bbl.).
Stocks: Checkered hard rubber.
Sights: Fixed, wide blade front, square notch rear adj. for w.
Price: Blued $92.00

SMITH & WESSON MODEL 59 DOUBLE ACTION

Caliber: 9mm Luger, 14-shot clip.
Barrel: 4".
Length: 7⁷/₁₆" over-all. **Weight:** 27½ oz., without clip.
Stocks: Checkered high impact moulded nylon.
Sights: ⅛" serrated ramp front, square notch rear adj. for w.
Features: Double action automatic. Furnished with two magazines. Blue finish.
Price: Blued $252.00
Price: Nickel $275.00

SMITH & WESSON 9mm MODEL 39 AUTO PISTOL

Caliber: 9mm Luger, 8-shot clip.
Barrel: 4".
Length: 7⁷/₁₆". **Weight:** 26½ oz., without magazine.
Stocks: Checkered walnut.
Sights: ⅛" serrated ramp front, adjustable rear.
Features: Magazine disconnector, positive firing pin lock and hammer-release safety; alloy frame with lanyard loop; locked-breech, short-recoil double action; slide locks open on last shot.
Price: Blued .... $210.50   Nickeled $232.00

STAR MODEL PD AUTO PISTOL

Caliber: 45 ACP, 7-shot magazine.
Barrel: 3.94".
Weight: 25 oz. **Length:** 7" over-all.
Stocks: Checkered walnut.
Sights: Ramp front, fully adjustable rear.
Features: Rear sight milled into slide; thumb safety; grooved non-slip front strap; nylon recoil buffer; inertia firing pin; no grip or magazine safeties. From Interarms.
Price: Blue $255.00

HANDGUNS — AUTOLOADERS, SERVICE & SPORT

STAR BM/BKM AUTO PISTOL
Caliber: 9mm Para., 8-shot magazine.
Barrel: 3.9″.
Weight: 25 oz.
Stocks: Checkered walnut.
Sights: Fixed.
Features: Blue or chrome finish. Magazine and manual safeties, external hammer. Imported from Spain by Interarms.
Price: Blue, BM and BKM $215.00
Price: Chrome, BM $230.00

STERLING MODEL 450 D.A. AUTO
Caliber: 45 ACP, 8-shot magazine.
Barrel: 4¼″.
Weight: 35 ozs. **Length:** 7½″ over-all.
Stocks: Checkered walnut.
Sights: Blade front, rear adj. for w. & e.
Features: All steel, reversible safety, inertia firing pin. Introduced 1977.
Price: Blue only $269.95

STERLING MODEL 302
Caliber: 22 LR, 6-shot.
Barrel: 2½″.
Length: 4½″ over-all. **Weight:** 13 oz.
Stocks: Cycolac, black or white.
Sights: Fixed.
Features: All steel construction.
Price: Blue $89.95
Price: Stainless steel $108.95

STERLING MODEL 300
Caliber: 25 ACP, 6-shot.
Barrel: 2½″.
Length: 4½″ over-all. **Weight:** 13 oz.
Stocks: Cycolac, black or white.
Sights: Fixed.
Features: All steel construction.
Price: Blued $89.95
Price: Stainless steel $108.95

STERLING MODEL 400 MK II DOUBLE ACTION
Caliber: 380 ACP, 7-shot.
Barrel: 3¾″.
Length: 6½″ over-all. **Weight:** 18 oz.
Stocks: Checkered walnut.
Features: All steel construction. Double action.
Price: Blued $199.95
Price: Stainless steel $249.95

TDE "BACKUP" AUTO PISTOL
Caliber: 380 ACP, 5-shot magazine
Barrel: 2½".
Weight: 17 oz. **Length:** 5" over-all.
Stocks: Smooth wood.
Sights: Fixed, open, recessed.
Features: Concealed hammer, blowback operation; manual and grip safeties. All stainless steel construction. Smallest domestically-produced pistol in 380. From AMT.
Price: About **$235.00**

TARGA MODELS GT32, GT380 AUTO PISTOLS
Caliber: 32 ACP or 380 ACP, 7-shot magazine
Barrel: 4⅞".
Weight: 26 oz. **Length:** 7⅜" over-all.
Stocks: Checkered nylon with thumb rest. Walnut optional.
Sights: Fixed blade front; rear drift-adj. for w.
Features: Chrome or blue finish; magazine, thumb, and firing pin safeties; external hammer; safety lever take-down. Imported from Italy by Excam, Inc.
Price: 32 cal., blue . . . . **$ 95.00**
Price: 32 cal., chrome . . . . **$ 99.00**
Price: 380 cal., blue **$109.00**
Price: 380 cal., chrome **$116.00**
Price: 380 cal., chrome, engraved, wooden grips **$152.00**
Price: 380 cal., blue, engraved, wooden grips **$147.00**

TARGA MODEL GT27 AUTO PISTOL
Caliber: 25 ACP, 6-shot magazine
Barrel: 2⁷⁄₁₆".
Weight: 12 oz. **Length:** 4⅝" over-all.
Stocks: Checkered nylon.
Sights: Fixed.
Features: Safety lever take-down; external hammer with half-cock. Made in U.S. by Excam, Inc.
Price: Blue **$48.50**
Price: Chrome **$53.00**

WALTHER PP AUTO PISTOL
Caliber: 22 LR, 8-shot; 32 ACP, 380 ACP, 7-shot.
Barrel: 3.86".
Weight: 23½ oz. **Length:** 6.7"
Stocks: Checkered plastic.
Sights: Fixed, white markings.
Features: Double action, manual safety blocks firing pin and drops hammer, chamber loaded indicator on 32 and 380, extra finger rest magazine provided. Imported from Germany by Interarms.
Price: (22 LR) **$425.00**
Price: (32 and 380) **$405.00**
Price: Engraved models . . . . **On request**

Walther PPK/S Auto Pistol
Same as PP except bbl. 3.27", length 6.1" o.a.
Price: 22 LR **$415.00**
Price: 32 or 380 ACP **$395.00**
Price: Engraved models . . . . **On request**

WALTHER P-38 AUTO PISTOL
Caliber: 22 LR, 30 Luger or 9mm Luger, 8-shot.
Barrel: 4¹⁵⁄₁₆" (9mm and 30), 5¹⁄₁₆" (22 LR).
Weight: 28 oz. **Length:** 8½"
Stock: Checkered plastic.
Sights: Fixed.
Features: Double action, safety blocks firing pin and drops hammer, chamber loaded indicator. Matte finish standard, polished blue, engraving and/or plating available. Imported from Germany by Interarms.
Price: 22 LR **$690.00**
Price: 9mm or 30 Luger **$600.00**
Price: Engraved models . . . . **On request**

Walther P-38K Auto Pistol
Streamlined version of the P-38; 2¾" barrel, 6⅜" over-all, weight 26 ozs. Strengthened slide (no dust cover), recoil bearing cross-bolt. Rear sight adj. for windage, both front and rear sights have white accents. Hammer decocking lever. Non-reflective matte finish. Imported from Germany by Interarms. Introduced 1977.
Price: **$650.00**

Walther P-38IV Auto Pistol
Same as P-38K except has longer barrel (4½"); over-all length is 8", weight is 29 ozs. Sights are non-adjustable. Introduced 1977. Imported by Interarms.
Price: **$650.00**

WILDEY AUTO PISTOL

Caliber: 9mm Win. Mag. (14 shots), 45 Win. Mag. (8 shots).
Barrel: 5'', 6'', 7'', 8'' or 10''; vent rib.
Weight: About 51 oz. (6'' bbl.).
Stocks: Select hardwood, target style optional.
Sights: Adjustable for windage and elevation; red or white inserts optional.
Features: Patented gas operation; selective single or autoloading capability; 5-lug rotary bolt; fixed barrel; stainless steel construction; double-action trigger mechanism. Has positive hammer block and magazine safety. From Wildey Firearms.
Price: 9mm Win. Mag., 5″ bbl. $389.95
Price: 45 Win. Mag., 8″ bbl. $399.95

HANDGUNS—REVOLVERS, SERVICE & SPORT

ARMINIUS REVOLVERS

Caliber: 38 Special, 357 Mag., 32 S&W (6-shot); 22 Magnum, 22 LR (8-shot).
Barrel: 4″ (38 Spec., 357 Mag., 32 S&W, 22 LR); 6″ (38 Spec., 22 LR/22 Mag., 357 Mag.); 8⅜″ (357 Mag.).
Weight: 35 oz. (6″ bbl.). **Length:** 11″ (6″ bbl. 38).
Stocks: Checkered plastic, walnut optional at $14.95.
Sights: Ramp front, fixed rear on standard models, w. & e. adj. on target models.
Features: Ventilated rib, solid frame, swing-out cylinder. Interchangeable 22 Mag. cylinder available with 22 cal. versions. Also available in 357 Mag. 3″, 4″, 6″ barrel, adj. sights. Imported from West Germany by F.I.E. Corp.
Price: .... $89.95 to $170.95

ASTRA 357 MAGNUM REVOLVER

Caliber: 357 Magnum, 6-shot.
Barrel: 3″, 4″, 6″, 8½″.
Weight: 40 oz. (6″ bbl.). **Length:** 11¼″ (6″ bbl.).
Stocks: Checkered walnut.
Sights: Fixed front, rear adj. for w. and e.
Features: Swing-out cylinder with countersunk chambers, floating firing pin. Target-type hammer and trigger. Imported from Spain by Interarms.
Price: 3″, 4″, 6″ $235.00
Price: 8½″ $245.00

CHARTER TARGET BULLDOG

Caliber: 357 Mag., 44 Spec., 5-shot.
Barrel: 4″ or 6″.
Weight: 20½ oz. **Length:** 8½″ over-all.
Stocks: Checkered American walnut, square butt.
Sights: Full-length ramp front, fully adj., milled channel, square notch rear.
Features: Blue finish only. Enclosed ejector rod, full length ejection of fired cases.
Price: **$165.00**

CHARTER ARMS BULLDOG

Caliber: 357 Mag., 44 Special, 5-shot.
Barrel: 3″, 6″.
Weight: 19 oz. **Length:** 7½″ over-all.
Stocks: Hand checkered walnut; Square butt.
Sights: Patridge type 9/64″ front, square notch rear.
Features: Wide trigger and hammer, chrome-moly steel frame, unbreakable firing pin, transfer bar ignition.
Price: 44 Spec., 3″ **$150.00**
Price: 357 Mag., 6″ **$150.00**

CHARTER ARMS POLICE BULLDOG

Caliber: 38 Special, 6-shot.
Barrel: 4″.
Weight: 20½ oz. **Length:** 8½″ over-all.
Stocks: Hand checkered American walnut; square butt.
Sights: Full length ramp front; fully adj. combat rear.
Features: Accepts both regular and high velocity ammunition; enclosed ejector rod; full length ejection of fired cases.
Price: Blue only, approx. **$149.00**

CHARTER ARMS UNDERCOVER REVOLVER

Caliber: 38 Special, 5 shot; 32 S & W Long, 6 shot.
Barrel: 2″, 3″.
Weight: 16 oz. (2″). **Length:** 6¼″ (2″).
Stocks: Smooth walnut or checkered square butt.
Sights: Patridge-type ramp front, notched rear.
Features: Wide trigger and hammer spur. Steel frame.
Price: Polished Blue . . . . . . **$130.00** Nickel **$142.00**
Price: With checkered square butt grips, blue, 3″ **$139.00**
Price: 32 S & W Long, blue, 2″ **$130.00**

Charter Arms Pathfinder

Same as Undercover but in 22 LR caliber, and has 3″ or 6″ bbl. Fitted with adjustable rear sight, ramp front. Weight 18½ oz.
Price: 22 LR, blue, 3″ **$144.00**
Price: 22 LR, square butt, 6″ **$153.00**
Price: 22 Mag., square butt, 3″ **$158.00**
Price: 22 Mag, square butt, 6″ **$158.00**

COLT DETECTIVE SPECIAL

Caliber: 38 Special, 6-shot.
Barrel: 2″.
Length: 6⅝″ over-all. **Weight:** 22 oz.
Stocks: Full, checkered walnut, round butt.
Sights: Fixed, ramp front, square notch rear.
Features: Glare-proofed sights, smooth trigger. Nickel finish, hammer shroud available as options.
Price: Blue **$225.00**

COLT DIAMONDBACK REVOLVER
Caliber: 22 LR, or 38 Special, 6 shot.
Barrel: 4", or 6" with ventilated rib.
Length: 9" (4" bbl.). **Weight:** 28½ oz. (4" bbl.).
Stocks: Checkered walnut, target type, square butt.
Sights: Ramp front, adj. notch rear.
Features: Ventilated rib; grooved, crisp trigger; swing-out cylinder; wide hammer spur.
Price: Blue, 4" bbl., 38 Spec. $261.00
Price: Blue, 22-cal., 6" bbl. $265.00

COLT POLICE POSITIVE
Caliber: 38 Special, 6-shot.
Barrel: 4".
Weight: 26½ oz.
Stocks: Checkered walnut, wrap-around.
Sights: Ramp-style front, fixed square notch rear.
Features: Steel frame, smooth trigger, shrouded ejector rod. Uses Colt Cobra frame. Introduced 1977.
Price: Blue $225.00

COLT LAWMAN MK III REVOLVER
Caliber: 357 Mag., 6 shot.
Barrel: 2" or 4", heavy.
Weight: 33 oz.
Length: 9⅜".
Stocks: Checkered walnut, service style.
Sights: Fixed, glare-proofed ramp front, square notch rear.
Price: Blued $215.95
Price: Nickel $229.95

COLT TROOPER MK III REVOLVER
Caliber: 22 LR, 22 WMR, 357 Magnum, 6-shot.
Barrel: 4" 6".
Length: 9½" (4" bbl.). **Weight:** 39 oz. (4" bbl.), 42 oz, (6" bbl.).
Stocks: Checkered walnut, square butt. Grooved trigger.
Sights: Fixed ramp front with ⅛" blade, adj. notch rear.
Price: Blued with target hammer and target stocks $264.95
Price: Nickeled (357 only) $286.50

F.I.E. MODEL F38 "Titan Tiger" REVOLVER
Caliber: 38 Special.
Barrel: 2" or 4".
Length: 6¼" over-all. (2" bbl.). **Weight:** 27 oz.
Stocks: Checkered plastic, Bulldog style. Walnut optional ($10.95).
Sights: Fixed.
Features: Swing-out cylinder, one stroke ejection. Made in U.S.A. by F.I.E. Corp.
Price: Blued 2" or 4" .. $87.95   Nickel, 2" or 4" bbl. .. $109.95
Price: Blue/gold combo finish $114.95

HARRINGTON & RICHARDSON M622 REVOLVER
Caliber: 22 S, L or LR, 6 shot.
Barrel: 2½", 4", round bbl.
Weight: 20 oz. (2½" bbl.).
Stocks: Checkered black Cycolac.
Sights: Fixed, blade front, square notch rear.
Features: Solid steel, Bantamweight frame; pull-pin safety rim cylinder; non-glare finish on frame; coil springs.
Price: Blued, 2½", 4" bbl. $59.50
Price: Model 632 (32 cal.) $67.50
Price: Model 623, nickel, 2½", 4" $64.50
Price: Model 633, nickel, 2½" $72.50

HARRINGTON & RICHARDSON M732 GUARDSMAN
Caliber: 32 S&W or 32 S&W Long, 6 shot.
Barrel: 2½" or 4" round barrel.
Weight: 23½ oz. (2½" bbl.), 26 oz. (4" bbl.).
Stocks: Checkered, black Cycolac.
Sights: Blade front; adjustable rear on 4" model.
Features: Swing-out cylinder with auto. extractor return. Pat. safety rim cylinder. Grooved trigger.
Price: Blued, 2½" bbl. **$79.50** Nickel (Model 733), 2½" bbl. **$84.50**
Price: Blued, 4" bbl. . **$79.50** Nickel, 4" bbl. **$84.50**

H&R MODEL 940 ULTRA "SIDE-KICK" REVOLVER
Caliber: 22 S, L or LR, 9 shot.
Barrel: 6″ target weight with ventilated rib.
Weight: 36 oz.
Stocks: Checkered walnut-finished hardwood with thumbrest.
Sights: Ramp front; rear adjustable for w. and e.
Features: Swing-out, safety rim cylinder.
Price: H&R Crown-Lustre Blue $99.50

H&R Model 939 Ultra "Side-Kick" Revolver
Like the Model 940 but with a flat-sided barrel.
Price: H&R Crown-Lustre Blue $99.50

HARRINGTON & RICHARDSON MODEL 666
Caliber: 22 LR/22 Mag., 6-shot.
Barrel: 6″.
Weight: 28 oz.
Stocks: Checkered black Cycolac.
Sights: Blade front, fixed rear.
Features: Comes with two cylinders. Double action. H & R Crown Lustre blue finish.
Price: $74.50

Harrington & Richardson Model 649 Revolver
Similar to model 666 except has 5½″ barrel, one piece wrap around walnut-finished hardwood grips, western-type blade front sight, adjustable rear. Loads and ejects from side. Weighs 32 oz.
Price: $89.50
Price: Model 650—as above except nickel finish $94.50

HARRINGTON & RICHARDSON M676 REVOLVER
Caliber: 22 LR/22 WMRF, 6-shot.
Barrel: 4½″, 5½″, 7½″ or 12″.
Weight: 31 oz. (4½″), 41 oz. (12″).
Stocks: One piece smooth walnut-finished hardwood.
Sights: Western type blade front, adj. rear.
Features: Blue barrel and cylinder, "antique" color case-hardened frame, ejector tube and trigger. Comes with extra cylinder.
Price: 4½″, 5½″, 7½″ bbl. .... $ 99.50
Price: 12″ bbl. $125.00

HARRINGTON & RICHARDSON MODEL 922
Caliber: 22 S, L, LR, 9-shot.
Barrel: 2½″, 4″, 6″.
Weight: 20 oz. (2½″).
Stocks: Checkered black Cycolac.
Sights: Blade front, fixed rear.
Features: Double action. Cylinder is removed for ejection and loading. H & R Crown Lustre Blue cylinder and trigger guard.
Price: Blue $67.50
Price: Model 923, as above in nickel $69.50

HARRINGTON & RICHARDSON M949 FORTY-NINER
Caliber: 22 S, L or LR, 9 shot.
Barrel: 5½″ round with ejector rod.
Weight: 31 oz.
Stocks: One-piece smooth frontier style wrap-around walnut-finished hardwood.
Sights: estern-type blade front, rear adj. for w.
Features: Contoured loading gate; wide hmmer spur; single and double action. Western type ejector-housing.
Price: H&R Crown-Luster Blue $79.50
Price: Nickel (Model 950) $84.50

HARRINGTON & RICHARDSON M929 "SIDE-KICK"
Caliber: 22 S, L or LR, 9 shot.
Barrel: 2½″, 4″ or 6″.
Weight: 26 oz. (4″ bbl.).
Stocks: Checkered, black Cycolac.
Sights: Blade front; adjustable rear on 4″ and 6″ models.
Features: Swing-out cylinder with auto. extractor return. Pat. safety rim cylinder. Grooved trigger. Round-grip frame.
Price: Blued, 2½″, 4″ or 6″ bbl. $79.50
Price: Nickel (Model 930), 2½″ or 4″ bbl. $84.50

H&R SPORTSMAN MODEL 999 REVOLVER

Caliber: 22 S, L or LR, 9 shot, 32 S&W Long, 6-shot.
Barrel: 4", 6" top-break (16" twist), integral vent rib, fluted.
Length: 10½". **Weight:** 34 oz. (6", 22 cal.).
Stocks: Checkered walnut-finished hardwood.
Sights: Front adjustable for elevation, rear for windage.
Features: Simultaneous automatic ejection. Trigger guard extension. H&R Crown Lustre Blue finish.
Price: Blued, 4" either cal. $120.00
Price: Blued, 6", either cal. $125.00

HIGH STANDARD CRUSADER COMMEMORATIVE RE-VOLVER

Caliber: 357 Mag., 44 Mag., 45 Long Colt.
Barrel: 4¼", 6½", 8-3/8".
Weight: 48 oz. (4-1/8").
Stocks: Smooth Zebrawood.
Sights: Blade front on ramp, fully adj. rear.
Features: Unique gear-segment mechanism. Smooth, light double-action trigger pull. First production devoted to the commemorative; later (1979) guns of plain, standard configuration.
Price: 4¼" $335.50
Price: 6½" $340.00
Price: 8-3/8" (357, 44 only) $345.50

HI-STANDARD SENTINEL 9390 AND 9392

Caliber: 22 LR, 22 Mag., 9-shot.
Barrel: 2" (9390), 4" (9392).
Weight: 22 oz. (2"). **Length:** 6⅞" over-all (2" bbl.).
Stocks: Checkered walnut.
Sights: ⅛" ramp front, fixed or adj. rear.
Features: Blue finish only. Steel frame. Dual swing-out cylinder.
Price: Fixed sights $159.25
Price: Adj. sights $168.50

Hi-Standard Camp Gun

Same as Sentinel 9390 except has 6" barrel, adjustable sights, checkered walnut grips. Blue only.
Price: 22 LR/22 Mag. combo $156.00

HIGH STANDARD DOUBLE-NINE CONVERTIBLE

Caliber: 22 S, L or LR, 9-shot (22 WRM with extra cylinder).
Barrel: 5½", dummy ejector rod fitted.
Length: 11" over-all. **Weight:** 32 oz.
Stocks: Smooth walnut, frontier style.
Sights: Fixed blade front, notched rear.
Features: Western styling; rebounding hammer with auto safety block; spring-loaded ejection. Swing-out cylinder.
Price: Blued $159.50
Price: With adjustable sights $173.25

High Standard Long Horn Convertible

Same as the Double-Nine convertible but with a 9½" bbl., adjustable sights, blued only, Weight: 40 oz.
Price: With adjustable sights $176.75

HIGH STANDARD HIGH SIERRA DOUBLE ACTION

Caliber: 22 LR and 22 LR/22 Mag., 9-shot.
Barrel: 7" octagonal.
Weight: 36 oz. **Length:** 12½" over-all.
Stocks: Smooth walnut.
Sights: Blade front, adj. rear.
Features: Gold plated backstrap and trigger guard. Swing-out cylinder.
Price: Adj. sights, dual cyl. $176.77

LLAMA COMANCHE REVOLVERS
Caliber: 22 LR, 38 Special, 357 Mag., 44 Mag.
Barrel: 6", 4" (except 22 LR, 6" only).
Weight: 22 LR 24 oz., 38 Special 31 oz. **Length:** 9¼" (4" bbl.).
Stocks: Checkered walnut.
Sights: Fixed blade front, rear adj. for w. & e.
Features: Ventilated rib, wide spur hammer. Chrome plating, engraved finishes available. Imported from Spain by Stoeger Industries.
Price: 22 LR, 38 Spec. $199.95
Price: Comanche 357 Mag $209.95
Price: Satin chrome, 357 only $266.95
Price: Super Comanche 44 Mag. $349.95

> Consult our Directory pages for
> the location of firms mentioned.

RG 14 REVOLVER
Caliber: 22 LR, 6-shot.
Barrel: 1¾" or 3".
Weight: 15 ozs. (1¾" bbl.) **Length:** 5½" over-all.
Stocks: Checkered plastic.
Sights: Fixed.
Features: Blue finish. Cylinder swings out when pin is removed. Imported by RG Industries.
Price: $34.00
Price: Model 23 (central ejector no pin to remove) $44.00

RG 31 REVOLVER
Caliber: 32 S & W (6-shot), 38 Spec. (5-shot).
Barrel: 2".
Weight: 24 ozs. **Length:** 6¾" over-all.
Stocks: Checkered plastic.
Sights: Fixed.
Features: Cylinder swings out when pin is removed. Blue finish. Imported by RG Industries.
Price: 32 cal. $58.95
Price: 38 cal. $58.95

RG 40 REVOLVER
Caliber: 38 Spec., 6-shot.
Barrel: 2″.
Weight: 29 ozs. **Length:** 7¼″ over-all.
Stocks: Checkered plastic.
Sights: Fixed.
Features: Swing-out cylinder with spring ejector. Imported by RG Industries.
Price: $76.00

RG 38S REVOLVER
Caliber: 38 Special, 6-shot.
Barrel: 3″ and 4″.
Weight: 3″, 31 oz.; 4″, 34 oz. **Length:** 3″, 8½″; 4″, 9¼″.
Stocks: Checkered plastic.
Sights: Fixed front, rear adj. for w.
Features: Swing out cylinder with spring ejector. Imported from Germany by RG Industries.
Price: Blue $77.95

RG MODEL 88 REVOLVER
Caliber: 38 Spec., 357 Mag.
Barrel: 4″.
Weight: 33 oz. **Length:** 9″ over-all.
Stocks: Checkered walnut.
Sights: Fixed.
Features: Swing out cylinder, spring ejector. Wide spur hammer and trigger. Imported by RG Industries.
Price: $199.50

RG 57 REVOLVER
Caliber: 357 Magnum, 41 Mag., 44 Mag., 45 Colt.
Barrel: 4″, 6″.
Weight: 44 oz. **Length:** 9½″.
Stocks: Checkered plastic.
Sights: Fixed rear.
Features: Swing out cylinder, spring ejector, steel frame. Imported from Germany by RG Industries.
Price: .... $197.00 to $242.00

ROSSI MODELS 68, 69 & 70 DA REVOLVERS
Caliber: 22 LR (M 70), 32 S & W (M 69), 38 Spec. (M 68).
Barrel: 3″.
Weight: 22 oz.
Stocks: Checkered wood.
Sights: Ramp front, low profile adj. rear.
Features: All-steel frame. Thumb latch operated swing-out cylinder. Introduced 1978. Imported by Interarms.
Price: 22, 32 or 38, blue or nickel $105.00
Price: As above, 38 Spec. only with 4″ bbl. as M 31 .... $110.00

RUGER SECURITY-SIX Model 117
Caliber: 357 Mag. (also fires 38 Spec.), 6-shot.
Barrel: 2¾″, 4″ or 6″, or 4″ heavy barrel.
Weight: 33½ oz. (4″ bbl.) **Length:** 9¼″ (4″ bbl.) over-all.
Stocks: Hand checkered American walnut, semi-target style.
Sights: Patridge-type front on ramp, rear adj. for w. and e.
Features: Music wire coil springs throughout. Hardened steel construction. Integral ejector rod shroud and sighting rib. Can be disassembled using only a coin.
Price: 2¾″, 4″, 6″ and 4″ heavy bbl. $177.50
Price: 4″ HB, 6″ Big Grip $193.00

RUGER STAINLESS SECURITY-SIX Model 717
Caliber: 357 Mag. (also fires 38 Spec.), 6-shot.
Barrel: 2¾″, 4″ or 6″.
Weight: 33 oz. (4 bbl.). **Length:** 9¼″ (4″ bbl.) over-all.
Stocks: Hand checkered American walnut.
Sights: Patridge-type front, fully adj. rear.
Features: All metal parts except sights made of stainless steel. Sights are black alloy for maximum visibility. Same mechanism and features found in regular Security-Six.
Price: 2¾″, 4″, 6″ and 4″ heavy bbl. $192.00
Price: 4″ HB, 6″ Big Grip $207.50

RUGER POLICE SERVICE-SIX Models 107, 108
Caliber: 357 (Model 107), 38 Spec. (Model 108), 6-shot.
Barrel: 2¾″ or 4″, and 4″ heavy barrel.
Weight: 33½ oz (4″ bbl.). **Length:** 9¼″ (4 bbl.) over-all.
Stocks: Checkered American walnut, semi-target style.
Sights: Patridge-type front, square notch rear.
Features: Solid frame with barrel, rib and ejector rod housing combined in one unit. All steel construction. Field strips without tools.
Price: Model 107 (357) $140.00
Price: Model 108 (38) $140.00
Price: Mod. 707 (357), Stainless, 4″, 4″ HB $154.00
Price: Mod. 708 (38), Stainless, 4″, 4″ HB $154.00

RUGER SPEED-SIX Models 207, 208
Caliber: 357 (Model 207), 38 Spec. (Model 208), 6-shot.
Barrel: 2¾" or 4".
Weight: 31 oz. (2¾" bbl.). **Length:** 7¾" over-all (2¾" bbl.).
Stocks: Round butt design, diamond pattern checkered American walnut.
Sights: Patridge-type front, square-notch rear.
Features: Same basic mechanism as Security-Six. Hammer without spur available on special order. All steel construction. Music wire coil springs used throughout.
Price: Model 207 (357 Mag.) $140.00
Price: Model 208 (38 Spec. only) $140.00
Price: Mod. 737 (357), Stainless $154.00
Price: Mod. 738 (38), Stainless $154.00

SMITH & WESSON M&P Model 10 REVOLVER
Caliber: 38 Special, 6 shot.
Barrel: 2", 4", 5" or 6"
Length: 9¼" (4" bbl.). **Weight:** 30½ oz. (4" bbl.).
Stocks: Checkered walnut, Magna. Round or square butt.
Sights: Fixed. 1/8" ramp front, square notch rear.
Price: Blued ....$125.50   Nickeled $137.00

Smith & Wesson 38 M&P Heavy Barrel Model 10
Same as regular M&P except: 4" ribbed bbl. with 1/8" ramp front sight, square rear, square butt, wgt. 34 oz.
Price: Blued ....$125.50   Nickeled $137.00

SMITH & WESSON 38 M&P AIRWEIGHT Model 12
Caliber: 38 Special, 6 shot.
Barrel: 2 or 4 inches.
Length: 6⅞" over-all. **Weight:** 18 oz. (2" bbl.)
Stocks: Checkered walnut, Magna. Round or square butt.
Sights: Fixed, 1/8" serrated ramp front, square notch rear.
Price: Blued ....$166.00   Nickeled $188.50

SMITH & WESSON Model 13 H.B. M&P
Caliber: 357 and 38 Special, 6 shot.
Barrel: 4".
Weight: 34 oz. **Length:** 9¼" over-all.
Stocks: Checkered walnut, service.
Sights: 1/8" serrated ramp front, fixed square notch rear.
Features: Heavy barrel, K-frame, square butt.
Price: Blue only, M-13 .... $139.00
Price: Nickel $152.00
Price: Model 65, as above in stainless steel $154.00

SMITH & WESSON Model 14 K-38 MASTERPIECE
Caliber: 38 Spec., 6-shot.
Barrel: 6", 8⅜".
Weight: 38½ oz. (6" bbl.). **Length:** 11⅛" over-all (6" bbl.)
Stock: Checkered walnut, service.
Sights: 1/8" Patridge front, micro click rear adj. for w. and e.
Price: 6" bbl. $195.50
Price: 8⅜" bbl. $205.00

SMITH & WESSON 357 COMBAT MAGNUM Model 19
Caliber: 357 Magnum and 38 Special, 6 shot.
Barrel: 2½", 4", 6".
Length: 9½" (4" bbl.). **Weight:** 35 oz.
Stocks: Checkered Goncala Alves, target. Grooved tangs and trigger.
Sights: Front, 1/8" Baughman Quick Draw on 2½" or 4" bbl., Patridge on 6" bbl., micro click rear adjustable for w. and e.
Price: S&W Bright Blue or Nickel $202.00

SMITH & WESSON 44 MAGNUM Model 29 REVOLVER
Caliber: 44 Magnum, 44 Special or 44 Russian, 6 shot.
Barrel: 4", 6½", 8⅜".
Length: 11⅞" (6½" bbl.). **Weight:** 47 oz. (6½" bbl.), 43 oz. (4" bbl.).
Stocks: Oversize target type, checkered Goncala Alves. Tangs and target trigger grooved, checkered target hammer.
Sights: ⅛" red ramp-front, micro. click rear, adjustable for w. and e.
Features: Includes presentation case.
Price: S&W Bright Blue or Nickel 4", 6½" $331.50
Price: 8-3/8" bbl. $342.00
Price: Model 629 (stainless steel) . . . . **Not available**

SMITH & WESSON 357 MAGNUM M-27 REVOLVER
Caliber: 357 Magnum and 38 Special, 6 shot.
Barrel: 3½", 5", 6", 8⅜".
Length: 11¼" (6" bbl.). **Weight:** 44 oz. (6" bbl.).
Stocks: Checkered walnut, Magna. Grooved tangs and trigger.
Sights: Any S&W target front, micro click rear, adjustable for w. and e.
Price: S&W Bright Blue or Nickel, 3½", 5", 6" $303.00
Price: 8⅜" bbl. $314.50

SMITH & WESSON HIGHWAY PATROLMAN Model 28
Caliber: 357 Magnum and 38 Special, 6 shot.
Barrel: 4", 6".
Length: 11¼" (6" bbl.). **Weight:** 44 oz. (6" bbl.).
Stocks: Checkered walnut, Magna. Grooved tangs and trigger.
Sights: Front, ⅛" Baughman Quick Draw, on plain ramp. micro click rear, adjustable for w. and e.
Price: S&W Satin Blue, sandblasted frame edging and barrel top **$190.50**
Price: With target stocks $205.50

SMITH & WESSON 32 REGULATION POLICE Model 31
Caliber: 32 S&W Long, 6 shot.
Barrel: 2", 3", 4".
Length: 8½" (4" bbl.). **Weight:** 18¾ oz. (4" bbl.).
Stocks: Checkered walnut, Magna.
Sights: Fixed, 1/10" serrated ramp front, square notch rear.
Price: Blued . . . . **$156.00**   Nickeled $170.00

SMITH & WESSON 1953 Model 34, 22/32 KIT GUN
Caliber: 22 LR, 6 shot.
Barrel: 2", 4".
Length: 8" (4" bbl. and round butt). **Weight:** 22½ oz. (4" bbl.).
Stocks: Checkered walnut, round or square butt.
Sights: Front, 1/10" serrated ramp, micro. click rear, adjustable for w. & e.
Price: Blued . . . . **$159.00**   Nickeled $172.50
Price: Model 63, as above in stainless, 4" $187.00

SMITH & WESSON 38 CHIEFS SPECIAL & AIRWEIGHT
Caliber: 38 Special, 5 shot.
Barrel: 2", 3"
Length: 6½" (2" bbl. and round butt). **Weight:** 19 oz. (2" bbl.); 14 oz. (AIR-WEIGHT)
Stocks: Checkered walnut, Magna. Round or square butt.
Sights: Fixed, 1/10" serrated ramp front, square notch rear.
Price: Blued std. M-36 . . **$147.50**   Standard weight Nickel . .**$160.00**
Price: Blued AIR'W M-37 **$164.00**   AIRWEIGHT Nickel **$185.50**

Smith & Wesson 60 Chiefs Special Stainless
Same as Model 36 except: 2" bbl. and round butt only.
Price: Stainless steel $181.50

SMITH & WESSON BODYGUARD MODEL 38 RE-VOLVER
Caliber: 38 Special; 5 shot, double action revolver.
Barrel: 2".
Length: 6⅜". **Weight:** 14½ oz.
Features: Alloy frame; integral hammer shroud.
Stocks: Checkered walnut, Magna.
Sights: Fixed 1/10" serrated ramp front, square notch rear.
Price: Blued . . . . **$171.00**   Nickeled $193.00

Smith & Wesson Bodyguard Model 49 Revolver
Same as Model 38 except steel construction. Weight 20½ oz.
Price: Blued . . . . **$159.00**   Nickeled $172.00

SMITH & WESSON 41 MAGNUM Model 57 REVOLVER
Caliber: 41 Magnum, 6 shot.
Barrel: 4″, 6″ or 8⅜″.
Length: 11⅜″ (6″ bbl.). **Weight:** 48 oz. (6″ bbl.).
Stocks: Oversize target type checkered Goncala Alves wood and target hammer. Tang and target trigger grooved.
Sights: ⅛″ red ramp front, micro. click rear, adj. for w. and e.
Price: S&W Bright Blue or Nickel 4″, 6″ $331.50
Price: 8⅜″ bbl. $342.00

SMITH & WESSON MODEL 64 STAINLESS M&P
Caliber: 38 Special, 6-shot.
Barrel: 4″.
Length: 9½″ over-all. **Weight:** 30½ oz.
Stocks: Checkered walnut, service style.
Sights: Fixed, ⅛″ serrated ramp front, square notch rear.
Features: Satin finished stainless steel, square butt.
Price: $145.00

SMITH & WESSON MODEL 66 STAINLESS COMBAT MAGNUM
Caliber: 357 Magnum and 38 Special, 6-shot.
Barrel: 2½″, 4″, 6″.
Length: 9½″ over-all. **Weight:** 35 oz.
Stocks: Checkered Goncala Alves target.
Sights: Front, ⅛″ Baughman Quick Draw on plain ramp, micro click rear adj. for w. and e.
Features: Satin finish stainless steel, grooved trigger with adj. stop.
Price: $208.00

SMITH & WESSON MODEL 67 K-38 STAINLESS COMBAT MASTERPIECE
Caliber: 38 special, 6-shot.
Barrel: 4″.
Length: 9⅛″ over-all. **Weight:** 34 oz. (loaded).
Stocks: Checkered walnut, service style.
Sights: Front, ⅛″ Baughman Quick Draw on ramp, micro click rear adj. for w. and e.
Features: Stainless steel. Square butt frame with grooved tangs, grooved trigger with adj. stop.
Price: $187.50

TAURUS MODEL 66 REVOLVER
Caliber: 357 Magnum, 6-shot.
Barrel: 3″, 4″, 6″.
Weight: 35 ozs.
Stocks: Checkered walnut, target-type.
Sights: Serrated ramp front, micro click rear adjustable for w. and e.
Features: Wide target-type hammer spur, floating firing pin, heavy barrel with shrouded ejector rod. Introduced 1978. From International Distributors.
Price: Blue only, about $175.00
Price: Model 65 (as above except has fixed rear sight, ramp front), about $161.00

TAURUS MODEL 80 STANDARD REVOLVER
Caliber: 38 Spec., 6-shot.
Barrel: 3″ or 4″.
Weight: 31 oz. (4″ bbl.). **Length:** 9¼″ over-all (4″ bbl.).
Stocks: Checkered Brazilian walnut.
Sights: Serrated ramp front, square notch rear.
Features: Imported from Brazil by International Distributors.
Price: Blue, about $108.00
Price: Nickel, about $125.00

TAURUS MODEL 83 REVOLVER
Caliber: 38 Spec., 6-shot.
Barrel: 4" only, heavy.
Weight: 34½ ozs.
Stocks: Over-size checkered walnut.
Sights: Ramp front, micro. click rear adj. for w. & e.
Features: Blue or nickel finish. Introduced 1977. From International Distributors.
Price: Blue, about **$115.00**
Price: Nickel, about **$130.00**

TAURUS MODEL 82 HEAVY BARREL REVOLVER
Caliber: 38 Spec., 6-shot.
Barrel: 3" or 4", heavy.
Weight: 33 oz. (4" bbl.). **Length:** 9¼" over-all (4" bbl.).
Stocks: Checkered Brazilian walnut.
Sights: Serrated ramp front, square notch rear.
Features: Imported from Brazil by International Distributors.
Price: Blue, about **$113.00**
Price: Nickel, about **$127.00**

TAURUS MODEL 84 SPORT REVOLVER
Caliber: 38 Spec., 6-shot.
Barrel: 4".
Weight: 30 oz. **Length:** 9¼" over-all.
Stocks: Checkered Brazilian walnut.
Sights: Serrated ramp front, rear adj. for w. and e.
Features: Imported from Brazil by International Distributors.
Price: Blue, about **$115.00**
Price: Nickel, about **$130.00**

TAURUS MODEL 74 SPORT REVOLVER
Caliber: 32 S&W Long, 6-shot.
Barrel: 3".
Weight: 22 oz. **Length:** 8¼" over-all.
Stocks: Oversize target-type, checkered Brazilian walnut.
Sights: Serrated ramp front, rear adj. for w. and e.
Features: Imported from Brazil by International Distributers.
Price: Blue, about **$113.00**
Price: Nickel, about **$127.00**

DAN WESSON MODEL 8-2 & MODEL 14-2
Caliber: 38 Special (Model 8-2); 357 (Model 14-2), both 6 shot.
Barrel: 2", 4", 6", 8". "Quickshift" interchangeable barrels.
Weight: 34 oz. (4" bbl.). **Length:** 9¼" over-all (4" bbl.).
Stocks: "Quickshift" checkered walnut. Interchangeable with three other styles.
Sights: ⅛" serrated ramp front, rear fixed.
Features: Interchangeable barrels; 4 interchangeable grips; few moving parts, easy disassembly.
Price: 2" barrel **$164.50**
Price: 4" barrel **$170.55**
Price: 6" barrel **$176.55**
Price: 8" barrel **$182.75**
Price: Pistol Pac (cased with all above bbls.) **$383.80**

DAN WESSON MODEL 9-2 & MODEL 15-2
Caliber: 38 Special (Model 9-2); 357 (Model 15-2), both 6 shot.
Barrel: 2", 4", 6", 8", 10", 12", 15". "Quickshift" interchangeable barrels.
Weight: 36 oz. (4" bbl.). **Length:** 9¼" over-all (4" bbl.).
Stocks: "Quickshift" checkered walnut. Interchangeable with three other styles.
Sights: ⅛" serrated blade front with red insert (Std.), white or yellow insert optional, as is Patridge. White outline, rear adj. for w. & e.
Features: Interchangeable barrels; four interchangeable grips; few moving parts, easy disassembly; Bright Blue finish only. Contact Dan Wesson for additional models not listed here. 10", 12" and 15" barrels also available with vent. rib.
Price: 9-2H, 15-2H (bull barrel shroud) 2" **$230.90**
Price: 9-2H, 15-2H, 6" bbl. **$248.25**
Price: 9-2V, 15-2V (vent. rib) 8" **$260.45**
Price: 9-2V, 15-2V, 10" **$286.90**
Price: 9-2VH, 15-2VH (heavy vent. shroud) 12" **$334.60**
Price: Pistol Pac, VH **$620.05**
Price: 9-2, 15-2 (Std. shroud) 2" **$211.75**
Price: 9-2, 15-2, 6" **$227.45**
Price: 9-2, 15-2, 8" **$235.35**
Price: 9-2, 15-2, 15" **$308.25**
Price: 9-2, 15-2, Pistol Pac **$449.95**

Consult our Directory pages for
the location of firms mentioned.

ABILENE SINGLE ACTION REVOLVER
Caliber: 357 Mag., 44 Mag., 6 shot.
Barrel: 4⅝", 5½", 6½", 7½", and 8½" (44 Mag. only).
Weight: About 48 oz.
Stocks: Smooth walnut.
Sights: Serrated ramp front, click adj. rear for w. and e.
Features: Transfer bar ignition, wide hammer spur. Blue or stainless steel. From United States Arms Corp.
Price: Blue, 357, 4⅝", 5½", 6½" **$192.45**
Price: Blue, 44 Mag., 7½", 8½" **$219.95**

BISON SINGLE ACTION REVOLVER
Caliber: 22 LR.
Barrel: 4¾".
Weight: 20 oz.
Stocks: Imitation stag.
Sights: Fixed front, adj. rear.
Features: 22 WRM cylinder also available ($9.00 additional). Imported from Germany by Jana.
Price: **$50.00**

COLT SINGLE ACTION ARMY REVOLVER
Caliber: 357 Magnum, 44 Spec. or 45 Colt, 6 shot.
Barrel: 4¾", 5½" or 7½".
Length: 10⅞" (5½" bbl.). **Weight:** 37 oz. (5½" bbl.).
Stocks: Black composite rubber with eagle and shield crest.
Sights: Fixed. Grooved top strap, blade front.
Price: Blued and case hardened 4¾", 5½" bbl. **$367.95**
Price: Nickel with walnut stocks **$431.95**
Price: With 7½" bbl. **$374.50**

Colt Single Action Army—New Frontier
Same specifications as standard Single Action Army except: flat-top frame; high polished finish, blue and case colored; ramp front sight and target rear adj. for windage and elevation; smooth walnut stocks with silver medallion.
Price: **$431.95**

FREEDOM ARMS MINI REVOLVER
Caliber: 22 Short, Long, 5-shot.
Barrel: 1" or 1¾".
Weight: 4 oz. **Length:** 4" over-all with 1" bbl.
Stocks: Black ebonite.
Sights: Blade front, notch rear.
Features: Made of stainless steel, simple take down; half-cock safety; sheathed trigger; cartridge rims recessed in cylinder. Comes in presentation case.
Price: Short barrel **$109.50**
Price: Long barrel **$112.80**

FREEDOM ARMS 454 CASULL
Caliber: 454 Casull, 5-shot. Also fires 45 Long Colt.
Barrel: 7½".
Weight: 3 lbs., 2 oz. **Length:** 14" over-all.
Stocks: One piece hardwood.
Sights: Blade front, notched rear in top strap.
Features: Completely stainless steel, bright polish finish. New safety mechanism allows hammer-down carry on loaded chamber. Cylinder chambers counter bored to enclose case rim. Commercial ammunition will be available. From Freedom Arms.
Price: .... **Not available**

F.I.E. E15 BUFFALO SCOUT REVOLVER
Caliber: 22 LR/22 Mag., 6-shot.
Barrel: 4¾", 7", 9".
Length: 10" over-all. **Weight:** 32 oz.
Stocks: Black checkered nylon.
Sights: Blade front, fixed rear.
Features: Slide spring ejector. Blue, chrome or blue with brass backstrap and trigger guard models available.
Price: Blued, 22 LR **$39.95**
Price: Blue, 22 combo **$50.65**
Price: Chrome, 22 LR **$44.95**
Price: Chrome, combo **$54.95**
Price: Blue/brass, combo **$53.95**

F.I.E. "LEGEND" SINGLE ACTION REVOLVER
Caliber: 22 LR/22 Mag.,
Barrel: 4¾".
Stocks: Smooth walnut or black checkered nylon. Walnut optional, ($14.95).
Sights: Blade front, fixed rear.
Features: Positive hammer block system. Brass backstrap and trigger guard. Color case hardened steel frame. From F.I.E. Corp.
Price: 22 LR **$84.95**
Price: 22 combo **$99.95**

HAWES FEDERAL MARSHAL REVOLVER
Caliber: 357, 44 Mag., 45 L.C.
Barrel: 6".
Weight: 44 oz. **Length:** 11¾" over-all.
Stock: Smooth walnut.
Sights: Blade front, fixed rear.
Features: Color case hardened frame, brass backstrap and trigger guard. Barrel, cylinder and frame are blued. Imported by Hawes Firearms.
Price: .... **$203.35 to $212.95**

HAWES CHIEF MARSHAL REVOLVER
Caliber: 357 Magnum, 44 Magnum, 45 Long Colt; 6-shot.
Barrel: 6".
Weight: 48 oz. **Length:** 11¾".
Stocks: Extra large smooth rosewood.
Sights: Ramp target front, rear adj. for w. & e.
Features: Single action. Extra heavy frame. Imported from West Germany by Hawes.
Price: 357, 45LC **$200.90**
Price: 44 Mag. **$210.95**

HANDGUNS—SINGLE ACTION REVOLVERS

HAWES SAUER WESTERN MARSHAL REVOLVERS
Caliber: 357 Magnum, 44 Magnum, 45 Long Colt, 6-shot.
Barrel: 6" (357 Mag., 44 Mag., 45).
Weight: 44 oz. **Length:** 11¾".
Stocks: Rosewood.
Sight: Blade front.
Features: Single action. Imported from West Germany by Hawes.
Price: 357 Mag., 45 LC $166.70
Price: 44 Mag. $174.50

Hawes Montana Marshal Revolver
Same as Western Marshal except with solid brass backstrap and trigger guard.
Price: .... $189.70 to $198.95

Hawes Texas Marshal Revolver
Same as Western Marshal except full nickel finish and white Pearlite grips.
Price: .... $193.65 to $203.35

HAWES SILVER CITY MARSHAL REVOLVER
Caliber: 357, 44 Mag., 45 L.C.
Barrel: 6" (357, 44, 45), 5½" (22 cal.).
Weight: 44 oz. **Length:** 11¾" over-all.
Stocks: White Pearlite.
Sights: Fixed.
Features: Nickel plated frame, brass backstrap and trigger guard, blue barrel and cylinder. Imported by Hawes Firearms.
Price: .... $201.95 to $211.95

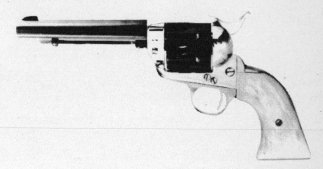

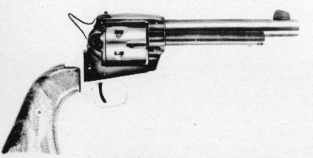

HAWES DEPUTY MARSHAL REVOLVER
Caliber: 22 LR, 22 LR/22 WRM.
Barrel: 5½".
Weight: 34 oz. **Length:** 11" over-all.
Stocks: Black or white plastic.
Sights: Fixed.
Features: Available in std. blue finish with black grips, with brass backstrap and trigger guard and wood grips, with completely chromed finish and white grips, or with chrome frame, brass backstrap and trigger guard, blue cylinder and barrel and white grips. Imported by Hawes Firearms.
Price: .... $68.95 to $106.50

IVER JOHNSON CATTLEMAN TRAILBLAZER
Caliber: 22 S, L, LR, 22 Mag.
Barrel: 5½" or 6½".
Weight: 2½ lbs.
Stocks: Smooth walnut.
Sights: Ramp front, rear adj. for w. and e.
Features: Comes with interchangeable magnum cylinder. Single action. Case-hardened frame, brass backstrap and trigger guard. Imported by Iver Johnson.
Price: .... Not available

I. J. CATTLEMAN BUCKHORN MAGNUM
Caliber: 357, 38 Spec., 44 Mag., 45 LC.
Barrel: 6½", 7½" (44 Mag.), 5¾" or 7½" (357, 38, 45).
Weight: 2¾ lbs.
Stocks: Smooth walnut.
Sights: Ramp front, rear adj. for w. and e.
Features: Single action. Blued barrel, case-hardened frame, brass backstrap and trigger guard. Imported by Iver Johnson.
Price: 357, 38 Spec., 45 LC .... Not available
Price: 44 Mag. .... Not available

I. J. CATTLEMAN BUNTLINE BUCKHORN MAGNUM
Caliber: 357, 38 Spec., 44 Mag., 45 LC, 6-shot.
Barrel: 18".
Weight: 3½ lbs.
Stocks: Smooth walnut.
Sights: Ramp front, rear adj. for w. and e.
Features: Single action. Blued barrel, case-hardened frame, brass trigger guard and backstrap. Comes with detachable shoulder stock. Imported by Iver Johnson.
Price: 357, 45 LC ... Not available 44 Mag. .... Not available

IVER JOHNSON CATTLEMAN MAGNUM

Caliber: 357, 44 Mag., 45 LC, 6-shot.
Barrel: 4¾", 5½" or 7½". 44 Mag. avail. with 6", 6¼" or 7½".
Weight: 2½ lbs.
Stocks: Smooth walnut.
Sights: Fixed.
Features: Case-hardened frame, single action, blued barrel, brass backstrap and trigger guard. Imported by Iver Johnson.
Price: 357, 45 LC ... **Not available**   44 Mag. .... **Not available**

RG 66 SUPER SINGLE ACTION REVOLVER

Caliber: 22 LR, 22 Mag., 6-shot.
Barrel: 4¾", 6" or 9".
Weight: 32 oz. **Length:** 10".
Stocks: Checkered plastic.
Sights: Fixed front, rear adj.
Features: Slide ejector rod, blue finish. Model 66M is combo set with both 22 LR and 22 mag. cylinders. Imported from Germany by R. G. Industries.
Price: Blue, about ....$52.00; (Model 66M) $60.50
Price: Blue (6"), about .... $55.75; Magnum $65.50
Price: Blue (9"), about .... $59.00; Magnum $68.00
Price: RG86 (same as above except steel frame) $95.95

RUGER NEW MODEL SUPER SINGLE-SIX CONVERTI-BLE REVOLVER

Caliber: 22 S, L, LR, 6-shot. 22 WMR in extra cylinder.
Barrel: 4⅝", 5½", 6½" or 9½" (6-groove).
Weight: 34½ oz. (6½" bbl.) **Length:** 11¹³⁄₁₆" over-all (6½" bbl.).
Stocks: Smooth American walnut.
Sights: Improved patridge front on ramp, fully adj. rear protected by integral frame ribs.
Features: New Ruger "interlocked" mechanism, transfer bar ignition, gate-controlled loading, hardened chrome-moly steel frame, wide trigger, music wire springs throughout, independent firing pin.
Price: 4⅝", 5½", 6½", 9½" barrel $141.50
Price: 5½", 6½" bbl., stainless steel $174.50

RUGER NEW MODEL BLACKHAWK REVOLVER

Caliber: 357 or 41 Mag., 6-shot.
Barrel: 4⅝" or 6½", either caliber.
Weight: 42 oz. (6½" bbl.). **Length:** 12¼" over-all (6½" bbl.).
Stocks: American walnut.
Sights: ⅛" ramp front, micro click rear adj. for w. and e.
Features: New Ruger interlocked mechanism, independent firing pin, hardened chrome-moly steel frame, music wire springs throughout.
Price: Blued $179.75
Price: Stainless steel (357) $195.80

Ruger New Model 357/9mm Blackhawk

Same as the 357 Magnum except furnished with interchangeable cylinders for 9mm Parabellum and 357 Magnum cartridges $196.90
9mm cylinder, fitted to your 357 Blackhawk (less shipping & handling) $34.00

RUGER NEW MODEL SUPER BLACKHAWK
Caliber: 44 Magnum, 6-shot. Also fires 44 Spec.
Barrel: 7½" (6-groove, 20" twist).
Weight: 48 oz. **Length:** 13⅜" over-all.
Stocks: Genuine American walnut.
Sights: ⅛" ramp front, micro click rear adj. for w. and e.
Features: New Ruger interlocked mechanism, non-fluted cylinder, steel grip and cylinder frame, square back trigger guard, wide serrated trigger and wide spur hammer. Deep Ruger blue.
Price: **$207.00**

RUGER NEW MODEL CONVERTIBLE BLACKHAWK
Caliber: 45 Colt or 45 Colt/45 ACP (extra cylinder).
Barrel: 4⅝" or 7½" (6-groove, 16" twist).
Weight: 40 oz. (7½" bbl.). **Length:** 13⅛" (7½" bbl.).
Stocks: Smooth American walnut.
Sights: ⅛" ramp front, micro click rear adj. for w. and e.
Features: Similar to Super Blackhawk, Ruger interlocked mechanism. Convertible furnished with interchangeable cylinder for 45 ACP.
Price: Blued, 45 Colt **$179.95**
Price: Convertible **$196.90**

Ruger New Model 30 Carbine Blackhawk
Specifications similar to 45 Blackhawk. Fluted cylinder, round-back trigger guard. Weight 44 oz., length 13⅛" over-all, 7½" barrel only.
Price: **$179.95**

> Consult our Directory pages for
> the location of firms mentioned.

SMITH & WESSON K-38 S.A. M-14
Caliber: 38 Spec., 6-shot.
Barrel: 6".
Length: 11⅛" over-all (6" bbl.). **Weight:** 38½ oz. (6" bbl.).
Stocks: Checkered walnut, service type.
Sights: ⅛" Patridge front, micro click rear adj. for w. and e.
Features: Same as Model 14 except single action only, target hammer and trigger.
Price: 6" bbl. **$244.50**

TANARMI S.A. REVOLVER MODEL TA22S
Caliber: 22 S, L, LR, 22 LR/22 Mag., 6-shot.
Barrel: 4¾".
Weight: 32 oz. **Length:** 10" over-all.
Stocks: Walnut.
Sights: Blade front, rear adj. for w. & e.
Features: Manual hammer block safety; color hardened steel frame; brass backstrap and trigger guard. Imported from Italy by Excam.
Price: 22/22 Mag. with walnut grips, target sights **$95.00**

TANARMI SINGLE ACTION MODEL TA76
Same as TA22 models except blue backstrap and trigger guard.
Price: 22 LR, blue **$50.50**
Price: Combo, blue **$61.75**
Price: 22 LR, chrome **$56.25**
Price: Combo, chrome **$68.25**

THE VIRGINIAN DRAGOON REVOLVER
Caliber: 357 Mag., 44 Mag., 45 Colt.
Barrel: 44 Mag., 6", 7½", 8⅜"; 357 Mag. and 45 Colt, 5", 6", 7½"
Weight: 48 ozs. (6" barrel). **Length:** 11⅞" over-all (6" barrel).
Stocks: Smooth walnut.
Sights: Ramp-type Patridge front blade, micro. adj. target rear.
Features: Color case-hardened frame, spring-loaded floating firing pin, coil main spring. Firing pin is lock-fitted with a steel bushing. Introduced 1977. Made in the U.S. by Interarms Industries, Inc.
Price: 6", 7½", 8⅜" **$229.00**
Price: 12" Buntline (44 Mag. only) **$319.00**

F.I.E. MODEL D-38 DERRINGER
Caliber: 38 Special or 38 S&W.
Barrel: 3".
Weight: 14 oz.
Stocks: Checkered white nylon.
Sights: Fixed.
Features: Chrome finish. Spur trigger. Tip-up barrel, extractors. Made in U.S.A. by F.I.E. Corp.
Price: **$64.95**

HI-STANDARD 9194 AND 9306 DERRINGER
Caliber: 22 Rimfire Magnum. 2 shot.
Barrel: 3½", over and under, rifled.
Length: 5" over-all. **Weight:** 11 oz.
Stocks: Smooth plastic.
Sights: Fixed, open.
Features: Hammerless, integral safety hammerblock, all steel unit is encased in a black, anodized alloy housing. Recessed chamber. Dual extraction. Top break, double action.
Price: Blued (M9194) ..... **$94.50** Nickel (M9306) **$109.50**

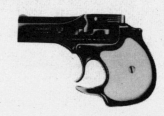

MERRILL SPORTSMAN'S SINGLE SHOT PISTOL
Caliber: 22 LR, 22 WMR, 22 Hornet, 22 Jet, 25-35 Win., 256 Win. Mag., 357 Mag., 357/44 B & D, 30-30 Win., 30 Herrett, 35 Herrett, .41 Mag., 44 Mag.
Barrel: 9" or 12", semi-octagonal; .450" wide vent. rib, matted to prevent glare.
Weight: About 54 ozs. **Length:** 10½" over-all (9" bbl.)
Stocks: Smooth walnut with thumb and heel rest. Rosewood optional at extra cost.
Sights: Front .125" blade; rear "Micro Sight" adj. for w. and e.
Features: Polished blue finish. Barrel is grooved for scope mounting. Cocking indicator visible from rear of gun. Has spring-loaded barrel lock, positive thumb safety. Wrist rest attachment (optional) is adjustable, can be swung out of way for holster carry. Scope and mount shown are not included.
Price: 9" barrel, with Micro sight **$269.50**
Price: 12" barrel, with Micro sight **$289.50**
Price: Extra barrel, 9" .... **$79.50** 12" **$99.50**
Price: Wrist rest attachment **$20.75**

ROLLING BLOCK SINGLE SHOT PISTOL
Caliber: 22 LR, 357 mag.
Barrel: 8".
Weight: 2 lbs. **Length:** 12"
Stocks: Walnut.
Sights: Front adj. for w., buckhorn adj. for e.
Features: Polished brass trigger guard. Imported by Navy Arms.
Price: **$135.00**

REMINGTON MODEL XP-100 Bolt Action Pistol
Caliber: 221 Fireball, single shot.
Barrel: 10½ inches, ventilated rib.
Length: 16¾ inches. **Weight:** 60 oz.
Stocks: Brown nylon one-piece, checkered grip with white spacers.
Features: Fits left or right hand, is shaped to fit fingers and heel of hand. Grooved trigger. Rotating thumb safety, cavity in fore-end permits insertion of up to five 38 cal., 130-gr. metal jacketed bullets to adjust weight and balance. Included is a black vinyl, zippered case.
Sights: Fixed front, rear adj. for w. and e. Tapped for scope mount.
Price: Including case **$239.95**

SEMMERLING LM-4 PISTOL
Caliber: 45 ACP.
Barrel: 3½".
Weight: 24 ozs. **Length:** 5.2" over-all.
Stocks: Checkered black plastic.
Sights: Ramp front, fixed rear.
Features: Manually operated repeater. Over-all dimensions are 5.2" x 3.7" x 1". Has a four-shot magazine capacity. Comes with manual, leather carrying case, spare stock screw and wrench. From Semmerling Corp.
Price: Complete **$645.00**
Price: Thin Version (blue sideplate instead of grips) **$645.00**

TANARMI O/U DERRINGER
Caliber: 38 Special.
Barrel: 3".
Weight: 14 oz. **Length:** 4¾" over-all.
Stocks: Checkered white nylon.
Sights: Fixed.
Features: Blue finish; tip-up barrel. Made in U.S. by Excam, Inc.
Price: **$59.50**

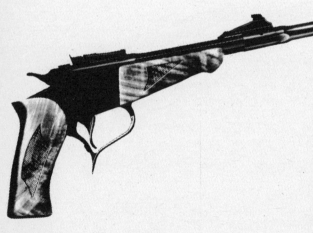

THOMPSON-CENTER ARMS CONTENDER
Caliber: 218 Bee, 221 Rem., 25-35 Win., 30-30 Win., 22 S, L, LR, 22 WMR, 22 Rem. Jet, 22 Hornet, 22 K Hornet, 256 Win., 257 Mag., also 222 Rem., 45 ACP, 44 Mag., 5mm Rem., 45 Long Colt, 45 Win. Mag.
Barrel: 8¾", 10", tapered octagon. Single shot.
Length: 13¼" (10" bbl.). **Weight:** 43 oz. (10" bbl.).
Stocks: Select checkered walnut grip and fore-end, with thumb rest. Right or left hand.
Sights: Under cut blade ramp front, rear adj. for w. & e.
Features: Break open action with auto-safety. Single action only. Interchangeable bbls., both caliber (rim & center fire), and length. Drilled and tapped for scope. Engraved frame.
Price: Blued (rimfire cals.) **$190.00**
Price: Blued (centerfire cals.) **$190.00**
Price: Extra bbls. (standard octagon) . . . . **$ 75.00**
Price: 30 Herrett and 357 Herrett bull bbl. with fore-end,
  less sights . . . . **$ 70.00**
Price: As above except with sights . . . . **$ 75.00**
Price: Bushnell Phantom scope base . . . . **$ 8.75**
Price: Fitted walnut case . . . . **$ 39.50**
Price: 357 and 44 Mag. vent. rib, internal choke bbl. . . . . **$ 85.00**

Thompson-Center Super 14 Contender
Similar to regular Contender except has 14" barrel with fully adjustable target-type sights. Available in 30 Herrett, 357 Herrett, 30-30 Win., 35 Rem., 41, 44 Mag. and 45 Win. Mag. only. Introduced 1978.
Price: **$210.00**
Price: Extra barrels . . . . **$ 85.00**

DIRECTORY OF MANUFACTURERS

AMMUNITION (Commercial)

Alcan Shells, (See Smith & Wesson Ammunition Co.)
Cascade Cartridge Inc., (See Omark)
Federal Cartridge Co., 2700 Foshay Tower, Minneapolis, Minn. 55402
Frontier Cartridge Co., Inc., Box 1848, Grand Island, Neb. 68801
H&H Cartridge Corp., Box 294, Greensburg, IN 42240 (Super Vel)
Lee E. Jurras & Assoc., Drawer F, Hagerman, NM 88232 (Jurras calibers)
Omark-CCI/Speer, Inc., Box 856, Lewiston, ID 83501
Remington Arms Co., Bridgeport, Conn. 06602
Service Armament, 689 Bergen Blvd., Ridgefield, N.J. 07657
Speer, Inc. (See Omark)
Smith & Wesson Ammunition Co., 2399 Forman Rd., Rock Creek, OH 44084
Winchester-Western, East Alton, Ill. 62024

AMMUNITION (Custom)

Beal's Bullets, 170 W. Marshall Rd., Lansdowne, PA 19050 (Auto Mag Specialists)
Brass Extrusion Labs. Ltd., 800 W. Maple Lane, Bensenville, IL 60106
Glaser Safety Slug, Inc., Box 1975, McAllen, TX 78501
KTW, Inc., 710 Cooper-Foster Park Road West, Lorain, OH 44053 (metal piercing bullets and ammo; sales to police only)
Lomont Precision Bullets, 4421 S. Wayne Ave., Ft. Wayne, IN 45807 (custom bullets)
Numrich Arms Corp., 203 Broadway, W. Hurley, N.Y. 12491
Anthony F. Sailer-Ammunition, P.O. Box L, Owen, WI 54460
Geo. Spence, P.O. Box 222, Steele, MO 63877 (Boxer-primed cartridges)

AMMUNITION (Foreign)

Canadian Ind. Ltd. (C.I.L.), Ammo Div., Howard House, Brownsburg, Que., Canada, JOV 1AO
Dynamit Nobel of America, Inc., 910, 17 St. NW, Suite 709, Washington, DC 20006
Eastern Sports Distributors Co., Inc., P.O. Box 28, Milford, NH 03055 (RWS; Geco)
Gevelot of Canada, Box 1593, Saskatoon, Sask., Canada
Hirtenberger Patronen-, Zundhutchen- & Metallwarenfabrik, A.G., Leobersdorfer Str. 33, A2552 Hirtenberg, Austria
NORMA-Precision, Lansing, NY 14882
RWS (Rheinische-Westfalische Sprengstoff) see: Eastern

AMMUNITION COMPONENTS — BULLETS, POWDER, PRIMERS

Alcan, (see: Smith & Wesson Ammunition Co.)
Brass Extrusion Laboratories, Ltd., 800 W. Maple Lane, Bensenville, IL 60106
Kenneth E. Clark, 18738 Highway 99, Madera, CA 93637 (Bullets)
Colorado Custom Bullets, P.O. Box 215, American Fork, UT 84003
DuPont, Explosives Dept., Wilmington, Del. 19898
Elk Mountain Shooters Supply, 1719 Marie, Pasco, WA 99301 (Alaskan bullets)
Federal Cartridge Co., 2700 Foshay Tower, Minneapolis, MN 55402
Forty Five Ranch Enterprises, 119 S. Main, Miami, Okla. 74354
Godfrey Reloading Supply, R.R. 1, Box 688, Brighton, Ill. 62012 (cast bullets)
Hercules Powder Co., 910 Market St., Wilmington, Del. 19899
Herter's Inc., Waseca, Minn. 56093
Hodgdon Powder Co. Inc., 7710 W. 50th Hwy., Shawnee Mission, KS 66202
Hornady Mfg. Co., Box 1848, Grand Island, Neb. 68801
L.L.F. Die Shop, 1281 Highway 99 North, Eugene, Ore. 97402
Lomont Precision Bullets, 4421 S. Wayne Ave., Ft. Wayne, IN 46807 (custom bullets)
Lyman Gun Sight Products, Middlefield, Conn. 06455
Markell, Inc., 4115 Judah St., San Francisco, Calif. 94112
Norma-Precision, Lansing, NY 14882
Omark-CCI/Speer, Inc., Box 856, Lewiston, ID 83501
Remington-Peters, Bridgeport, Conn. 06602
Sierra Bullets Inc., 10532 Painter Ave., Santa Fe Springs, CA 90670
Smith & Wesson Ammunition Co., 2399 Forman Rd., Rock Creek, OH 44084
Speer, Inc. (See Omark)
Texas Contenders Firearms, 4127 Weslow St., Houston, TX 77087 (Herrett brass)
Thompson/Center Arms Corp., RFD 4, Box 2426, Rochester, NH 03867
Winchester-Western, 275 Winchester Ave., New Haven, CT 06504

BULLET & CASE LUBRICANTS

Birchwood-Casey Co., Inc., 7900 Fuller Rd., Eden Prairie, Minn. 55343 (Anderol)
Brownell's, Inc., Rt. 2, Box 1, Montezuma, IA 50171
Choate Machine & Tool Co., Box 218, Bald Knob, AR 72010 (bullet lubes)
Cooper-Woodward, Box 972, Riverside, Cal. 92502 (Perfect Lube)
D.R. Corbin, Box 758, Phoenix, OR 97535 (bullet jackets, swaging supplies)
Herter's, Inc., Waseca, Minn. 56903 (Perfect Lubricant)
H-R Research & Mfg., Box 25888, Los Angeles, CA 90025 (Formula 99 bullet lube)
IPCO (Industrial Products Co.), Box 14, Bedford, MA 01730
Jet-Aer Corp., 100 Sixth Ave., Paterson, N.J. 07524
Lyman Gun Sight Products, Middlefield, Conn. 06455 (Size-Ezy)
Micro Shooter's Supply, Box 213, Las Cruces, N. Mex. 88001 (Micro-Lube)

Omark-RCBS Operations, Box 1919, Oroville, CA 95965
Pacific Tool Co., P.O. Drawer 2048, Ordnance Plant Rd., Grand Island, NB 68801
Phelps Rel. Inc., Box 4004, E. Orange, N.J. 07019
Precision Ammunition & Rel., 122 Hildenboro Square, Agincourt, Ont. M1W 1Y3, Canada
RCBS, Inc. (See Omark)
SAECO Rel. Inc., P.O. Box 778, Carpinteria, CA 93103
Scientific Lubricants Co., 3753 Lawrence Ave., Chicago, Ill. 60625
Testing Systems, Inc., 2832 Mt. Carmel, Glenside, PA 19038

BULLET SWAGE DIES AND TOOLS

C-H Tool & Die Corp., P.O. Box L, Owen, WI 54460
Clymer Mfg. Co., 14241 W. 11 Mile Rd., Oak Park, MI 48237
Lester Coats, 416 Simpson St., North Bend, OR 97459 (lead wire cutter)
D.R. Corbin, Box 758, Phoenix, OR 97535 (bullet jackets, swaging supplies)
Herter's Inc., Waseca, MN 56093
Independent Machine & Gun Shop, 1416 N. Hayes, Pocatello, ID 83201 (TNT bullet dies)
L.L.F. Die Shop, 1281 Highway 99 North, Eugene, OR 97402

CHRONOGRAPHS AND PRESSURE TOOLS

B-Square Co., Box 11281, Ft. Worth, Tex. 76110
Chronograph Specialists, Box 309, Mira Loma, CA 91752
Custom Chronograph Co., 3518 1st Ave. N.W., Seattle, WA 98107
Display Electronics, Box 1044, Littleton, CO 80120
Herter's, Waseca, Minn. 56093
Micro-Sight Co., 242 Harbor Blvd., Belmont, Calif. 94002 (Techsonic)
Oehler Research, P.O. Box 9135, Austin, Tex. 78756
Precisionics, Box 502, Moss Point, MS 39563 (Speed-Meter)
Scharon Fabricators, 2145 East Dr., St. Louis, MO 63131
Schmidt-Weston Co., Box 9, West Islip, NY 11795
Sundtek Co., P.O. Box 744, Springfield, Ore. 97477
Teal Electronics, 15124 Weststate St., Westminster, CA 92683
Time Electro Systems, Inc., P.O. Box 2703, Colorado Springs, CO 80901 (Kronoscope)
M. York, 19381 Keymar Way, Gaithersburg, MD 20760 (press. tool)

CLEANING & REFINISHING SUPPLIES

Armoloy, 204 E. Daggett St., Ft. Worth, TX 76104
Ber Big Enterprises, P.O. Box 291, Huntington, CA 90255 (gunsoap)
Birchwood-Casey Chem. Co., 7900 Fuller Rd., Eden Prairie, Minn. 55343 (Anderol, etc.)
Bisonite Co., Inc., P.O. Box 84, Kenmore Station, Buffalo, NY 14217
Break-Free (See San/Bar Corp.)
Jim Brobst, 299 Poplar St., Hamburg, Pa. 19526 (J-B Compound)
GB Prods, Dept., H&R, Inc., Industrial Rowe, Gardner, MA 01440
Brownell's, Inc., Rt. 2, Box 1, Montezuma, IA 50171
Browning Arms, Rt. 4, Box 624-B, Arnold, Mo. 63010
J.M. Bucheimer Co., Airport Rd., Frederick, MD 21701
Dri-Slide, Inc., Industrial Park, Fremont, Mich. 49412
Garcia Sptg. Arms Corp., 329 Alfred Ave., Teaneck, N.J. 07666
Gun-All Products, Box 244, Dowagiac, Mich. 49047
Frank C. Hoppe Div., P.O. Box 97, Parkesburg, Pa. 19365
Jet-Aer Corp., 100 Sixth Ave., Paterson, N.J. 07524 (blues & oils)
LPS Res. Labs. Inc., 2050 Cotner Ave., Los Angeles, Calif. 90025
LEM Gun Spec., Box 31, College Park, Ga 30337 (Lewis Lead Remover)
Liquid Wrench, Box 10628, Charlotte, N.C. 28201 (pen. oil)
Marble Arms Co., 420 Industrial Pk., Gladstone, Mich. 49837
Micro Sight Co., 242 Harbor Blvd., Belmont, Ca. 94002 (bedding)
Mill Run Prod., 1360 W. 9th, Cleveland, O. 44113 (Brite-Bore Kits)
Mirror-Lube, P.O. Box 693, San Juan Capistrano, Ca 92675
Mitchell Chemical Co., Wampus Lane, Milford, CT 06460 (Gun Guard)
New Method Mfg. Co., Box 175, Bradford, Pa. 16701 (gun blue)
Northern Instruments, Inc., 6680 North Highway 49, Lino Lake, MN 55014 (Stor-Safe rust preventer)
Numrich Arms Co., West Hurley, N.Y. 12491 (44-40 gun blue)
Ordnance Parkerizing, 1511 Waverly Ave., Florence, SC 29501
Outers Laboratories, Box 37, Onalaska, Wis. 54650 (Gunslick kits)
Rig Products Co., Box 279, Oregon, Ill. 61061 (Rig Grease)
Rocket Chemical Co., Inc., 5390 Napa St., San Diego, Calif. 92110 (WD-40)
Rusteprufe Labs., 605 Wolcott St., Sparta, Wis. 54656
San/Bar Corp., Box 11787, Santa Ana, CA 92711 (Break-Free)
Saunders Sptg. Gds., 338 Somerset, No. Plainfield, NJ 07060 (Save-Bore)
Silicote Corp., Box 359, Oshkosh, Wis. 54901 (Silicone cloths)
Silver Dollar Guns, P.O. Box 489, 10 Frances St., Franklin, NH 03235 (Silicone oil)
Sportsmen's Labs., Inc., Box 732, Anoka, Minn. 55303 (Gun Life lube)
Surcon, Inc., P.O. Box 277, Zieglerville, Pa. 19492
Taylor & Robbins, Box 164, Rixford, Pa. 16745 (Throat Saver)
Testing Systems, Inc., 2832 Mt. Carmel, Glenside, PA 19038 (gun lube)
C.S. Van Gorden, 120 Tenth Ave., Eau Claire, Wis. 54701 (Instant Blue)
WD-40 Co., 1061 Cudahy Pl., San Diego, CA 92110
West Coast Secoa, Inc., Rt. 5, Box 138, Lakeland, FL 33801 (Teflon coatings)
Williams Gun Sight, 7389 Lapeer Rd., Davison, Mich. 48423 (finish kit)
Woodstream Corp., P.O. Box 327, Lititz, Pa. 17543 (Mask)

CUSTOM GUNSMITHS

Bain and Davis Sptg. Gds., 599 W. Las Tunas Dr., San Gabriel, Calif. 91776
Mashburn Arms Co., 1218 N. Pennsylvania, Oklahoma City, OK 73107
Mathews & Sons Gunsmithing, 10224 South Paramount Blvd., Downey, CA 90241
Pachmayr Gun Works, 1220 S. Grand Ave., Los Angeles, Calif. 90015
George H. Sheldon, P.O. Box 489, Franklin, NH 03235 (45 autos & M-1 carbines only)
Silver Dollar Guns, P.O. Box 489, 10 Frances St., Franklin, NH 03235 (45 autos & M-1 carbines only)
A.D. Swenson's 45 Shop, P.O. Box 606, Fallbrook, CA 92028
Upper Missouri Trading Co., Inc., Box 181, Crofton, MO 68730
Walker Arms Co., R. 2, Box 73, Selma, AL 36701
Williams Gunsmithing, 704 E. Commonwealth, Fullerton, CA 92631

GUN PARTS, U.S. AND FOREIGN

Badger Shooter's Supply, Box 397, Owen, WI 54460
Numrich Arms Co., West Hurley, N.Y. 12491
Martin B. Retting, Inc., 11029 Washington, Culver City, Cal. 90230
Sherwood Distr. Inc., 18714 Parthenia St., Northridge, CA 91324
Triple-K Mfg. Co., 568 6th Ave., San Diego, CA 92101 (pistol magazines)

GUNS (Foreign)

Browning, Rt. 4, Box 624-B, Arnold, Mo. 63010
Connecticut Valley Arms Co., Saybrook Rd., Haddam, CT 06438 (CVA)
Dixie Gun Works, Inc., Hwy 51, South, Union City, Tenn. 38261
Firearms Center Inc. (FCI), 113 Spokane, Victoria, TX 77901
Firearms International Corp., 17801 Indian Head Hwy., Accokeek, MD 20607
Garcia Sptg. Arms Corp., 329 Alfred Ave., Teaneck, N.J. 07666
Hawes National Corp., 15424 Cabrito Rd., Van Nuys, CA 91406
Herter's, Waseca, Minn. 56093
Interarmco, see: Interarms (Walther)
Interarms Ltd., 10 Prince St., Alexandria, Va. 22313 (Mauser, Valmet M-62/S)
International Distr., Inc., 7290 S.W. 42nd St., Miami, FL 33155 (Taurus rev.)
Kerr's Sport Shop, Inc., 9584 Wilshire Blvd., Beverly Hills, CA 90212
L.A. Distributors, 4 Centre Market Pl., New York, N.Y. 10013
L.E.S., 3640 Dempster, Skokie, Il 60076 (Steyr, Mannlicher-Schoenauer)
Navy Arms Co., 689 Bergen Blvd., Ridgefield, N.J. 07657
Pachmayr Gun Works, 1220 S. Grand Ave., Los Angeles, CA 90015
Precise, 3 Chestnut, Suffern, NY 10901
Security Arms Co., 1815 No. Ft. Myer Dr., Arlington, VA 22209 (Heckler/Koch)
Sherwood Dist., Inc., 18714 Parthenia St., Northridge, CA 91324
Stoeger Arms Co., 55 Ruta Ct., S. Hackensack, N.J. 07606
Universal Sporting Goods, Inc., 7920 N.W. 76th Ave., Medley, FL 33166

GUNS, U.S.-made

A-J Ordnance, Inc. (Alexander-James), 1066 E. Edna Pl., Covina, CA 91722 (Thomas auto pistol)
Bauer Firearms, 34750 Klein Ave., Fraser, MI 48026
Brownell's, Inc., Rt. 2, Box 1, Montezuma, IA 50171
Challanger Mfg. Corp., 118 Pearl St., Mt. Vernon, NY 10550 (Hopkins & Allen)
Charter Arms Corp., 430 Sniffens Ln., Stratford, CT 06497
Colt, 150 Huyshope Ave., Hartford, CT 06102
Day Arms Corp., 2412 S.W. Loop 410, San Antonio, TX 78227
EMF Co. Inc., Box 1248, Studio City, CA 91604 (T.D.A. rev.)
Firearms Imp. & Exp. Co., 2470 N.W. 21st St., Miami, FL 33142 (FIE)
Firearms Intl. Corp., (see: Garcia)
Harrington & Richardson, Industrial Rowe, Gardner, MA 01440
High Standard Sporting Firearms, 31 Prestige Park Circle, East Hartford, CT 06108
Hopkins & Allen, see: High Standard
Ithaca Gun Co., Ithaca, N.Y. 14850
Iver Johnson Arms & Cycle Works, Fitchburg, Mass. 01420
Lee E. Jurras & Assoc., Drawer F, Hagerman, NM 88232
Merrill Company, 704 E. Commonwealth, Fullerton, CA 92631 (Merrill Sportsman)
Numrich Arms Corp., W. Hurley, N.Y. 12491
Plainfield Machine Co., Inc., Box 447, Dunellen, N.J. 08812
Plainfield Ordnance Co., P.O. Box 251, Middlesex, NJ 08846
Remington Arms Co., Bridgeport, Conn. 06602
Ruger (see Sturm, Ruger & Co.)
Security Industries of America, Inc., 31 Bergen Turnpike, Little Ferry, NJ 07643
Smith & Wesson, Inc., 2100 Roosevelt Ave., Springfield, MA 01101
Sterling Arms Corp., 4436 Prospect St., Gasport, NY 14067
Sturm, Ruger & Co., Southport, Conn. 06490
TDE Marketing Corp., 11658 McBean Dr., El Monte, CA 91732 (380 ACP Back Up pistol & Auto Mag)
Thompson/Center Arms Corp., RFD 4, Box 2426, Rochester, NH 03867
Universal Sporting Goods. Inc. 7920 N.W. 76th, Miami, FL 33166
Dan Wesson Arms, 293 So. Main St., Monson, Mass. 01057
Winchester Repeating Arms Co., New Haven, Conn. 06504

HANDGUN ACCESSORIES

Baramie Corp., 6250 E. 7 Mile Rd., Detroit, MI 48234 (Hip-Grip)
Bar-Sto Precision Machine, 633 S. Victory Blvd., Burbank, CA 91502 (stainless barrels)
B.L. Broadway, Rte. 1, Box 381, Alpine, CA 92001 (machine rest)
C'Arco, Box 308, Highland, CA 92346 (Ransom rest)
Case Master, 4675 E. 10 Ave., Miami, Fla. 33013
Central Specialities Co., 6030 Northwest Hwy., Chicago, Ill. 60631
Bill Dyer, 503 Midwest Bldg., Oklahoma City, Okla. 73102 (grip caps)
Essex Arms, Box 345, Phaerring St., Island Pond, VT 05846 (45 Auto frames)
R.S. Frielich, 396 Broome St., New York, N.Y. 10013 (cases)
R.G. Jensen, 16153½ Parthenia, Sepulveda, Calif. 91343 (auxiliary chambers)
Lee E. Jurras & Assoc., Drawer F, Hagerman, NM 88232
Laka Tool Co., 62 Kinkel St., Westbury, L.I., NY 11590 (stainless steel 45 Auto parts)
Lee Custom Eng., Inc., 46 E. Jackson, Hartford, WI 53027 (pistol rest holders)
Matich Loader, 10439 Rush St., South El Monte, Ca 91733 (Quick Load)
W.A. Miller Co., Inc., Mingo Loop, Oguossoc, ME 04964 (cases)
Pachmayr, 1220 S. Grand, Los Angeles, Calif. 90015 (cases)
Pelson Inc., 13918 Equitable Rd., Cerritos, CA 90701 (cases)
Pistolsafe. Dr. L., N. Chili, NY 14514 (handgun safe)
Platt Luggage, Inc., 2301 S. Prairie, Chicago, Ill. 60616 (cases)
Joseph E. Smith, 1114 W. McKinley Ave., Sunnyvale, CA 94086 (Magna-Trigger Safety)
Texas Contenders Firearms, 4127 Weslow St., Houston, TX 77087 (Contender accessories)
M. Tyler, 1326 W. Britton, Oklahoma City, Okla. 73114 (grip adaptor)
Dave Woodruff, 116 Stahl Ave., Wilmington Manor, New Castle, DE 19720 (relining and conversions)

HANDGUN GRIPS

Beckelhymer's, Hidalgo & San Bernardo, Laredo, Tex. 78040
Belmont Prods., Rte. No. 1. Friendsville. TN 37737
Custom Grips, 148 Sheperd Ave., Brooklyn, N.Y. 11208
Fitz, Box 49697, Los Angeles, Calif. 90049
Herrett's, Box 741, Twin Falls, Ida. 83301
Hogue Custom Combat Grips, c/o Gateway Shooters' Supply, Inc., 10145 103rd St., Jacksonville, FL 32210
Mershon Co., Inc., 1230 S. Grand Ave., Los Angeles, Calif. 90015
Mustang Firearms, Inc., 28715 Via Montezuma, Temecula, CA 92390 (Mustang grips)
Safety Grip Corp., Box 456, Riverside St., Miami, Fla. 33135
Sanderson Custom Pistol Stocks, 17695 Fenton, Detroit, Mich. 48219
Jay Scott, 81 Sherman Place, Garfield, N.J. 07026
Sile Dist., 7 Centre Market Pl., New York, N.Y. 10013
Sports Inc., P.O. Box 683, Park Ridge, IL 60068 (Franzite)

HEARING PROTECTORS

AO Safety Prods., Div. of American Optical Corp., 14 Mechanic St., Southbridge, MA 01550 (ear valve)
Bausch & Lomb, 635 St. Paul St., Rochester, N.Y. 14602
David Clark Co., 360 Franklin St., Worcester, Mass. 01604
Curtis Safety Prod. Co., Box 61, Webster Sq. Sta., Worcester, Mass. 01603 (ear valve)
Hodgdon, 7710 W. 50 Hiway, Shawnee Mission, Kans. 66202
Sigma Eng. Co., 11320 Burbank Blvd., No. Hollywood, Ca. 91601 (Lee-Sonic ear valve)
Safety Direct, P.O. Box 8907, Reno, NV 89507 (Silencio)
Smith & Wesson, 2100 Roosevelt Ave., Springfield, MA 01101
Vector Scientific, P.O. Box 21106, Ft. Lauderdale, FL 33316
Willson Safety Prods. Div., P.O. Box 622, Reading, PA 19603

HOLSTERS & LEATHER GOODS

American Sales & Mfg. Co., P.O. Box 677, Laredo, Tex. 78040
Andy Anderson, P.O. Box 225, North Hollywood, CA 91603 (Gunfighter Custom Holsters)
Bianchi Holster Co., 100 Calle Cortez, Temecula, CA 92390
Boyt Co., Div. of Welch Sptg., Box 1108, Iowa Falls. Ia. 51026
Brauer Bros. Mfg. Co., 817 N. 17th, St. Louis, Mo. 63106
Browning, Rt. 4, Box 624-B, Arnold, MO 63010
J.M. Bucheimer Co., Airport Rd., Frederick, Md. 21701
Colt's, 150 Huyshope Ave., Hartford, Conn. 06102
Goerg Ent., 6543-140th Pl. N.E., Redmond, WA 98052
Hoyt Holster Co., P.O. Box 1783, Costa Mesa, Cal. 92626
Don Hume, Box 351, Miami, Okla 74354
The Hunter Co., 3300 W. 71st Ave. Westminster, Co 80030
Jumbo Sports Prods., P.O. Box 280, Airport Rd., Frederick, MD 21701
George Lawrence Co., 306 S. W. First Ave., Portland, OR 97204
Leathercrafters, 710 S. Washington, Alexandria, VA 22314
MMGR Corp., 5710 12th Ave., Brooklyn, N.Y. 11219
Pete Mason/The Armoury, RR2, Bluffton, Alberta T0C 0M0 Canada
S.D. Myres Saddle Co., 5530 E. Paisano, El Paso, TX 79905
Pony Express Sport Shop Inc., 17460 Ventura Blvd., Encino, CA 91316
Red Head Brand Co., 4100 Platinum Way, Dallas, Tex. 75237
Rickenbacker's, P.O. Box 532, State Ave., Holly Hill, SC 29059
R.E. Roseberry, 810 W. 38th, Anderson, Ind. 46014
Roy's Custom Leather Goods, P.O. Box 852, Magnolia, AR 71753
Safariland Leather Products, 1941 Walker Ave., Monrovia, Calif. 91016
Safety Speed Holster, Inc., 910 So. Vail, Montebello, Calif. 90640
Saguaro Holsters, 1508 Del Carlo Circle, Seagoville, TX 75159 (custom)
Buddy Schoellkopf Products Inc., 4949 Joseph Hardin Dr., Dallas, TX 75236
Sile Distr., 7 Centre Market Pl., New York, N.Y. 10013
Smith & Wesson Leather Co., 83 Stevens St., Springfield, MA 01104
Stein Holsters & Accessories, Inc., Drawer B, Wakefield Sta., Bronx, NY 10466
Swiss-Craft Co., Inc., 33 Arctic St., Worcester, MA 01604
Tandy Leather Co., 1001 Foch, Fort Worth, Texas 76107

Torel, Inc., 1053 N. South St., Yoakum, TX 77995 (gun slings)
Triple-K Mfg. Co., 568 Sixth Ave., San Diego, CA 92101
Whitco, Box 1712, Brownsville, Tex. 78520 (Hide-A-Way)

LABELS, BOXES, CARTRIDGE HOLDERS

Milton Brynin, Box 162, Fleetwood Station, Mount Vernon, NY 10552 (cartridge box labels)
E-Z Loader, Del Rey Products, P.O. Box 91561, Los Angeles, CA 90009
Jasco, J.A. Somers Co., P.O. Box 49751, Los Angeles, CA 90049 (cartridge box labels)
Peterson Label Co., P.O. Box 186, Redding Ridge, CT 06876 (cartridge box labels; Targ-Dots)
N.H. Schiffman, 963 Malibu, Pocatello, ID 83201 (cartridge carrier)

LOAD TESTING and PRODUCT TESTING, CHRONOGRAPHING, BALLISTIC STUDIES

Custom Ballistics' Lab., 3354 Cumberland Dr., San Angelo, Tex. 76901
Horton Ballistics, North Waterford, Me. 04267
Kennon's, 5408 Biffle, Stone Mountain, Ga. 30083
Kent Lomont, 4421 S. Wayne Ave., Ft. Wayne, IN 46807
Plum City Ballistics Range, Rte. 1, Box 29A, Plum City, Wis. 54761
H.P. White Lab., Box 331, Bel Air, Md. 21014

PISTOLSMITHS

Alamo Heat Treating, Box 55345, Houston, Tex. 77055
Allen Assoc., 7448 Limekiln Pike, Philadelphia, Pa. 19138 (speed-cock lever for 45 ACP)
Bain and Davis Sptg. Gds., 559 W. Las Tunas Dr., San Gabriel, Cal. 91776
Bar-Sto Precision Machine, 633 So. Victory Blvd., Burbank, CA 91502
Behlert. see: Custom Gun Shop
F. Bob Chow, Gun Shop, 3158 Mission, San Francisco, Calif. 94110
J.E. Clark, Rte. 2, Box 22A, Keithville, LA 71047
Custom Gun Shop, 725 Lehigh Ave., Union, NJ 07083
Day Arms Corp., 2412 S.W. Loop 410, San Antonio, TX 78227
Alton S. Dinan, Jr., P.O. Box 6674, Canaan, Conn. 06018
Dominic DiStefano, 4303 Friar Lane, Colorado Springs, CO 80907 (accurizing)
Dan Dwyer, 915 W. Washington, San Diego, Calif. 92103
Ehresman Tool Co., Inc., 5425 Planeview Dr., Ft. Wayne, IN 46805 (custom)
Giles' 45 Shop, Rt. 2, Box 847, Odessa, FL 33556
H.H. Harris, 1237 So. State, Chicago, Ill. 60605
Lee E. Jurras & Assoc., Drawer F, Hagerman, NM 88232
R.W. Loveless, Box 7836, Riverside, CA 92503 (M41 S&W Field Gun conversion and custom Colt Commander)
Rudolf Marent, 9711 Tiltree, Houston, TX 77075 (Hammerli)
Maryland Gun Exchange, Inc., Rte. 40 W., RD 5, Frederick, MD, 21701
Match Arms Co., 831 Mary St., Springdale, Pa. 15144
Mathews & Sons Gunsmithing, 10224 South Paramount Blvd., Downey, CA 90241
Nu-Line Guns, 3727 Jennings Rd., St. Louis, MO 63121
Pachmayr Gun Works, 1220 S. Grand Ave., Los Angeles Calif. 90015
L.W. Seecamp Co., Inc., Box 225, New Haven, CT 06502 (DA Colt' auto conversions)
R.L. Shockey Guns, Inc., 1614 S. Choctaw, E. Reno, Okla. 73036
Silver Dollar Guns, P.O. Box 489, 10 Frances St., Franklin, NH 03235 (45 ACP)
Sportsmens Equipmt. Co., 915 W. Washington, San Diego, Calif. 92130
Irving O. Stone, Jr., 633 S. Victory Blvd., Burbank, CA 91502
Victor W. Strawbridge, 6 Pineview Dr., Dover Pt., Dover, NH 03820
A.D. Swenson's 45 Shop, P.O. Box 606, Fallbrook, CA 92028
Dennis A. Ulrich, 2511 S. 57th Ave., Cicero, IL 60650
Williams Gunsmithing, 704 E. Commonwealth, Fullerton, CA 92631
Tom Wilson Co., 1406 S. Oak Cliff Blvd., Dallas, TX 75208
Dave Woodruff, Box 5, Bear, DE 19701

RELOADING TOOLS AND ACCESSORIES

Advanced Mfg. Co., Inc., 18619 W. 7 Mile Rd., Detroit, MI 48219 (super fillerprimer tube)
B-Square Eng. Co., Box 11281, Ft. Worth, Tex. 76110
Bahler Die Shop, Rte. 1, 412 Hemlock, Florence, OR 97439
Bill Ballard, P.O. Box 656, Billings, MT 59103
Bonanza Sports, Inc., 412 Western Ave., Faribault, Minn. 55021
C-H Tool & Die Corp., Box L, Owen, Wis. 54460
Camdex, Inc., 23880 Hoover Rd., Warren, MI 48089
Carbide Die & Mfg. Co., Box 226, Covina, CA 91724
Cascade Cartridge, Inc., (See Omark)
Clymer Mfg. Co., 14241 W. 11 Mile Rd., Oak Park, MI 48237 (½-jack. swaging dies)
Lester Coats, 416 Simpson St., No. Bend. Ore. 97459 (core cutter)

Cooper-Woodward, Box 972, Riverside, Calif. 92502 (Perfect Lube)
D.R. Corbin, Box 758, Phoenix, OR 97535 (bullet jackets, swaging supplies)
Fitz, Box 49697, Los Angeles, Calif. 90049 (Fitz Flipper)
Flambeau Plastics, 801 Lynn, Baraboo, Wis. 53913
Forster Products Inc., 82 E. Lanark Ave., Lanark, Ill. 61046
Geo. M. Fullmer, 2499 Mavis St., Oakland, CA 94601 (seating die)
Goerg Enterprises, 6543 140th Pl. N.E., Redmond, WA 98052
Gopher Shooter's Supply, Box 278, Faribault, MN 55021
The Gun Clinic, 81 Kale St., Mahtomedi, Minn. 55115
Hensley & Gibbs, Box 10, Murphy, Ore. 97533
Herter's Inc., RR1, Waseca, Minn. 56093
B.E. Hodgdon, Inc., 7710 W. 50 Hiway, Shawnee Mission, Kans. 66202
Hornady (see: Pacific)
Hulme Firearm Serv., Box 83, Millbrae, Calif. 94030 (Star case feeder)
JASCO, Box 49751, Los Angeles, Calif. 90049
Kexplore, 9450 Harwig No. G, Houston, TX 77036
Lee Custom Engineering, 46 E. Jackson, Hartford, WI 53027
Lee Precision, Inc., Hwy "U" Hartford. WI 53027
L.L.F. Die Shop, 1281 Highway 99 N., Eugene, Ore. 97402
Lyman Gun Sight Products, Middlefield, Conn. 06455
MTM Molded Prod., 5680 Webster St., Dayton, OH 45414
Magma Eng. Co., P.O. Box 881, Chandler, AZ 85224
Merit Gun Sight Co., P.O. Box 995, Sequim, Wash. 98382
Ohaus Scale Corp., 29 Hanover Rd., Florham Park, N.J. 07932
Omark-RCBS Operations, Box 1919, Oroville, CA 95965
Omark-CCI/Speer, Inc., Box 856, Lewiston, ID 83501
Pacific Tool Co., P.O. Drawer 2048, Ordnance Plant Rd., Grand Island, NB 68801
Ferris Pindell, R.R. 3, Box 205, Connersville, IN 47331
Plum City Ballistics Range, Rte. 1, Box 29A Plum City, Wis. 54761
Marian Powley, 19 Sugarplum Rd., Levitown, Pa. 10956
Precise Alloys Inc., 69 Kinkel St., Westbury, NY 11590 (bullet wire)
Quinetics Corp., Box 13237, San Antonio, TX 78213 (kinetic bullet puller)
RCBS, Inc. (See Omark)
Redding Inc., 114 Starr Rd., Cortland, NY 13045
Remco, 1404 Whitesboro St., Utica, NY 13502 (shot capsules)
Republic Tool Mfg. Co., P.O. Box 112, Caldwell, NJ 07006 (port. rel. stand)
Rochester Lead Works, Rochester, N.Y. 14608 (leadwire)
SAECO Rel. Inc., P.O. Box 778, Carpinteria, Calif. 93013
Sandia Die & Cartridge Co., Rte. 5, Box 5400, Albuquerque, NM 87123
Saunders Gun & Machine Shop, 145 Delhi Rd., Manchester, IA 52057 (primer feed tray)
Scientific Lubricants Co., 3753 Lawrence Ave., Chicago, Ill. 60625
Smith & Wesson Ammunition Co., Inc., 2399 Forman Rd., Rock Creek, OH 44084
J.A. Somers Co., P.O. Box 49751, Los Angeles, CA 90049 (Jasco)
D.E. Stanley, P.O. Box 323, Arvin, CA 93202 (Kake-Kutter)
Star Machine, Inc., 418 10th Ave., San Diego, CA 92101
Texan Reloaders, Inc., P.O. Box 5355, Dallas, Tex. 75222
Webster Scale Mfg. Co., Box 188, Sebring, Fla. 33870
L.E. Wilson, Inc., P.O. Box 324, 404 Pioneer Ave., Cashmere, WA 98815
Zenith Ent., 361 Flagler Rd., Nordland, WA 98358

SIGHTS, OPTICAL (FOR HANDGUN USE)

B-Square Eng. Co., Box 11281, Ft. Worth, TX 76110 (scope mounts)
Bushnell Optical Co., 2828 E. Foothill Blvd., Pasadena, CA 91107 (Phantom scope)
Maynard P. Buehler, 17 Orinda Hwy., Orinda, CA 94563 (scope mounts)
Conetrol Scope Mounts, Hwy. 123 South, Seguin, TX 78155
Fontaine Industries (See Thompson/Center Arms)
Jim Herringshaw, 1221 Iroquoise, Mayfield Hts., OH 44124 (Maxi-Mount)
Leupold & Stevens, Box 688, Beaverton, OR 97005 (pistol scopes, mounts)
Redfield, 5800 E. Jewell Ave., Denver, CO 80224 (pistol scopes, mounts)
Thompson/Center Arms, Farmington Rd., Rochester, NH 03867 (Lobo, Silhouette, Insta-Sight and mounts)
W.R. Weaver, 7125 Industrial Ave., El Paso, TX 79915 (scope mounts)

SIGHTS, METALLIC

B-Square Eng. Co., Box 11281, Ft. Worth, Tex. 76110
Bo-Mar Tool & Mfg. Co., Box 168, Carthage, Tex. 75633
Maynard P. Buehler, Inc., 17 Orinda Highway, Orinda, Calif. 94563
Christy Gun Works, 875 57th St., Sacramento, Calif. 95819
Lyman Gun Sight Products, Middlefield, Conn. 06455
Merit Gunsight Co., P.O. Box 995, Sequim, Wash. 98382
Micro Sight Co., 242 Harbor Blvd., Belmont, Calif. 94002
Miniature Machine Co., 212 E. Spruce, Deming, N.M. 88030
Williams Gun Sight Co., 6810 Lapeer Rd., Davison, MI 48423